Where did
Why a
Where are we g

Solving
the BIG QUESTIONS
As if Thinking Matters

Third Edition
Revised-Simplified-Updated

The only book that sets aside evolutionary and
religious bias to reveal the truth manifest by
reason, evidence, and experience.

DR. RANDY WYSONG

WHERE DID WE COME FROM?
WHY ARE WE HERE?
WHERE ARE WE GOING?

SOLVING THE
BIG QUESTIONS
AS IF THINKING MATTERS

THIRD EDITION
REVISED-SIMPLIFIED-UPDATED

THE ONLY BOOK THAT SETS ASIDE EVOLUTIONARY
AND RELIGIOUS BIAS TO REVEAL THE TRUTH
MANIFEST BY REASON, EVIDENCE, AND EXPERIENCE.

DR. RANDY WYSONG

Solving the Big Questions As If Thinking Matters
Third Edition *Revised-Simplified-Updated*
Dr. Randy Wysong, Author

Solving the Big Questions As If Thinking Matters 1ˢᵗ Edition
Printed—2010

Solving the Big Questions As If Thinking Matters 2ⁿᵈ Edition
First printing—July, 2018
Second printing *with additions and revisions*—February, 2019

Solving the Big Questions As If Thinking Matters 3ʳᵈ Edition
Printed—January, 2021

Published by Inquiry Press
7550 Eastman Avenue
Midland, MI 48642
989-631-0009
inquirypress@inquirypress.com

Includes bibliographical references and index

(Hardcover)
ISBN 0-918112-31-6
978-0-918112-31-6

(Paperback)
ISBN 0-918112-30-9
978-0-918112-30-9

(eBook)
ISBN 0-918112-24-8
978-0-918112-24-8

Library of Congress Control Number: 2018945215

Distributed by: Inquiry Press

DEDICATION

To those unafraid to challenge cherished beliefs, and for whom the open-minded search for truth, no matter where it might lead, is the breath of life.

WYSONG

Solving the Big Questions As If Thinking Matters
Third Edition *Revised-Simplified-Updated*

SECTION E

The Real Reality

SECTION F

Our True Nature and Destiny

INTRODUCTION

You come to this book with at least some notion of answers to the Big Questions. Perhaps you believe what your parents believed, what was taught in school, or simply went along with popular opinion. Out of a sense of duty, respect, peer pressure, or the feeling of inadequacy in the face of such daunting questions, you may have never questioned these early formed beliefs. Or, if you did, it's likely that you sought affirmation from authorities who believe as you do and can help you sweep doubts away.

Nobody is looking to have their cherished beliefs overturned. Change, for most people, must be easier and less consequential than habit. Moreover, once beliefs are in place, we wrap our brains and lives around them. If challenged, we dig our heels in. That makes it harder to convince us we've been fooled, than to fool us.

As you think back to the source of the answers you have, they always trace to other humans. Unfortunately, all source people have vested interests, including being in love with their own ideas. So, nobody can be implicitly trusted. That's why we really have no business relying on others. Therefore, if you haven't earned your beliefs with open-minded inquiry weighing all the pros and cons, but were handed them by an institution or person, you're most likely wrong.

Wrong answers derive from ignoring reality. Reality is not the millions of ideas conjured in the heads of other people. It's not the mysterious etchings on a Bronze Age parchment, the musings of a philosopher thousands of years ago, or the speculations and hypotheses of modern-day intellectuals and scientists. Reality—truth as it can be known in the world we experience moment by moment—is accessed through our own intuition (common sense), reason, conscience, and experience, as well as consideration of evidence and nature's laws.

This book is intended to convince you that you are fully capable of using reality to determine truthful answers to the Big Questions. It's heuristic, meaning it will reacquaint you with your own reasoning powers. Facts and logic presented will affirm what you already intuitively know but have set aside in favor of belief in someone else's belief. Thus, you'll likely find exhilarating "I knew that" realizations that you can own because you unearthed them from your own mind.

The truth-seeking process is just that, a process. It requires establishing truthful foundations consistent with reality and building from there. That is the way this book is constructed. So please read sequentially since each chapter provides the basis for the following ones.

I know emotions run high on this subject. Beliefs are so dear. But if truth is your goal, don't expect to end up where you started. Expect that open- mindedly unleashing your reasoning powers will overturn your erroneous prior beliefs. That's not a cause for dismay. Truth is what we all have to bend to eventually anyway, so why not discover it now and experience its peace and fruits.

Feel free to contact me with your thoughts or questions at: drwysong@asifthinkingmatters.com.

Thinking about . . .

SEARCHING FOR TRUTH

In This Section: There is truth in an absolute sense, out there waiting for discovery. But finding it will not be as simple as keeping beliefs we were spoon fed as a child or following popular opinion. Let's start at the only place from which truth can be hoped to be viewed but where few people dare to begin: with the honesty of an open mind and the courage to fill it only by reason and evidence.

1
RULES FOR FINDING TRUTH

If scientists and engineers want to build a skyscraper, put a person on the moon, develop a recyclable plastic, maintain a nuclear power plant, improve crops, or make parachutes, they must follow rules. Those rules are derived from the truthful natural laws of math, geometry, chemistry, physics, genetics, and so on. They dictate reality and thus success or failure.

All of us in our day to day lives must follow the same rules, be it for driving the car, cooking a meal, or balancing the checkbook. Even putting one foot in front of another must be in tune with these absolute laws. Although we may not know how to make their precise calculations, we know the laws intuitively. We also learn about them by experience, like a child discovering the law of gravity by falling from a tree, or the laws of motion by taking a corner too sharply and fast with a bike. It's called coming to grips with reality, the truth as it can be known.

When you get right down to it, other than our free will, everything is locked in to the laws of nature. Only to the extent we discover these laws and principles can we learn truth. Since that's the case, then truthful answers to the Big Questions must be consistent with these laws.

Nobody approaches the Big Questions from this obvious starting point. Epistemology (the investigation of the difference between justified belief and opinion) is ignored in favor of faith, hope, and preconceived ideas. Such human notions can float absolutely free from reality. However, insofar as these disregard and conflict with the real laws of nature, they are wrong. As wrong as asserting that apples don't fall to the ground, but rather shoot out into space.

The disregard for natural laws began long ago when they were not understood. Birth, death, and all aspects of nature and the heavens were mysterious and scary. State religious leaders took advantage of this ignorance and came up with their own explanations to give the impression that they were in control of nature. The ignorant masses had no way of refuting the dogmas and no will to flout powerful leaders and suffer the consequences.

Today there is sophisticated understanding of natural laws. But nothing has really changed. Dogmas still prevail. Since easy answers to the Big Questions don't immediately come to mind, and people prefer to believe in something rather than nothing, they surrender, follow, vow, and pledge allegiance to the authorities and institutions promulgating the dogmas. Although this compliance is no longer demanded under threat of burning at the stake or torture, there are social and personal forces. For many, being wrong doesn't matter; being part of a group or consensus is better than being right all alone. Peer pressure, ego, economic ties, livelihood interests, loyalty to parents, and obedience to teachers all can influence what is believed.

Moreover, modern political correctness venerates opinion, belief, and faith. They are thought to be like sacred personal rights, private, and concern the bearer of them alone. But, in fact, what we put in our heads as dogma creates ideologies that serve as the "mission control" guiding life and the world. Enshrining nonsense with belief and faith has shrouded the planet in ignorance and misery from time immemorial. Think Mayan human sacrifices, Inquisitions, Crusades, witch trials, Nazi Germany, Stalinist Russia, Jonestown, religious ostracisms, jihads, medical myths . . . and so on.

(When using the terms belief and faith, I am using them synonymously with dogma: an idea accepted from an authoritarian as incontrovertibly true without being questioned or doubted and then retained using only selective and superficial information input. Please keep in mind the distinction between valid belief and faith, like in the law of gravity and 2+2=4, and dogmatic belief and faith.)

Dogma leaves no room for discussion, denies any mechanism for testing and revision, and excludes alternate explanations by assuring their defeat before they're fairly considered. Dogma creates bias and intolerance resulting in contempt prior to investigation. Faith is the go-to word to consecrate and further immunize a dogma against challenge.

3

The nebulous realms of belief, faith, and dogma are refuges where people go when they tire of thinking. The resultant ignorance may be bliss, but it makes us unaware of our incompetence, not knowing what we do not know. If we don't have time or capability for study, analysis, introspection, and a sober and open examination of the evidence, we should have no time or capability for belief, faith, or even an opinion.

In our Internet age, there is no excuse for being unaware of how the facts may contradict our dogmas. One's access to knowledge is not limited by the scope of the local library, one's willingness to travel there and use it properly, or by what was learned at school or in the encyclopedia set at home. Search any word or phrase and a world of knowledge opens. The Internet is the best truth facilitator ever invented.

But in spite of the wealth of information now at our fingertips, we're inherently lazy and tend toward reliance. Searching and thinking is hard; shifting work to others is easy. We look for easy fixes and quick neatly packaged beliefs to give us succor and fill empty spaces in our brains.

When I say we, I include myself. At some time in my life, I have taken on beliefs for all the wrong reasons listed above. I now look back on that history with shame. But it was a necessary gauntlet I needed to pass through to awaken myself. This book is a sort of biography of my coming out from under all the naïve false ideas. Hopefully, I can short circuit that path for you.

I now feel embarrassed because I've come to learn that morally and ethically, I had a legitimate claim to a belief only so far as reason and evidence stood at its back. Instead, effectively, I heeded the words of the great sage, Willy Wonka: "Let us never ever doubt, what no one is sure about."

Clifford, the ethicist, so aptly wrote: "It is wrong always, everywhere, and for anyone to believe anything on insufficient evidence . . . If a man, holding a belief which he was taught in childhood or persuaded of afterwards, keeps down and pushes away any doubts which arise about it in his mind, purposely avoids the reading of books and the company of men that call in question or discuss it, and regards as impious these questions which cannot easily be asked without disturbing it—the life of that man is one long sin against mankind."

Wrong beliefs begin with wrong premises and wrong motives. If we assume a certain thing is true, or we simply want it to be, we'll seek and accept only those facts that fit. The result is endless and contradictory political, religious, health, and scientific views that have forever plagued the world. Each may appear logical, given the starting premises and using only the evidence that fits, but usually turn out to be silly when measured against natural law, reason, intuition, conscience, experience, and the full array of evidence.

SORTING THINKING FROM NONTHINKING

Choosing the Right Thinking – We should be in a constant struggle with ourselves to suppress the tendency toward indoctrination and bias on the one hand, and enliven the open pursuit of truth on the other. The above contrasts the common tactics of those who wish to only support and advance their prejudices, with those who are interested in exploring life and our world as if thinking matters.

Techniques of Non-Thinkers	Techniques of Thinkers
1. Use generalizations – 'Allness' statements: always, completely, only, never.	1. Use qualifiers – Stipulations and limiting statements (usually, sometimes, almost, perhaps), statements supported with specific references and data.
2. One sided – Opposing views are ignored, misrepresented, under-represented, denigrated, or made strawmen.	2. Circumspect – Issues examined from many points of view. Opposition fairly represented.
3. Card stacking – Data carefully selected to present only the best or worst possible case while contrary facts are concealed.	3. Balanced – Samples from a wide range of available data. Purpose is to reveal.
4. Skews the numbers – Misleading use of statistics.	4. Numbers are qualified – Size, duration, conditions, controls, source, subsidies, and interests are revealed.
5. Lumpism – Ignores distinctions and subtle differences. Lumps superficially similar elements together. Reasoning by analogy.	5. Discrimination – Differences and subtle distinctions are conceded. Analogies are used carefully so as to distinguish where nonapplicable.
6. False dilemma (either/or) – There are only two solutions to the problem, or two ways of viewing an issue, the arguer's way or the wrong way.	6. Alternatives - There may be many ways of solving a problem or viewing an issue.
7. Appeals to authority – Only the selected expert knows.	7. Appeals to reason – Statements by authority are only used to stimulate thought and discussion since 'experts' seldom agree.
8. Appeals to consensus (bandwagon) –'Everybody's doing it' so it must be right.	8. Appeals to reason – Uses emotionally neutral words and illustrations.
9. Appeals to emotions – Uses strong emotional connections and built-in biases.	9. Avoids labels and derogatory language – Addresses the argument, not the people.
10. Ignores and denies assumptions and biases.	10. Explores assumptions and built-in biases.
11. Inhibit inquiry and awareness beyond the approved bias.	11. Language usage promotes greater awareness.

© Wysong

Figure 001

2
TRUTH IS REAL AND ACCESSIBLE

Truth is commonly thought to be relative, an open arena in which anyone can throw in their hat of opinion. But that denies the fact that absolute truth actually exists.

Not only are there day-to-day truths like black not being white and cars on empty not going anywhere, but also truths about the biggest questions we ever face: Where did we come from? Why are we here? Where are we going?

Wishy Washy Truth

Some say truth is subjective and dependent upon individual experience, "Your reality is not my reality." Others say it is a collection of perceptions and memories or a cultural artifact. Tolerance and political correctness also make truth wishy-washy. You've heard it, how everyone has a "right to their opinion" and that it's polite to "agree to disagree." All such permissive attitudes lead people to conclude that there can be no absolute truth.

Socrates said, thousands of years ago, "All I know is that I know nothing." But that's a contradiction, an oxymoron. Today, some 2,500 years later it's fashionable to assert that it's truth that there is no truth. But that's an oxymoron as well.

Truth Exists

All such reasons for dismissing absolute truth are defeated by the logical fact that truth must exist. Otherwise there would be no certainty anywhere at any time and our very existence would be impossible.

The only question is whether we can come to know it. We can and do. The laws of nature and facts of reality are truths. Reality truths are empirical, verifiable, repeatable, consistent, observable, and supported by reason, experience, and the full array of evidence.

I believe it's absolutely true that there is no such thing as absolute truth.

© Wysong   Figure 003

Truths we know as a matter of course, include and are determined by:

- **Nature's laws**: 2+2 always equals 4, stones thrown into the air will return to the ground, water turns to ice when it gets really cold, ordered things will get messy unless we intervene . . . and so on. Such truths are common sense and intuitive. If they weren't, we could not function in day-to-day living nor do anything productive.

- **Facts**: pieces of evidence and phenomena that can be observed or otherwise sensed.

- **Reason**: white is not black, up is not down, a lie is not the truth, $2+2=4$ . . .

- **Consistency**: true things remain the same and apply everywhere to everything.

- **Non-contradiction**: a truth cannot contradict itself or other truths.

- **Justice and ethics**: truths are obvious to everyone, predictable, even-handed, and meld with our conscience. They provide a deontology (system of ethics) with no harm resulting unless they are violated.

These reality truths are like railroad tracks that mandate the course of a train. Passengers may argue and debate about whether the train is moving, its speed, mechanics, destination, or even its existence. They might pray for divine intervention to make it turn a different way or ignore its movement and step out onto the ground to their peril. But the train moves along inexorably fixed on the truth of the tracks, oblivious to what we may want to believe about it.

No beneficial technology would be possible without obedience to these reality truths. All the comforts of modern life are the result of thought and action that obeys them. Since the truths of reality work so well with practical matters, like building bridges, space ships, and parachutes, why stop there? They should also serve as an organon to expose the false beliefs that thwart solving not only govenrmental, health, environmental, economic, and the rest of our social problems, but the big questions of existence as well.

Violating the Truths of Reality Has Consequences

Reality truths are necessary for survival. Not just for us, but for the world. Write more checks than your balance adds to, step off a cliff, or decide to not eat and this will become quickly apparent. When truth is ignored in industry, science, medicine, politics, education, and commerce, you, society, and even the whole world can suffer.

We don't get to ignore reality, truth, make up any cockamamie belief, ossify it in our mind, and go out into the world and act it out without insidious consequences somewhere at some time.

For example, religions outrightly laud the virtues of belief and faith without regard to reality truths. The result has been millions maimed and killed in Crusades, Inquisitions, witch trials, jihads, and religiously motivated conflicts.

Science is promoted as the cure for religion's failings. But it is not the sober, analytical, and indifferent gatekeeper of truth commonly thought. That's because science, like religion, is done by opinionated people with unmerited beliefs as well as egocentric and financial interests.

There is a fantasy that truth is all taken care of in peer-reviewed (conformity policed) scientific journals. But scientific literature abounds with contradictory data and conclusions, even fraud. Moreover, there are 2.5 million new scientific papers each year and 50 million articles in the archives dating back to 1665. Real truth does not change on the first of each month when all the thousands of new journals come out.

Just like religious dogmas have resulted in immense human harm, so too have the dogmas held by scientists. The dogma that peer-reviewed literature is like sacred text, leads to flawed conclusions and disastrous effects. For example, hundreds of drugs have been "scientifically proven" safe and effective, but once released on the public have maimed and killed. Modern medicine, buttressed by scientists and peer reviewed literature, has become the number one killer.

Millions of people and their pets suffer and die due to scientifically proven and government-approved foods and official scientifically-backed dietary advice. Scientifically proven agriculture poisons and diminishes fertile land and its crops. Almost every modern intrusion into the natural order threatens life on the planet. Yet they are justified by scientific studies and experts.

Then there's the money. The scientific community runs on it. Scientific "truth," too often, becomes whatever creates grants, profit, or secures careers.

Underlying modern science are the unproven dogmas of materialism and evolution that now permeate education, media, and politics. These dogmas lead to the conclusion that we are biological robots in a meaningless universe. If we are nothing more than moving mounds of atoms derived spontaneously from a primordial brew and under a survival of the fittest imperative, all ethical bets are off.

Duty to Truth Is a Personal Responsibility

We cannot trust others or the consensus view on matters of truth. Nor can we inherit truth by osmosis from family, society, or authoritarian institutions.

Follow the Money – Modern society moves by the flow of money. Any idea that creates money and resultant livelihoods, security, and prestige becomes entrenched without regard to whether it is correct or beneficial. Our only safeguard is to keep our brain intact by being critical of popular thinking, particularly if it creates economic benefit to someone somewhere.

© Wysong — Figure 005

That leaves us where we should have begun in the first place, with ourselves. Disintermediation, removing the middle men, between us individually and the truth is the key. All that's required is setting aside the unearned beliefs we learned as children or adopted from others during adulthood, and then opening the mind to the obvious truths of reality.

Unfortunately, opinions and beliefs are more popular than truth-seeking. That's because they require no effort. They are prepackaged for convenience by countless belief vendors. At no charge—other than our mind--we can pick from a bounteous inventory whatever suits our desired behavior, selfish interests, and placates fears. Once locked in place, a blindness takes over that precludes truth even if it stares us in the face or threatens our very existence.

The most important duty in life is to truth. To achieve that end requires that the sleepy givens be disturbed. The best place to begin is to objectively critique the foundational beliefs that have entrapped society. Thus, materialism, evolutionism, atheism, and religion, the predominant assumed answers to

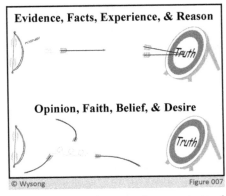

the Big Questions of existence and purpose, must be openly scrutinized by measuring them against reality truths.

That may seem daunting. But finding truth is quite simple, regardless of a person's circumstance or education. And, surprisingly, real truth won't be a surprise since it will be like coming home to what we knew all along. It was just hidden under the clutter of cherished beliefs and faiths given to us by others.

TRUTH FILTERS

•*Does the idea have a significant history? Truth is sticky and just keeps hanging around.*

•*Does it match the real world that can be studied? It must fit all the facts.*

•*Does it fit experience? Personal experience can be the most dependable of all because everything else comes to us secondhand.*

•*Does the idea accommodate all of reality? We don't get to ignore contradictory facts.*

•*Is the belief falsifiable? There must be clear criteria by which a proposition can be proven false.*

•*Does it extrapolate to a good and harmonious conclusion? If everyone believed it, and its applications were expanded on a wide scale, would the world be a better or worse place?*

•*What do our conscience and intuition tell us? If it feels right and we are being honest with ourselves, we are probably on the right track.*

• *Are we fearlessly willing to embrace whatever conclusions emerge from open and honest investigation? That is what real honesty is, and it's the only path to truth.*

© Wysong   Figure 008

Thinking about . . .

ORIGINS

In This Section: The origin of humans and the world in which we live is one of the most intriguing and important questions we ever face. Religions claim to have the answer. Evolutionists say they have a better one. Perhaps one is right or perhaps they are both wrong. We will never know unless we leave our beliefs behind, approach the question as if thinking matters, and let the evidence lead.

3
ORIGIN CHOICES

The predominant opposing views on the origin of the universe and life are religion and materialism (abiogenesis and evolution). But there is a third one too, secular creation, although that option is virtually ignored by everyone.

We won't though.

THREE CHOICES
1. Materialism
2. Religion
3. Secular Creation

Let's define and consider the implications of each of these three.

1. Materialistic Evolution

Materialism is the belief that natural laws, the universe, and life can and did arise spontaneously.

As one popular science writer put it, "We are, after all, evolved comets and sunbeams. From stardust we are born and to stardust we will return."

Scientists believe it either because it's what they were taught or because the assumed alternative, religion, is rationally untenable and morally repugnant to them. They can't put the Creator in a test tube to examine, forgive the atrocities committed by religion throughout history, or reconcile a just god with the tragedies in our world.

But belief in materialism has its own ethical implications. Matter, energy, and randomness, the gods of evolution, say nothing about stealing or killing. Moreover, peace would be an oxymoron since evolution's mechanism is struggle and conflict, with only the fittest surviving.

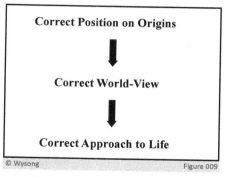

This is not to say that evolutionists are keen to hurl atomic bombs about, or that humanistic evolutionists cannot be wonderfully kind and decent. It's just that the materialistic evolutionary philosophy would logically accommodate any variation of amorality one would like to compose.

2. Religion

Religions contend that life was created by a god as revealed in the Bible or other religious texts.

Holy book religions either take their creation accounts literally, or not wanting to be at odds with current scientific opinion, bend their scriptures and adopt evolution (god-directed) into their beliefs.

Although religion is thought to represent goodness, and it often does, every manner of unethical behavior has also been justified by religion. Holy books and guesses about the will of each religion's god create doctrines. Doctrines dictate right and wrong without regard to the sensibilities of individual conscience. Each religion imagines their god and doctrines as true, and the gods and doctrines of other religions as false. This creates a war of doctrines, as well as literal wars that have wrought misery upon humankind for thousands of years.

3. Secular Creation

The ignored third option is that we were created, but the Creator has nothing to do with human-made religions.

This third alternative, creation without religion, argues that reason and science force the conclusion that there is an intelligent Creator.

The ethics of this position are derived from individual conscience created within us.

Evolutionists don't consider the secular creation position because they think their belief is a closed case. They also suspect any mention of creation as an evangelistic ruse to push holy books into schools. Evolutionists fear a return to the Dark Ages with schools becoming catechisms indoctrinating children with a fundamentalist mindset hostile to science and reason.

On the other hand, religionists don't consider secular intelligent creation because they see atheism and evolution as the only alternatives to religion. They're also vested emotionally and socially and believe religious edicts are necessary for humans to know right from wrong.

Finding Truth – requires an unencumbered open mind. No baggage allowed.

© Wysong   Figure 010

Nothing could be more important than the underpinnings that sow the seeds for why we decide to do what we do in life. So, the question of origins is not a mere academic exercise. It's vitally important to each of us and the world at large.

Consistency with natural law, reason, and evidence are the only means by which the truth can be determined from among the three alternatives.

To determine which idea will survive such scrutiny, we must suppress our biases and make finding truth the only goal.

4
THE LAWS OF
THERMODYNAMICS

Don't let this title scare you. The takeaway from this chapter—things can't come from nothing and things get messy—is so simple every child knows it.

Materialism means that physical reality holds within itself the capability to cause the origin of itself and the universe. Moreover, matter, energy, and natural laws serve as the only needed raw materials for the appearance of the universe and life and its transformation into increasingly complex organisms.

The First Law of Thermodynamics

Evolutionists ignore the problem of the origin of their starting materials. They are taken as freebies, reminding me of a joke. It goes something like this: A materialist was explaining to school children that the origin of the universe was no big deal. A student remarked, "Well then how would you do it?" The teacher said, "Sure thing, first you start with some dust . . ." The student interrupts, "Hold on! Get your own dust."

Natural laws, energy, and matter must be accounted for but there is nothing within them that can account for their own origin.

Moreover, the first law of thermodynamics, also known as the law of conservation of energy, states that energy can neither be created nor destroyed. Energy can be thought of as matter (mass) since Einstein showed the two to be equivalent in the famous equation: $E=MC^2$.

This means matter (mass) can be energy and vice versa: $M=E/C^2$ (C is the velocity of light). If energy (matter) cannot be created, the universe (including us) made of energy (matter) should not exist. But it does.

Thus, the materialistic tenet that the universe appeared spontaneously from nothing violates the First Law of Thermodynamics, a known truth. Ideas that contradict truth are false.

The Second Law of Thermodynamics

Even if we allow materialists to have starting materials and laws for a Big Bang, nothing is solved. In fact, things get even worse.

That's because abiogenesis and evolution means a progression from simple to complex. First, natural laws had to emerge from nothing. Then energy from nothing. Then atoms, perpetually moving and energized dynamos, had to appear. A Big Bang explosion had to form everything else using unaccounted for preexisting natural laws, thermal noise (energy), and hydrogen gas (matter). Then simple atoms had to combine to form cells and then humans.

The most apparent question is, hearkening to our common sense, how can these transformations be true when they contradict what we observe and experience in everyday life? We don't see (keep in mind that science is observation) natural laws, energy, or atoms coming into existence from nothing and then further organizing. Rather, things rust, decay, break, fall apart, get disorganized and messy. Functionally complex things turn into dust; dust does not turn into increasingly functionally complex things.

Science backs up our common sense and experience.

Real World Thermodynamics – The Second Law exerts itself everywhere. Without concerted intelligent effort everything gets messy and degrades.

The Second Law of Thermodynamics demands that things proceed to maximum disorder. According to this law, the entire universe is headed one way with time's arrow: toward a bleak, dark, cold, uniform equilibrium of randomness.

The reverence that working scientists have for the Second Law is typified by the famed Sir Arthur Eddington: ". . . a supreme metaphysical law of the entire universe . . . If your theory is found to be against the Second Law of Thermodynamics, I can give you no hope, there is nothing for it but to collapse in deepest humiliation."

It is the Second Law that prevents perpetual motion machines. No matter how efficient a machine is made, it eventually wears down, degrades, and disassembles. Leonardo da Vinci (1494) wrote: "Oh ye seekers after perpetual motion, how many vain chimeras have you pursued? Go and take your place with the alchemists." Now then, if great minds over the course of centuries can't defy nature's Second Law, unattended nature most certainly wouldn't either. But defying the Second Law is exactly what the alchemy of materialism means.

Against the backdrop of a universe that is headed inexorably toward absolute chaos, evolutionists contend that atoms, energy, and then biology do cartwheels uphill over every other spontaneous material thing headed thermodynamically downhill.

To counter this, materialists say the law only applies to "closed" thermodynamic systems. They argue that life could emerge and evolve on Earth because it is not closed. It is open to the energy from the sun. But they fail to prove that sunbeams can cause atoms to aggregate into living cells, or those cells complexifying into the myriad life forms on the planet. In effect, their argument voids the second law and would permit the spontaneous appearance of computers, space ships, or the assembly of landfills into cities. All that would be needed would be atoms and sunbeams.

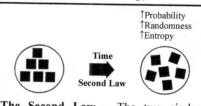

The Second Law – The two circles represent a closed (no energy exchanges with the outside) thermodynamic system. The blocks represent the degree of order therein. The Second Law of Thermodynamics says that all systems will spontaneously tend toward the state of greatest probability, greatest randomization and highest entropy.

© Wysong   Figure 012

17

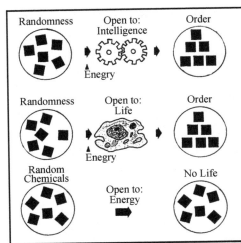

Open Thermodynamic Systems – The three circles on the left represent random arrangements of building blocks. In the top drawing, if the blocks are acted upon by energy (an open system) and intelligence, order can result. In like manner, in the second drawing, random chemicals acted upon by energy (open system) and the intelligent order within life, can also create ordered products. If the random building blocks in the third drawing are only acted upon by energy (open system), increased randomness will result, not order. Open-system thermodynamics does not solve the problem of spontaneously forming the functional complexity of life. Raw energy only expedites the removal of whatever order exists.

© Wysong   Figure 013

The existence of the tremendous functional complexity of life in the context of a universe that is infected with a thermodynamic virus causing universal degradation and uselessness presents a conundrum. Since evolution means simple to complex, the very material science evolution hails, including the Second Law, is the very science that denies the possibility of evolution.

Another problem is presented in that evolution demands an infinitely old universe. But the Second Law says that if the universe is infinitely old, the order that we see in it—planets, galaxies, hot spot stars, and us—would have long since breathed its last gasp and now be absolutely cold and without order. Everything should be just a

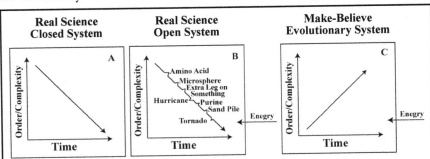

Closed and Open Systems – Real science tells us that in a closed thermodynamic system (A) with no energy or information coming into it, the system's order will degrade over time. Real science also tells us that if a thermodynamic system is open to the input of energy (B), that it will also degrade over time. There may be some blips here and there, but the inevitable degrading of order continues. It is make-believe science to argue that a system will increase in order by being open to energy – but that is exactly what evolution (C) requires.

© Wysong   Figure 014

homogeneous mix of energy and elementary particles evenly distributed throughout the universe. But that's clearly not the case.

The inference from the Second Law is that since all things run down, they all must be wound up to start. A sufficient winder upper can't be matter/energy itself since that's the stuff for which we're trying to account. And besides, the Second Law governs matter and says it cannot wind up all on its own, but must instead wind down.

Therefore, the fundamental materialistic tenet that things spontaneously increase in order and complexity violates the Second Law of Thermodynamics, a known truth. Ideas that contradict truth are false.

On the other hand, a creative intelligence not bound by the laws of thermodynamics is a sufficient explanation for the incredible functional complexity of the universe and life. This conclusion doesn't require any religious predisposition nor does it foster one. We're simply letting known truths speak to us.

Any materialist who disagrees is free to prove by evidence or experiment that complex things on the scale of complexity found even in the simplest living organism can arise spontaneously. So far, in spite of millions of pages of scientific literature and hundreds of years, nada, nothing. Just proclamations about how true evolution is. That's faith, not science.

In Your Face Thermodynamics — We too are subject to the Second Law. Not only does the genome for any given species degrade over time, the expression of that genome, life, also degrades, ages, dies, and turns to random dust.

Figure 015

5
THE LAW OF INFORMATION

It used to be thought that babies grew from a very small version of themselves—termed a homunculus. From a Bible perspective, this neatly explained how it was that "in Adam, all had sinned." The whole of humanity resided within his loins (homunculi within homunculi within homunculi . . .) Therefore, when he sinned so did all of his contained homunculi, giving us all an "original sin" requiring a savior.

Our modern understanding of genetics retired the cute little baby in a sperm homunculus idea. However, although DNA in a fertilized ovum may not be a preformed homunculus human, its program is a blueprint for a human.

To any thinking person, it is a consternating wonder that something as unimaginably complex and functional as a human could form from an egg the size of the period at the end of this sentence. The source of the complex information embedded in its DNA is an even greater wonder.

DNA is comprised of smaller molecules that in turn come from atoms which are in turn comprised of quanta. But none of these individual components have the inherent potential to create the information, the blueprint, to form a human.

There is an obvious difference between the information in sperm and eggs and that which is within their component atoms.

The Homunculus

The famous homunculus drawing by Hartsoeker in the late 1600's. Miniature people were believed to reside in the sperm, and miniature people in their sperm and on and on backwards for as many as it takes to account for an entire line of people.

© Hartsoeker   Figure 016

Search as they may, atomic physicists never find so much as even a hint of anything akin to the information characterizing life residing there. Any given atom only contains information about how to be that atom or how to randomly combine with other atoms.

If atoms had the ability to self-organize into prodigious information, such as in DNA, laboratories around the world would be churning out every imaginable sort of creature. (That would be incorrectly assuming life is nothing more than organized DNA letters.) But not even the simplest living thing has ever spontaneously formed from atoms in spite of the ability to create every imaginable experimental circumstance.

The Evolutionist's Homunculus

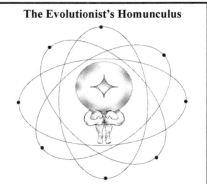

Since it is argued that all the information to create a human resides in matter itself, then it must reside in the atoms that make up the DNA molecule. No evolutionist would admit to such a thing, but that is exactly what their hypothesis demands.

© Wysong   Figure 017

The period in this box represents the size of a human egg. We all begin with such a start. Inside of that dot-sized egg is all the information required to form you and all your functions—trillions of bits of information. Nobody can explain—step-by-step with chemical specificity— much less create a human egg.

© Wysong   Figure 018

Add every materialistic explanation for the origin of life up, such as incrementalism, draw a line, and the same impossible conclusion emerges: massive amounts of information must arise from no information.

Complex functional things— like life—must come from a sufficient cause. The injection of intelligent information is always necessary to take fundamental things beyond their intrinsic nature. On their own, water molecules don't become ice sculptures, letters don't become books, dust doesn't create skyscrapers, and atoms don't create DNA.

| A. | Little Information | ——————————————→ | Massive Information | = | Creation of Massive Information |
| B. | Little Information | → (Millions of Small Steps) → | Massive Information | = | Creation of Massive Information |

The Ploy of Incrementalism – It makes no difference whether information comes about suddenly (**A**) or by small increments (**B**), the bottom line is the same: massive information of the useful directed sort found in life cannot come from lesser information.

© Wysong   Figure 019

Moreover, it's an immutable law that things naturally lose information, they don't gain it. Start at one end of a group of people and whisper to the person: "Earth science describes nature's machinations." Then ask that it be whispered one to another to the end of the group. When it gets to the end it will be something like: "Washing machines clean Earth."

At the end of any series of random events acting upon information, the loss of information always exceeds any random gains.

On July 22, 1962, the Mariner 1 space probe was exploded shortly after liftoff. The omission of a single hyphen in the guidance software information led to a series of false course correction signals. The rocket was then deliberately detonated to prevent it from crashing down in a populated area. The rocket was worth between $80 and $150 million, a loss due to a single typo error. The point is that even a small inadvertent error can fatally destroy functional information. Imagine what random changes can do.

Neither the formation of or inevitable degradation of information over time jibes with materialism. Science is about observation and facts. But there are no observations or facts demonstrating the spontaneous formation of information or its increase in the absence of outside intelligent agency.

Matter can naturally manifest in different forms that, at first glance, appear to be something other and more complex than what they were to begin with. A snowflake is an intricate pattern that does not look at all like a water molecule. But the snowflake is nothing more than a manifestation of the preexisting information in the molecule. Even though there are trillions of different snowflake configurations, they are all an expression of a preexistent capacity held within water molecules. But aside from the ability to form water, clouds, and snowflakes, as well as evaporate, sublimate, combine with or disassociate other chemicals, and expand upon freezing, that's about all the information that water molecules contain. The encyclopedia within water molecules never so much as adds even a meaningful word. It is what it is and that's it.

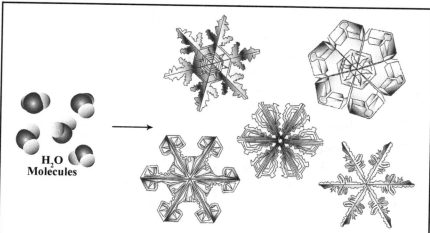

Water Information – Water molecules (left) contain within them the information to create apparently limitless configurations of exquisitely beautiful snowflakes (right). This transformation does not defy the Law of Information or the Second Law of Thermodynamics, nor does it represent order emerging from disorder. Snowflakes, like any crystal, are just a different manifestation of order that is already present within the atoms. To parallel what is proposed in evolution, the water molecules would have to order themselves into a variety of ice sculptures that move with free will, in other words create whole new orders of information, function, and complexity beyond that inherent in the molecules.

© Wysong   Figure 020

Organisms are the effect of information. The DNA molecule is made of four nucleotides, represented by the letters A, C, G, T (adenine, cytosine, guanine, thymine). This is a quaternary code, as opposed to the binary code of computers. These molecular letters are in turn organized into genetic codons, genes, operons, regulons, and chromosomes which are like words, sentences, paragraphs, chapters, and books.

The prodigious DNA information in even one human cell is staggering. The 100 trillion cells in the entire body would equal 1,000,000,000,000,000 (1015) copies of this book. That's enough books, stacked side-by-side, as in a library, to reach to the sun well over fifty times.

The information-carrying capacity of DNA outstrips the man-made inorganic data-storage devices such as flash memory, hard disks, or even storage based on quantum-computing methods. It's estimated that about a teaspoon of DNA in 2011 could have held all human-generated information up to that time. That would include everything from the ancient Greeks through every selfie, text, movie, and album.

With present silicon chip technology, by 2040 the amount of world data accumulated for instant access would require a facility costing billions and decades to build. This is not to mention consuming hundreds of megawatts of power and exhausting the world's supply of computer-grade silicon. On the other hand, only about two pounds of DNA would be required and would consume about 0.04 watts per gigabyte.

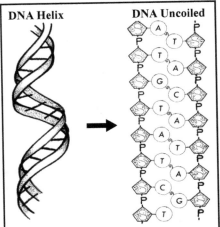

DNA Helix   **DNA Uncoiled**

DNA Language – The DNA molecule consists of a four letter alphabet (A,T,G,C) that is arranged into genetic sentences, paragraphs, chapters, books, and libraries. The resulting information instructs chemicals to form the protein structures of life. That information has nothing to do with the characteristics of the atoms composing the DNA molecule any more than ink has anything to do with the information in a blueprint. Manipulation of letters (English or DNA) into information requires intelligent input.

© Wysong   Figure 021

In addition to recognizing the extraordinary information-carrying capacity of DNA, the critical point to understand is that DNA is beyond the characteristics and information of the atoms composing its structure. Atoms simply do not have the know-how on their own to form DNA or any other information-carrying biochemical that could result in functional complexity.

Information is an entity in and of itself and apart from the letters and vocabulary it uses. It is neither energy dependent nor matter dependent. It is other. Something had to encode ("tell") quanta, neutrons, protons, cells, organs, physiological systems, bodies, planets, stars, and galaxies to be what they are and behave as they do. Nothing discovered within nature can account for this, other than preexisting information.

Information requires an information giver, an intelligence, a mind. We know this to be true because when things that contain functional information, such as blueprints, music, language, instructions, and computer HTML are constructed, they require mind. We also know that once in place, such information remains as it is or degrades with time. There is no exception to the rule and that is as good as science can get. It's simple, obvious, common sense, and requires no data to be excluded.

Everything is what it is because of information. Everything stays what it is because of information. Randomness and time are destroyers of information, not its creators.

Information requires mind. That is an inviolable law, a universal truth. No evidence or experiment proves otherwise.

This conclusion doesn't require any religious predisposition nor does it lead to one. We're simply letting facts and reason guide us.

6
THE LAW OF IMPOSSIBILITY

From a practical standpoint, our lives are guided by what we believe to be possible and what is not. I think it's impossible to fix the hard-drive in my computer with a hammer. I think it's possible that a computer technician can fix it. Such practical reasoning occurs on a daily basis with all of us and makes life livable.

As we look about our world at its incomprehensible complexity, it's easy to conclude that it's not the mere product of chance. That conclusion can be schooled out, but it still haunts us.

Since we actually know so little, it seems reasonable to believe that anything is possible. But that would mean there can be no certainty about anything. If true, all science would end and we would fear to put one foot in front of the other because of the "possibility" of the floor turning to quicksand or disappearing entirely.

Moreover, if anything is possible, then the chance that any one belief is correct (like the belief that anything is impossible) is infinitely small.

Nature's laws, not odds or opinions, define truths. Things fall to the ground, north poles attract south poles, negative charges attract positive charges, mass and energy are never destroyed, they just change places . . . and so on through all of science and mathematics. Laws, by definition, are 100% correct and any opinion contrary to them is 100% wrong.

The laws of probability are part of nature's laws and can be applied to the chance formation of life. Two critical precursors to life are proteins and nucleic acids (DNA, RNA). The odds of even a simple protein found in life coming into existence by chance is $1/10^{78,000}$. That's one chance in one followed by 78,000 zeros. The most important proteins, enzymes, cannot form without nucleic acids. Nor can information-carrying nucleic acids, as found in life, form without enzymes. If both were to form spontaneously and independently, the probability of them forming at the same time is one in $10^{168,000}$. (For details on these calculations, do an Internet search on origin of life probabilities or see my previous book, The Creation-Evolution Controversy.)

Moving on to the probability for an actual living organism. Morowitz calculated the odds to be one in $10^{340,000,000}$. Sagan said the odds of such an event was one in $10^{2,000,000,000}$. (Don't underestimate these numbers. For perspective, the entire universe contains 10^{80} elementary particles, and is 10^{17} seconds old.)

Probabilities determine truths we, and the technical, industrial, and commercial worlds rely on every day. For example, casinos win approximately 52% of the time, their patrons win 48% of the time. The fastest growing city in America, lavish Las Vegas, is being built with such a small probability advantage.

Using Sagan's above figure of one chance in $10^{2,000,000,000}$ for life to form by chance, the odds are 99.99999 . . . for about two billion more 9's % against. If the casino's 52% is certain, this 99. + about a billion 9s % equals impossible.

Nevertheless, when faced with these dire probabilities, materialists will argue that there is still a numerator of one in Sagan's one chance in $10^{2,000,000,000}$. That, they say, means there is still a chance.

But the one in the numerator is effectively vaporized by the denominator. Probability experts calculate that odds greater than one chance in 10^{150} would be impossible. Some say one chance in 10^{50} is impossible. Morowitz's $10^{340,000,000}$, Sagan's $10^{2,000,000,000}$ or my $10^{168,000}$ are definitely beyond even the most generous impossible probability of 10^{150}.

Making these numbers even more impossible is the estimate by mathematicians that the maximum number of chance events that could have occurred in the universe since its inception is 10^{120}. That would make Morowits's, Sagan's, and my odds impossible to even play out. It would be like trying to flip heads five times in a row but only being allowed to flip the coin once.

Another tactic used to overcome the law of impossibility is to load the dice with infinite universes, vast time, and an appeal to gaps in our understanding. But there's a sample size of only one universe. Furthermore, time is the enemy of improbable events. In casinos, time always makes their slight edge pan out for them, not the gamblers. As for basing a belief upon what we do not understand or know, that would justify any belief in anything. It would also make such a belief unfalsifiable, which is the opposite of truth.

"... and then a miracle happens."

© Wysong   Figure 022

A leaf could jump to Pluto rather than fall to the ground (it is possible). One could calculate the odds for such a ridiculous thing and there would be a 1 in the numerator. But it won't happen because there's a law of gravity and several others that declare it won't. It's not a matter of odds; it's a matter of law.

Nature's laws demand that order and information (as in life) cannot emerge from chaos. That denies abiogenesis. Further, once order is present it cannot compound its order and information and improve upon itself. That denies evolution.

The only thing that can change the odds and create functionally complex order out of chaos is an intelligent agency.

This conclusion doesn't require any religious predisposition nor does it lead to one. We're simply opening our eyes to reason, evidence, and nature's laws.

Those who disagree that abiogenesis is impossible must prove by evidence or experiment that functional complexity on the scale found in even the simplest living organism can beat the odds and arise spontaneously and then further complexify. Stories, hypotheticals, extrapolations, and faith in future discovery do not qualify as proof.

7
THE LAW OF BIOGENESIS

Spontaneous generation is an old belief that life automatically arises from nonliving matter. It was a reasonable thing to assume in the pre-scientific era since there were no microscopes to identify what caused critters to pop out of manure and mud.

Spontaneous Generation is Disproven

Now, in every introductory biology textbook, the disproof of spontaneous generation is featured as part of the proud history of the march of science. Experiments by Redi, Spallanzani, and Pasteur demonstrated that if the starting materials in a flask were sealed and rendered lifeless by cooking, no life appeared. Life arose only if there was preexisting life in the flask.

This resulted in the Law of Biogenesis: life can only come from preexisting life.

But the ambitious goal of proving spontaneous generation took on new life with Darwin's evolutionary ideas. It's now disguised by renaming it "evolution," "abiogenesis," or "biopoiesis," giving it a more modern and credible scientific flare.

Pellegrino, in his book, Ghosts of Vesuvius, confidently describes the saga of abiogenesis as follows:

"In the beginning, there was little besides the strong and the weak forces, gravitation, and electromagnetism . . . hydrogen and helium, with a little lithium here and there; but from the lights in the heavens, you might have guessed that these were enough . . . Life was inevitable . . . warm, wet zones . . . were trying to make life . . . From atoms and empty space . . . From the dust of stars . . . the phenomenon we call life is but the most likely outcome of some very common elements, if stirred together and kept warm enough and wet enough for long enough . . . We are the dust of the universe trying to understand itself . . . volcanically heated water . . . to act as primitive catalytic centers . . . nudging atoms of carbon forcefully and with statistical inevitability in the direction of biochemistry . . . life . . . would appear to have been pulled from a curiously simple bag of tricks . . . Life from nonlife. You could probably start the process in your own kitchen."

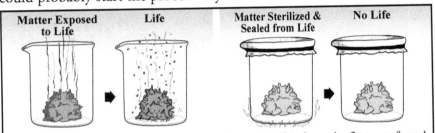

Spontaneous Generation Disproved – Matter exposed to bacteria, fly eggs, fungal spores, etc., may generate populations of life. Superficially it appears as though life is coming from the matter itself. However, as shown by Redi, Pasteur and Spallanzani, if matter is sterilized and then sealed from preexisting life, no life arises.

© Wysong   Figure 024

Really? We're to believe we could do in our kitchen what thousands of scientists for hundreds of years have been unable to do? Not one experiment using the best brains on the planet has demonstrated life can come from nonlife. To this day, no living thing has ever emerged from a lab where the starting materials were simple atoms.

Even if life were the mere assemblage of atoms and molecules, which it isn't since dead things have those composites, the sheer scope of the problem is beyond human capability. A "simple" bacterium contains 50 billion atoms in precise ratios and specific functionally complex arrangements all interrelated in precise machine-like ways.

Invented Words Do Not Prove Evolution

That doesn't mean there aren't plenty of proposed scenarios about life's early moorings. But these guesses are propped up by creating new words, not life. Speculative precursors are given evocative bio-seductive names like proteinoids, protocells, bions, protobionts, eobionts,

Spontaneous Generation – Students the world over are taught the historical and scientific greatness of the disproof of spontaneous generation and the establishment of the law of biogenesis (life only comes from pre-existing life). Nonetheless, evolutionist teachers dogmatically assert that life first arose on Earth by spontaneous generation.

© Wysong

Figure 026

microspheres, and biomorphs. These words, the words alone, are then promoted as transitional steps on the living cell's ascent from inorganic soup. There's talk of "membranes," "organelles," "reproduction," and "vesicles," words normally associated with real living things. But that's only proof by linguistic hobnobbing. The definition of life is even broadened to help accommodate such potential ancestors and to make it near impossible to differentiate life from nonlife.

The stories about life from non-life, as technically sophisticated as they may be at times, are still just stories of make-believe—"once upon a time, long, long ago . . ." The words, the invented tendentious words themselves (abiogenesis, biopoiesis, protobionts, biomorphs, etc.), not real facts and proof are the crux of the origin of life case.

Scientists today—3.8 billion years after life supposedly bubbled up out of the primordial broth—with all of the 21st-century technology at their disposal, have yet to even synthesize one cell or even one functional part (organelle) of a cell, or even any but the very simplest of the 6000 known enzymes essential to life. It can't be done with all our brainpower, but stewing little eddies at the base of volcanoes 3.8 billion years ago supposedly did it all on their own.

That conclusion is only possible if any conceivable alternative explanation for the origin of life is dismissed a priori.

31

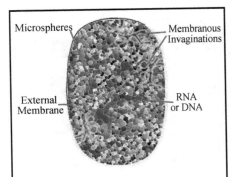

Microspheres

External Membrane

Membranous Invaginations

RNA or DNA

Sci Fi Protobiont – Although no such creature has ever been found or created, this is how this little imaginary life precursor is described: "Protobionts were the evolutionary precursors of the first prokaryotic cells. Protobionts were originated by the convergence of microspheres of proteins, carbohydrates, lipids, nucleic acids (RNA and DNA), and other organic substances, generally enclosed by lipidic membranes. Water was the most significant factor for the configuration of the protobionts' endoplasm. Microspheres were grouped into membranous envelopes to assemble organelles dedicated to specialized functions. We think that the RNA was the first nucleic acid in protobionts. RNA was competent to produce autocatalytic and non-autocatalytic proteins. Some of those autocatalytic proteins helped self-synthesis of RNA molecules. When climate was too hot, the enzymes for the synthesis of DNA could not work properly, mainly because the DNA was unsteady at very high temperatures. After, when the environmental conditions were more propitious, the molecules of RNA built molecules of DNA. Gradually, several sectors of the external membrane invaginated into the endoplasm, forming organelles as endoplasmic reticulum, Golgi apparatus, lysosomes, peroxysomes, vacuoles, and other membranous structures. Most primitive protobionts lacked a nuclear membrane (nuclear envelope)."

Although the author is to be applauded for giving it a shot, not one of the steps forward from the starting materials is scientifically feasible or experimentally reproducible. Looks good and sounds good unless any single detail is scrutinized.

© Nasif Nahle, biocab.org   Figure 027

Dead Things Are Not Alive

For hundreds of years, explorers have tried to find the right mixture of chemicals to create life. We know that amino acids, proteins, carbohydrates, nucleic acids, minerals, vitamins and so on are necessary for life. If an abiogenesis chemist creates any one of these components in a laboratory, there is great excitement. The accomplishment is heralded as proof that life is no big mystery. All that is needed is a little more time, more research, more funding . . . and manufacturers will be creating life with as much ease as they now produce plastic spoons and noodles.

But there's something amiss in this enthusiasm. During my medical life, I have seen many deaths. One second a person or animal is alive, the next moment they're dead. For medical practitioners, it's incredibly frustrating to see this happen when the material composition of the organism is still all there. Reversing death, even when all the necessary biochemical components are there, preformed in the dead body, has proven to be impossible.

If an entire organism with all of its trillions of chemical parts and pieces in place, once dead, remains dead, there is no reason to believe that a chemist's ability to create a few of these parts in a laboratory proves that life can come from nonlife. Faith, not evidence or reason, is the only basis for such belief.

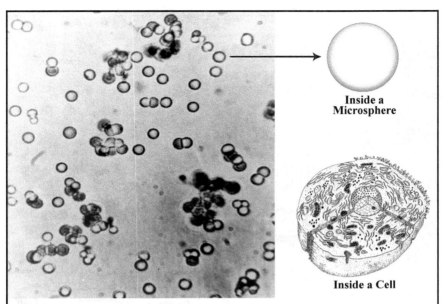

Inside a Microsphere

Inside a Cell

Microsphere Forms – A photograph of microspheres magnified x 450. These typify the "life-like" forms microspheres can take. The twin forms and "microsphere division" are generally produced by pressing on the microscope coverslip. Microspheres are mere physical phenomena like the foam bubbles on a seashore or the droplets of oil in a vinegar salad dressing. They are dead-ended and do not reproduce in a biological sense. They are as close to a living thing as a grain of sand is to a modern skyscraper.

Left: © S. W. Fox. | Right: © Wysong   Figure 028

Moreover, the technology is now available to analyze an organism and quantitate the precise percentages of its different atoms. If life and health could result from the mere assemblage of atoms, alchemists would have long ago created life, and doctors would have long ago solved the problems of disease and death. Instead, only lifeless pretenses emerge in the modern-day alchemist's laboratory, and death and disease increase in proportion to the degree that doctors treat life as if it were merely an assemblage of chemicals. Life is clearly more than a mixture of its chemical components and cannot be explained by them.

No Cheating

Even if someday scientists create life in the laboratory starting with atoms, spontaneous generation would not be proven. Millions of working hours in laboratories by Nobel laureates over hundreds of years would hardly qualify as convincing evidence that no intelligence is necessary to create life.

© Wysong · Figure 029

Life's Components Are Fragile

Another stickler is that the materials and forces that are supposed to have caused the formation of the biochemicals of life—water, heat, lightning bolts, and so on—are actually most effective at disassembling, not creating them. For example, enzymes are chains of amino acids configured in elaborate three-dimensional forms and are essential to virtually every life process. They would have had to form for life to emerge out of the bubbling volcanic goo. But they are destroyed at temperatures above only 118°F (not to mention the killer impact of ultraviolet light, cosmic rays, acidity, concurrent noxious chemicals, oxidizing and chelating minerals, hydration, acidity, alkalinity—all present in a volcanic setting). One lightning bolt blazing in at 55,000°F would nix any abiogenesis hopes in short order.

The Law of Biogenesis stands. It affirms the laws of thermodynamics, information, and probability and points to intelligent causation. Either scientific laws are wrong, or abiogenesis is wrong.

These conclusions require no religious predisposition. We're simply letting known truths guide us.

Anyone who disagrees is free to prove by evidence or experiment that complex things on the scale of complexity found even in the simplest living organism can arise spontaneously.

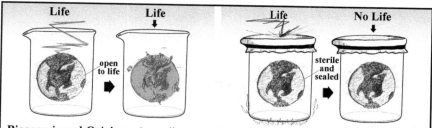

Biogenesis and Origins – According to the law of biogenesis, life cannot spring from lifeless matter. Therefore, if the primordial Earth were exposed to life, more life could arise. If there were no life to begin with, no life could result.

© Wysong

Figure 025

8
THE LAWS OF CHEMISTRY

For life to arise spontaneously out of inorganic matter, basic building blocks such as amino acids (precursors to proteins and enzymes), sugars (precursors to carbohydrates), glycerol and fatty acids (precursors to lipids), and nucleotides (precursors to DNA and RNA) must first form.

Amino Acids and Proteins

Within living organisms, chains of amino acids form proteins that comprise enzymes, the catalysts that drive life's machinery. All the components of life could be present, but without enzymes, nothing further would happen other than Second Law degradation.

However, the spontaneous formation of enzymes would violate nature's laws. Here's how:

1. Chemicals (carbon, nitrogen, hydrogen, oxygen, sulfur) that comprise amino acids can form millions of molecules other than amino acids. Although a few amino acids have formed in experiments attempting to duplicate imagined early Earth conditions favorable to forming amino acids, an intelligently designed experiment proves intelligence, not spontaneity. Nevertheless, such experiments are used as proof of the spontaneous generation of life. But even then, an amino acid is not life any more than a water molecule is. Compounding the problem further is the fact that if any of the 500 or so amino acids found in life were to form spontaneously in the early Earth,

they would then need to find one another to link up in a very specific way to form enzymes. The probability of this happening is way beyond the limit of possibility of one chance in 10^{150}.

2. Amino acids can exist in either right- or left-handed forms (called D- and L-enantiomers). They are mirror images of each other. Approximately a 50:50 mix forms in laboratory amino acid syntheses. That's also what would have occurred (if it ever really did occur) in the broths nestled on the lightning scorched volcanic landscape at the dawn of prehistory. But life's proteins are not composed of a mixture of D- (dextro) and L- (levo) amino acid enantiomers. They are almost exclusively left-handed (levo, L-). Spontaneous chemistry cannot account for this.

3. Proteins are not just straight strings of amino acids. They have a secondary, tertiary, and quaternary structure that arises as the string twists and folds upon itself to create a three-dimensional form. This folded, globular-like structure is critical to function. In living organisms, once the primary amino acid strings form, they take on a mind of their own and proceed to fold into a specific three-dimensional shape in a matter of seconds or minutes. This folded structure is critical because it exposes reactive sites in specific positions on the surface to permit specific biological and catalytic functions.

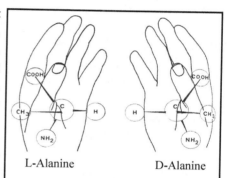

L-Alanine   D-Alanine

Enantiomers – Most amino acids can exist as D and L enantiomers. The enantiomers of the same amino acid are alike in containing the same atoms, but are different three-dimensionally. They are mirror images of one another but not superimposable. So, just as the right and left hand cannot be matched when superimposed, or a right-handed glove cannot fit a left hand, neither can the D and L forms of alanine be matched when superimposed.

© Wysong   Figure 030

Even a tiny protein of a hundred amino acids has potentially trillions of folded forms. But only one shape will do in living organisms. This specificity defies explanation by random spontaneous processes. It is known as the Levinthal paradox.

The importance of proper folding is manifest in diseases. For example, brain proteins that fold wrong create prion diseases (transmissible spongiform encephalopathies) such as mad cow disease, sheep scrapie, chronic wasting disease in deer, Kuru, fatal familial insomnia, and Creutzfeldt-Jakob disease in humans. Other diseases and degenerative conditions such as Alzheimer's, dementia, and Parkinson's are also related to aberrant protein folding.

The propensity of proteins to fold and stick together creates the threat of amyloid formation (the default option) if chaperone proteins are not simultaneously present to orchestrate the proper folding. When beta-amyloids lose the three-dimensional conformation that hides their sticky parts, they become insoluble and toxic. In the brain, they form plaques that degrade neural function resulting in diseases such as Alzheimer's if

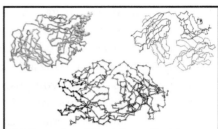

3-Dimensional Proteins – Proteins are far more than just chains of amino acids. The three-dimensional shape that a protein takes is very specific and critical to life functions. This configuration is dictated by the sequence of amino acids and will be fatally altered if even one amino acid is incorrect.

© Wysong   Figure 031

protective mechanisms aren't in place. But there were no chaperone proteins and protective mechanisms in the early Earth scenario. In spite of these impediments, scientists propose toxic beta-amyloids as one of the first steps in the formation of life.

The specificity of proteins is further illustrated in sickle cell anemia. In this disease, only two of the 574 amino acids in the blood's oxygen-carrying hemoglobin molecule are wrong. Each red blood cell contains about 280 million molecules of hemoglobin. This defect causes them to distort and even rupture. Death can result.

There are hundreds of thousands of proteins and other sequenced molecules of specific structure and shape in every cell. Things have to be perfect for life to exist. Random chemistry is totally incapable of accounting for such perfection.

4. It must also be considered that amino acids could go through all the work of assembling into a chain of L-amino acids, fold in a precise three-dimensional way to have enzymatic activity, and then be scuttled if the temperature ever rises above 118° F. That's highly likely on an early Earth starting at 4000° F and then continuously pockmarked with steaming volcanoes.

5. Before enzymes come to an inglorious hellish end in the primordial soup, their precursors would not know how to assemble and fold without preexistent DNA. On top of that, not only do enzymes need DNA, DNA cannot form without enzymes. Both must exist at the same time in order for either to exist.

Nevertheless, materialists imagine enzymes and DNA developing step-by-step on their own without ever laying out the step-by-step chemistry, or proving that one could occur without the other.

6. Hundreds of toxic problems can occur if the components of DNA and enzymes are just mixed together, as abiogenesis proposes and as occurs in your kitchen when you cook meals. For example, the ribose in DNA is a reducing sugar that will combine with amino acids in a Maillard reaction. The resulting advanced glycation end products (AGEs) are toxic. In living organisms, they can be a factor in aging and degenerative diseases, such as diabetes, atherosclerosis, chronic kidney disease, and Alzheimer's.

Water Problems

You've probably heard that since our body fluids are similar to seawater, we must have come from the sea. But when scientists try to make the biochemicals of life in seawater, nothing happens. This is, in part, because of the Law of Mass Action.

In a chemical reaction, there are starting ingredients and end products. Most biochemical reactions are reversible and can go either way, toward the end products or back toward the starting materials. The direction the reaction takes depends upon the relative amounts (mass) of the materials on each side of the chemical reaction. The more ingredients, the more pressure to form products; the more products, or things like products, like water, the more back pressure to revert to ingredients.

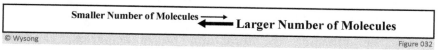

Smaller Number of Molecules ⟶ ⟵ **Larger Number of Molecules**

© Wysong   Figure 032

Many of the chemical reactions that form life's biochemicals are condensation reactions, meaning ingredients combine and form water as one of the products.

This is how the reaction looks if proteins were to be formed in the ocean:

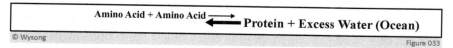

Amino Acid + Amino Acid ⟶ ⟵ **Protein + Excess Water (Ocean)**

© Wysong   Figure 033

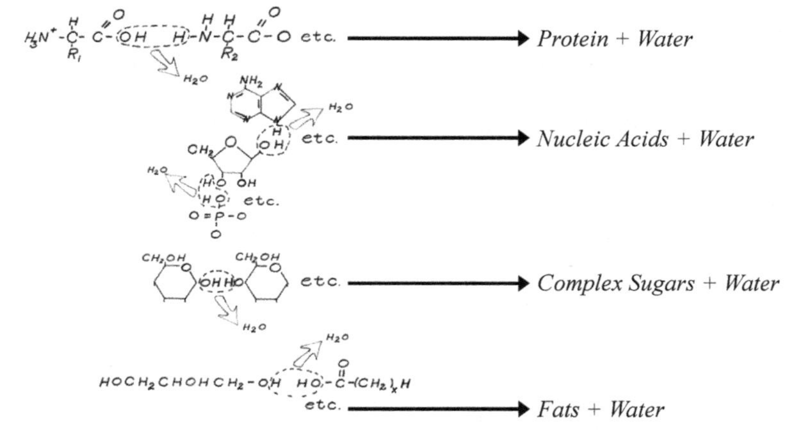

Condensation Reactions – The chemical reactions that form proteins, nucleic acids (DNA, RNA), complex sugars (polysaccharides), and fats (lipids) are known as condensation reactions. As the polymers are built up from subunits (e.g. proteins from amino acids), water is liberated. After the water is released, the subunits join: the c=o of one amino acid will attach to the N of the next amino acid. These condensation reactions are reversible, and in the presence of excess water (the primitive oceans?) will proceed from the complex to the simple rather than from the simple to the complex.

© Wysong   Figure 036

Note that water would be the predominant component in an early Earth milieu. That means, according to the Law of Mass Action, the reaction would not go to the right toward the formation of proteins, but rather, to the left toward their disassembly into the starting amino acids.

The only reason the reactions go to the right inside a watery living organism (70% water) is that enzymes drive the reactions to the right. But there were no enzymes back in the primordial sea because enzymes are proteins and cannot form in the sea because of the law of mass action. It's a heck of a pickle.

Further impeding the formation of amino acids, or their degradation if formed, would be heat, light, and oxidation. Thus, the ingredients for proteins and enzymes would be foiled before they even had a chance to try a doomed condensation reaction.

Lipids

Lipids are a class of compounds that include fats, sterols, and oils. They are important to life because virtually every biological membrane is made of a sandwich of these molecules called the bilipid membrane.

They are also essential in forming hormones, and cell, tissue, and immune regulators called eicosanoids. The popular press and brochures in your doctor's office promote the outdated idea that fats and cholesterol are unhealthy. However, lipids are actually critical to life—in their unaltered natural state.

Fatty Acid Configurations – Fatty acids can exist in rigid straight configurations as in saturated and trans- forms or, in bent more dynamic cis- forms. Water, heat, minerals, oxygen, acid, and myriad other factors in raw nature can destroy, inhibit formation, or convert them into toxins. Their precise form is essential to life and they can only be safely synthesized and maintained within living tissue.

© Wysong   Figure 034

For life to arise, lipids are necessary. But since they form via condensation reactions, they, and life, could not arise spontaneously in a watery milieu.

Additionally, the essential fatty acids that are so important to metabolism are highly vulnerable to oxidation (like biological rusting). Oxidizing minerals, heat, oxygen, acidity, and even light will not only render them useless but convert them to free radical and trans-fat toxins. (For a more thorough discussion of this topic see my books, *Lipid Nutrition*, and *The Cholesterol Myth*.)

No early Earth environment can even be conceived in which these complicated long-chain fragile lipid molecules could arise by chance, remain biologically promising, and nontoxic. There would have been photo-oxidizing sunlight back then and lots of oxidizing minerals. At some point, there was oxidizing oxygen, electrical discharges, and heat cooking things up. Such a noxious cauldron would never do for either forming or protecting essential fatty acids so they could evolve.

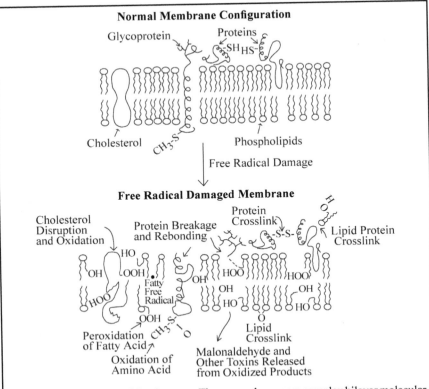

Free Radical Damage to Membranes – Tissue membranes are complex bilayer molecular structures capable of undergoing disruption from free radicals. The resulting membrane loses structural and functional integrity resulting in characteristic aging, wrinkles, drying, and predisposition to neoplasia (cancer). This schematic of what happens to skin tissue due to free radical damage reflects what can happen throughout body tissues.

© Wysong   Figure 035

DNA

DNA and RNA hold the promise of replication, which is fundamental to life.

However, aside from the toxic glycation mentioned above, the ribose sugars (Deoxyribose, the D part of DNA) that form the backbone of DNA are of only one enantiomer, in this case, the right- handed (D-, dextro) variety. But when these sugars form outside of living tissue, they are a 50:50 mixture of D- and L- forms.

What's more, the mass action of water gets in the way of DNA synthesis driving the condensation reactions to the left, back toward the simpler ingredients. On top of that, remember that the ribose sugars cannot form if amino acids are present. But amino acids need to be present because they form enzymes, and enzymes are necessary to join the subunits (nucleotides) of DNA.

By far, the biggest abiogenic problem with DNA is its prodigious information. Information cannot arise without the input of intelligence.

This doesn't take into account the fact that functional DNA is not a bare molecule in cells. The new science of epigenetics demonstrates that proteins and other complex biochemicals shroud the helix and serve as switches to turn sections of the molecule on and off. All of the above chemical and probability impossibilities would apply to the origin of these critical shrouding epigenetic molecules.

Epigenetics – DNA is not a bare molecule nor does it solely determine genetic expression. It is shrouded in complex epigenetic molecules that serve as switches and can be modified by environmental factors. The existence of these molecules and the epigenetic mechanism can no more be explained by evolution than can DNA.

© Wysong

Figure 037

Dead Ends

Any progression of chemicals to more complex states would require incremental steps. But an event such as the formation of an amino acid has no memory; it's dead-ended. It doesn't know to hold its form until the next improbable event occurs to build it up to a more complex next step.

The spontaneous formation of life would require the piling on of millions of functional complexities, step by step, all remembered, held, and improved upon. Such progressive functional complexity occurs nowhere in our reality, other than within already formed living organisms.

There are no footholds upon which one event can advance to the next, just forbidding chemical and probability laws, and a slippery thermodynamic slope where everything slides back to where it began, or less.

The laws of chemistry deny the spontaneous formation of life and affirm intelligent intervention.

This conclusion doesn't require any religious predisposition. We are simply letting known truths guide us.

Cilia/Flagella	Mitochondria	Rough Endoplasmic Reticulum
Intracellular Fluid	Peroxisome	Smooth Endoplasmic Reticulum
Potassium	Ribosome	Nuclear Envelope
Magnesium	Lysosome	Nuclear Pores
Phosphate ions	Lipase	Nucleus
Extracellular Fluid	Carbohydrase	Nucleoplasm
Sodium ions	Protease	Nuclear matrix
Chloride ions	Nuclease	DNA
Cell Membrane	Vacuole	Chromatin
Proteins	Water	Euchromatin
Phospholipids	Waste products	Heterochromatin
Cholesterol	Maintain acidic	Nucleolus
Polysaccharides	internal pH	Fibrilla Centers
Cytoplasm	Centriole	Dense Fibrilla Component
Enzymes	Microtubule	Granular Fibrilla Component
Carbohydrates	Cytoskeleton	tRNA
Salts	Actin filament	Ribosomes
Proteins	Intermediate filaments	
RNA	Microtubles	
Ions	Microtrabecule	
Macromolecules	Golgi Apparatus	
Organelles		
Cystol		
Water		
Salt		
Enzymes		
Organic molecules		

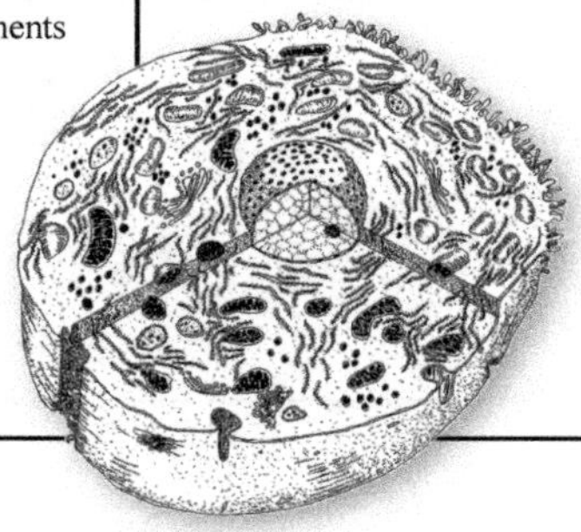

Cellular Components – A partial list of the composition of living cells. Note the word *partial*. Every single item must be accounted for. The spontaneous generation of life is obviously not just about forming amino acids, a protein, or a nucleic acid. It must account for all parts and pieces, and their parts and pieces, in a synchronous fashion, in the right proportions, in the right stereoisomeric and three-dimensional forms, and all this out of a harsh physical environment. Even if they were to all form, life would not result since science can put the chemical components of these things together right now and the mix remains lifeless.

Figure 038

9
THE LAW OF TIME

Vast time is thought to be the solution to the improbability of life arising spontaneously by chance and then evolving into the myriad creatures on Earth.

The universe is said to be 17 billion years old, and the Earth about 4.7 billion years old. Those ages, as will be explained, are by no means absolute. They are selected from among many possible ages to give abiogenesis and evolution breathing room.

The Uncertainty of Dating Methods

Any dating method that takes us beyond observable history is a guess.

Nobody was around for billions of years to observe and record events that could affect dating clocks. We can't know with certainty that ice at the poles has always been laid down at today's rate, that tree rings only record 365-day years, or that sediment has always accumulated at the rate we now see it accumulating. Even the sacrosanct rate of radioactive decay is not certain.

In fact, cataclysms have occurred which have both accelerated and slowed clocks. That would make it impossible to extrapolate from rates observed today into the past and date anything with certainty. (See my *Creation-Evolution Controversy* book for a more thorough discussion of many popular dating methods and their weaknesses.)

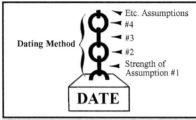

Dating Assumptions – All dating methods rely on a set of assumptions. They are like links in a chain holding up the date that was determined. The certainty of the date can only be as strong as the weakest link. Since the strength of links that extend beyond direct observation cannot be known, all such dates are assumptions.

© Wysong   Figure 039

For example, in 1991 Oxford University used the radiocarbon method to date a rock painting found in Africa and determined it to be 1,200 years old. But later a Cape Town artist identified the painting as her recent creation and explained it was stolen from her garden.

The Harvard Institute of Geophysics used the potassium-argon method to assign an age to lava of 3 billion years. But the lava was known to have formed in 1801. In another case, lava that was known to be 1,000 years old from historical records was dated at 465,000 years old.

Different dating methods used for the same sample can also yield vastly disparate ages. Examples could be enumerated almost endlessly.

As a rule, when there are dates that do not accord with presuppositions about how old a certain thing is expected to be, they are ignored or set aside as anomalous.

Evolutionists are not alone in their bias about the age of the Earth. Archbishop James Ussher, in 1650, read the Bible and decided creation took place in 4004 BC. Dr. John Lightfoot, a professor at Cambridge University, one-upped Ussher and added more precision. He agreed that creation occurred in that year, but narrowed it down to October 23rd at 9:00 AM. These confident fellows, like evolutionists, also based conclusions on prior belief. Contrary evidence was summarily rejected.

Catastrophes

It is assumed that it takes millions of years to create the vast depths of sedimentary rocks in the Earth's crust. Dating these rocks would be a simple matter of measuring how much sediment is laid down today by rivers, oceans, and floods (about 0.2 millimeters per year on average), and dividing the 0.2 millimeters into the depth of the strata. This sounds reasonable enough—as long as there were no cataclysms that accelerated deposition or erosion.

But scientists have now come to understand that Earth history does not always move uniformly or glacially slow. Earth has a history of catastrophes. Modern examples show the dramatic impact such events can have on geology. For example, when Mount St. Helens erupted in 1980, 18 billion cubic feet of material laid down 600 feet of sediment. Subsequently, a 100-foot deep canyon was cut. The walls of this canyon show a layering like the walls of canyons all over the world that are used to prove billions of years of history.

Deep Canyon Created by Mount St. Helens' Eruption – The flat plain of pumice deposited on May 18, 1980, was eroded to a depth of more than 100 feet by August 1984. Obviously Grand Canyon style geological formations do not require millions of years.

© 1984 Geoscience Research Institute   Figure 040

Mount St. Helens' Aftermath – Photograph taken in August 1983. Man provides scale. The gorge was created by the mudflow of March 19, 1982. Mass wasting of the sides and water erosion of the channel have kept the gorge open, forming part of the new drainage network on the pumice plain at the headwaters of the North Fork of the Toutle River.

© 1984 Geoscience Research Institute   Figure 041

Vast and quick sedimentation with sudden burial is necessary for fossil formation. Otherwise, huge dinosaurs and mammoths could not get preserved as fossils. Some creatures were killed and mummified so quickly that food is still in their mouths and undigested in their stomachs.

Fossil Proof of Catastrophe – The Eocene varves of Fossil Lake in Wyoming yielded this fossil of a perch swallowing a herring. It is estimated by evolutionists that a foot of rock here would require 2,000 years to form. This fossil proves that theory false since not only would dead fish not be fossilized by a slow build up of silt, but most certainly not a live one in the middle of a meal.

© Princeton Museum of Natural History   Figure 042

Millions of marine creatures that would normally die, be eaten, or decay are preserved as fossils. Trees are fossilized upright coursing through 40 feet of coal. But no tree could avoid disintegration while millions of years of coal were formed around it. Extremely fragile tissue such as skin, fish scales, and eyes have even been preserved. Such would demand instantaneous burial and encasement.

Fossils don't prove vast time. They prove sudden catastrophe.

Fossil Ripples – These are ripple marks fossilized in the Red Deer River in Alberta. Such ephemeral markings in sand could never be preserved by slow geological processes. Sudden burial by catastrophe is the only reasonable explanation.

© Princeton Museum Natural History   Figure 043

A Young Universe

Evolutionists start with the presumption of vast time and select those dating methods in support. Religionists start with the presumption of a young universe and select those dating methods in support.

Neither can prove their beliefs with certainty using dates.

Time is Irrelevant

Polystrate Tree – This Lepidodendrid tree trunk found in Tennessee, has its base on the Pewee coal seam and extends twenty feet through sedimentary rock. It would be impossible for a tree to be preserved in this way by the slow build up of silt around it over millions of years. Go to any forest and note what happens to trees and other organic material. Time returns them to dust, it does not create fossils.

© Steve Minkin   Figure 044

Our physical reality is like a machine, and machines will not function without all elements simultaneously present. We're part of an infinite machine consisting of organs, cells, and biochemicals connected to an ecological web of millions of organisms, connected to air, water, light, and innumerable physical forces generated in a cosmic web of planets, stars, galaxies, and perhaps other universes. Such machine-like interdependency demands sudden creation.

SOME YOUNG UNIVERSE DATING METHODS

Examples of indicators and dating methods that show the Earth and universe to be young — in some cases just thousands of years old. (For further detail see my book, The Creation-Evolution Controversy, pages 147-151.) Also, Internet search: evidence for a young Earth.

- The amount of salt and other minerals in the ocean
- Oxygen and helium in the air
- Depth of moon dust
- Planetary ring detail
- Magnetic moment decay
- Scarcity of meteors in sedimentary rock
- Distinctness of galaxy spirals
- Cooling of outer solar system planets
- Entropy in the universe
- Comet decay
- Second stage supernova remnants
- Ice cores—250 feet of ice accumulating in only 50 years
- Pressure in oil gushers

- Carbon-14 production versus disintegration
- Carbon-14 found in coal
- Lack of supernova remnants
- Existence of large stars
- Delta filling
- Sea ooze and sediment
- Tree age
- Volcanic water and rocks
- Rate of canyon erosion such as at Niagara Falls
- Influx of cosmic dust
- Mutation load
- Human population
- Stellar radiation
- Cosmic dust velocity
- Level of micrometeoroids

- Meteorite distribution in Earth rocks
- Rate of loss of Earth's heat
- Lunar inert gases
- Stalactites and stalagmites
- Hydrogen in the universe
- Moon rock radiation and short-lived isotopes
- Drag, torque and interdistance between the Earth and moon— extrapolated backwards for the time argued by evolutionists, would put the moon in contact with Earth
- The rate of sun shrinkage (five feet per hour)—would mean that even 100,000 years ago the sun would have been so large that life could not have existed on Earth

© Wysong   Figure 045

Creation would scrap the reliability of all dating methods. Sudden creation would immediately create the appearance of age. One-second old creatures could appear decades old and one-second old galaxies could appear to be billions of years old.

Although the idea of sudden creation may seem ridiculous to us four- dimensionally bound creatures, in the physics of quantum reality time is irrelevant. Everything, past and future, exists simultaneously and is connected. (This mind-numbing fact is discussed more fully in a coming chapter.)

The integration and codependency of all elements of our reality is an impenetrable blockade to any attempt at a step-by-step evolution, no matter how much time is granted. It also conflicts with the religious notion of creation in "day" steps.

The Law of Time demolishes evolution. The more time, the more degradation and disorder. That's the opposite of what evolution needs. Moreover, degradation and disorder point backward to a winder upper. But the only sufficient winder upper would be intelligence. That's where logic and science lead and has nothing to do with religion.

10
FOSSIL PROBLEMS

The geological and evolutionary sequence laid out in textbook charts and in artfully crafted displays in museums can be found nowhere on the planet itself. It was created based upon the assumption that evolution is true. Therefore, a simple fossil organism must be in really old rocks and really old rocks must contain simple organisms. Contrary evidence is ignored.

Bible religionists have been guilty of bias as well. As late as the 1800s it was thought heretical to believe that any death could have occurred before the fall of Adam and Eve. Therefore, fossils couldn't have been dead things predating humans. So, they were explained away, such as being bones dropped by travelers. Contrary evidence was ignored.

It's true that often "simple" creatures are found deeper in the rocks than the larger, more complex ones. But that's expected with the conditions that permit fossilization, such as flooding and sudden burial with sedimentation. In general, small and dense creatures are going to settle in sediment more quickly than large, less dense ones. So they would predominate in the lower rocks. Larger organisms more capable of fleeing a natural disaster would be the last captured by sediment. Watery cataclysm explains such a tendency toward simple to complex progression in the rocks, but also explains the inversions and randomness also found.

The Living Fossil Problem

There are countless animals alive today that look identical to their ancient fossil kin. Creatures that have been on earth for millions of years and have not changed, contradict progressive, simple to complex evolution.

The age of the Earth has been set by evolutionary scientists at 4.6 billion years. They say the first time conditions would have been propitious for the spontaneous generation of life would be 3.8 billion years ago, when they believe the Earth cooled enough for water to form.

Contradicting this timeline are fossils of proteobacteria in rocks dated to 3.8 billion years. One would expect, if abiogenesis is true, that only nascent chemistry would be occurring at this time, not fully formed organisms.

Era	Period	Epoch	Records of Distinctive Life	Millions of Years Ago
Cenozoic ▼	Quaternary	Recent		
		Pleistocene	Early Man	2+
		Pliocene	Large Carnivores	10
	Tertiary	Miocene	Whales, Apes, Grazers	27
		Oligocene	Large Browsing Animals	38
		Eocene	Rise of Flowering Plants	55
		Paleocene	First Placental Animals	70
Mesozoic ▼	Cretaceous		Dinosaurs Extinct Modem Floras	130
	Jurassic		Dinosaurs Zenith Primitive Birds First Small Mammals	180
	Triassic		Appearance of Dinosaurs	225
Paleozoic ▼	Permian		Conifers Abundant Reptiles Developed	260
	Carboniferous: •Pennsylvanian		First Reptiles Coal Forests	300
	•Mississippian		Sharks Abundant	340
	Devonian		Rise of Amphibians Fishes Abundant	405
	Silurian		Earliest Land Plants and Animals	435
	Ordovician		First Primitive Fishes	480
	Cambrian		All Subkingdoms of Invertebrate Animals Trilobites Brachiopods	570
Proterozoic Archeozoic	Precambrian		No Indisputable Fossils	570 to 1,500 +

Geologic Column and Timetable – The classical geological column portrayed in textbooks and museums. There is no place on Earth where this column is found. Fossils are used to date rocks, and rocks are used to date fossils – leaving out all the evidence that contradicts the simple to complex hypothesis. This is a mythical column built with hypothesis laid upon hypothesis.

© Wysong   Figure 046

Port Jackson Shark (left) – The Port Jackson Shark, Heterodontus Japonicus, is believed to have remained unchanged for "181 million years," according to evolutionists. Likewise, the cow shark has been traced back "166 million years" and the cat shark "136 million years."

Sea Lily (right) – This sea lily, Rhizocrinus Lofotensis, not a plant but an animal, is identical with fossils "160 million years old."

There is no reasonable explanation for why such creatures remained unchanged, while countless others, including us, evolved into existence.

Figure 047

Metasequoia – This tree, Metasequoia Glyptosroboides, a deciduous conifer, prior to 1945 was found only as a fossil in Mesozoic strata "60 million years old." This specimen is one of several on the Michigan State University campus.

Ginkgo – This Ginkgo tree, with its distinctive leaves in fan shape, grows on the Michigan State University. campus and looks identical to fossils "20 million years old." My children, under the Ginkgo, supposedly evolved from ape-like precursors in less time.

© Wysong   Figure 048

Vast time was supposedly necessary for the spontaneous formation of enzymes, DNA, RNA, organelles, cell walls, and the other complexities found in proteobacteria. But there is no evidence of precursors to stromatolites.

Further complicating the evolutionary picture is the presence of proteobacteria alive and well today in stromatolites around the world. Since the earliest life forms have not evolved, there is no reason to believe evolution has occurred at all.

Stromatolites – These mineral accretions housing proteobacteria (prokaryotes—no nucleus) are found around the world, from Australia, to the Bahamas, Indian Ocean, Yellowstone, and elsewhere. They are identical to their fossils 3.8 billion years old. These oldest known forms of life could not be precursors to us and all other life and at the same time remain unchanged.

© Paul Harrison   Figure 049

Fossil Whoops

Our putative human ancestors, such as Homo erectus, are said to have arrived on scene 1.5 million years ago. Australopithecus afarensis, a variety of ape beguilingly named Lucy, is the alleged earliest progenitor and dated 3.2 million years. That means, of course, fully formed humans could not coexist with or predate their evolutionary beginnings.

However, consider these facts (dates are by methods used by evolutionists):

Lucy reconstruction (3.2M)

Lucy is believed to be our ape-like precursor dating to 3.2 million years.

© The respective copyright holders.   Figure 050

- Fully human skeleton in Olduvai Gorge, Africa 1.15 million years old.
- Fossilized human footprints in volcanic ash 3.7 million years old.
- Human tool use 25 million years ago.
- A shell with a human face carving, 2 million years old.
- Paleoliths (human artifacts), 20-38 million years old.
- Bolas, signs of fire making, and a stone arrowhead embedded in the femur of a 3-5 million-year-old Pliocene species.
- Stone tools in California gold mines in undisturbed 55-million-year-old lava.
- Coins, hammer handles, and other tools, 36 million years old.
- Letter-like shapes in a solid block of marble, 600 million years old.
- A nail in 360-408 million-year-old rocks.
- Gold thread embedded in stone, 380 million years old.
- A metallic vessel inlaid with ornate silver, 600 million years old.
- A Nampa figurine, 12 million years old.
- A gold chain, 300 million years old.
- An iron pot, 312 million years old.
- Shoe sole with well defined sewn thread, 248 million years old.
- Fossil shoe imprint with a 500 million-year-old trilobite squashed in it.

(More evidence of humans on Earth over a billion [that's a B] years ago is documented at mcremo.com.)

Nampa Image – The Nampa figurine retrieved from rocks estimated at 12 million years old. This artifact, apparently made by humans, predates when evolutionists contend humans came into existence.

Figure 053

Coelacanth – Once thought to be a fossil link between fish and amphibians, coelacanths have been found alive and well off the coast of Africa at depths of 1,640 feet. They look exactly like their fossil remains millions of years old and thus could not be a link to anything other than themselves.

Figure 052

Hammer in Stone – Found in a rock that was split open outside of London, Texas. The rock was nestled among others dated 75-100 million years old. Part of the handle is coalified and the unusual metal (iron, chlorine, and sulfur—no carbon) had no corrosion and was cast with no bubbles—a feat very difficult to achieve to this day.

Figure 055

Cycad – The Cycad tree has remained unchanged for over "200 million years" according to evolutionists.

Figure 051

If facts from the rocks are going to be used as proof, then all the evidence from the rocks must be let in. The above facts and what follows are not found in any school text. They can't be, of course, or the case for the geological column, evolutionary timetable, and simple to complex biological gradation would be clearly untenable.

Laetoli Footprints – Roughly three and three-quarter million years ago, a volcano erupted in what is now northern Tanzania, blanketing the landscape with volcanic ash. Rain fell, causing the ashy surface to take on the properties of plaster. Across this ground numerous animals walked, leaving their footprints in the wet volcanic ash to be preserved as it turned into a hard cement. One of the creatures that passed across this landscape 3.6 million years ago had footprints indistinguishable from modern humans. In this trail are at least two individuals, child and adult. Some of the prints are superimposed with smaller prints from a child lengthening its stride to walk in the adult print. Since evolutionists know that modern-type humans could not predate their hominid precursors, they attribute these prints to *Australopithecus* afarensis, a supposed human precursor, and say this is proof of "bipedalism." This is actually proof that the human mind will see what it wants to see.

Figure 054

The atheist evolutionist Dawkins admitted, ". . . evolution makes the strong prediction that if a single fossil turned up in the wrong geological stratum, the theory would be blown out of the water." He then follows up by saying, "No such anachronistic fossils have ever been found . . ."

Dinosaurs as Meals and Pets

According to the evolutionary timetable, dinosaurs predated humans by almost 250 million years. However:

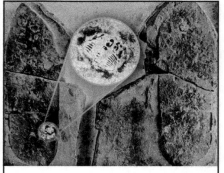

Squashed Trilobites – This fossil shoe impression has trilobites squashed in the toe and heel. (The magnified portion shows a trilobite in the heel.) But evolutionists say trilobites went extinct 252 million years ago, which is long before they say humans appeared.

Figure 056

- The Kuku Yalanji aborigines of Queensland have lore and paintings of plesiosaurs. They even drew the digestive tract in overlay indicating that they apparently hunted and butchered the creatures.

- The Doheny expedition into the Grand Canyon in the early 1900s discovered cave drawings of duck-billed dinosaurs.

- Carvings on rocks in Peru show long-necked and spine-crested sauropods, brontosaurs, T. rex, stegosaurs, and pterodactyls in great variety in the same scene with humans—as reported by the head of the Department of Medicine at the University of Lima.

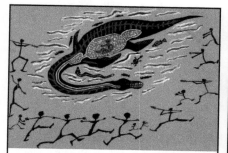

Plesiosaur Pictograph – This is a painting of a plesiosaur-like creature made by the KuKu Yalanji tribe of far North Queensland, Australia. Note the depiction of the digestive tract, indicating that they probably killed and butchered these creatures. Evolution does not allow for humans and dinosaurs being contemporaneous.

© Wysong   Figure 057

Dinosaur Pictograph – If this pictograph is actually a representation of a dinosaur, about 250 million years of the geologic column is collapsed.

© The respective copyright holders.   Figure 058

- Ancient Sumatran art depicts head-crested hadrosaurs and a Corythosaurus.

- A drawing by North American Indians shows a warrior and an apatosaurus-like creature.

- A painting on an urn artifact from Asia Minor, dated 530 B.C., depicts a Mosasaurus in a scene with an octopus and dolphin.

- An Egyptian seal dated to about 1300 B.C. has a depiction of a pterosaur hunting a gazelle.

- An Egyptian statue shows a pterosaur hunting a falcon.

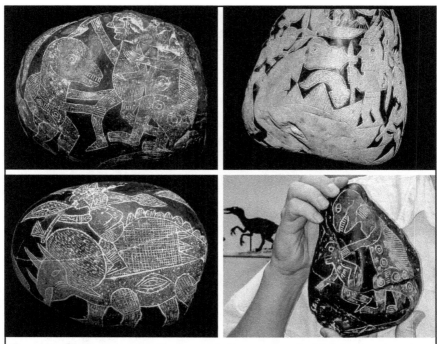

Domestic Dinosaurs – Specific types of dinosaurs are depicted in Peruvian stone engravings from 2000 years ago. A huge collection can be found in Dr. Javier's Museum in Ica. Triceratops, Tyrannosaurus, Pterodactyl, Stegosaurus, Diplodocus, Allosaurus, and Pterosaurs are shown. Sauropod spines are shown along the back, but paleontologists did not discover this in fossils until 1992. Some appear to have been domesticated (if scale is correct, by giant humans), others were definitely not.

Figure 059

Fossil Fraud

In my 1974 Creation-Evolution Controversy book, I showed pictures of human footprints alongside dinosaur footprints in the Texas Paluxy riverbed. I have since seen reports that some such evidence may have been doctored. If that's true, it's no surprise. Both sides in this debate have been found guilty of such shenanigans. But an instance of fraud cannot be taken to mean that all evidence showing humans coeval with dinosaurs is void.

Moreover, if an incident of fraud is sufficient to categorically reject an argument, then evolutionists are most certainly in trouble.

In 1868, the evolutionist Haekel discussed a creature he named Pithecanthropus alalus, a link between ape and man. There was no evidence for it whatsoever. It was created out of sheer belief.

Neanderthal and Piltdown Man – The Neanderthal reconstruction (left), giving a brutish appearance, is based on a diseased specimen. Neanderthal was fully human. Piltdown Man (right), Eoanthropus Dawsoni, was fraudulently reconstructed from ape and human parts. Such fabrications represent an unscientific and dishonest desire to press facts into the service of a belief.

© 1960 Zdeněk Burian (left) Figure 061

Piltdown Man was a forged missing link. Java Man (another Pithecanthropus) was created with a few fragments from an extinct Gibbon-like creature. Peking Man, Nebraska Man, Southwest Colorado Man, Ramapithecus, Australopithecus africanus, and Homo habilis were proposed as evolutionary links but were either outright frauds, creatures other than links, real humans, or fanciful reconstructions.

Haeckel's Pithecanthropus alalus – (speechless ape-man) as depicted in 1894 by the painter Gabriel Max. There is not a shred of evidence, not even a chip off a tooth, to support that this creature ever existed. This reified image negatively influenced at least two decades of hominid specimen interpretation and was included in evolutionary trees. Its only reality is the officious name.

© 1894 Franz Hanfstaengl Figure 060

Hesperopithecus was a supposed human precursor. It was reconstructed from a single pig's tooth. Many missing links are reconstructed from a few bone fragments or teeth. That's creative imagination, not science.

Cro-Magnon Man had to be retired from missing link status when specimens showed larger brain capacity than modern humans.

Some reconstructions of Neanderthal Man were based on an older arthritic specimen—perfect for showing a stooped ape-like posture. Both Neanderthal and Cro-Magnon are now considered fully human.

This is what fossils prove:

- The sudden appearance of life
- Earth cataclysms and rapid burial
- No change between contemporary creatures and their fossils
- Coexistence of highly developed organisms with their supposed progenitors

The golden ages of evolution that are thought to be buried in the fossil record are presented in textbooks as if there is clear evidence that life emerged spontaneously and then gradually evolved from simple to complex.

However, the fossil record shows the sudden appearance of a profusion of life at the Cambrian Period with no antecedents. Fossils distributed throughout the strata are fully formed and identical to their modern-day offspring. Other than variations within defined organisms (syngameons), there is no evidence of a step-by-step evolution of life on Earth.

This conclusion does not require any religious predisposition. We're simply letting reason and facts guide us.

11
HAVE HUMANS EVOLVED?

If we examine actual human history and artifacts, evolution is absent. There is no proof that humans have, for example, gained intelligence. If anything, we seem to have devolved and are less capable than our ancestors.

That is what we would expect given the immutable laws of nature. Complex functional things, like us and our genetics, do not improve over time, they degrade.

Our modern technological advancements show the effect of accumulated knowledge (or input from some extraneous source?), not an intrinsic improvement in humans.

Megaliths

Consider the accomplishments of our ancestors. The hanging gardens of Babylon, the Rhodes Colossus, the statue of Zeus, the Artemus temple at Ephesus, the Mausoleum at Halicarnassus, Rome and its infrastructure and Coliseum, the Alexandria lighthouse, Jewish Temples, the Parthenon, and the gigantic and ornate cathedrals and castles spread throughout Europe. These speak to high intelligence and skills. Such is surpassed only by the following which predated them by thousands of years.

Megaliths are large artificial stone structures. Examples include the huge mound structures in the Ohio valley, the complex of Baalbek in Lebanon, Gobekli Tepe in Turkey dated 10,000 years BC, Malta's megaliths, Tiahuanaco and Puma Puku in Bolivia, Machu Picchu and Sacsayhuaman in Peru, Angkor Wat in Cambodia, the huge temples in Mexico and Central America, a structure underwater off the coast of the island of Yonaguni in Japan which is part of a complex stretching for hundreds of miles (also dating possibly to 10,000 BC) . . . to only begin a list.

Giza Pyramids

© 2006 Ricardo Liberato   Figure 062

The Great Pyramid of Egypt is forty stories high and was built with 2.3 million stones, each weighing three to four tons. Some were moved from 500 miles away. The pyramid stones could make a wall ten feet high by five feet wide stretching from Los Angeles to New York. The precision of the Great Pyramid is such that a fraction of an inch error in the base would end up as a twenty-foot or more deviation at the top. If that had occurred, all the work would have been for naught since such a tilt would result in the structure eventually collapsing on itself.

Conventional archeological (and evolutionary) thought is that it was built using crude copper tools in 20 years. This would require each of the 2.3 million, 3-4 ton stones being cut precisely, transported, elevated, and placed every two and a half minutes—assuming there were no errors.

The Sphinx in Giza is almost the length of a football field and six stories tall. It was carved out of a single stone thousands of years before the Egyptians discovered it in about 6000 B.C.

Sphinx – This is the largest single stone carving yet discovered. It was hewn thousands of years before the Egyptians discovered it and when technology was supposedly barely beyond the discovery of fire. It lies in a ravine and will cover with wind-blown sand unless constantly excavated. The damage to the face is not a result of erosion but from the Malumeks at the time of the Napoleonic wars using it for target practice with their brass cannon... if you can imagine ruining an artifact thousands of years old for fun!

© 2002 Paul James Cowie — Figure 063

Nan Madol, the Venice of the Pacific, is an 80-acre island in Pohnpei, Micronesia. It consists of 900 artificial islands. There are 750,000 metric tons of stones used in the 800-year-old structures. Some are more than 20 feet in length and weigh 50 tons. They are believed to have been transported from a volcanic site 20 miles away. Some of the walls are 30 feet high and 10 feet thick. They rest upon a foundation of similar huge stones either built underwater or when the ocean was much lower.

Nan Madol – This megalithic structure in Micronesia was constructed of gigantic stones and erected at a time when there were believed to be essentially no tools, no electricity, no diesel powered cranes. The evolutionary hypothesis demands a progression from simple and crude to complex. Thus such anachronisms are ignored.

© 2014 Civiltà antiche & Antichi misteri — Figure 064

A temple platform in Lebanon is made of five million square feet of stone blocks. Most of them weigh hundreds of tons. The trilithon consists of three single stones weighing over 1000 tons each. Another weighs 1,650 tons. They were quarried and moved ½ mile uphill to their placement. The stones are fitted so closely together that when first unearthed, they were thought to be one large stone. Nobody knows who made the structure and there is no evidence of any roadway from the mountain quarry from which they were taken to their destination in the temple..

Qasr al-Farid – carved out of a single rock thousands of years ago. It is five stories high and was abandoned in the middle of the desert.

© 2015 Richard.hargas   Figure 065

Trilithon – One of the Trilithon stones (black arrow) in Baalbek, Lebanon. It weighs approximately 1000 tons and was moved uphill from a great distance to be placed in the wall. Even modern equipment is not up to such a challenge. There is no evidence of a roadbed upon which it was moved and the people who did the feat are unknown. Note the comparative size of the person in the photo (white arrow).

© The respective copyright holders.   Figure 066

Equally astounding is the fact that many megaliths were oriented precisely for astronomical observations and predictions.

Although dating thousands of years BC, the billions of tons of worked megalithic stones found worldwide contain evidence of machining and technology we not only don't possess but can't imagine.

An extremely hard rock weighing hundreds of tons is polished to a mirror finish. Interior angles are made which are only possible today with laser machines the size of large rooms. Precise vertical notches and cuts course several meters perfectly straight and some curve perfectly. Some cuts are thinner than even modern jewelers can create.

Other cuts show imprints of circular saw blades three-sixteenths of an inch thick and eighteen feet in diameter. No such saws exist today. Perfect holes have been bored at a rate 500 times faster than possible with modern boring equipment. There are furrows in stones akin to pulling a finger or tool through soft clay suggesting that hard stones could be worked while transformed into some kind of plastic malleable state.

Walls

Figure 067

Holes and Hole Coring – Perfect holes are bored in granite rock. The coring machine that was used advanced faster than any modern machine can do. This is determined by measuring the spiral grooves left in the sidewalls of the hole. (see arrow)

Figure 069

Wall Detail – Perfectly stacked and dry-fitted stones are found around the world. Some weigh thousands of tons. Not only can we today not do this even using modern machinery, nobody knows how it even could be done.

Figure 068

Corners – Perfect rectangular inside corners require sophisticated machinery.

Figure 070

Line – Thin cuts in ancient stones are impossible with hand tools. Yet these are the only tools evolutionists believe existed at the time these structures were built.

Protuberances – To have these nubs on the stones would mean that the entire face of the stone was shaved leaving only the mysterious protuberances.

Figure 071 Figure 075

Stone Sawing – On left, kerf slices are seen in ancient stone apparently made by a power saw. Right, a slice on the face of a giant ancient stone apparently made by a circular saw blade. Arrows show that the diameter of the blade was enormous.

© The respective copyright holders.

Figure 072

Cut and Holes – Perfect tiny holes are cut inside of a perfect vertical cut.

© The respective copyright holders.

Figure 074

Trough and Hole – In this ancient stone, the hole appears to have been cut by a boring saw. The trough looks like it was formed when the stone was in a plastic state or by some special cutting machine.

© The respective copyright holders.

Figure 073

I've done some masonry and split and laid stones and blocks. Attempting to place a stone that weighs just 100 pounds, even when I get to fudge with mortar all around the joints, is a gigantic feat. I can't imagine how an army of even thousands of workers could quarry a thousand ton stone out of solid red granite and shape it into a perfect cube that would fit perfectly with other such stones. Nor have any of my supposedly highly evolved human contemporaries figured it out.

It is embarrassing that with all of our tools, engineering, machines, "advanced" brains, and accumulated history and technology, such feats lie outside all modern capabilities. We can neither figure these things out nor accomplish them, but supposedly our less-evolved ancestors could.

Personal Masonry Work – The left photo is of a dry set retaining wall I built from broken concrete about thirty years ago. Loose pea stones were used to help level them and fill gaps. The right photo is of a fireplace I built with fabricated stones using mortar to cement it and fudge in the joints. I impressed me very much until becoming aware of what "primitives" did many thousands of years ago. They used no fudging pea stones or mortar and quarried real stones 40,000 times heavier than I was struggling to handle.

Figure 076

History should be rewritten. But conventional science and archeology ignore the evidence because it contradicts the prevailing evolutionary bias. Those who attempt an explanation argue that tens of thousands of ancients with nothing better to do chipped away day and night with crude tools to create the megaliths. They then supposedly slid stones weighing millions of pounds across miles and up hills with twine made of twisted plants.

Modern-day Peruvians, Egyptians, and other civilizations around the world where megaliths are found are totally incapable of the ancient megalithic architecture and machining. For example, here you can see characteristic historical and modern Peruvian and Inca stonework (which looks similar to mine) placed on top of the advanced technology that preceded them.

Nazca Mountains – The entire top of Nazca mountains have been shaved off by unknown ancients with sophisticated capabilities.

Figure 079

The geoglyphs in Peru, also known as the Nazca lines, range in size up to 1000 feet and include a variety of geometrical and animal figures. They were sculpted 2000 years ago and are only recognized for what they represent when viewed from an airplane.

Megalithic City Stones – This photo shows what the Inca did when they found an abandoned megalithic city. The grey stone section on the right is typical megalithic perfection not possible by Incas in the Bronze Age or by modern masons. The stones are several feet thick with no gaps in the joints. The darker stones in the lower left were apparently found on the ground by the Inca and crudely stacked. Then to make the wall higher they used stones and mortar as is now common. The contrasting stone work proves a more technologically sophisticated people preceded the historical Inca. Similar contrasts can be found around the world.

© The respective copyright holders.   Figure 077

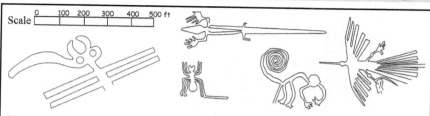

Nazca Lines in Peru – Aerial perspective of some of the geoglyphs stretching over a 53 mile area. They were created about 2000 years ago.

© Wysong   Figure 078

Hundreds of Costa Rican stone spheres estimated to be up to 4000 years old, range in size from a few inches to over eight feet in diameter. Many were hewn out of solid granite (although there is no immediate local source of granite) and weigh as much as sixteen tons. They are nearly perfectly spherical. One sphere with a diameter of over six feet varies only by 0.5 inches at any point in its circumference. And this imperfection is likely due to weathering over the 4000 year.

Stone Balls – Hundreds of stone balls made of granodiorite, a hard, igneous stone, have been discovered in Costa Rica. They are monolithic sculptures, not natural in origin. Dates range from 200 B.C. to A.D. 800. The balls range in size from a few inches to about eight feet in diameter, with weights up to sixteen tons. Amazingly, they are almost perfectly spherical and were made at a time, according to conventional evolution-tainted archeology, when there were little more than stone tools to work with. To this date, nobody knows how this feat was accomplished. Yet we are supposed to be more evolved than the artisans who made them over 2000 years ago.

© The respective copyright holders.   Figure 080

Anomalous Archeology

Considering that our modern technologies developed primarily in just the last few hundred years, the possibilities for what humans (or others?) may have done in the past over thousands or millions of years is unimaginable.

Consider the amazing Antikythera mechanism found on a sunken ship near Greece. Embedded in encrusted rock, this small device contains an estimated seventy gears. It's displayed in the Bronze Collection of the National Archeological Museum of Athens. Although dating to about 150 B.C., the mechanism works like a computer to precisely calculate astronomical positions from dates entered.

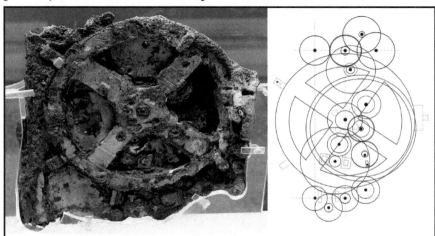

Antikythera Mechanism – This shoebox-size device, dated to 150 BC, was found in 1901 on a shipwreck in 150 feet of water off the coast of a Greek island. It has the capacity to calculate the position of the sun, moon, planets and other astronomical information when past or future dates are entered with a crank. Some 70 intermeshing gears of bronze have been found in the machine.

Figure 081

We can only marvel at the intelligence behind this machine built by hand before electricity and modern technology.

Other anomalous prehistory includes:

- Engines
- Machine cut optical lenses
- Tiny drills and ultra-sharp blades
- Fine jewelry

Bobbin – This bobbin, and many like it, appears to have been produced by a sophisticated machine thousands of years ago.

Figure 082

- Sophisticated dentistry and surgery

- High-speed drills and other machining tools

- Anesthesia

- Electrical lighting

- Sound waves used to move gigantic objects

- Detailed world maps including the poles prior to ice covering

- X-rays

- Rolls of sheet metal wallpaper

- Vast underground tunnels, cities, and auditoriums large enough to hold 60,000 people

- Automatic doors

- Microtechnology and nano-machines

- Dry-cell batteries

- Flying technology

- Plumbing technology . . .

- And more

(Internet search: anomalous archeology, or ancient artifacts, or Cremo forbidden archeology)

Devolution

At the age of 6, we have five times more neural connections in our brains than when we're adults. The number of connections is directly related to intellectual capacity. Some 80% of the neural mass in the neocortex (smart part of the brain with all those fancy folds) is dissolved by age 14. So as an adult, we have only 20% of the brain potential we had at 6. We use only about 5% of what's left.

Not only does the brain seem to physiologically and anatomically devolve, but so too does human capability. Take a modern-day course in philosophy and you'll be studying the thinking of Greeks who lived over 2,000 years ago. Language was invented long before that. The astronomical knowledge of ancient sages and mariners has only been slightly tweaked since their time. The skill at prose, poetry, music, architecture, and art by those in the distant past working under candlelight is enviable. The letters of Civil War teenagers possess an eloquence that would be hard to find in today's college graduates.

EIGHTH GRADE FINAL EXAM

Final Exam – This is an 'eighth-grade final exam' from 1895 in Salina, KS, USA. It was taken from the original document on file at the Smokey Valley Genealogical Society and Library in Salina, KS, and reprinted by the Salina Journal. Most of today's high school graduates could not pass this test. Many could not read or understand it! So much for cultural, intellectual and educational evolution.

Grammar (Time, one hour)

Give nine rules for the use of Capital Letters. Name the Parts of Speech and define those that have no Modifications.

1. Define Verse, Stanza and Paragraph.
2. What are the Principal Parts of a verb?
3. Give Principal parts of lie, lay and run.
4. Define Case, Illustrate each Case.
5. What is Punctuation? Give rules for principal marks of Punctuation.
6. Write a composition of about 150 words and show therein that you understand the practical use of the rules of grammar.

Arithmetic (Time, 1.25 hours)

1. Name and define the Fundamental Rules of Arithmetic.
2. A wagon box is 2 ft. deep, 10 ft. long, and 3 ft. wide. How many bushels of wheat will it hold?
3. If a load of wheat weighs 3942 lbs., what is it worth at 50 cts./bushel, deducting 1050 lbs. for tare?
4. District No. 33 has a valuation of $35,000. What is the necessary levy to carry on a school seven months at $50 per month, and have $104 for incidentals?
5. Find cost of 6720 lbs. coal at $6.00 per ton.
6. Find the interest of $512.60 for 8 months and 18 days at 7 percent.
7. What is the cost of 40 boards 12 inches wide and 16 ft. long at $20 per meter?
8. Find bank discount on $300 for 90 days (no grace) at 10 percent.
9. What is the cost of a square farm at $15 per acre, the distance around which is 640 rods?
10. Write a Bank Check, a Promissory Note, and a Receipt.

Orthography (Time, one hour)

1. What is meant by the following: Alphabet, phonetic, orthography, etymology, syllabication?
2. What are elementary sounds? How classified?
3. What are the following, and give examples of each: Trigraph, sub vocals, diphthong, cognate letters, linguals?
4. Give four substitutes for caret 'u'.
5. Give two rules for spelling words with final 'e.' Name two exceptions under each rule.
6. Give two uses of silent letters in spelling. Illustrate each.
7. Define the following prefixes and use in connection with a word: bi, dis, mis, pre, semi, post, non, inter, mono, sup.

8. Mark diacritically and divide into syllables the following, and name the sign that indicates the sound: card, ball, mercy, sir, odd, cell, rise, blood, fare, last.
9. Use the following correctly in sentences: cite, site, sight, fane, fain, feign, vane, vain, vein, raze, raise, rays.
10. Write 10 words frequently mispronounced and indicate pronunciation by use of diacritical marks and by syllabication.

U. S. History (Time, 45 minutes)

1. Give the epochs into which U. S. History is divided.
2. Give an account of the discovery of America by Columbus.
3. Relate the causes and results of the Revolutionary War.
4. Show the territorial growth of the United States.
5. Tell what you can of the history of Kansas.
6. Describe three of the most prominent battles of the Rebellion.
7. Who were the following: Morse, Whitney, Fulton, Bell, Lincoln, Penn, and Howe?
8. Name events connected with the following dates: 1607, 1620, 1800, 1849, 1865.

Geography (Time, one hour)

1. What is climate? Upon what does climate depend?
2. How do you account for the extremes of climate in Kansas?
3. Of what use are rivers? Of what use is the ocean?
4. Describe the mountains of North America.
5. Name and describe the following: Monrovia, Odessa, Denver, Manitoba, Hecla, Yukon, St. Helena, Juan Fernandez, Aspinwall & Orinoco.
6. Name and locate the principal trade centers of the U.S.
7. Name all the republics of Europe and give the capital of each.
8. Why is the Atlantic Coast colder than the Pacific in the same latitude?
9. Describe the process by which the water of the ocean returns to the sources of rivers.
10. Describe the movements of the earth. Give the inclination of the earth.

Figure 083

The vocabulary of today's high school student is less than half what it was in 1950. Fifteen years ago people could distinguish 300,000 sounds. Today the average is 180,000, and many children can't exceed 100,000. Twenty years ago the average person could distinguish 350 shades of a particular color. Today they struggle to differentiate 130.

Other than being the ben-eficiaries of accumulated know-ledge and technology, humans are slipping, not evolving to a higher state. That's exactly what the degrading effects of natural laws would predict and is consistent with an original pristine creation at the mercy of those laws.

How Kids Evolve

© Wysong

Figure 084

12
ARE WE SELECTED MUTANTS?

The engine that is supposed to propel evolution needs to have the muscle for shape-shifting one kind of creature into another. That engine is described as neo-Darwinism, the combination of mutations to create genetic variations, and natural selection to winnow out the fittest variants.

An immediate problem arises in that this mechanism must explain all features of all creatures in every environment. The fin of the fish and the legs of the crab must both be explained by water. The short neck of the elephant and long neck of the giraffe must both be explained by leaf food . . . and so on through all of nature. Every environmental niche contains myriad creatures with different physical features and abilities. But on the same piece of geography can be found bacteria, insects, fish, reptiles, amphibians, birds, mammals . . . all manner of creature in every imaginable color, size, and configuration.

It would seem, if evolution were true, there should be just one "most fit" "naturally selected" creature in each niche. If natural selection effectively dictated form and function, the desert would have one kind of creature, the ocean another, the forest another, and the air yet another. Instead, there are millions of varieties in each of these habitats, about nine million total species. This effectively denies that evolution is a powerful and exacting force sufficient to explain the biological world.

Sometimes there is variation in response to environmental pressure, but such variation is subtle and never does something like create a new beneficial organ or a whole new creature. The distinction of creatures one from another that exists in the world, frankly, fits better creative ingenuity and even artistic flair.

Each Step and Detail Must Be Explained

Consider just the eyelid. It includes skin cells, muscles, nerves, blood vessels, lymphatics, connective tissue, mucosal tissue, sweat glands, sebaceous glands, lashes, hormones, immune cells and so forth, all arranged in a precise three-dimensional shape, and wired and plumbed to the rest of the body so it can function both voluntarily and on autopilot. Each of those parts, in turn, has millions of cell, organelle, and biochemical parts. Evolution must account for every single detail down to the placement of each atom.

But explaining such detail has never been done other than in very broad, and sweeping terms, such as: "The eyelid evolved because it was necessary to protect and lubricate the eye. Those with lids were more fit than those without them. Thus our 'lidded' ancestors had a selective advantage."

Such simplistic conjecture doesn't explain the origin and step-by-step transformation of any of the millions of components.

Irreducible Complexity

It is assumed that life is a mere summation of parts, a philosophy known as materialistic reductionism. Thus, like machines, organisms are thought to be understood by taking them apart.

Such exploration has revealed some aspects of how living things work but does not point to evolutionary origin. That's because functional things are irreducibly complex. Mutate (remove, damage, or add) parts and creatures either do not work (die) or become less functional (diseased). Yet all evolutionary precursors supposedly had less developed, and thus nonfunctional, parts. Thus, living things cannot evolve—add and remove parts—they are irreducibly complex and thus could not incrementally mutate to be less or more than what they are.

Mutations Are Not Nice Things

To make evolution happen, mutations must be called upon again and again to create complex and beneficial changes. But mutations are random disruptions of the information contained in DNA. The human genome, for example, contains the equivalent of the information in 3 quadrillion (3×10^{15}) fact-filled books. All human experience proves that changes to information result in degradation, not improvement.

The pressure in nature is always from complex to random no matter how much natural selection is applied. That's why, in practice, mutations are essentially 100% lethal or disadvantageous. In humans, mutations are linked to dwarfism, albinism, Huntington's Chorea, Down's syndrome, cystic fibrosis, familial hypercholesterolemia, cancer aging . . . to only begin the list of hundreds of deleterious effects.

The inability, or reduced capacity, of humans to synthesize certain nutrients, such as the 22 essential amino acids, vitamins, long-chain fatty acids, antioxidants, and others without which we suffer disease and death is likely traceable to mutational damage. For example, the essentiality of vitamin C is traced to a mutation in the GULO (gulonolactone oxidase) gene. Minus this vitamin in our diet, scurvy and an array of pleomorphic (various form) diseases and weaknesses occur. At our beginning, unspoiled by mutational damage, we were likely far more nutritionally self-sufficient.

Cancer is now devastating modern society with 1600 people in the US, and 21,000 worldwide dying from it each day. Causes ultimately relate to disrupted normal metabolism or altered genetics. All carcinogens (chemicals that cause cancer) are mutagens. For the same reasons you don't want to store nuclear waste under your bed, you don't want an existence driven by mutations.

There is not one example of a beneficial mutation that increases the functional complexity of an organism. An increase in functional complexity—needed for evolution in the molecule-to-man sense—should not be confused with mutations that may increase survivability. For example, the AIDS virus is thought to mutate resistance to drugs. But the AIDS virus does not become something more complex, such as a bacterium or protozoan. If given reprieve from the drugs, it will just revert to its original wild type. In fact, it may not even be mutations that create such resistance. Epigenetics demonstrates that new characteristics in organisms are not new and are not mutations, but rather the molecular switching on and off of existing genetic codes.

The Anti-Evolution DNA Mechanism

Each day thousands of mutations occur throughout the body. These result from ionizing radiation, cosmic rays, chemicals, and other factors. We wouldn't survive if not for biochemical systems within cells that have the ability to detect, excise, and repair mutations. These DNA repair mechanisms are not trivial. Some 4,600 biochemicals are engaged in the moment-by-moment repair of mutated DNA.

Think of that. We live because we have automatic mechanisms that repair mutations. These repair mechanisms not only help keep us alive, but they also lock creatures into what they are. They are evolution preventers and our survival depends on them.

The Ultimate Survivor

Fast-reproducing microorganisms have a high mutation rate and should have long ago evolved out of their single-celled retardation. They should no longer exist. But they do—and they look just like their progenitors, no matter how far back in time we go or how many trillions of reproductive cycles occur. Recall the 3.8 billion-year-old stromatolite proteobacteria that still exist today, unchanged.

Then there's this guy, a Tardigrade, commonly known as a water bear. It can survive and reproduce in the vacuum of outer space, on the highest peaks, frozen in Antarctica, boiling in hot springs, and enduring 16,000 psi at the bottom of the ocean. They survive high radiation, heat to over 300°F, and being frozen almost to absolute zero. They can be desiccated for years and brought back to life by just adding water. Their estimated life span is 200 years.

Figure 287

Since survivability is the thesis of evolution, life should have stayed as microbes and Tardigrades, not evolved into more specialized and thus more vulnerable creatures. Better yet, life should have not even begun, since the inorganic elements of which it is composed is virtually indestructible. Better even yet, stay just energy that is totally indestructible.

The Missing Links

If evolution is true, the world should abound with transitional mutated organs and organisms. There would be no need to search for "missing links" since they would be everywhere in the fossil record and alive today.

Forming new organs would require millions of transitional steps because billions of different chemical parts need to be developed, transformed, and interlinked with one another. These steps should be clearly evident everywhere in living and fossilized creatures in countless gradations.

Given evolution, it would now be impossible to clearly differentiate one sort of creature from another. But the biota is not a blur. Rather, it is demarcated by distinct, recognizable, and well-developed forms, called syngameons, that remain true to their kind. Humans stay humans, chimps stay chimps, dogs stay dogs.

Culling the Transitions

If a step occurred toward a new trait but was not functional and advantageous, it would make the organism less fit. A budding wing cannot know, it just hangs in there, that a million years hence it will be a functional flight organ. Instead, natural selection would cull out organisms with useless appendages that are in the developmental stages.

There is no survival value of a nub destined to be a wing in a million years or so, or a flopping appendage that has a few, scraggly, wannabe feathers emerging here and there. Any random change in an existing organism will make the creature genetically discombobulated, less fit than the form from which it was derived. Natural selection is not a savior, it is a pitiless executioner.

Impossible to Explain by Evolution

The planthopper, Laternaria servillei, has at one end the perfect shape of a small alligator's head and has painted on its back the perfect likeness of alligator teeth, eyes, nostrils, and markings. The only obvious purpose is to scare away predators. Evolutionary transitions leading to this likeness would have been amorphous white blotches signaling to predators, "Come eat me." Thus, the transitions would have been gobbled up. If there were no transitions, there could be no planthopper. But there is. There is no mutational or genetic mechanism that could account for such a feature. The only reasonable conclusion is that the likeness was created fully formed.

Laternaria – The bug that decided to look like an alligator because evolution supposedly willed it.

Figure 085

Macaws live in a rain forest that contains some 40,000 varieties of trees. Only about ten produce edible fruit for the birds. Of the ten, most only bear fruit a few days each year and some only do so every several years. With no written language or maps, how was the macaw ability to find the right trees developed or transmitted? The capability could not arise by chance mutations and selection. The forest floor would have long ago been fertilized with the exhausted bodies of macaws waiting for the right mutations enabling them to find the right ten trees at the right times of the year.

The orb-weaver spider (Plesiometa argyra) lives in the rain forest of Costa Rica. It spins a round (orb) web. A parasitic wasp (Hymenoepimecis sp.) can temporarily paralyze the spider by stinging it in the mouth. The wasp then attaches a wasp egg to the spider's abdomen. A larva hatches from the egg, pierces the abdomen of the spider and dines on hemolymph (spider blood). The larva knows how to do this in such a way that the spider remains alive long enough to sustain the larva's development. The night the larva finally kills the spider, it gorges on the remaining contents of the spider and discards the empty shell to the forest floor.

Orb Spider – The left web is the configuration of a normal web spun by an orb spider. The right web with beefed-up cabling is the configuration of the web it spins when parasitized by a wasp.

Figure 086

But before that grotesque end, the larva communicates instructions to the spider to change its web weaving to a rectangular shape supported by beefed-up cabling. The new web shape accommodates the weight of the wasp larva so it can spin a cocoon to pupate and metamorphose into a wasp to begin the whole macabre cycle all over again. The special web protects the cocoon from heavy rains and the emerging wasp from being entangled in the spider's normal web.

It's impossible to prove in detail the step-by-step evolution of such a complex parasitic relationship, much less the wasp larvas' ability to communicate to the spider the new shape of a web to build to accommodate its executioner.

The end result is a new wasp that sets about finding other spiders to suck the life out of, boss around, and kill. By natural selection rules, this spider is more fit than its precursors that didn't let wasps kill them or force them to create a hatchery for their killers.

Speaking of cocoons, consider the impossibility of a specific step-by-step evolutionary mechanism (biochemical and genetic detail) enabling a worm to transform itself into a wasp. moth, or butterfly. Even if the mechanism were there, where would the desire for such a transformation come from?

The entire biological world is filled with such conundrums. Evolutionists ignore them or call them temporary gaps in understanding. The problem is, all of evolution is filled with such gaps.

The astounding complexity of organisms cannot be proven to result from evolution. Nor would any organism dare change significantly from its functional and surviving self. Natural selection occurs, but it is an excellent mechanism for preventing genetic aberrations (like mutations) from changing, vitiating, or destroying a species.

The failure of evidence and lack of any logical or proven mechanism, by Darwin's own words, defeats evolution. In *The Origin of Species*, he wrote:

"If it could be demonstrated that any complex organ existed which could not possibly have been formed by numerous, successive, slight modifications, my theory would absolutely break down."

13
FAVORITE EVOLUTION PROOFS

Evolution and abiogenesis are presented to the public under the banner of science. But science is about facts, experimental proofs, and repeatability. Yet there are no facts or repeatable experiments proving life came from nonlife, new beneficial organs appear spontaneously, or creatures transmutate into different and more functionally complex organisms that will not revert to their progenitors.

This is not to say there isn't a lot of voice and ink declaring that evolution is an established fact. Here are examples of the proofs that are used.

Similarity

Similar features are used to prove evolutionary ancestry. But similarity presents more contradictions than evidence.

If similarity proved relationship, the beak of the platypus would relate it to the goose, its hair to a bear, the tail to a beaver, webbed feet to a duck, claws to a reptile, spurs on its hind legs to a rooster, venom to a scorpion, and eggs to a snake. It detects prey like an eel, and produces milk but has no nipples. (Platypus fossils date back 167 million years and have the identical features of the present platypus.)

An insect can look like a leaf or stick, but insects are clearly not related to leaves or sticks. Cytochrome C is a biochemical that is similar in the carp, bullfrog, turtle, chicken, rabbit, and horse. But no evolutionary tree shows these creatures related.

Human hemoglobin (the red blood cell pigment), is very similar to that in worms and we share about the same number of protein-coding genes. But we are far removed from worms in evolutionary trees. Antigen receptors in camels and nurse sharks are more similar to each other than to creatures in their supposed evolutionary lines. The GULO enzyme is similar in New World and Old World

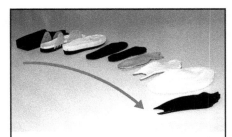

Insoles – These are some of the prototypes created in my development of an ergonomic insole. The similarities do not mean they evolved into each other, but rather reflect the thinking of a common designer.

© Wysong   Figure 087

monkeys. However, humans would seem to be more closely related to fruit bats, hamsters, and guinea pigs since we and they are absent GULO enzymes. We share about 50% of our DNA with bananas.

Evolution requires a gradation of simple to complex, less to more. Therefore, it would seem that larger, more complex organisms should have more DNA than simpler ones. However, toads and lilies have far more DNA per cell than humans, salamanders have twenty times more, and some insects have twice as much. Based on chromosome count, humans are similar to deer and lower on the evolutionary ladder than chimps.

Similarities can also be selected to support evolution. But since they can be used to both prove and disprove evolution, they are not a useful argument.

Vestigial Organs

Evolutionists say that some body parts are useless and only present as leftovers from evolutionary ancestors. Such parts are thus called vestigial.

In 1893, Wiedersheim listed 180 such organs. As knowledge has been gained, the list gets whittled down. It should be zero. Lack of understanding of a body part's function doesn't mean it's useless.

The belief in vestigial organs has justified countless surgeries to remove them. Sadly, every such surgery removing a non-diseased body part renders the person less healthy in the long term. All parts of the human body have a function. Ignorance of that function doesn't justify surgical pruning.

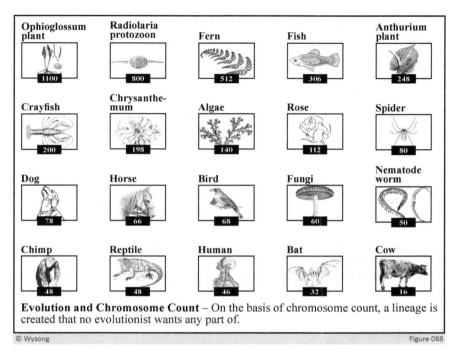

Evolution and Chromosome Count – On the basis of chromosome count, a lineage is created that no evolutionist wants any part of.

© Wysong   Figure 088

Moreover, if there is a body part with no function or a detrimental one, that would most likely be the result of mutations or other Second Law degenerations of the human genome.

The other factor to consider is epigenetics which permits the inhibition or expression of different parts of the genome depending upon the needs. For example, wisdom teeth may have been more important in the past because of a diet requiring more mastication than now. Goosebumps, thought to be a vestige, may have been more important in the primitive past when we had lots of body hair to insulate us and were in constant threat of predation and other violence. The muscles in the skin that cause goose bumps would cause the hair to rise up when we were threatened to make us look bigger and more intimidating, just as occurs in a cat. Now, when threatened, all we get are bumps because clothes obviated our need for lots of body hair. Epigenetics—switching genes on and off—not evolution is at play.

Here are some examples of body parts labeled mistakenly as vestigial or unimportant at one time or another, and their subsequent proven functions:

- Wisdom teeth—improve mastication
- Body hair—insulates and increases tactile senses
- Tailbones—provide an anchor for muscles, tendons, and ligaments
- Thyroid—secretes thyroid hormones
- Pineal gland—controls growth, sexual, and circadian cycles
- Vomeronasal organ—detects pheromones
- Appendix—part of the immune system
- Tonsils—part of the immune system
- Adenoids—part of the immune system
- Thymus—produces immune elements

Notice the last four in that list. Given that no health or healing ever occurs without the immune system, it's unthinkable that doctors lopped off millions of functional immune organs. They justified it with their evolutionary belief in vestigial organs and the presumption that they prevented disease by removing them.

Embryology

Virtually every textbook attempting to prove evolution will line up the embryological stages of humans and show their similarities to our supposed ancestors. This is called ontogeny (our individual life history) recapitulating phylogeny (our supposed evolutionary history).

The drawings originally used to demonstrate this were fudged by Haeckel (1866) to make the evolutionary case.

If ontology is actually recapitulating phylogeny, then women would miscarry fish, amphibians, reptiles, and sub-human primates. But that never happens.

Embryology isn't a memory of the past. It's the succession of stages necessary to create the creature it is designed to be. It would be impossible to develop in the womb from one cell (zygote) into a human without going through transitions that might look like less complex organisms.

Archaeopteryx

Archaeopteryx is a fossil used to show that birds evolved from dinosaurs. It had feathers like birds and teeth similar to reptiles. However, no intermediaries have been found leading to it or away from it. Nor have any fossils been found showing the evolution of feathers.

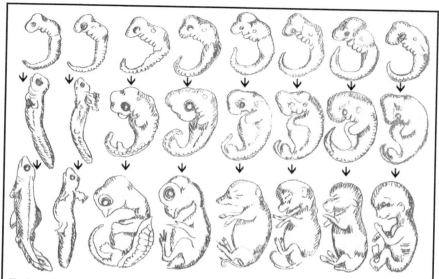

Embryology Does Not Recapitulate Phylogeny – These doctored drawings of embryos by Ernst Haeckel have been used for over a century to attempt to prove evolution.

Figure 090

Archaeopteryx is clearly just a type of bird, a syngameon. It began as an Archaeopteryx and stayed an Archaeopteryx. Moreover, dinosaurs like Velociraptor and Deinonychus are found in rocks of the same age as well as in those 75 million years younger than those containing Archeopteryx. That would make Archaeopteryx and other birds predecessors and contemporaries of dinosaurs, not their evolved progeny.

Archaeopteryx – This fossil is argued by evolutionists to be a link between dinosaurs and birds. However, it is a true bird in all respects and is found contemporaneous with dinosaurs in the same strata.

Figure 091

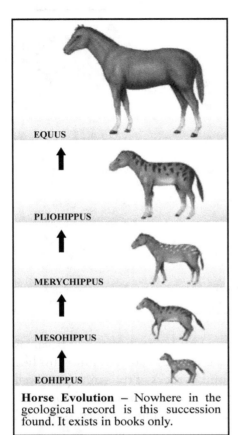

EQUUS

PLIOHIPPUS

MERYCHIPPUS

MESOHIPPUS

EOHIPPUS

Horse Evolution – Nowhere in the geological record is this succession found. It exists in books only.

© Wysong   Figure 092

Horses

Various horse-like animals are commonly arrayed in evolutionary trees. The pictures, drawings, and arrows are a fabricated sequence. This is proven by the fact that the fossils of supposed transitional forms can be found out of sync with the evolutionary progression. That means "precursors" are found younger than their "progeny." That's like saying children beget parents.

The fossil record of horses shows variety within a kind, or horse-like animals that are kinds (syngameons) in their own right.

Variety Is Not Evolution

Variation, such as breeds of horses, dogs, varieties of fruit flies and corn, antibiotic resistance in bacteria, and insecticide resistance by insects should not be confused with the shape-shifting hypothesized in macroevolution, meaning the change of one kind of organism into another. Variety within a syngameon (kind) is not the same thing as the evolution of new creatures.

Even after hundreds of years of breeding and genetic manipulation, creatures remain essentially the same. Cows stay cows and wheat stays wheat. Each interbreeding syngameon has a finite pool of genes. Size, shape, color, strength, speed, and personality all may vary to a degree in a population as a result of random or directed breeding. If the environment favors a particular variation, that creature and its progeny may fare better and predominate.

Nobody disagrees that such variation happens to a degree and that it helps creatures survive. The key word here is degree. Variety, yes; evolutionary transmutation, no.

Moth Melanism – The predominance of one color of moth over another in rural versus urban habitat is taken as proof of evolution. Note that they are still moths, have always been moths and, according to scientific laws, will always be moths.

© Chiswick Chap

Figure 108

Geneticists constantly try to push the envelope but they always reach a barrier. For example, since the time of Napoleon sugar beets have been selectively bred to increase sugar yield. They're now at about 18% sugar. In spite of the huge economic reward for moving that % higher, the limit of the sugar beet syngameon has apparently been reached.

Over 800 different breeds of cattle have been created (all are still cows). Milk production per dairy cow udder has increased three-fold in just the past few decades. Those changes can't be extrapolated to prove that one day a cow will evolve into something that is 99% udder.

A Chihuahua is dramatically different in size from a Great Dane or Bulldog. But no amount of breeding will stretch that limit so that dogs cannot be identified as dogs.

Fruit flies will vary the number of bristles between 25 and 56. After over a century of experimentation and hundreds of thousands of generations, that's the limit. Not only that, if the flies are left to interbreed naturally, they'll revert to the original average of 36.

Darwin used finches to make his case for speciation (the development of new species).

World's tallest and shortest humans are still humans.

© Guinness World Records

Figure 093

87

Finches separated geographically had slightly different beaks. He saw this as evidence of natural selection creating new species. However, all of the new finch varieties can interbreed. They're just varieties of one kind of bird syngameon.

In just the time since the discovery of the bacterium, E. coli, in the late 1800s, there have been almost five million E. coli generations. But E. coli is still E. coli. The total generations of bacteria since life supposedly first appeared would be trillions upon trillions. Yet they have remained the same. On the other hand, we are to believe, if evolution is true, that humans supposedly evolved from chimp-like creatures in just 300,000 generations.

The Middle, Not the Edge, Is Safe

When creatures go out to the extreme edges of their genetic potential, they become sterile and less fit, not more evolved. For example, a mule is a cross between a donkey and a horse but it's usually sterile. Fruit flies with 56 bristles, rather than the average 36, will usually be short-lived and sterile. The genetic drift pressure is always back to the average wild-type—the mutt—not new novel varieties onward and upward in an evolutionary tree.

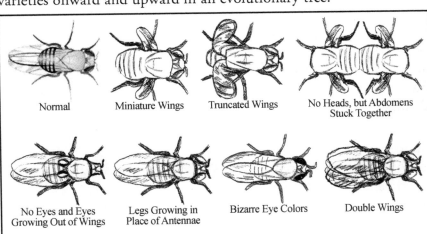

| Normal | Miniature Wings | Truncated Wings | No Heads, but Abdomens Stuck Together |

| No Eyes and Eyes Growing Out of Wings | Legs Growing in Place of Antennae | Bizarre Eye Colors | Double Wings |

Mutant Fruit Flies – include bizarre eye colors of pink, purple, maroon; truncated wings or miniature wings, or no wings at all; legs growing where their antennae or mouth should be; perfectly formed, functional eyes growing out of their wings, or on their legs, or at the tips of their antennae; two sets of wings instead of one; and no heads but two abdomens stuck end to end. But no new, improved fruit flies and no new species, even after the equivalent of millions of years of laboratory-attempted evolution. The bottom line is that highly complex genetic information does not upgrade when randomly shuffled or damaged, it degenerates.

© Wysong   Figure 104

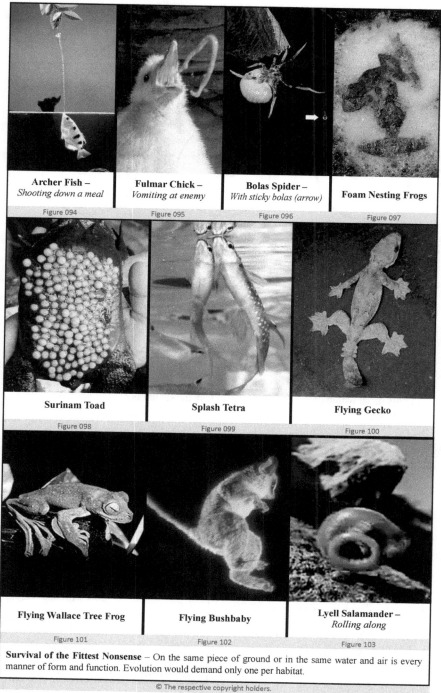

Archer Fish –
Shooting down a meal

Figure 094

Fulmar Chick –
Vomiting at enemy

Figure 095

Bolas Spider –
With sticky bolas (arrow)

Figure 096

Foam Nesting Frogs

Figure 097

Surinam Toad

Figure 098

Splash Tetra

Figure 099

Flying Gecko

Figure 100

Flying Wallace Tree Frog

Figure 101

Flying Bushbaby

Figure 102

Lyell Salamander –
Rolling along

Figure 103

Survival of the Fittest Nonsense – On the same piece of ground or in the same water and air is every manner of form and function. Evolution would demand only one per habitat.

Natural selection works, but it puts pressure on a population toward the middle, toward home base, not out to the weird and novel genetic edges where evolution needs to take place.

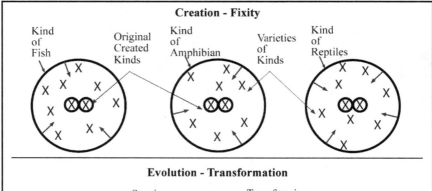

Creation - Fixity

Kind of Fish — Original Created Kinds — Kind of Amphibian — Varieties of Kinds — Kind of Reptiles

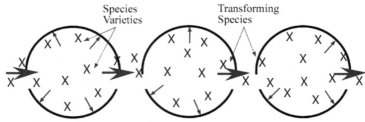

Evolution - Transformation

Species Varieties — Transforming Species

Fixity Vs. Transformation – Although species can vary, adapt, mutate and change, they will only do so within prescribed bounds (circles), the set limits of their kinds. Evolution, on the other hand, argues that species have the inherent ability, through the aid of time, mutations and selection, to transmutate from one form into another. Thus, according to evolution, life forms are not enclosed by genetic barriers restricting the amount of change possible. Which position is more scientific is determined by the evidence.

© Wysong   Figure 105

Extrapolation

The dictionary definition of evolution makes it easy to conflate the fact that technology, cars, computers, dress, food . . . "evolves," with the extrapolated notion that life has evolved from atoms.

Extrapolation is a wonderful tool of reason and we all use it every day. However, breeding different sizes, shapes, and colors

Both evolutionists and religionists base beliefs on human created words, rather than reason and facts.

© Wysong   Figure 106

of dogs doesn't prove that dogs came from guppies. Mutating fruit flies into all kinds of freaky fruit flies doesn't prove fruit flies came from stardust or that they will one day evolve into eagles. Biological variation is to evolution as a firefly is to lightning.

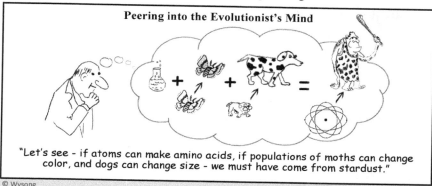

"Let's see - if atoms can make amino acids, if populations of moths can change color, and dogs can change size - we must have come from stardust."

© Wysong

Figure 107

Rather than a true account of biology, evolution is a lineup of hopeful extrapolations culminating in a belief that does not logically follow from the facts or the laws that govern the universe.

Biological variation is not evolution, it is the mere result of various genetic functions including regulator genes, genetic drift, recombinations, and epigenetics (switching genes on and off) and proves nothing except that creatures can vary, adapt, and be different to a degree based upon existing genetic potential.

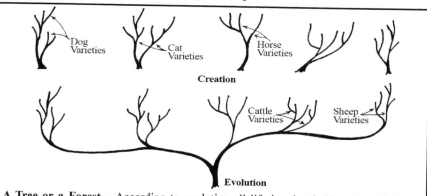

A Tree or a Forest – According to evolution all life is related. Therefore all living things should be traceable to a common origin (monophyletic origin) and all living things should belong to one tree. On the other hand, the creation model would stipulate that geneological trees would terminate in the original created organisms (polyphyletic origins), and not merge with other trunks. So the issue is not whether organisms can vary (have branches) but whether the trunks of all geneological trees join at the base.

© Wysong

Figure 109

The star witness for abiogenesis and evolution never comes forward to nail it. We never actually see any direct proof that life can spontaneously come from nonlife or that creatures can or did evolve into new and distinct creatures with new organs and traits. Instead, there are just speculative extrapolations. That is not science.

14
WHY MATERIALISM
IS BELIEVED

The tenacity with which materialism (abiogenesis and evolution) is held is in large part because it's thought to be the only alternative to untenable religions. It also seems intellectual since it's taught in schools and prestigious scientists and thinkers believe it. Philosophically, it's attractive because it justifies amoral freedom and unaccountability. Facts, logic, and evidence barely have a chance against such powerful reasons to accept and retain this belief.

Hobnobbing With Science

Lacking evidence to the contrary, the materialistic explanation of origins appears to have been accepted into the fraternity of science without passing the initiation rigors of observation and experimentation. That would make it a pretender that has slipped in through the back door. Then, by raising the banner of science and hobnobbing with people who do real science it has become an assumed scientific truth.

Science is a method of exploring the world, it's not a dogma that demands compliance. Science requires observation and repeatability first, conclusions second. But neither spontaneous generation nor cell-to-man evolution has been observed nor repeated in a laboratory. Moreover, unlike true science, these beliefs have done nothing in a material or philosophical way to better the world.

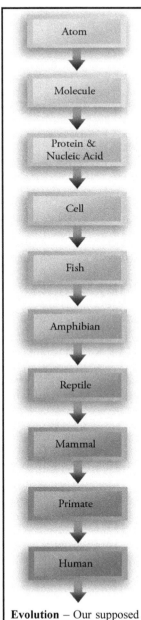

Atom

Molecule

Protein & Nucleic Acid

Cell

Fish

Amphibian

Reptile

Mammal

Primate

Human

Evolution – Our supposed ancestry is entirely speculation based upon the presupposition of materialism, the false idea that reality is reducible to matter.

© Wysong   Figure 110

But it's persuasive when the same people who do real science sing the praises of materialism. After all, if a person is smart enough to split and splice genes and atoms, or explain astrophysics, then they must be right when they talk about origins. And talk they do. It's hard to find any biological or cosmological literature that isn't seeded with references to evolution. This is done even though evolution has nothing to do with discovery or salutary value.

Those on the outside looking into the esoteric world of scientists and brainwashed in schools presenting evolution as fact assume there is a scientific consensus. That in itself persuades laypeople. But there is no consensus. For example, at dissentfromdarwin.org, hundreds of scientists and professors sign a statement that they are skeptical of the basic tenets of evolution. But even if there were consensus on either side of the issue, popularity proves nothing.

Evolution has become the intellectual word du jour without ever being critically examined on its own merits. The word could be replaced with "design," or "creation" in any text of value and no beneficial information nor understanding of reality would be lost.

Even many religionists have been cowed. Seeking to appear progressive and enlightened, they hybridize their religious faith with the evolutionary faith. But this doesn't deem them with the credibility they seek. First, it makes no sense that the Creator would do a special case continuous violation of its own natural laws to accommodate evolution. Second, it makes no sense that the Creator would comport with an atheistic materialistic view that denies the Creator's existence.

94

Alchemy, Shape Shifting, and Fairy Tales

Alchemists of old hoped to be able to brew gold and create elixirs for eternal youth. The idea of magical transformations has seeded mythology for thousands of years. Read Grimm's Fairy Tales, Ovid's Metamorphoses, or the Italian epics. People change into gods, gods change into people, animals become human, and humans become animals.

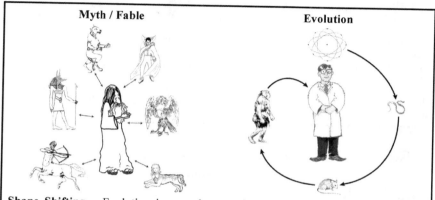

Myth / Fable   **Evolution**

Shape Shifting – Evolution is a modern version of shape shifting that is widely believed, even called science, even though there is no proof and no known mechanism for such a thing to happen.

© Wysong   Figure 112

Evolution is the same kind of mythology. Although the story is drawn out into smaller and seemingly more plausible steps, the end result is life popping into existence from stardust, and creatures magically transforming into new, more functionally complicated creatures. Since such transformations violate nature's evidence and natural laws, evolution, if it actually did occur, would be beyond nature. In other words, supernatural.

Panspermia Solves Nothing

Some evolutionary scientists recognize the paucity of evidence and, in desperation, invoke panspermia—the seeding of life on Earth from outer space. Crick, the co-discoverer of DNA, invented "directed panspermia" which invokes aliens bringing life here on spacecraft so it's protected from the interstellar elements.

But that doesn't really solve the problem of the origin of life, it merely displaces it to the aliens' planet where the same problems of origin remain.

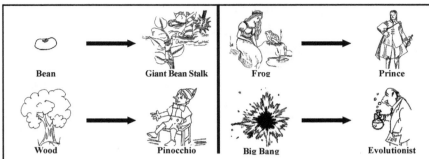

Fairy Tales – Things that are not plausible are called fairy tales. It is considered implausible that a bean could grow a gigantic bean stalk for a boy to climb, that wood from a tree could create a talking little boy and that a frog could turn into a prince. Even though in each case the starting materials are living things, we automatically dismiss the idea of them converting to something more complex. But evolutionists would like us to believe that inanimate exploding stardust can create the entire panorama of life.

© Wysong   Figure 111

Keeping a Distance from Religion

Perhaps the most common underlying reason evolution is believed is that the only alternative there is thought to be is religion. Religions commonly anthropomorphize a Creator thus making it intellectually and ethically difficult to reconcile the evil, suffering, and injustice in the world with a god who can intervene like we think we would. (I will address this issue more thoroughly later in the book.)

Also, a return to the darkness of religious authority is terrifying. If it were not for the intervention of the secular state, religion would still be mandating the torturing and killing of those who don't believe

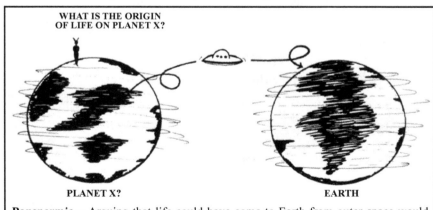

Panspermia – Arguing that life could have come to Earth from outer space would simply remove the question of origins to another planet.

© Wysong   Figure 113

in a domed heaven, circling sun, flat Earth, fire breathing dragons, talking snakes and donkeys, magnetic islands that pulled ships to them, Cyclops, witches, demon-possessed cats, and curing disease with holy water enemas.

The Bible-based belief that the sun revolved around the Earth held sway for 1500 years. When Copernicus published his contrary theory of heliocentricity in 1530, it was prefaced with a disclaimer so its author would not meet the flames of the Holy Inquisition. An infallible pope placed the book on the don't read list in Index Librorum Prohibitorum where it remained until another infallible pope removed it in 1835.

Giordano Bruno openly advocated the double motion of Earth (the Earth revolves on its axis and around the sun). For this anti-Biblical heresy, he was incinerated in 1600. Galileo (1564- 1642) provided further proof of Earth's double motion, but his observations were considered heretical because he used a telescope rather than the Bible and syllogisms. Under threat of torture by the Inquisitors, he recanted: "I, Galileo, being in my seventieth year, being a prisoner and on my knees, and before your Eminence, having before my eyes the Holy Gospel, which I touch with my hands, abjure, curse, and detest the error and the heresy of the movement of the Earth."

Shedding the authority of religion allowed the Earth to move correctly and brought us into the light of reason and evidence. For those aware of this history, turning back is unthinkable.

However, the fact that scientists discovered that disease could be caused by germs, and not from skimping on tithes, is no reason to believe any pronouncement scientists may make.

Unfortunately, in the haste to flee from religious belief and faith, people have uncritically adopted faith and belief in materialistic origins.

The idea of evolution has percolated through society taking on a grandeur that does not fit its intellectually homely underpinnings. It's a story repeated so often in the most prestigious circles, that the story itself has become the evidence.

When people want to believe something, they'll torture the facts however necessary into the service of the belief. This isn't mere innocent folly. Flying away on the wings of belief betrays the duty to truth and threatens the self and the entire planet.

There is an alternative to materialism, abiogenesis, evolution, and religion. Recognizing it requires admitting ignorance and intellect beyond our own.

Why People Can't Think

Evolutionist   Religionist

© Wysong   Figure 114

The Psychology of Prior Commitment – Both religionists and materialists build their cases on pillars of sand.

© Walt Horton   Figure 115

That does not mean a return to the Dark Ages, sacrificing lambs, blowing ourselves up in a jihad, or kissing the boots of church leaders. Science doesn't end if nature is found to have the footprint of a creative consciousness that has nothing whatsoever to do with the anthropomorphized gods of man-made religions.

Thinking about . . .

THE FINGERPRINT OF MIND

In This Section: The application of logic and a fair consideration of the evidence proves that mind, not matter, underlies our reality.

15
FREE WILL PROVES CREATION

If our reality is the mere product of matter and energy interacting over vast stretches of time, the qualities we and the universe possess should be fully attributable to those agents.

And the materialist has confidence that this is so. After all, if there's a question about why a bulldozer works, just start disassembling it into its gears, nuts, and bolts until the answer emerges. Such experience with human-made devices is then extrapolated to apply to everything in nature. For example, to understand how the body works, it's dissected to its smallest components. This reductionist approach is central in today's sciences of anatomy, physiology, histology, cytology, and biochemistry.

Practical successes with examining parts and pieces have brought us great technological advances and created confidence that all answers will lie within the components of matter. However, break things down far enough and a problem emerges. For example, there is nothing about the iron atoms in the bulldozer that would explain how the bulldozer works, why it's broken, or what made it. Similarly, the atoms in color pigments don't explain the design and beauty that emerges from a painting or flower. There's nothing about hydrogen and oxygen that would predict the properties of water when they combine as H2O.

Nor is there anything within the nature of atoms that would suggest, or even hint at a fully functioning human. In fact, the proton in a neuron in your brain is identical to a proton in the door handle on your car.

At the atomic level, atoms simply obey natural laws that make their behavior perfectly predictable. (I am not ignoring quantum uncertainty, which I address elsewhere.) Obedient atoms are what allow chemists to mix a batch of certain atoms and molecules together to produce plastic food wrap and count on not getting Coca-Cola coming out of the extruder.

Atoms, or parts of atoms, don't have little engineering drawings in their hip pockets describing how to build a bulldozer, flower, painting, human, frog, or aardvark. Nor do atoms have the free will to choose to assemble in such complex functional ways. They are bound by law, they aren't volitionally free and creative.

There's clearly a missing factor between elemental pieces of matter and the higher-level complicated and functionally ordered qualities that we see in our reality. The intelligent painter's choices, not atoms, are the cause of the beauty in a painting. The intelligent engineer's choices, not atoms, are responsible for the functional complexity and feats of a bulldozer.

But materialists attempt to rebut this with determinism, a philosophy that denies will and argues that materialistic forces cause all things.

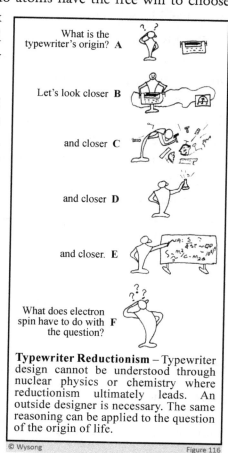

Typewriter Reductionism – Typewriter design cannot be understood through nuclear physics or chemistry where reductionism ultimately leads. An outside designer is necessary. The same reasoning can be applied to the question of the origin of life.

© Wysong   Figure 116

Consider their reasoning on a coin toss. They say, and it is true, that subtleties in the way the coin is held, the laws governing the forces from your thumb, air currents, barometric pressure, humidity, and symmetry of the coin all determine exactly what will turn up with each flip. If the forces acting upon the coin could be calculated, heads or tails could be predicted every time.

Materialists take this reasoning a gigantic step further and claim the same determinism applies to all things, including us and the choices we make. The contention is that every particle in your body, every action you take, and your existence could be explained if one were long-winded and smart enough to detail the history of every atom and how the laws of the universe affected them. To determinists, we are nothing more than biological robots.

By this reasoning, the entire history and future of the universe are locked in, determined, with no surprises. All of our actions would be just an effect of underlying chemical reactions that are the inevitable end result of a long chain of other chemical collisions, all interlinked and cascading from one to the other since the Big Bang. If one atom anywhere since the beginning of time would have been in a different spot, that would have impacted all other atoms through time and I would not now be me writing these words and you would not be you reading them.

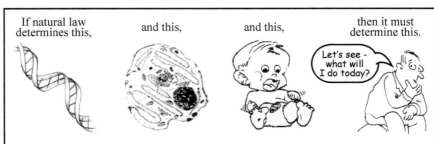

If natural law determines this, and this, and this, then it must determine this.

Let's see - what will I do today?

Determinism – If matter is guided solely by the action of natural laws – gravity, magneticism, inertia, nuclear forces and so forth – then atomic action is determined. Molecules such as DNA are also determined; there is no free choice. Cells, which are composites of chemicals and DNA, would also be determined. Since humans are made of chemicals and cells, they should also be determined. But they aren't. The fact that humans have free choice argues that they are composed of something other than matter and the forces that govern it.

© Wysong   Figure 117

At first glance, determinism seems a reasonable sort of thing since the motions of the planets, the speed of an apple falling from a tree, and the strength of the steel necessary to hold up a bridge are all determined and predicted by matter and natural laws.

Determinists then extrapolate from this that we are no different than the planets, apples, and bridges. All thought, which they claim is the result of the particular atoms a person has in their brain, would be the mere consequence of atoms interacting with each other since the Big Bang. Therefore, there would be no free will that could violate this progression of inexorable forces. Assuming all thought comes from matter in the brain, atoms would not be choosing, any more than blacktop atoms on roadways have a choice of whether to get excited and generate heat when exposed to the sun, or a ball set atop a plank elevated at one end decides whether to roll downhill or not.

However, determinism is demolished by the existence of free will. Unlike atoms, molecules, and other material things that blindly obey natural laws, we can choose among endless options. Will (choice) is the antithesis of blind obligatory obedience to law.

Granted, many of our day-to-day acts, particularly in our modern world of consumerism and obedience, may seem reactive, deterministic, even robotic. We eat, sleep, don or shed clothes depending on the weather, and move to sexual urges. But, clearly, at any point in this flow of life, we can make alternate choices.

On the other hand, nonliving things are only deterministic. They obey natural law only. A rock does what the laws governing its atoms dictate. A machine does what its parts permit. Even a computer can make no choices beyond its program code and the laws governing its electronics and other physical parts.

Further complicating matters for determinists are the collectives of people in nation-states, religions, and society that settle on the same ideologies, and ontologies. From a materialistic stance, it's not possible to explain how the atoms in various brains, all having unique histories since the Big Bang, settle upon the same beliefs.

It's a self-evident fact assumed by virtually all of humanity that we have free will. It's embedded in language with hundreds of words and phrases, such as choosing, choice, deciding, decision, ambivalence, quandary, uncertainty, freedom, latitude, leeway, liberty, prerogative, dilemma, adjudge, guess, waver, unsettle, prefer, discriminate between, and so on.

If determinism is true, languages worldwide would have to be purged of all such words indicating choice. Replacing all the deletions would be one word, determined, and its derivatives. Moreover, all the millions of non-fiction writings in stores and libraries with references to choices and deciding would have to be moved over to the fiction aisles.

This practical implication highlights the absurdity of denying free will. But determinism requires holding to its denial because free will would nullify the materialistic faith that atoms and energy are an ultimate explanation of reality. It would also mean the free choice to believe in materialistic determinism would prove that materialistic determinism cannot be true.

Compounding the logical and practical sinkhole that results from denying free will is an ethical dilemma. Ethics cannot be derived from atoms no matter how they interact. This, combined with evolutionary survival of the fittest, not only sets the stage for amorality but brutal competitiveness as well.

In a world absent free will, no dastardly deed could be prosecuted. People under the force of dog-eat-dog evolution and the brain's forced obedience to the laws of chemistry and physics would be blameless. Courtrooms and prisons would be empty since nobody could logically be held accountable for their actions. Every manner of behavior could be deterministically justified. This is actually creeping into our judicial system which is peopled with lawyers and lawyer-judges schooled in materialism, evolution, and determinism.

Such dire consequences signal wrong premises, just like the horrors visited upon mankind by the church-state through millennia are due to wrong premises. Wrong ideas create wrong results.

"Let me out! My atoms forced me to murder, rape, and pillage!"

© Wysong   Figure 272

Materialists must explain away these socially destructive implications of determinism. Secular humanism serves that end. It's a doctrine of acceptable ethics not unlike the basic precepts of most religions and what can be derived from one's own conscience. However, ethics cannot reasonably be concluded from materialism, determinism, or evolution.

Free will can only be reasonably denied if, as a starting point, materialism is presumed true. But there is no proof that life can emerge from lifeless matter or transform itself into ever more complex forms.

Whoa! Please release me. I promise to throw my telescope away and use the Bible to learn about astronomy.

© Wysong   Figure 273

The denial of free will also has the bonus of supporting materialists' anti-religious stance since choice is integral to religious moral codes, redemption, salvation, and so on. But human-made religions have nothing to do with whether we have free will or not.

The reality of free will stands and demands other, other than matter, other than natural law. The prospect that our essence is "other," something beyond the reach of microscopes and test tubes, is just not something the materialist-evolutionist-determinist mind can tolerate.

Nor can the inevitable conclusion that something other than matter would have to account for our free will be tolerated. A sufficient cause for such an extraordinary departure from obedience to natural physical laws would have to be the extraordinary intelligence and free will of an extradimensional nonmaterial Creator.

Keep in mind that no religious predisposition is required for this logic. Nor does concluding that an intelligence underlies our reality substantiate any human-made religion or holy book. We're simply permitting truth, to the degree we can know it, to speak to us.

On the other hand, materialists can set about proving, by actual science, not just philosophical musings, that free will can be traced to atoms. But that has not only never been done, it can't be. The truth of fixed natural laws prevents it.

16
DESIGN

On the face of it, the detailed intricacy, roiling complexity, and staggering functionality of the natural world point to intelligence. That's the common-sense conclusion humans have made since the beginning of time.

For example, a crudely chipped flint stone in a dig is considered an artifact produced by an intelligence who chose to create it. If such rudiments of organization and functionality signify intelligence, something stupendously more dynamic, complex, and functional, such as the simplest of living cells, must also point to an intelligence choosing to create them.

NASA (National Aeronautics and Space Administration) and SETI (Search for Extraterrestrial Intelligence) probe space for extraterrestrial life by looking for order and patterns that would signify intelligent choice.

Forensic science, cryptography, and archeology are also beset with the problem of discerning what is due to chance and what is due to intelligent intervention. The criteria these scientific specialties use to determine intelligent origin are complexity, information, probabilities, repeating patterns, and choice.

Our entire world, from subatomic quanta, to atoms, viruses, amoebas, ants, elephants, us, stars, and galaxies contains the unmistakable earmarks of purpose and design. Purpose and design point to mind, not self-causation or randomness.

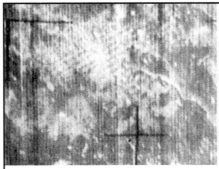 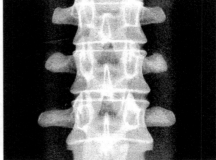

Signs of Intelligence – The left photo is from a Tiros weather satellite, of a region in Ontario. The parallel lines (logging swaths) are a sign of intelligent life on Earth. Scientists look for similar signs on other planets to indicate intelligent life. The right photograph is a radiograph of three human lumbar vertebrae. Do the parallel lines and order seen here suggest an intelligent creator?

Figure 119

Beauty

Nature is suffused with exquisite beauty for which there is no apparent cause or purpose. A peacock's fanned tail does not need to be that beautiful to attract a mate. A monarch butterfly's wings don't have to be so elaborately ornate in order to signal to predators that it's poisonous. The venation in a leaf doesn't need to be beautiful for any reason whatsoever. A Bengal tiger is an incredible work of art and simply does not need to be so perfect. Flowers may attract insects, but really, must they be that breathtaking? There are even exquisitely beautiful flowers that don't even need to attract anything, other than, apparently, our awe and enjoyment.

Beauty in Nature – Although the beauty in nature can serve some functions, such as camouflage or mate attraction, the degree of intricate beauty cannot be explained by any evolutionary function that is necessary for the creature possessing it. In many respects, nature is like a montage of art, a gigantic art exhibit to be appreciated by an audience.

Figure 120

Orchid Mantis – The same arguments apply to this praying mantis with bulbous features identical to the parts in flowers where it lies in wait for insect prey.

Leaf Insect – Evolutionists explain this insect by saying that it developed the leaf mimicry in order to hide from predators. While it is true that the camouflage may help its survival, that is an effect. Effects do not prove cause. Evolutionists must explain with logic, scientific proofs, and biochemical detail how every single square nanometer of the leaf features, including the frayed edges, came to be step by step, with each step making the insect more survivable than the previous step. No such explanation exists. Intelligence, not natural law, best explains the art in nature.

Figure 121

The elaborate beauty and diversity in nature cry out to us that something other than necessity, chemical mixing, and degrading mutations are at play.

Irreducible Complexity and The Eye

Everything in nature is irreducibly complex. That means that if something is made to be less complex than it is, it doesn't work. Functionally complex things (cars, washing machines, computers, organs, and creatures) work because all the parts are there and in sync.

If any part of the eye is removed, it will not work properly. If something less than the eye preceded the eye it would not have worked, would have had no survival value, and the creature having it would have been culled out of the population (natural selection).

Consider the eyelids. If they were smaller than needed to cover the eye, the cornea would become damaged from exposure and from not being properly lubricated. The cornea would then ulcerate and eventually, vision would be lost. If the lids were too big, they would not seal properly to protect the globe. If the eyelashes are not placed properly (distichiasis), they may rub on the cornea and ulcerate it. (A condition frequently seen in certain dog breeds and needing veterinary intervention.) Lash length is also critical in permitting the correct airflow over the cornea (why long false eyelashes are not a good idea). If tear lubricants aren't present, that too can result in ulceration. If all the parts and pieces, the skin, glands, blood vessels, lymphatics, and neurons made up of the five million or so cells in the lid are not there, that will result in a faulty lid and potential loss of vision as well. The eyelid doesn't need just to be a little close, it needs to be pretty much right on the money, or the eye will not function at its optimum or will be damaged resulting in loss of vision. The same stipulations and caveats can be detailed about every other structure related to the eye or any other organ or part of the body for that matter.

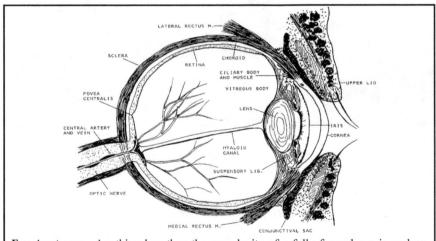

Eye Anatomy – Anything less than the complexity of a fully formed eye is useless. Thus the eye could not have developed piecemeal through eons of time because natural selection would cull the "less fit" developing steps. Natural selection is the nemesis of evolution, not its savior.

© Wysong   Figure 122

The eye is a machine able to convert light into an image that we can "see" with our brains. That's just the beginning of the story. Here's more detail.

Light passes through the cornea and iris to the retina at the back of the eye, a paper-thin membrane consisting of (in part) about 150 million rod and cone cells for detecting intensity and color.

There a photon, within picoseconds, converts 11-cis-retinal to trans-retinal. This causes a change in the shape of the attached protein, rhodopsin, converting it to metarhodopsin II, which attaches to another protein called transducin that has attached to it a small molecule called GDP. Then GDP splits off, and a molecule called GTP binds to transducin. GTP-transducin-metarhodopsin II then binds to the protein phosphodiesterase. Phosphodiesterase, in turn, reduces the concentration of a molecule called cGMP. This results in ion channel changes by way of pumps that vary the level of sodium ions, creating a charge differential and thus a current that can be transmitted down a million optic nerve fibers to the brain's vision center.

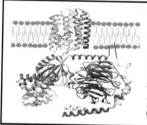

Rhodopsin II – A simplified schematic of Rhodopsin II with C- terminus and N-terminus embedded in a lipid bilayer cell membrane with transducin, Gtα, Gtβ, and Gtγ. A GDP molecule is bound in the Gtα-subunit and retinal is bound in the rhodopsin. Within the squiggly representations of molecules are thousands of individual atoms, and within them millions of subatomic particles all needing to behave precisely for sight to occur. Anything less than this perfection (like an evolutionary step) would mean blindness.

© Dpryan, wikipedia

Figure 123

As complex as that sounds, it's pathetically under-understated. It's like me explaining how my laptop works by describing that I plug in the power, open the top, and press the on button.

The above description only paints broad strokes about what is so far known about one photon striking the eye. Nothing was said about the infinite other photons that enter the cornea second by second are sorted out by the brain, how the spectrum of 370 nanometers of colors, hues, brightness, shapes, and motion is captured in the retina, and how two eyes can create one united image.

The retina can see one photon in the dark, then tune down bright light containing trillions of photons. It can handle light intensity of ten billion to one. By comparison, the best camera film can only handle an intensity of 1000 to one. None of this addresses the question of how all these processes can happen simultaneously from moment to moment as we look about, or how everything must be instantly set back to start to capture the next view.

The complexity of the eye is not an anomaly. Everything in nature has this order of complexity. Evolution will have to account for every minute chemical, structural, and physiological detail if it is to be a sound explanation. Little wonder that does not happen. Instead, there are simplistic stories like this: light-sensitive pigment evolved to light-sensitive cells, then to a primitive eyespot, to a deeply recessed eyespot, to a pinhole lens eye, and finally to the complex eye. The proof, aside from the a priori belief that evolution is true, is that there are creatures alive today that have each of the supposed precursors to the eye.

But that very fact contains the disproof that any of these sight organs evolved from one to the other. If supposedly semi-evolved precursor eye organs are fully functional for the creatures that have them, there is no need for them to evolve further. That's why evolutionists must suggest that the eye evolved dozens of different times along separate lines. Explaining one is impossible, explaining dozens is, well, it's whatever dozens times impossible is.

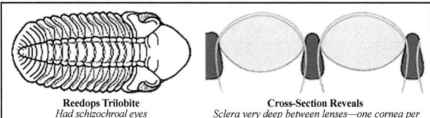

Reedops Trilobite
Had schizochroal eyes

Cross-Section Reveals
Sclera very deep between lenses—one cornea per lens—corneal membrane extends into sclera

Trilobites – Trilobites have one of the most advanced visual systems in the animal kingdom. Vertebrate lenses (such as our own) can change shape (accommodate) to focus on objects at varying distances. Trilobite eyes, in contrast, had rigid, crystalline lenses, and therefore no accommodation. Instead, an internal doublet structure (two lens layers of different refractive indices acting in combination) corrected for focusing problems that result from rigid lenses. The result is that, even without the benefit of accommodation, the rigid trilobite doublet lens had remarkable depth of field (that is, allowed for objects both near and far to remain in relatively good focus) and minimal spherical aberration (distortion of image). The shapes of some trilobite lenses, in fact, match those derived by optical scientists "over 300 million years later" to answer similar needs.

The doublet lens schizochroal eyes are made up of a few to more than 700 relatively large, thick lenses, each covered by a separate cornea. Each lens is positioned in a conical or cylindrical mounting and is separated from its neighbors by sclera (cuticular exoskeleton material) that extends deeply, providing an anchor for the corneal membrane, which extends downward into the sclera, where it is called intrascleral membrane.

Such incredible complexity is way too 'low' in the record of the rocks. How could eyes rivaling or even superior to ours be already formed and fully functioning about the time our eyes were supposed to be evolving from some sort of rudimentary light sensitive pigment?

Figure 124

I watched a recent educational television program that was supposedly going to sort out whether Darwinism or creationism is true. One scientist, to explain how the focusing ability of the eye evolved, shined a light at each of a series of shapes ranging from a flat surface to a globe-shaped like an eyeball. As the shape got more like a globe, the light increasingly focused onto a screen in back of the objects. This was the proof that the eye evolved. In other words, because the eye is a globe that focuses light, that proves it evolved.

You don't get to prove something by using that something to prove itself.

As of yet, nobody can even fathom a detailed mechanism for creating even one part of the eye.

Walt Whitman wrote, "a mouse is miracle enough to stagger sextillions of infidels."

Design = Designer

Figure 126

And speaking of mice, I am reminded of Beast, our family's cat. He is a partly domestic cat, combined with lynx and bobcat. A gorgeous creature in so many ways. He can run like a cheetah, jump several feet in the air, climb trees to show off for us, talk to us, hiss when he gets upset—like when he's too hot, hungry, not getting his love, or just plain cranky because things are not going quite his way. But never mean. His markings are beautiful and completely camouflage him in the woods. His eyes are like perfect gemstones and his lean musculature knots under his skin, yet he has never done one curl, squat, or deadlift. Rough and tumble play with us is always measured so that he carefully pulls his punches by keeping his claws retracted. (He's polydactyl with six toes on each front foot, making a particularly lethal arrangement.)

Not only is it totally baffling how such creatures could have originated by mere chemical mixing and natural forces, but how the trillions of elements and functions in Beast's body could form from a speck-of-dust-egg gestating inside another such creature in just 65 days. Evolutionists must explain with specificity every nanometer of every hair on his body and every cell and their constituents in the rest of his physique, let alone the countless elements of his brain and personality. No such explanation is even attempted. Yet learned people worldwide claim evolution to be a fact.

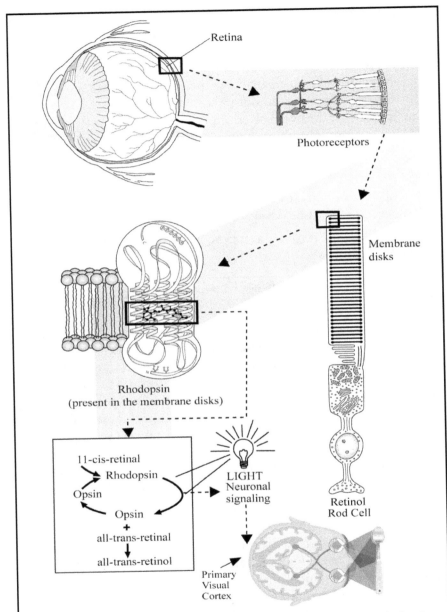

Retina

Photoreceptors

Membrane
disks

Rhodopsin
(present in the membrane disks)

11-cis-retinal
Rhodopsin
Opsin
Opsin
+
all-trans-retinal
all-trans-retinol

LIGHT
Neuronal
signaling

Retinol
Rod Cell

Primary
Visual
Cortex

The Visual Pathway – This is a simplified schematic of the structures and biochemistry used in sight. Millions of elements interplay. Nobody has ever explained with specificity how any one of these elements came to be by evolutionary means. Anything less than the whole functioning affair would either cause faulty, or no sight. Yet evolution demands that every component of this pathway evolved from something less than it is.

Figure 125

Beast – This is my cat, part bobcat, lynx, and domestic. An incredible and loving marvel whose existence can only be explained by an incredible mind.

© Wysong   Figure 127

Beast likes to interrupt my writing of this book by jumping up on my lap, wedging himself between me and the keyboard. I push the computer away giving him his due space and he then starts his purring motor and makes cookies with his two gigantic front paws (our label; it's a kneading similar to what they do when they are nursing as kittens). Then he rolls over, exposing a scrumptious belly of soft fur for petting. If I tell him what a good boy he is, he will twitch his bobtail, look me straight in the eyes, and give a sort of chirping sound. If I ask him a question, he chirps back. He will try to snuggle up close to my face to give me a few licks and then go into the most relaxed sleep in an upside-down contorted position of complete trust.

Last night my daughter came into my room looking for him. She just smiled at how silly we both looked with him all sprawled out and me leaning back in the chair to give room for his almost three and a half foot length. She came over to pet him and marvel at his beauty. He just looked up, gave a chirp, and purred even louder. She's helping proofread this book for me, so knowing she would follow my train of thought, I said to her, "Yep, no problem, just mix up atoms for a few billion years and this is what comes out." She said, "Sure thing, Dad."

As I write this and reflect upon Beast and all the rest of the phantasmagoric world in which we live I feel silly for even having to go through all this argumentation. Intelligent design in nature is so staggeringly common sense and so obvious it's absurd.

115

17
BIOLOGICAL MACHINES

If you were on the outside looking in on our universe, you would see not only order, complexity, and repeating patterns, but motion as well. Our universe is an outlandish array of moving machines within machines. There are lightning-fast quantum and atom machines, molecular and biochemical machines, worm and elephant machines, and solar system and galaxy machines. And they all interrelate with one another in a gigantic, intricate, and interconnected moving web machine.

Hundreds of thousands of scientific papers have been written on biological topics. Not one has ever proven with detail how any biological machine, process, or feature came piecemeal into existence by chance, natural law, or evolution.

There is a scientific publication called the Journal of Molecular Evolution. Remarkably, as convincing as that title sounds, there are zero papers discussing detailed proven intermediates in the development of complex biomolecular machines. Not even detailed speculative models are presented.

Evolutionists have put themselves in the untenable position of hoping that damage to machines (mutations) will provide useful and innovative novelty to cause bigger and better machines. Ask any mechanic or serviceman what he thinks of that prospect.

We tend to think of the physical and biological worlds as static structures. But nothing is actually standing still. Everything is a dynamic machine consisting of smaller dynamic machines down through the smallest things known.

Within life are atom machines making up protein, nucleic acid, lipid, carbohydrate, vitamin, and cellular organelle machines. And everything is moving and interrelated.

The web that a spider's spinning machine produces is so strong and resilient that if a spider were the size of humans and strung a proportionate web in the sky, it would have the ability to catch a passenger airplane flying full throttle. Spiders contain machines that can weave threads less than 1/1000th of a millimeter in diameter having twenty times the strength of steel. A cord of spider silk the diameter of the thumb could easily carry the weight of a jumbo jet.

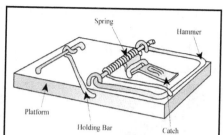

Spring Hammer

Platform

Holding Bar Catch

Mousetrap – An apparently simple machine which is still irreducibly complex. If any element is removed it will not work. Compare this to the far more intricate machines pictured in these pages that are found in, and are, living organisms. If a mousetrap is obviously designed by an intelligence, how could it be reasoned that the far more complex biomachines are not?

© Wysong   Figure 128

Fish skin machines secrete a crystal ¼ the wavelength of the incident light—seven-millionths of a centimeter—that helps them appear invisible in water.

Biological timing machines include tree fruiting, migration, sleep cycle, puberty, menstrual cycle, estrus cycle, the seventeen-year crop cycle of the asparagus, the emergence of baby, adult and wisdom teeth, flowering of bamboo trees every 117 years, cacti flowering every 12 years, insects that lie in the ground for 17 years and then all emerge at the same time, and coat and plumage changes with the seasons.

Albatross machines will return with food to a nesting site where there are hundreds of thousands of young chicks. Each mom will immediately find her own offspring.

Bird and small mammal machines hide seeds and nuts over widely scattered areas and then return months later to the precise locations and dig out the food, even when hidden deep under snow.

Monarch butterfly machines begin with an egg laid on a poisonous milkweed plant. To prevent glue in the plant from sticking to the mouth, the larva machine interrupts leaf circulation with a specific eating pattern. The larva uses the poison from the plant to deter predators and turns itself into a gorgeous butterfly machine that migrates as much as 5000 miles from Canada to South America using a brain the size of the period at the end of this sentence. Weighing only one-half gram, this amazing machine flies at up to 30 mph (plus tailwind) with wings akin to wisps of tissue paper.

Two-pound Sooty Shearwater bird machines can fly 700 miles in a day, dive 225 feet deep into the sea after food, and travel 46,000 miles, covering practically the entire globe.

Tern vs. DC-9 – The arctic Tern can migrate some 14,000 miles. For man to accomplish similar navigation, sophisticated instrumentation such as seen in this DC-9, is needed. Neither can be accounted for by anything other than intelligence.

© AWeith (left) | © 1971 LostFlights File Photo (right)   Figure 129

Loggerhead turtle machines will migrate as much as 9000 miles at one mile per hour to get back to the exact beach where they were hatched to lay their eggs.

The male Mallee Fowl machine spends eleven months of each year building a mound nest of compost weighing 6000 pounds. He then invites his sweetheart to lay her eggs in holes he digs in the mound. During the incubation period, the male adjusts the layering in the mound to maintain the perfect 930F temperature. The hatched chicks fly away having all the same talents yet have no contact with the parents.

Some bird machines allow the cuckoo bird machine to lay eggs in their nest resulting in all the foster mother's eggs getting pushed out of the nest by the hatched cuckoo. The cuckoo then migrates 12,000 miles to South Africa to join the parents who abandoned it.

The coat of the northern sea otter machine consists of one million hairs per square inch permitting it to live in lethally frigid water. Fish machines have no hair at all, permitting them to live in the same lethally frigid water. Evolution supposedly mandated both hair and scales for the exact same environment.

The Australian Mallee Fowl Bird – incubates its eggs in a huge mound consisting of soil, leaves and twigs. The temperature is tested by the beak and maintained within about one to two degrees of the ideal by constant adjustment of the mound compost. These anatomic and behavioral capabilities defy explanation by evolutionary mechanisms.

© Jocelyn Lindner   Figure 130

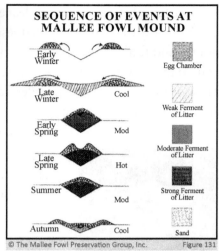

SEQUENCE OF EVENTS AT MALLEE FOWL MOUND

Early Winter

Late Winter — Cool

Early Spring — Mod

Late Spring — Hot

Summer — Mod

Autumn — Cool

Egg Chamber

Weak Ferment of Litter

Moderate Ferment of Litter

Strong Ferment of Litter

Sand

© The Mallee Fowl Preservation Group, Inc.   Figure 131

Dog machines can differentiate the smell of the feces of a killer whale, black bear, grizzly bear, lynx, bobcat, puma, maned wolf, wolverine, and fisher. They can also sniff out marijuana, heroin, cocaine, and crack, as well as diagnose skin, prostate, breast, and lung cancer by whiffing patients' urine and breath.

Rat nose machines can smell landmines as well as detect tuberculosis by sniffing human sputum. Laboratory machines can analyze twenty samples a day. A rat machine can do 150 tuberculosis tests in thirty minutes with greater accuracy.

The amazing flying ability of insect machines includes marvels such as delayed stall, rotational circulation, wake capture, as well as speeds over 70 mph. Some beat their wings more than 63,000 times per minute. As far back as fossils can be examined in stones and amber, supposedly hundreds of millions of years ago, insect wing machines looked exactly like they look today. No wannabe wing nubs found anywhere.

An ant machine can lift fifty times its body weight. An equivalent lift by a human would be about four tons. Certain honeypot ants engorge themselves with honeydew to the point that they can't walk. They just hang from the ceiling of the ant nest and become regurgitation food machines for the rest of the colony.

Honeypot Ant

© The respective copyright holders.   Figure 132

Leaf-cutter ants can't digest leaves so they culture edible fungus machines on the leaves they harvest. The African acacia tree machine houses and feeds a special ant that clears all competing plants and vines and attacks any creature that threatens the tree. Dairying ants farm and protect aphid machines in order to milk them for food. Some army ants have mouthpart machinery so suited for fighting off enemies that they must be fed by others in the colony.

Bombarder Beetle

© The respective copyright holders.   Figure 133

The bombardier beetle machine defends itself by ejecting a boiling hot 212° F jet spray at 500 pulsed combustions per second.

Bacteria machines can survive polar temperatures over an extended time, zero humidity, the edges of boiling hot geysers, even hotter undersea fumaroles, and the inside of nuclear reactors. This begs the question, why would such resilient creatures ever "evolve"?

Gecko machines can hang upside down from a smooth surface by one toe. Each foot machine has a half-million microscopic setae hairs which have on their ends hundreds of projections smaller than the wavelength of light. The gecko machine instantly engages and disengages these sticky molecular forces as it scurries about.

Gecko – Hanging upside down from one toe attached to glass.

© Wysong   Figure 134

Some species of fig tree machines depend upon wasp machines to pollinate them. The wasps depend upon the fruit machine to lay their young. A nematode parasite machine depends upon both the fig and the wasp for its survival. Evolutionists must explain how widely separated organisms (machines)—trees, insects, and worms—slowly evolved absolute dependency to become one composite tree-insect-worm machine.

Hummingbird machines can flap their wings at 200 beats per second and have a heartbeat of 1200 per minute. Heliconia flower machines have developed specialized structures (machines) to accommodate the feeding mouthparts of certain species of hummingbirds. Neither bird nor plant machine could survive without the other, yet they supposedly evolved at widely separated times.

Anglerfish

© The respective copyright holders. Figure 135

The three-inch-long anglerfish machine attracts prey with a bioluminescent light bulb on the end of a stalk on the top of its head. The bulb is powered by Photobacteria—light-producing bacteria machines. The male mates with the female by biting into her flesh and fusing with her body such that the two blood supplies join and his body atrophies (withers away) until only testicles remain. The female thus becomes a hermaphrodite machine.

The Venus Flower Basket Sponge machine grows fiber optic cables the width of a hair that are up to seven inches long. Unlike synthetic fiber optics that are produced with high heat and are fragile, the sponge's cables are produced at cold temperatures and can be tied in a knot without cracking or breaking.

Feather machines are complex affairs consisting of shafts, vanes, barbs, barbules, hooks, and ridges. They contain sliding joints needing lubrication from a preening gland machine. They insulate, waterproof, provide ornate color, and self-regenerate. There is no evidence anywhere of anything evolving into a feather machine.

To have survival value, biological machines can't be just a little bit right; they have to be right on from the get-go with all the parts present and perfected. Moreover, it's the nature of biological machines to be running, i.e., alive. That means, if evolution is true, all such machines would have had to accomplish the impossible feat of running while alterations were being made.

Every component of every biological machine in existence cries out intelligent engineering.

18
NUTS, BOLTS, GEARS, AND ROTORS PROVE INTELLIGENT DESIGN

Let's say you were strolling on the beach looking for nice seashells and came across a set of perfectly intermeshing gears. You looked to the side, and there was also a bolt with a nut screwed onto it. Beside that was a rotary mechanism.

You'd conclude the obvious, that some intelligent person made them. And you wouldn't be alone. Any person on the planet would conclude the same.

Archeologists and anthropologists finding even crudely chipped stones conclude that such artifacts are the product of intelligence. The Oldowan stone tools found in Africa are an example.

If that's the obvious conclusion about chipped stones, there could be no other conclusion if we found gears, nuts, bolts, and rotors.

Here are gears wired to a neural circuit, muscles, brain, optics, and all of the other paraphernalia found in living creatures. Billions of components all interconnected in a machine that is not just thousands, but millions of years old.

This tiny plant hopper insect-machine, one-tenth of an inch long, can bullet skyward faster than the eye can see and accelerate in 2 milliseconds to 400 g's, more than 20 times what the human body can withstand without tearing apart.

(Video can be found at youtu.be/4KmMzpQdwwk)

Oldowan Stone Tools – from Olduvai Gorge in Tanzania, Africa are dated by evolutionists at about two million years. They are thought to have been used for food processing, cutting, and scraping. When these chipped tools made from basalt or chert are found, they tell archeologists that intelligent life was present. In this case the tools are believed to have been used by Homo habilis or some other human precursor. If such crude and simple items that have only a hint of order and design prove intelligence was necessary for their origin, how could living creatures, which are infinitely more complex and ordered, be products of chance?

Figure 118

The gears are located in the hip of the Issus and, in 1/300,000th of a second, synchronize the legs for the jump. Unlike kangaroos and us, where neural feedback loops permit coordination of the jump, the Issus' jump occurs faster than the six milliseconds it takes for nerve transmission to and from the brain. Thus, the need to lock the legs with gears so the insect doesn't spiral out of control.

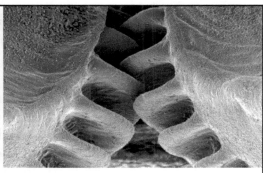

Issus Gears

Figure 136

It is only in the young molts of the Issus machine that the hip gears are found. In the adult version, another design in its program takes over whereby the gears are gone, and the legs lock together as occurs in other jumping insects. In other words, the Issus has not only one jumping mechanism, but two.

Issus Planthopper

Figure 137

Gears, as we know them, were not invented until the genius of the Swiss mathematician Leonhard Euler in the 18th century. So, there must have been genius that invented the Issus gears millions of years before.

Planthopper nymph's gears as seen through a confocal microscope.
All samples treated with KOH/H2O2, stained with Congo Red, imaged with Zeiss LSM 710, 10x NA 0.45

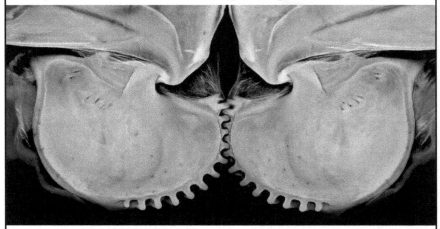

Posterior, dorsal and ventral views of the trochanteral gears of the Acanalonia conica (Green Coneheaded Planthopper) nymph. Colors represent depth (depth color coding).

© photomacrography.net, blepharopsis, Igor Siwanowicz   Figure 286

Rotor Mechanism of Flagellum – How could such structural and functional complexity arise by natural law and chance?

© The respective copyright holders.   Figure 138

Bacterial Rotors

The bacterium, *E. coli*, is just one cell, but it contains many machines. A remarkable one that gives it locomotion is the flagellum, a whip-like strand that propels the organism through liquid. To describe this mechanism, terms must be used that are identical to those used by engineers: reversible rotary motor (acid-driven at 20,000 revolutions per minute), flexible coupling, universal joint, propeller, stator, and bushing.

Like with gears, humans didn't invent such mechanical elements of machines until the 1800s. Their creation was heralded as genius and gave rise to electric motors, helicopters, and other machines propelling the Industrial Revolution. None of these great accomplishments has ever been attributed to anything other than great intelligence.

The same rotor elements existed in bacteria 3.5 billion years ago. Nothing less than great intelligence can account for them.

Nuts and Bolts

Then there's the nuts and bolts in the *Trigonopterus oblongus* weevil legs. Instead of the ball and socket like we have for our hip-leg joint, the weevil has a bolt-screw on the leg that seats into a nut-thread in the hip. Technically, the coxa is the thread, and the trochanter is the screw.

© Science/AAAS

Figure 281

This weevil nut-and-bolt mechanism locks the legs and stabilizes the beetle for certain feeding actions when moved to the extreme of the thread in one direction, and then frees up for walking when unscrewed.

Nuts and bolts weren't invented and integrated into machines until about 1500 CE. The weevil machine is dated at 100 million years old. If intelligent humans had to invent nuts and bolts, intelligence a hundred million years ago would have been required to invent the beetle's leg machine.

No step-by-step biochemical evolutionary progression can be proven. Nor is there even one observed example of any machine anywhere at any time coming into existence spontaneously. (The fact that such machinery comes into existence each time an organism reproduces, is a reflection of the preexisting information and engineering of the parents. That parental engineering and information cannot be proven to arise by spontaneous evolutionary processes.)

Keep in mind as you look at these mechanisms, or any other part of any living organism, even a single cell, that they are comprised of trillions of integrated biochemical machine components constantly moving about at blinding speed. It cannot be proven that these components came to be, step-by-step.

125

Biochemical Machines

The following diagram represents a snapshot fraction of the dynamics of what goes on in a minuscule bit of living tissue—biochemical gears, nuts, bolts, and rotors within and upon interlinked mechanism after mechanism. No part of which can exist on its own.

Biochemical knowledge, as reflected in such drawings of chemical pathways, is an incomplete snapshot of present incomplete knowledge and does not reflect the dynamics and speed of what actually happens second by second in living tissue. The trillions of complex machine-like interactions occurring at lightning speed every second for life to happen are incomprehensible.

Nevertheless, all such machines and mechanisms are thought by evolutionists to have arisen spontaneously. For example, this is the headline from an article about Issus gears in Scientific American: "Working Gears Evolved in Plant-Hopping Insect" Popular Mechanics states that the Issus "evolved its acrobatic prowess because it needs to flee dangerous situations . . . there's been enormous evolutionary pressure to become faster and faster, and jump further and further away." Similar quotes can be found for the bacterial rotor and for the weevil's nuts and bolts.

No detailed genetic or biochemical mechanisms and pathways are provided for how this evolution over time could occur. No fossils are provided showing the incremental development. No experiments. Not even an attempt at actual proof. Instead, there are just statements of faith about how gear, nut, bolt, rotor, and biochemical machines magically appeared because they were needed for evolution.

But if someone else says intelligence is responsible, even when intelligent design is clearly written all over life's gears, rotors, nuts, bolts, and millions of other mechanisms, that's supposedly absurd.

The Takeaway

1. Gears, rotors, nuts, and bolts require intelligent origin.

2. Organisms have gears, rotors, nuts, and bolts.

3. Therefore, organisms require an intelligent origin.

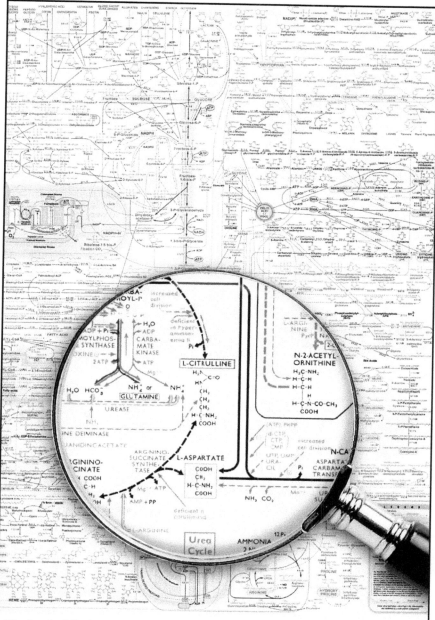

Biochemical Pathways – The incredible complexity of life is partially reflected in the biochemical pathways represented here. Note not only the scale of complexity, but how everything is interrelated. Also keep in mind that this is a mere snapshot. The reality is a moving dynamic with millions of interactions per second.

Figure 139

19
HUMANS DEFY EVOLUTION

All life is a staggering array of "in your face" mystery and complexity all the way down to their atomic and quantum levels. Humans, in particular, defy a materialistic evolutionary explanation.

By explanation, I mean accounting for the placement of each atom. Just saying this or that feature arises because of "survival value," "time," "mutations," need," "or "natural selection," is not the scientific detailed proof necessary for the following.

Cells

If the library of DNA within human cells was uncoiled and placed end to end it would be twice the diameter of the solar system.

Mitochondria, produce ATP (adenosine triphosphate), the energy currency of the body, at a rate of about 900000000000000000000 (9×10^{20}) per second. The total surface area of mitochondrial inner membranes where this takes place is almost four acres. We produce our body weight in ATP every day and could not survive more than fifteen seconds if the production shut down. During the course of the day, phosphates are attached and detached from the molecule to deliver this energy. Once ATP is formed, it's used up within a minute.

If all cells from one human were placed side by side, they could encircle the Earth 200 times. There are almost 300 different kinds of cells known in the human body, about 100 trillion total.

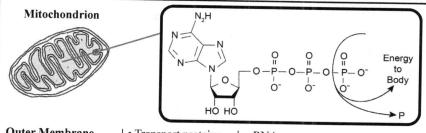

Outer Membrane	• Transport proteins	• rRNA
• Phospholipid Bilayer	• Hydrogen ions	• Pyruvate
• Porins	• Calcium ions	• Nicotinamide adenine dinucleotide (NAD+)
• Ribozymes	• ADP	• Flavin adenine dinucleotide (FAD+)
Inner Membrane	• ATP	• Flavin adenine mononucleotide (FMN)
• Cristae	• Electrons	• Ubiquinone
• Polypeptides	• Inorganic phosphate	• Cytochrome C
• Cardiolipin	• Dissolved oxygen	• Iron sulfur proteins
Matrix	• Water	• NADH - CoQ oxidoreductase
• Ribosomes	• DNA	• Succinate CoQ oxidoreductase
• ATP synthetase complex	• mRNA	• NADH dehydrogenase
• ATPase	• tRNA	• CoQ Cytochrome C oxidoreductase

Mitochondrial Structure – Mitochondria are organelles within cells that serve as power plants. **ATP (adenosine triphosphate)** is the primary energy currency used by our bodies. Enzymes extract energy from the food we eat and attach it to this molecule. It, in turn, delivers the energy to our muscles and metabolism to keep us alive. Once spent it goes back and is reenergized. Humans have never come close to fabricating such an amazing machine, but we are to believe this biological machine emerged by natural mechanisms and chance.

© Wysong

Figure 140

All human cells contain the same genetic information, yet somehow each one selects just that portion of the genetic information that dictates its specialized activity. A fat cell swells with fat, muscle cells contract, and immune cells destroy invading microbes.

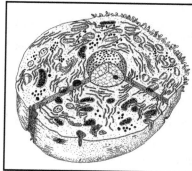

Living Cell – This cross section of a living cell gives a partial glimpse of its complexity. Human intellect has never come close to even approximating such an intricate, self-sustaining mechanism. Not only can our engineering not compete with it, after hundreds of years of study we still have only the faintest understanding of it. Yet we are to believe it is a product of spontaneous and random events. Surely if a crude stone tool (a trillion times less complex than a single cell) proves intelligent intervention, the complexity of living cells should as well.

© Wysong

Figure 141

129

This and every bit of cellular capability and complexity needs to be explained with reason and facts if evolution wants to take credit for it.

Sex

From a survival standpoint, it would have been far more efficient and survivable to stay simple asexual cells and divide into, or bud offspring. While microbes did and do just that, we supposedly evolved as two elaborate sexes simultaneously.

A woman's egg only contains half her genes, and a man's spermatozoan only contains half his. That way, when the sperm combines with the egg, the resulting zygote (fertilized egg) has the correct diploid number of genes to grow a full human. No evolutionary mechanism can prove the spontaneous origin of somatic (body) cells that decide to divide into two like versions (mitosis) containing the full complement of genetic material, whereas other cells (eggs and sperm) decide to divide (meiosis) so only half the genetic material ends up in their progeny cells.

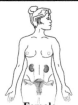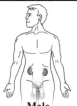

Female	Male
• Ovaries	• Testes
Mesovarium	Epididymis
Ovarian ligaments	Seminal (vas deferens)
Suspensory ligaments	Seminal vesicles
• Fallopian Tubes	Sertoli cells
Infundibulum	Germinal cells
Fimbriae	Leydig cells
Ampulla	Ejaculatory duct
Isthmus	Urethra
• Uterus	• Scrotum
• Vagina	Raphe
• External Genitalia	• Penis
Vulva	Glans penis
Pudendum	Bulb of penis
Mons pubis	Prepuce (foreskin)
Pubic symphysis	Corpus Cavernosa
Labia majora	Corpus spongiosa
Labia minora	• Prostate Gland
Clitoris	• Urethra
• Breasts	Prostatic urethra
Mammary gland	Spongy urethra
Nipple	Bulbourethral glands
Areola	• Spermatic Cord
• Ovary Structure	Testicular artery
Cortex	Testicular vein
Germinal layer	• Spermatogenesis
Primary ovarian follicles	Spermatogonia (mitosis)
Ovum	Primary spermatocytes (meiosis I)
Follicular cells	Secondary Spermatocytes (meiosis II)
Zona pelucida	Spermatids
Theca folliculi	Sperm
Atretic follicles	
Graafian follicle	
Cumulus oophorous	
Corona radiata	
Granulose cells	
Corpus hemorrhagicum	
Corpus luteum	
Corpus albicans	

Sex – Man and woman are both human but dramatically different in many ways. Such complementary features could not have evolved simultaneously. Why on earth would nature go to all the trouble of evolving complex sexes that must develop in synchrony when it would be so much easier to stay as a budding or simple dividing cell? Budding and dividing cells exist today and do just great—so what forces could have made some of them "ascend" all the way to man and woman?

© Wysong   Figure 142

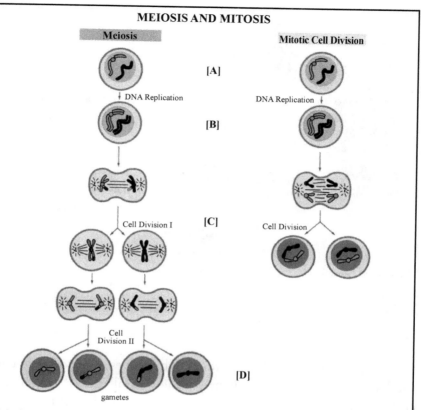

MEIOSIS AND MITOSIS

Meiosis and Mitosis – Each cell contains two complete sets of chromosomes [A]. Mitosis and meiosis both begin with the replication of these chromosomes into four complete sets [B]. The cell then divides into two identical daughter cells, each containing two complete sets of chromosomes like the original parent cell [C]. In meiosis, these cells undergo another cellular division resulting in four daughter cells that each contains only one complete set of chromosomes (half the number of the original cell) [D]. Nobody has the slightest idea how these two mechanisms could evolve in the same creature.

Figure 143

Cardiovascular System

The heart beats 24 hours a day for a lifetime (almost 3 billion times by the age of 75). The tiny sinoatrial node in the heart contains about 10,000 pacemaker cells. These are the timer cells that discharge electricity to the heart muscle causing it to contract in a rhythm . . . lub dub, lub dub. All 10,000 automatically discharge in synchrony. There is no feasible step-by-step origination of each cell in the heart and its pacemaker.

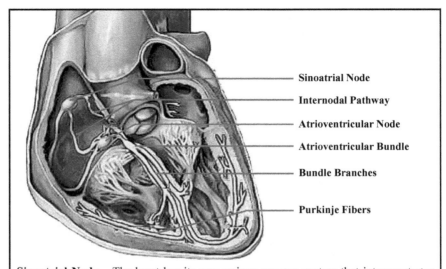

Sinoatrial Node
Internodal Pathway
Atrioventricular Node
Atrioventricular Bundle
Bundle Branches
Purkinje Fibers

Sinoatrial Node – The heart has its own unique nervous system that interpenetrates all of its muscle tissue. The rhythm of the heart is synchronized by nodes that self fire impulses. They are in turn tuned to the needs of the body and increase or decrease heart rate and strength of contractions. One cannot even attempt to imagine how such a complex, automatic timing mechanism could come to be by evolutionary mechanisms.

Figure 144

The body contains 100,000 miles of blood vessels, enough to circle the Earth eight times, and nineteen billion capillaries. If the thinnest cross-section possible were sliced at any point along these miles, billions of chemical elements would be revealed in the cells sliced through. Each one of these slices must be accounted for along the entire hundred thousand miles—as well as how they are interlinked with the trillions of other slices and the trillions of other elements in the body.

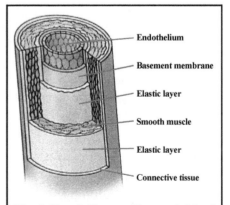

Endothelium
Basement membrane
Elastic layer
Smooth muscle
Elastic layer
Connective tissue

Blood Vessel Composition – A blood vessel is not just a tube. Every inch of it contains countless parts that must work together perfectly. It's impossible to explain this with piecemeal evolution.

Figure 145

Digestive System

Consider the coordination necessary for the tongue to dodge the teeth while we eat. Not only do we do it, we don't even think about it.

Evolutionary buds of tongues would be chewed off, lacerated, macerated, infected, swallowed, and mutilated along the evolutionary path, making eating either too painful or impossible to do. Death would be the outcome for creatures attempting to evolve tongues. But since we are here with tongues, we must not have gotten here by such a process.

The anatomy and coordination necessary in the back of the throat to shunt food down the right tube are essential to life. If even once the food is swallowed down the wrong tube—the trachea instead of the esophagus— death could occur from asphyxiation or pneumonia from the food rotting in the bronchi and lungs. But we put food down the right tube millions of times over a lifetime without even thinking about it.

The stomach produces and secretes hydrochloric acid strong enough to dissolve a coin. This acid is responsible in large part for breaking down the protein foods, including tripe (stomach). As the stomach supposedly evolved, stomachs and bodies would have been self-digested as evolution worked out how the body could contain a chemical that was strong enough to dissolve the very tissues that produced it.

How every inch of the 30 feet of human intestine evolved all of its billions of components simultaneously is a mystery never explained with step-by-step detail. How our predecessors with partially evolved intestinal tracts could have survived the supposed millions of years of transitional and faulty stages is certainly a mystery as well.

Auditory System

In response to some frequencies, the eardrum vibrates only one-tenth the diameter of a hydrogen atom. The membrane in the middle ear then vibrates only 300/1000-millionth of an inch in response. After recognition of the slightest sound, the ear returns to its ready state in about five-thousandths of a second. Sound is transmitted through three bones (malleus, incus, stapes) into fluid and to cilia that vibrate at 20,000 times per second. This causes atomic ions to move which in turn stimulates nerve transmission to the brain so the sound can be discerned. The ear can receive and separate the equivalent of notes from a piano with over 20,000 keys, as well as buffer any loud sounds.

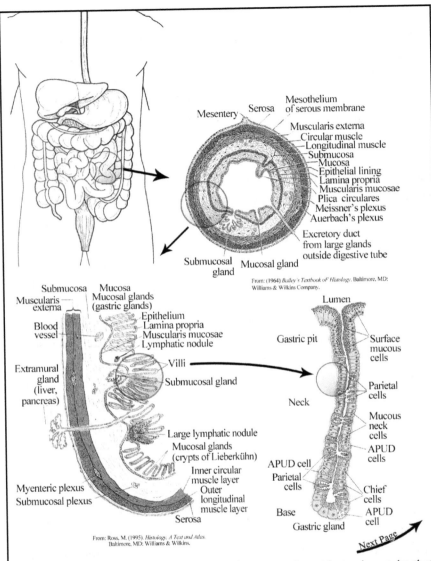

Mesothelium
Serosa of serous membrane
Mesentery
Muscularis externa
Circular muscle
Longitudinal muscle
Submucosa
Mucosa
Epithelial lining
Lamina propria
Muscularis mucosae
Plica circulares
Meissner's plexus
Auerbach's plexus

Excretory duct
from large glands
outside digestive tube

Submucosal   Mucosal gland
gland

From: (1964) *Bailey's Textbook of Histology.* Baltimore, MD:
Williams & Wilkins Company.

Submucosa   Mucosa
Muscularis   Mucosal glands
externa   (gastric glands)
Epithelium
Lamina propria
Blood   Muscularis mucosae
vessel   Lymphatic nodule

Extramural   Villi
gland   Submucosal gland
(liver,
pancreas)

Large lymphatic nodule
Mucosal glands
(crypts of Lieberkühn)
Inner circular
muscle layer
Myenteric plexus   Outer
Submucosal plexus   longitudinal
muscle layer
Serosa

Lumen

Gastric pit   Surface
mucous
cells

Parietal
cells
Neck

Mucous
neck
cells
APUD
cells
APUD cell
Parietal
cells   Chief
cells
Base   APUD
Gastric gland   cell

Next Page

From: Ross, M. (1995). *Histology. A Text and Atlas.*
Baltimore, MD: Williams & Wilkins.

The Human Intestinal Tract – Our digestive system is not just a long tube that absorbs nutrients and expels waste. Every millimeter along its entire length has complexity beyond imagination. This diagram breaks down some of what is known so far about that complexity. Every single molecule along every nanometer of the digestive system needs to be explained by evolutionary processes, i.e., how did each element come from something less than it is and coordinate with millions of others evolving in tandem, all the while creating a functioning digestive system? No such explanation exists, nor can it since the digestive system is an integrated holistic machine that is irreducibly complex and greater than the sum of its parts.

Figure 146

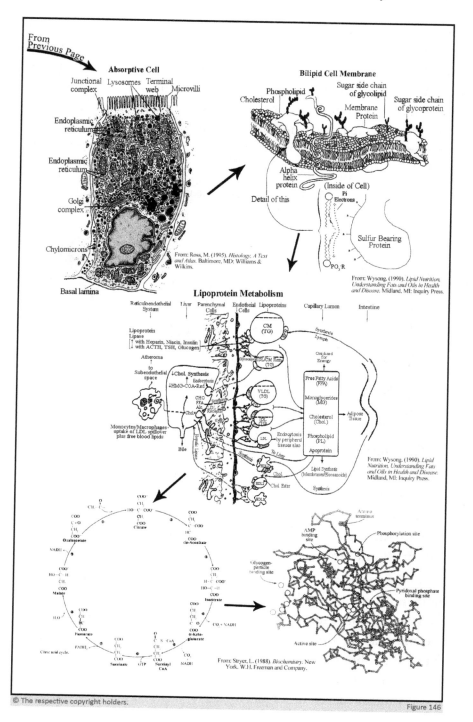

Figure 146

At the same time, the inner ear helps our sense of balance through the semicircular canals, equilibrates with atmospheric pressure through the Eustachian tube that connects to the back of the throat, and communicates in thousands of ways with the brain. That only begins the story of the complexity of hearing. Every minute step of formation must be explained mechanistically if evolution is to be believed.

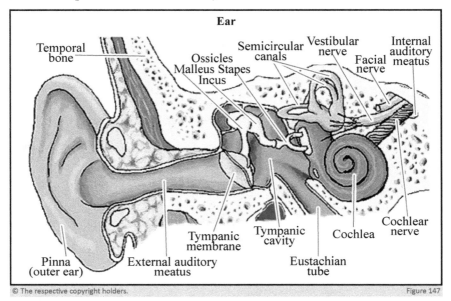

Figure 147

Olfactory System

The human nose can detect methyl mercaptan in rancid meat at a level of 1/400-billionth of a gram. It can also differentiate 4,000 other scents. This is made possible by about 150 million sensory cilia in the nose. They translate an odor into a specific neural transmission to the brain.

If that's not special enough, consider the smelling skills of our biological neighbors. The trace of sweat that seeps through shoes to the ground, and a few cells that drop off your skin to the ground as you move about through the day, is a million times more powerful than a bloodhound needs to track you down. An amorous silkworm moth can follow 1/10,000th of a milligram of a female's sexual attractant from seven miles away.

Central Nervous System

The brain contains 100 billion neurons, no two of which are alike. Evolution must account for each one of these. For the brain to function, the billions of neurons and trillions of interconnecting links transmitting signals through well over 60,000 miles of tendrils have to be wired correctly but yet permit hooking and rehooking of connections. It also makes no evolutionary sense that we presently have far more brain than we use and that it has the capacity for the artistic, musical, and mathematical genius not essential to survival.

Over the course of a lifetime the average human body does the following:

Quarts of urine produced	40,515
Heartbeats	2,700,000,000
Quarts of blood pumped	350,000,000
Tons of blood pumped	660,000
Breaths	740,000,000
Sperm produced	400,000,000,000
Eggs produced	400
Eye blinks	333,000,000
Finger joint flexes	25,000,000
Hair growth (scalp)	350 Miles
Nail growth	12 Feet per Finger
Laughs	540,000
Cries	3,000
Dreams/nightmares	127,507

The Human Miracle – This partial list of what goes on in the body – all on autopilot mind you – is staggering evidence that stupendous mind was responsible for our creation.

© Wysong   Figure 148

This brief review of complexity within the human body could go on and on through every single organ, tissue, and cell. A nose, section of skin, heart, liver, tooth, epiglottis, or knuckle present countless conundrums not solved by words like mutations and selection.

Callosities – We are born with thickened skin on the bottom of the feet exactly where it needs to be to help withstand the frictional demands of walking and running. But there are no such callosities elsewhere on the body to indicate that this was a trial and error process. From an evolutionary standpoint it is inexplicable why we do not have sections of thickened skin on the forehead, back, earlobe, etc.

© Wysong   Figure 149

Evolution proposes a process of trial, error, and nascent development increment-by-increment. All precursors would, therefore, have inevitable errors and budding functionless detrimental features. That means all precursor creatures attempting to climb an evolutionary ladder would be culled (selected) out. In effect, evolution defeats itself.

20
THE ANTHROPIC UNIVERSE

Over and over throughout the universe, there are countless circumstances perfect for the existence and continuance of life on Earth.

We could not be alive for another second were it not for the billions of coordinated events that occur so perfectly in our bodies. Outside the body, throughout the universe synchrony must also occur for us to exist. The universe is put together so perfectly, so anthropically, as it is called, to accommodate us.

A few examples:

- Protons and neutrons are held together by strong nuclear forces. A weaker force would have meant no atoms could ever have formed. A two percent reduction in the strong nuclear force would mean the only atom in the universe would be hydrogen. If the force were stronger, all the free protons in the universe would have been mopped up, preventing the formation of atoms—and us.

- If electrons did not spin and hold their negativity, or nuclei did not hold their precise positive charge, all atoms would either collapse or fly apart. (By the way, what powers an atom and what happens to it when it runs out of power—and when does that happen? Just asking. I don't know and apparently, nobody else does either. We just take these little miraculous nano- perpetual motion machines for granted.)

- If gravity were not extremely weak compared to nuclear forces and electromagnetism— 10,000,000,000,000,000,000,000,000,000,000,00 0,000,000,000 (1X10^{40}) times weaker—life could not exist.

- Life is impossible toward the center or heel of our galaxy. It can only happen two-thirds the distance to the center of a galaxy, such as the place where Earth is.

- The sun must be of a certain size. If it's too big and hot, it incinerates life. If it's too small, it is not hot enough to accommodate life.

- If Earth was closer to the sun, the tidal forces would break the rotational period, and life would not be possible. That's what makes Mercury and Venus inhospitable. Their rotational periods are several months, due to their proximity to the sun.

Solar Blast – This illustration shows nuclear blasts and solar wind directed toward Earth. Two to four days after the explosions, the cloud of incredible energy is seen being deflected around the Earth's magnetosphere. The paths emanating from the Earth's poles represent some of its magnetic field lines. The magnetic cloud of plasma from these storms can extend 30 million miles wide by the time they reach Earth and can disrupt communications, damage satellites, and cause blackouts. Without the magnetic field and the atmosphere, life would be extinguished virtually instantly. In the meantime, the photonic energy from the sun is the very source of the energy of life. It is hard to view this precarious position we find ourselves in and not feel wonder and awe that we are even here, much less that we continue to survive. In addition, it is hard to believe that we puny humans have things anywhere near all figured out.

Figure 150

- If the Earth required more or less than 24 hours to rotate on its axis, life would not be possible. A quicker spin would yield too many hurricanes and tornados. A slower spin would make the planet too frigid at night and too hot during the day. At present, it is spinning at 1,000 mph, yet we don't fly off.

- Our moon is just the right size and distance from Earth to stabilize its rotational axis to 23.5 degrees, making the ideal conditions for life to exist. Any change in any of these lunar-tidal-Earth circumstances and life on Earth would not be possible.

- If Jupiter was not present, was not so massive, was not five times more distant from the sun than us, the gravitational pull of Jupiter would not shield the Earth from most cosmic collisions.

- Earth experiences just the right amount of rain, winter, summer, volcanoes, hurricanes, earthquakes, and other natural phenomena to create a planet environmentally diverse and regenerating, yet stable enough for life to exist.

- The exact position of Earth in the galaxy is necessary for it to have enough heavy elements for life. For example, fluorine, an essential element, requires a very special galaxy (like ours) that has a white dwarf binary star (like ours).

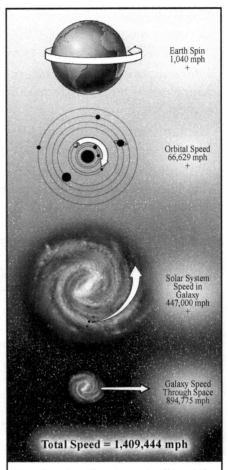

Earth Spin
1,040 mph
+

Orbital Speed
66,629 mph
+

Solar System
Speed in
Galaxy
447,000 mph
+

Galaxy Speed
Through Space
894,775 mph

Total Speed = 1,409,444 mph

Our Speed – If you are standing at the equator, the speed you are traveling as the Earth spins, orbits around the sun, the solar system orbits in the galaxy, and the galaxy moves through the universe is 1,409,444 mph. If this speed were to change any significant degree, life on Earth would cease.

© Wysong   Figure 151

- If there was a Big Bang, and it had been a billionth more powerful, galaxies and life could not exist.

- If the rate of the universe's expansion one second after the Big Bang had been smaller by even one part in 100,000,000,000, it would have collapsed into a fireball . . ..

That is only the beginning of such a list.

The interconnected intricacy of the universe, like the interconnected intricacy of living things, is irreducibly complex; it cannot evolve piecemeal.

The countless ongoing events to accommodate existence as we know it, are not only impossible (materialistically), they are terrifying. Just think, as you read this, that you are on a spaceship ball hurtling through space at 1.5 million miles per hour surrounded by countless galaxies, black holes, nebulas, stars, planets, moons, and rocks going at a similar speed. Our situation is so precarious. It is miraculous that we all don't just vanish at any second. But we don't, and we haven't.

And a final thought as I look out my window at the ice on our pond. It floats. Unlike other liquids that become denser with cold, water becomes less dense. If that were not the case and water behaved like other liquids, ice would sink, crushing not only all the life in my pond but in every other body of water subject to freezing. The spinoff effect would be catastrophic for all life on the planet.

Humility, not hubris is in order when we come to understand that this phantasmagoric Earth and universe machine that no human can claim any credit for hums along for a second, much less for billions of years.

21
EVOLUTION'S IMPACT

Origins is not just a question for science, academics, or casual musing. It's the foundation for belief, and belief has to do with how we live our lives and how we justify them. When we don't approach life and the questions it presents as if thinking matters, there are pragmatic and ethical consequences.

Hundreds of thousands of writings have been produced since Darwin with the word evolution lacing their pages. One would think that belief in evolution was essential to progress and human wellbeing. However, although evolution emerged when the Industrial Revolution was gearing up to nosebleed speed, it didn't contribute to that advance even in the slightest. Nothing in genetics, anatomy, physiology, medicine, biology, chemistry, physics, astronomy, or electronics was ever discovered, improved upon, or retired to obsolescence because of evolutionary thought. That is downright astonishing since evolution is treated as if it were a scientific law that would hamstring every scientist everywhere if it had not been conceived and believed with devotion.

Evolution does, however, affect people's view of existence. This, in turn, has a social impact. The detrimental effects evolution produces does not speak well for the worthiness of the belief. Bad ideas make bad results. For example:

- Millions of organs have been removed from people (tonsils, appendix, teeth, and other parts and organs) because doctors believe that some organs are merely useless remnants of evolution, vestigial. The result, if patients aren't damaged from the medical intervention itself, is people who are less fit, less whole, and more vulnerable to disease.

- The number one killer in our society is modern medicine. That's because doctors are trained into thinking the body is mere evolutionary matter that can be manipulated like any machine.

- The modern fields of nutrition and food processing assume food is only matter and nutrient analyses. The result is disease-producing foods based upon the evolutionary/materialistic assumption that since the body is mere percentages of matter, that's all food needs to be. The result is a world plagued by nutritionally generated diseases.

- Agriculture based upon materialism and evolution strip-mines the land and genetically manipulates crops to grow on paltry nitrogen-phosphorus-potassium (NPK) fertilizer and a toxic brew of insecticides and herbicides. The result is impoverished and toxic crops that vitiate health.

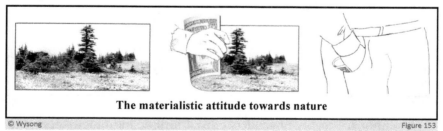

The materialistic attitude towards nature

- Many interpret evolution to mean that humans are its pinnacle achievement and that everything lower on the tree belongs to us to do with as we please. A might-makes-right imperative also logically leaves little room for a sense of responsibility toward the rest of the world. If we have the might, we have the evolutionary right.

- Class, racial struggles, and discrimination are justified by evolution.

• Most oppressive political systems, such as communism, fascism, and Nazism have philosophical roots in evolution. Herbert Spencer and eugenicists taught a social Darwinism that justified the nineteenth-century exploitation of immigrants by industrialists.

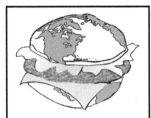

I don't mean to paint all evolutionists with broad evil strokes. Evolutionists can be good, kind, and even extraordinarily decent people. It's just that the belief they have yoked themselves to would permit an entirely different and base character. To be good, they must swim against the stream of their own ideas.

The Modern World View – Evolutionary and religious beliefs can lead to viewing the world as a mere substrate for humans to tool and consume as they wish.

© Wysong   Figure 154

How We Think Is How We Do – If we believe we are just the chance outcome of atoms then it makes little difference if we blow ourselves up and return to those atoms.

© Wysong   Figure 155

Evolutionary theory engenders ethical futility, meaninglessness, and purposelessness. Tell your kids bedtime stories every night about how they are nothing but biological robots, accidents of stardust, and burps from volcanic muck. Tell them how they are just a heap of atoms, and for atoms to bother contemplating right and wrong is absurd. Explain that no matter what they did that day or do the next, it is inconsequential. Since they have no free will, they can't be held responsible for what they do in life.

Human Evolution – It is very hard to see how humans have actually evolved in intelligence. We accumulate a lot of knowledge and technology but use it stupidly.

© Wysong   Figure 156

Tell them it makes no difference whether they are alive or dead and that their only mission in life (if they even wish to participate, since it all is unimportant) is to dominate the world and others.

If you don't tell them these intellectually and ethically X-rated materialistic and evolutionary stories, no matter, they'll watch it on television and get it hammered into them at school anyway.

In the meantime, we wonder why the world is going to hell in a hand-basket. Yes, we hear about goodness, high moral standards, the importance of right and wrong from evolutionist parents, teachers, judges, police officers, preachers, and politicians. But something is out of tune. There is a disconnect between the ethical void that logically flows from evolutionary philosophy that scientists and academicians are foisting on the public and the ironic call for the practice of probity and goodness.

© Wysong   Figure 157

Those smart enough to see this illogic may feel justified in brushing altruism and ethics aside and do what they must to serve their own selfish, riotous, evolutionary imperative. Or they may resign themselves to meaninglessness and live out a fruitless, vapid existence.

Only those who can espouse evolution, but deny its meaning, can live a fulfilling, contributing, and more selfless life. Thank goodness there are lots of those.

Our lives and the essential things from nature that sustain us and bring us happiness are not of our doing. They are gifts that come from elsewhere. Our ethical sense should nag that the "elsewhere" deserves acknowledgment. To wrongly assume that nature is self-explanatory, cold, and purposeless is to lose the wonder and respect that probing the universe, the atom, or the biological world should bring. There is a pleasure of appreciation and warmth of spirit from gazing at the stars or watching a sunset, a deer and its fawn, or even an amoeba. Such is lost or diminished by the blindness of evolution's hubris.

In the face of the impossibility of all circumstances coming together perfectly for the universe to function, for life to exist, and for us to breathe our next breath, humility can be the only reasonable reaction.

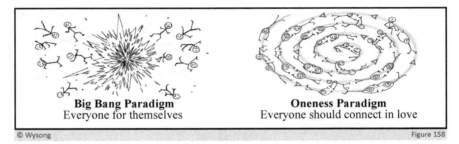

Big Bang Paradigm
Everyone for themselves

Oneness Paradigm
Everyone should connect in love

© Wysong

Figure 158

Thinking about . . .

RELIGION

In This Section: People do not come to the subject of religion using reason and evidence. Instead, belief and faith are thought necessary. But they aren't. The universe is scientifically true, rational, and without contradiction. The cause of that universe should have those same qualities, as should any religion that puts itself forth as representing that cause.

22
PUTTING RELIGION
ON THE TABLE

The disproof of abiogenesis, materialism and evolution. and the arguments in favor of intelligent design are used as proof for human-made religions and holy books. That's because religion is thought to be the only alternative.

However, just as science is misrepresented by evolution, the Creator is misrepresented by human-made religions.

This misdirection by religion is because we see things through human eyes. So, we assume that the source of us and our reality would want to communicate with us and answer our questions about why we're here, what we should be doing, and where we're going. Lacking a voice booming down from the heavens, people use their imagination and anthropomorphize the Creator. Surrogates, such as god institutions, god authorities, and god books satisfy the desires of many people to know their deity.

However, something capable of creating the incomprehensible complexities of the universe and life, and keeping it all together, is not in our league at all.

For that reason, "it," "source," or "Creator," rather than "He" and "God," are the more appropriate appellations for the Creator since "He" and "God" imply gender and human qualities.

All is not lost, however. We can, in fact, objectively know some things about the Creator by examining the creation and the laws governing it. Nature's laws are certain, consistent, and just. They are the best example of truth, the Creator, we can know in our Earthly reality.

Nature's laws dramatically demonstrate that materialism and evolution are false and that an intelligence is the only reasonable explanation for our existence. They are also what's responsible for every human advancement and for permitting us to safely and reliably navigate our day-to-day lives.

Most importantly, by the measure of nature's truths, we can understand what the Creator of our reality is not. Making the reasonable assumption that the Creator shares the qualities of the creation, the creator would not be contradictory, inconsistent with fact, nor untruthful. It would also not be unjust since injustice is the same thing as contradicting truth.

Contrary to popular opinion, the question of our maker is not a special case category requiring blind faith and belief. All ideas and beliefs, no matter how sacred they are thought to be, must be open to the challenge of reason and evidence. That's how we must approach life if we are ever to advance as a civilization; that's how we must approach the Big Questions if we are ever to understand where we came from, why we are here, and where we are going.

If by doing so we are not led to our prior beliefs, so what? If change means getting nearer to truth (the Creator), what more could we ask, and how thankful we should be.

Nobody comes to this subject without prior beliefs. Nor are they ready and eager to have them overturned. Everyone has a religious or irreligious opinion, and usually a stubbornly ingrained one.

But what's fair is fair. If we are moved to put materialism, evolution, atheism, or religions other than ours on the chopping block of rational scrutiny, honesty demands that we do the same with our own religious beliefs.

23
HOW RELIGION BEGINS
AND DEVELOPS

We are not born with the institutional ideas present in human-made religions. That much we know for sure. Religious ideas are schooled into us by fellow humans.

Moreover, way back at the beginning, there were no cathedrals, clergy, doctrines, or holy books. Humans began in a natural state, naked in the wild.

Primitive Personal Religion

No historian was there to record events, but we can reason on how religion must have begun. As a primitive person, you would have been dumbfounded by what you woke up to each day. You would have no idea why fruit appeared on trees, what caused babies, why autumn leaves fell, where you came from, and why there was death. The Earth would have seemed endless, the sun miraculous as it rose out of the Earth each morning and sank into it each evening. The heavens would be breathtaking. Lightning, thunder, fire, floods, volcanoes, tornados, hurricanes, and extreme hot or cold terrifying. You would certainly conclude that there were powerful forces behind it all and wonder what could be done to control them.

Imagined mysterious and powerful human-like gods filled the bill. Just talk to them, imagine what you would want if you were them, do it, and all would be well.

Tribal Religion

As populations grew and people assembled into families, tribes, and nations, rules and leadership developed. Since there was no god booming directives from the sky, the opportunity arose for someone to speak for god(s).

There was also the problem of conscience to contend with. Not wanting to do the hard work of weighing ethical choices ("don't make me decide, just tell me what to do"), and risking god ire, humans sought leaders who claimed the ability to know the will of the parent-like gods.

Since visual images exert far more influence than spoken words, religious icons were created. They took on the nature of the people who created them.

God Creations – Not by coincidence, the gods people worship always seem to take on the characteristics of the people who worship them.

© Joe Kirby (modified)   Figure 160

Not surprisingly, the gods always have the same language, hands, eyes, noses, emotions, enemies, worldview, writing style, and erroneous science as the people in the region where the god was created.

Having power over others is a natural thing for all living creatures, particularly for humans. However, a mere human leader would always be suspect. On the other hand, being able to speak for a god would put a person in the most powerful unquestioned position on Earth. Little wonder rulers throughout time have claimed to speak for gods, or that they were gods themselves.

Religious power could be gained and spread by military might—"I won the battle because god is on my side." Special abilities, such as making the moon disappear and reappear (ability to predict an eclipse), were helpful proofs of being god's earthly messenger. As the sun declined in the fall, and winter set in, people feared it would sink completely into the Earth and never return. Making the sun rise each day, and particularly at the winter solstice, by tearing the heart out of a person in sacrifice to the sun-god each morning, was convincing evidence as well.

151

Religious dynasties were created giving power automatically to progeny. Leaders put strict regulations in place, with special emphasis on veneration and obedience. Those who didn't recognize the authority of the god-leader were labeled as enemies (later as heretics and infidels). This brought the faithful closely together with the goal of vanquishing the nonbelievers.

Religious myths were passed orally with song and story. Later, when the tribal myths could be etched in stone or on parchments, they were better inoculated against doubt, as would befit any divine word from the gods. Also, being able to see words made the myths even more powerful through the unconscious bias of sight over sound (termed scriptism or graphocentrism). Such writings themselves became elevated and venerated as religious icons.

Idolatry Then and Now: Humans have the need to understand. Since a Creator is not readily apparent, human qualities are imposed upon it. In effect, bringing it down to our level, down to our brains and four dimensions. Many religions have used idols to accomplish this anthropomorphism and be the focus of worship and reliance. Others create books. There is really no difference since they are both man-made icons and have nothing to do with the Creator.

© Wysong

Figure 182

Holy writings and astrological meanings given to the stars had the added benefit of removing suspicion from the human leader. A mere human was not the author, he(usually) was just god's appointed agent for interpreting and passing the information on and executing it. However, and not accidentally, the human, as god's mouthpiece, became just like a god.

State Religion

With the advent of agriculture, society was able to transition from wandering hunter-gatherer tribes into more stationary concentrated populations. Industry and technology enabled the production of more food than could be immediately consumed. Stored food permitted the division of labor and the support of standing armies, legislators, enforcers, and ruling clergy. Society became what its belly allowed.

This is the time when people most dramatically separated into the rulers and the ruled. Those rulers held the reins of all religious, political, mercantile, and military power. The ruled became generic followers, some by force, some willingly.

Today we worry about gasoline, electricity, cell phones, medical insurance, and the price of groceries. In past times, survival had to do with brute nature and the favor of the state and its religion. Torture, human sacrifice, hangings, burnings, dungeons, flaying, and drawing and quartering to punish and ferret out disobedience (sin) were just the necessary duties of the religious leaders who, ostensibly, were protecting the population from a volcano or pestilence. If the predictions or protections of the clergy didn't work, that could only mean more torturing and sacrificial blood-letting was needed.

Religions Have to Be Intolerant

Religious leaders policed beliefs in order to maintain identity, cohesiveness, and power. Those who ruled in religions were never interested in the independent thinking of the ruled. Honest and creative thinking was, and is, labeled arrogance or heresy, while blind following and intellectual laziness (faith) rise to the rank of virtue.

Although all organizations must begin with a revolutionary individual who does the work of overturning the previous system (and being hated and persecuted for it), no established system encourages revolution against itself.

Religions tell inspiring tales of their heroic founders' sedition, but then must insist that the present organization is the ideal endpoint. No further change is needed other than a little incidental tweaking here and there as "new light" is revealed from the organization's "anointed" leaders.

153

No rabble-rousing apostates like Jesus, Mohammed, Luther, etc. allowed.

Religious Retreat and Regrouping

Here we will shift to a focus on Bible-based religions. Beginning around the sixteenth century, religious leaders had to increasingly contend with pesky intrusions by science, technology (like Gutenberg's printing press permitting people to learn on their own), and secular philosophy. It became increasingly difficult for the clergy to screen the knowledge accessible to the masses.

Pressure was on religion to defend, for instance, Bible-based geology that explained the broken and twisted crust of the Earth by invoking the fury of a wrathful god against a "fallen world." (St. Jerome) John Wesley, the founder of the Methodists, argued that "sin is the moral cause of Earthquakes, whatever their natural cause may be."

No longer could fossils be explained as "models made by the Creator" before he had fully made up his mind about how to go about the creation. Beringer (1725), a Wurzburg physician and university professor, defended his religion by stating that fossils are simply "stones of a peculiar sort, hidden by the Author of Nature for his own pleasure." Others concluded that fossils were put on earth as trials of human faith since they could not represent dead creatures because death could not have entered the world before Adam's sin.

Churches made presentations of bones proving the antediluvian giants spoken of in the Bible. (Genesis 6:4; Numbers 13:33) Displays were even erected proving that the height of Adam was 123 feet 9 inches, Eve 118 feet 9 inches. The bones were later found to be from a mastodon. (This doesn't mean that there may not have been human giants in the past, although not likely of the 123-foot variety.)

Veering from religious doctrine, as pontificated by those with a divine right to the Bible, was punishable by death or worse. Even possessing a Bible was punishable by death.

Fear was life's driving force. So trying to be enlightened in those days was about as likely as trying to be enlightened while walking the gangplank or facing a herd of charging buffalo. Questioning was easily set aside by the prospect of torture in the dungeons or being roasted alive in the town square.

Nevertheless, the scientific revolution eventually tightened the logical and factual noose and sent religion into retreat.

Since religion was fundamentally about the awesome forces of nature controlled by gods, explaining those forces logically and by scientific proof emasculated or retired one god after another. Over the course of about a century, three hundred years ago, religion's grip on nature dramatically weakened.

Once it was discovered that the Earth was not the center of the universe, it logically followed that man may not be the central and most important thing in the universe. This realization and the rest of the long list of embarrassing religious blunders exposed by advancing knowledge helped cause the rise of atheism, secularism, materialism, and evolution.

Not wanting further embarrassment and loss of parishioners, the Catholic Church backed away from a strict literalist Bible view. Anything in it that conflicted with science or reason was relabeled poetic moral metaphor. Luther and others were more tenacious. The protestant reformation argued that by just interpreting the Bible correctly and removing ecclesiastical excess and error, all problems between the Bible and science could be resolved.

Today religion has retreated into its primary bunker, faith. By definition, faith justifies belief in anything and is thus immune from reason, fact, and science. Reason and facts are useful in all areas of life, just not in religion except when by chance reason and facts happen to blend with belief.

A case in point is the resurgence of Bible fundamentalism fueled by the discovery that creation, not materialism and evolution, is consistent with science. This is then extrapolated to mean the book is true through and through. But that can only be determined by measuring all it says by reason, facts, consistency, and ethics.

So that's what we'll do next.

24
RELIGIONS CROSS POLLINATE

During college, I jettisoned the Christian religion of my youth and climbed on board the prevailing academic, evolutionist, materialistic, and atheistic train. Then, in my early medical years, I discovered the evidence and logic on origins presented in the previous section of this book. This was convincing of intelligent causation but gave no direction for where to go from there.

Curious about who this Creator was, various religions and holy books were examined. Critiques of non-Christian religions (written by Christians) and Bible proofs (used by Bible apologists) led me to believe that the Bible was the Creator's word. After all, the Creator, like a human father, would surely want to talk to its creation. I settled on a Bible-based religion that seemed most rational and faithful to the book.

This led to an immersion in Bible apologetics, hermeneutics, and critical evaluation of competing religions. After all, if this was the true religion, the others were false and had to be exposed so their followers could escape the Bible's imminent apocalypse.

Although reading contrary literature was strongly discouraged, it seemed that if this religion was the truth there should be no fear of any information. Such exploration resulted in discoveries and epiphanies that shook my beliefs.

I shared these with fellow believers. The headquarters of the religion was also contacted for rebuttals to Bible passages that seemed to disprove some of their doctrines. The result was a visit (trial of sorts) by a leader. Satisfactory answers weren't given and it became clear that compliance, not truth, was the real agenda of the organization. So, after about three years of this sidetrack in the quest for truth, I moved on.

The break was not nearly as clean and neat as that sounds. What I was doing was considered apostasy and heresy. Nor was it easy to leave behind so many friends, although several I spoke to about what I was discovering fell away along with me. The sense of belonging and comradery in this religion were powerful draws. Leaving behind a religion you commit to can be like having your world collapse in on you. But, truth was the goal. Living in a lie was not possible.

Looking back, the experience was an invaluable awakening to independent and open thinking and what it's like to be willingly brain-washed.

After leaving this religion, exploration widened to include information that challenged the very notion that the Bible was written (inspired) by the Creator of the universe.

In examining the earliest moorings of Judaism and Christianity, it was astonishing to learn that virtually everything in the Bible was known and practiced in cultures prior to the Bible. This included Minoan, Egyptian, Indus Valley, Etruscan, Greek, and Roman civilizations. The Egyptian Book of the Dead, the Hymn of Ra, the Gilgamesh Epic, Ovid's Metamorphoses, the Enuma Elish mythology, and many other religions/mythologies cross-pollinate the Bible and other holy books.

Features of gods, some dating back thousands of years before Christianity, include a heroic male demigod, often the son of a god and a mortal woman, miracles surrounding the birth, atonement, original sin, births announced by stars, birth at a December 25 solstice (Greco-Roman sun gods), tyrants trying to kill them in infancy, passion and violent death, bearing sins so humans could rise to heaven, rising from the dead, worshiped by "wise men," fasting for 40 days, baptism by water, twelve followers, miracles such as water walking and changing water into wine, the demigod being referred to as "king of kings," "lamb of god," "alpha and omega," "the truth," "the light," and likened to both a lion and a lamb, resurrection to eternal life, considered a savior and redeemer, and more.

CRUCIFIED SAVIORS BEFORE JESUS	GODS WHO BECAME MORTAL AND ASCENDED INTO HEAVEN
• Thulis of Egypt, 1700 B. C.	• Salivahana of Bermuda
• Krishna of India, 1200 B.C.	• Zulis or Zhule of Egypt
• Crite of Chaldea, 1200 B.C.	• Osiris of Egypt
• Atys of Phrygia, 1170 B.C.	• Oru of Egypt
• Thammuz or Tammuz of Syria, 1160 B.C.	• Odin of the Scandinavians
• Hesus or Eros 834 B.C.	• Zoroaster of Persia
• Bali of Orissa, 725 B.C.	• Baal of Phoenicia
• Indra of Thibet (Tibet), 725 B.C.	• Taut, "the only Begotten of God" of Phoenicia, inventor of letters
• Iao of Nepaul (Nepal), 622 B.C.	• Bali of Afghanistan
• Buddha Sakia (Muni) of India, 600 B.C.	• Xamolxis (Zalmoxis) of Thrace
• Mitra (Mithra) of Persia, 600 B.C.	• Zoar of the Bonzes
• Alcestos of Euripides, 600 B.C.	• Adad of Assyria
• Quezalcoatl of Mexico, 587 B.C.	• Deva Tat of Siam (Thailand)
• Wittoba of the Bilingonese, 552 B.C.	• Sammonocadam (Sommona-Codom) of Siam (Thailand)
• Prometheus or Æschylus of Caucasus, 547 B.C.	• Alcides of Thebes
• Quirinus of Rome, 506 B.C.	• Mikado of the Sintoos
• Thracian god Zalmoxis, before 425 B.C.	• Beddru of Japan
	• Bremrillah of the Druids
	• Thor son of Odin of the Gauls/Norse
	• Cadmus of Greece
	• Hil/Feta of the Mandaites
	• Gentaut of Mexico
	• Universal Monarch of the Sibyls
	• Ischy of Formosa (Taiwan)
	• Divine Teacher of Plato
	• Holy One of Xaca
	• (Fohi) of China
	• Tien of China
	• Adonis son of the virgin Io of Greece
	• Ixion of Rome
	• Mohamud or Mahomet of Arabia

From Graves and others, see Resource Section   Figure 275

Many gods before Christianity were worshipped as a trinity. For example, Brahma-Vishnu-Shiva; Horus-Isis-Osiris; Astarte-Anat-Quedesht; Dionysus-Demeter-Poseidon; Attis-Maia-Zeus; Astarte-Eshmun-Melkarth. Other pre-Christian doctrines include holy water, confession, penance, salvation based upon belief, priestly garb and ritual, Sunday worship, Saturday worship, temples, sacrificial blood, wine as blood (Dionysus cult), Eucharist communion, idolatrous reverence for holy writings, the cross symbol, three crosses with thieves to the side, halos, tithing, the Christmas tree, Easter, an end-time apocalypse, eternal punishment, a devil, hellfire, and more.

Consider the mythological god Attis, 1250 BC:
- Was born on December 25th of the Virgin Nana
- Was considered the "only begotten son" and killed for the salvation of humankind
- His followers had a meal of bread that represented him
- His priests were eunuchs
- He was both the Divine Son and the Father
- On Friday he was crucified on a tree
- He descended into the underworld
- After three days he was resurrected

Many Christian features trace back to ancient sun worship and the astrological zodiac. The sun made crops grow, brought warmth, gave light, and vanquished the terrifying predator-filled darkness. Little wonder it was worshiped as savior and light of the world. The sun was seen to pass through twelve major star constellations during a twelve-month year giving rise to the four-seasons in the cross of the zodiac. The sun was anthropomorphized as were the star constellations.

Notice the features of the Egyptian sun god Horus, 3000 BC, as compared to modern-day Christianity:
- Born December 25th
- Born of a virgin
- Birth accompanied by a star in the East
- Adored as a savior by three kings
- Child-teacher in a temple
- Baptized at 30 and began ministry
- 12 disciples
- Called a lamb, lion, and identified with a cross
- Trinity
- Performed miracles like healings, water walking, fishing bounty, seven loaves feeding a multitude, raising people from the dead
- Known as "truth," "the light," "God's anointed one," "lamb of god"
- Betrayed by a friend, crucified, dead for three days
- Resurrected
- A Millennial reign . . . (271 Egyptian-Christian parallels are found at asifthinkingmatters.com/preexistingdata)

159

The symbols in the zodiac are not just an artistic tool to track the sun, stars, and seasons. The zodiac doubles as a pagan religious symbol. For example, the bright star in the East is Sirius, which on December 24th aligns with the three kings. These stars in Orion's Belt point to the sunrise on December 25th. Thus the three kings "follow" the bright star in the East to locate the sunrise, the birth of the sun (son). This mimics the events surrounding the Christmas story.

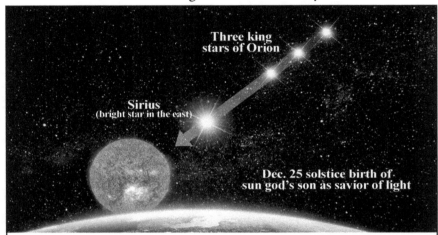

Three Kings – On December 25 the bright star in the east aligns with the three king stars of Orion to point to the sun. Then, what appears to be a dying sun, experiences a new birth as the days get longer. These astrological features correspond to saviors being born on December 25.

Figure 162

There are 12 parts of the astrological zodiac. Notice there are 12 disciples of Jesus, 12 tribes, kings, judges, and princes of Israel, 12 brothers of Joseph, and Jesus was at the temple at age 12.

Zodiac – The cross, sun, 12 segments and other features of the zodiac correspond to doctrines created in religions.

Figure 163

Jesus is often shown superimposed on the sun in the middle of the astrological cross. (Incidentally, the Romans crucified people on stakes, not crosses, if for no other reason than the impracticality of building stable crosses.)

Jesus superimposed on the sun god and zodiac.

Figure 164

In the Abrahamic religions of Judaism, Christianity, and Islam there are most especially common themes and doctrines. Christianity morphed out of Judaism and paganism, and Islam morphed out of both Judaism and Christianity. Judaism morphed out of the pagan religions preceding or concurrent with it, such as monotheistic Zoroastrianism.

Christianity thus appears as an amalgam of Jewish, Greek, and pagan beliefs. Since the early Christians lived among these cultures, it's little wonder that the people and the times would influence the Jesus story. There was also a practical aspect to this plagiarism. Christian states found it useful to adopt beliefs of the people they conquered to help assimilation and decrease the potential for rebellion.

Although this information was new to me, it was by no means new. For example, Higgins (1772-1833), in his Anacalypsis, concluded: "One thing is clear — the mythos of the Hindus, the mythos of the Jews and the mythos of the Greeks are all at bottom the same; and what is called their early histories are not histories of humankind, but are contrivances under the appearance of histories to perpetuate doctrines."

Most astonishing is the fact that a number of writers in the first four centuries, including Christians, knew of the plagiarism. For example, sainted Justin Martyr (100 CE), a pagan turned Christian, attempted to defend Christianity in the face of pagan claims that Christianity was nothing more than a rehash of their gods. Being well aware of pagan beliefs, Martyr didn't deny this but rather defended Christianity with his absurd "diabolical mimicry" argument: Satan read the Old Testament prophesies about the messiah and imitated Christ in the form of pagan gods prior to Jesus. In other words, any parallels to paganism are the devil's doing and should create no doubt that Jesus was god and did the things said of him. But pagan writers, such as Celsus, would have none of it. Pagans were used to syncretism (the amalgamation of different religions) among pagan religions and easily recognized Christian plagiarism.

Clearly, if Bible-based religions are truth and not human imaginings, they should stand alone, be unique, and historically first. So, it is shocking to learn that the mythological pagan gods anathematized and ridiculed by Christendom, were antecedents to all of Christendom's doctrines.

25
GODS WRITING BOOKS

Jesus, other Jews before him, Mohammed, and most founders of religions did not write holy books during their lives. Books attributed to them were not originally written in Middle-Age English or other modern languages, leather-bound with gold-embossed page edges, thumb notched, and then carefully guarded and passed down to this day.

Focusing here on the Bible, there was no consensus among Jews, even into the Christian era, as to which books were to be included in the Hebrew Bible (Old Testament). Some of present-day Judaism's most sacred books did not even exist at the time Columbus visited America. Catholic, Protestant, and Eastern Orthodox religions are also in disagreement about what is or is not the authentic Bible.

No Original Bibles

There is no uninterrupted Bible tradition beginning with the first printing for Adam and Eve, and then extending to Jesus, and from Jesus down to this day. Astonishingly, there are absolutely no original texts.

The earliest writings used in the New Testament are generally thought to be letters by Paul (who never met Jesus) and are believed to have been written about 50 to 60 A.D. (twenty to thirty years after the death of Jesus). The earliest Gospel is believed to have been written in a range of 70-200 A.D. The earliest actual document found is the P52 papyrus fragment of the Gospel of John. It is a copy of a copy of a copy . . . dated between 125-300 A.D. There are thousands of other fragments of copies of copies of copies . . . most dating to the ninth century.

Early Copy Differences

There are hundreds of thousands of differences between the various copies of copies of copies of mistakes of mistakes. There are more differences than there are words in the New Testament. There are words, lines, and pages omitted, spelling errors, and the insertion of the personal views of the scribes. Most are inconsequential to meaning, and some alter the meaning entirely. The greatest differences are among the earliest copies. Which, of course, suggests that the later versions were redacted to comport with one another and fit the ideas of people far removed from the actual events. Remember, since there are no originals the true degree of variance from the originals cannot be known.

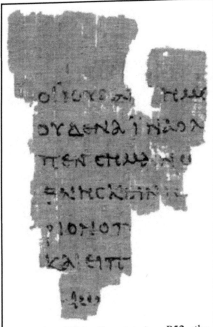

Christian Bible Fragment – P52, the earliest Christian Bible fragment in Greek dated between 125-300 CE. *Approximate actual size. (8.9 cm x 6 cm)*

© Wysong

Figure 166

Some of the more serious examples of omissions and contradictions include the famous story of Jesus telling those without sin to cast the first stones at an adulteress. (John 7:53-8:11) This is not found in the earliest manuscripts. The last 12 verses in Mark regarding speaking in tongues and snake handling are also not found in the oldest manuscripts. (Mark 16:9-20) How many people through the millennia have been injured and killed believing these were words of the Creator can only be guessed. Jesus' statement in Luke 23:34 asking the father to forgive his executioners for not knowing what they were doing is missing in the oldest texts. Whether Jesus is god or not, or part of a trinity, depends upon which part of the Bible is being read.

There are countless of such issues. Scholars around the world spend entire lives debating the comparisons between the copies of copies of copies of mistakes of mistakes. At stake is the inerrancy of the Bible. But, to repeat, there is no original by which any copied document can be compared to determine accuracy.

There were many stories about Jesus other than the few that were finally included in today's New Testament. For example, the "apocryphal" writings not included in the modern Bible were accepted by many Christians in the first four centuries. Books referred to in the Old Testament, such as Nathan, Jasher, Ahijah, Iddo, Jehu, and the Sayings of the Seers are not included. Catholics include numerous Apocryphal (Deuterocanonical) books while other religions exclude them. The Song of Solomon and Esther are included but never mention a divinity or any religious duty. Joseph Smith's translation of the Book of Mormon, supposedly created by putting a hat containing a seer stone over his face, is not included.

Many Different Christianities From the Beginning

Christianity in its beginnings was heterogeneous as it is now. Although today it's commonly argued by Bible-believing sects, including the one I followed for a time, that they have "gotten back to the original true Christianity." But there is no evidence that there was ever one original true Jesus religion. All versions were vying Jewish reformist and messianic movements, not something separate from Judaism. Christianity did not become separated from Judaism and unified until the pagan government stepped in hundreds of years A.D.

The human element is everywhere in the composition, editing, compilation, and transmission of the Bible. Over many hundreds of years, Christianity was codified based upon which group could gain the favor of worldly powers and suppress opponents. Decisions about what was official Bible were made through special interest, debate, and battle. The history of Christianity comes to us through the eyes of the victors. The losers were called heretics, the winners were called orthodox.

The New Testament came to be a selection of writings from among many, such as the omitted "heretical" Gnostic and Essene gospels. Only four gospels were chosen. Some scholars say that was due to the influence of myths such as the "four zones of the world" and the four corners of the zodiac cross.

There has never been a consensus of what should or should not be in the Bible. People such as Origen and Eusebius in earliest Christian times, later Martin Luther, and modern-day scholars debated and debate about what is or is not the authentic "word of god" Bible. Such debate remains alive and well because, again, there are no original texts by which to judge the thousands of copies of copies of copies.

The Bible has been repeatedly edited, then rewritten again and again, translated and re-translated, then given to kings for them to purge and compose to their liking, then edited, rewritten, and translated over and over, then modified by popes, then rewritten and re-edited to remove the parts they didn't like and keep their favorite parts. Any consistency found today is not because the eclectic original writings (which, again, do not exist) agreed with one another, but because of creative emendation by enthusiastic believers.

Constantine's Decisions

The official state-sanctioned assemblage of writings known as the Bible began when the Roman Emperor Constantine saw his empire increasingly divided by religious factions. In 325 A.D., while still embracing pagan Mithraism, he viewed the Christ god primarily as an effective war god. Constantine convened the Council of Nicaea to keep his kingdom united by establishing Christian orthodoxy. This was the first of several such councils to decide upon the makeup (canon) of the Bible.

Constantine – The pagan founder of modern Christian doctrines. Note the sun again in the background

© The respective copyright holders. Figure 167

Gospel of Peter Fragment

© The respective copyright holders. Figure 168

At the time of Constantine, councils to mandate beliefs were necessary because varying ideas were popping up everywhere. For example, Docetism, based upon the Gospel of Peter, one of the early books rejected, was widely spread. It taught that Jesus was not physically real, but rather an allegory for the spiritual awakening possible within any person. Many scholars today argue that all of Paul's letters reflect that same belief. Others disagree. (YouTube contains many debates on these subjects by scholars such as Ehrman, Price, and Carrier which, in spite of all the erudite knowledge displayed, solve nothing.)

At one counsel in ancient Chalcedon, it was decided that Christ was both human and divine. The opposition, called Monophysites, believed Christ was only divine. After the Council voted, the Monophysites were declared heretics.

In the 4th century, Pelagius refuted Augustine's original sin doctrine that man was predestined to be evil due to the fall of Adam and Eve. According to Pelagius, the mistakes of man do not come from inherent evil, but rather from failed conscience and the ability to choose. To him, guilt and sin were a matter of will, not moral genetics. Pelagianism was anathematized as heresy in the 6th century but continues to this day.

Pelagius

Figure 169

Origen

Figure 170

At the time of Constantine's Council of Nicaea, the prevalent view of Christian salvation, as evidenced in the Gnostic gospels (Nile River Gospels/Nag Hammadi Library) and as taught by early scholars such as Origen (third century), was that people reincarnated to learn and grow from a variety of Earth experiences. Christ could be "within" any person and any person could be a "son of God." People were their own redeemers on Earth.

A more favorable and utilitarian view to Constantine, himself coming from a long line of emperor gods and sons of gods, beginning with Julius Caesar in 49 B.C., was that salvation could only take place in heaven. Not surprisingly, to get to heaven people had to demonstrate appropriate obedience to earthly state religion creeds, ordained clergy, and their god leader, Constantine.

Arius argued Jesus could not be the same as god, but Constantine's council at Nicaea made Jesus an incarnate son of god just like Constantine declared himself to be.

Arius

Figure 171

To make sure there were no heirs of Jesus lingering about to compete with him, Constantine applied the pagan doctrine of god celibacy to the Jesus and Mary story. To be saved, people needed baptism into and confession of the Nicene and other creeds. People were executed for not believing what such councils decided.

Council of Nicaea

Figure 172

The early Christian reincarnation view was a threat to Constantine because it put people in charge of their own spirituality and posited salvation with no time limits. Constantine, of course, preferred the church-state in charge and putting people on notice that if they did not obey the church-state during their one shot on Earth (in his domain), hell awaited. It was a contest between individual spirituality on the one hand and the business of power religion and politics on the other.

A vote was taken and, not surprisingly, the church-state idea of heavenly salvation won. But there were still dissenters. Constantine immediately had rebels, such as Arius, branded as heretics and banished. All books contrary to the new orthodoxy were destroyed. Keeping one was punishable by death.

A second Nicaea vote was held. The dissenters weighed their options: vote with Constantine or be banished, or worse. Of course, Constantine's doctrine of heavenly salvation and the deity of Jesus won by a landslide. That became the Biblical word of god.

About a hundred years later, not wanting to contend with the persistent heretical Gnostics who challenged the Nicene Creed, and to make compliance doubly sure, Archbishop Cyril had as many of the Gnostic gospels and contrary books as he could find in Alexandria's libraries burned. (The only thing worse than book burning is not to read them.) Some early Christians hid their texts in earthen jars and placed them in caves to be preserved in the desert air. That's why some of the Gnostic Christian texts have survived to this day, such as the Nag Hammadi codices found in upper Egypt in 1945.

Pity those who disagreed with Constantine's new orthodoxy. The beautiful Alexandrian teacher, Hypatia, was dragged to the church, stripped by Cyril's holy monks, and flayed alive to the bone with oyster shells for her noncompliant reincarnation-flavored Christian philosophy. Imagine the degree of belief necessary to flay a living person! But

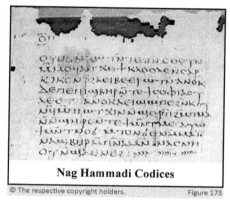

Nag Hammadi Codices

Figure 173

these early church fathers felt they were just doing god's bidding. And besides, they thought that if their god could torture people eternally in hellfire, they should emulate such cruelty and ferocity as best they could.

In celebration of Cyril's great contribution to holiness, he was made a saint upon his death.

Constantine the Great, who claimed "foreknowledge granted by God himself," has been revered even though he was responsible for the death of his wife Faustus, and son Crispus (in 326, one year after the council where he decreed what god says), and other atrocities.

Cyril –
Sainted

Figure 174

Hypatia –
Flayed alive by Cyril

Figure 175

This early history of the Bible, which had nothing to do with inspiration by the Creator of the universe, did not incline me to continue to labor over every Biblical word voted on by Constantine and the likes of Cyril.

Why Not a Perfect Book in Everyone's Hands?

If the Creator felt it important that humans have a perfect book to show a path to heaven and avoid divine wrath, then it would be reasonable to expect that billions of copies in each of the 10,000+ native languages should magically appear, one into each person's hands—a trivial feat for the Creator of the universe. Moreover, all people could be magically programmed to be literate and interpret them the same. After all, obedience and holiness should center on knowing truth, not the ability to decipher confusing and ambiguous ancient tongues.

As it is, religions vie with one another on what holy books say and mean, even venerating those claiming special apologetic and exegetical skills and knowledge of ancient languages. All for what? Certainly not to learn ethics. Not only can anyone derive morality from simply probing their own conscience, but holy book renderings have led to witch trials, the Inquisition, and countless other heinous acts.

Then there is the embarrassing fact that general access to the 700,000 printed putative words of the Creator in the Bible had to wait for Gutenberg in the fifteenth century, the inventor of the printing press, and modern mail services. That would make Gutenberg and mailmen among the holiest of all people.

Up to then, to keep the mystique and the clergy in power, the Bible was kept out of the hands of the populace for centuries. The flock was just spoon-fed official interpretations. In 1536 William Tyndale was garroted and burned at the stake. His sin was translating the Bible from Latin into English and thus making it more accessible to the common folk. Wycliffe was also burned alive by godly clergy for attempting translations.

But in spite of hundreds of years of printing, distribution, and evangelism no holy book (forgetting that most cannot be traced to an original) has yet been made available to all nations in all languages. One-third of the world has not even heard of the Bible. That means, since religions claim their holy books are essential, huge sections of the world are condemned. To create humans in need of a holy book and then place them in a holy book illiterate darkness would serve no purpose other than to condemn the world to wickedness and doom billions of souls. Attributing such an act to the Creator would make that Creator fiendish.

Religion is presented as a moral beacon. If the only way to get at morality is through a book, people would be faced with the impossible task of sorting through not only the thousands of religious interpretations of the Bible, but all other holy books as well. Finding and deciphering books is not morality.

Those serious about their holy book religions will spend their entire lives memorizing scriptures, studying original languages, and arguing doctrine and prophecy. I was on that path and still have the Bible I used with worn pages and hundreds of tiny notes and cross-references I made in the margins. Thousands of hours in study, but primarily to prove other religions wrong, while ignoring the sorts of things in these chapters that would cut the legs out from under any Bible religion's most fundamental tenets, including mine.

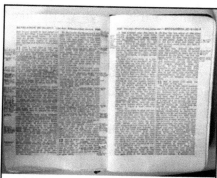

My Bible – I made notes in the margins with a fine point Rapidograph pen to permit lots of room for all my cross references and proofs. Inside of three years it was thumb-notched with the pages almost worn out. The more ragged the better since that was seen as like a badge of holy honor.

© Wysong   Figure 277

Uncertain Language

I was led to believe by my religion's leaders that an understanding of the original languages solves all Bible problems. So, I started to delve into the original languages of Bible writers (Hebrew, Aramaic, Greek). But that only made it clear that language itself creates generous room for disagreement and latitude. For example, Bible words in the native tongues, and those used in translations—Greek, Aramaic, Hebrew, Latin, Middle English, modern English, etc.—can have multiple meanings and cultural flavors.

Vowels were not added to the Hebrew language used in the Old Testament until the seventh century AD. There were no punctuations, sentence breaks, paragraphs, chapters, or headings in the early Bible texts. This made consistent copying and deciphering nearly impossible. I had to stop romanticizing about inspired Bible writers and face the reality of hundreds of ancients writing on skins and plant leaves without Word, Spellcheck, and the internet.

Even meanings for words change over time. "Wife" now means a woman married to a man. In Middle English, it meant simply a woman. This meaning remains to this day in words like "midwife" and "fishwife." Think of the Dutch one could get into imposing today's meaning

Former Meanings of Common Words
Extravagance = Strange
Meat = Food
Bully = Battering ram
Nice = Lewd
Secretary = Confidant
Awful = Inspiring awe
Fruition = Pleasurable use of something
Ovation = Ceremony for a victorious Roman general
Talent = Unit of weight

© Wysong   Figure 283

of "wife" on writings just a few hundred years old. Consider the possibilities with words thousands of years old in foreign languages.

Even the placement of a comma, if there are any, can make a huge difference in meaning. For example: "Woman, without her man, is nothing," versus, "Woman, without her, man is nothing." Simple commas can produce exact opposite meanings.

Or, consider the words of Jesus to the repentant thief hanging on the cross beside him: "Truly I say to you, today you will be with me in heaven." (Implying that at death they would both be in heaven) Or, "Truly I say to you today, you will be with me in heaven." (This implies that they may not get there until some undetermined time in the future.) Both versions are in today's official Bibles stamped as the Word of God.

CAN LANGUAGE BE PRECISE?

The bandage was wound around the wound.

The farm was used to produce produce.

The dump was so full that it had to refuse more refuse.

We must polish the Polish furniture.

He could lead if he would get the lead out.

The soldier decided to desert his dessert in the desert.

Since there is no time like the present, he thought it was time to present the present...and so on.

English – is a difficult language in part because so many words with the same spelling can take on different meanings. The same is true to one degree or another for all languages. The only way ambiguity can be sorted out is with experience with the language and with the time in which it is being spoken. Such a feat is impossible for languages spoken hundreds or thousands of years ago, particularly if one is attempting to parse the words with the precision necessary to claim they came from the Creator of the universe.

© Wysong   Figure 176

Presently there are some 40 English versions and over 1,400 translations of just the Bible. There is no "one" Bible or one other holy book. Nor are any of them better-written literature (as would be expected of the Creator) than humans can write.

Finding the Right Holy Book – There are hundreds of modern and ancient holy books. If a person is convinced that the Creator wrote one, the correct one could not be determined until each one was personally examined in detail. That means finding originals and reading them in their original language. No human lifetime could achieve such a feat. So, obviously, the Creator (the originator of truth and justice) would not write a book critical to human life and then ask humans to do the impossible.

Figure 276

Even if the Creator were a monoglot and all people on Earth spoke that language, and the canon of a holy book was undisputed, the problems of interpretation are not solved. For example, a legal contract in a tongue common to both parties can be interpreted differently. A judge and jury can also have different interpretations of it. A final judgment can cause debate in the legal profession for decades. That makes writings in a foreign tongue, translated over and over, written thousands of years ago, recounting oral traditions passed down through thousands of years before being written, impossible to be understood in one way by all people throughout all time. The thousands of vying religions extant today based on the same book testify to this.

Hubris

Today it's common in religions to romanticize the ancients by letting distance in geography or time lend enchantment to their words. I must admit to this as well. The sonorous words and mysterious writings of the ancients make it easy to mystify them. But the past and its languages are not sacred for being past. Truth is also not time-sensitive. What was true in antiquity can be found in the living present.

I reflected on the complexity of life and a universe holding more stars than grains of sand on Earth, and more atoms in a grain of sand than stars in the universe. (One of those trillions of stars, VY-Canis Majoris is so large that it would take a thousand years for a plane traveling a thousand miles per hour to circumnavigate it.) Given the scope of such reality, it seemed the ultimate hubris to believe that man fills the mind of a Creator who then stoops to converse in printed, flawed, and puny human languages.

"This is what I say, it says, you say."

Speaking for God – Arguably, for a human to speak for god and say that certain human writings are from him, is perhaps the most bold, presumptuous, arrogant, and audacious of human acts.

© Wysong   Figure 177

The "Word of God" Claim

It is embarrassing to admit that the Bible claim to being the word of god influenced me. Wanting to believe, I ignored other books, such as the Quran, making the same claim. Since all holy books making the claim contradict each other, the claim is worthless.

If the mere claim of god authorship is not sufficient proof, and learned scholars can disagree after spending entire lives trying to figure out what true scripture is or what it means, a layman, such as myself, could justifiably feel hopeless.

It says here it is the word of God so it must be.

What about this one?

© Wysong   Figure 178

But, for a time, I was able to deny doubt as most others do by reasoning that all things are possible with a Creator of infinite power. That would include guiding scriptural truths over eons through the quagmire of human scribes and their foibles. Embarrassingly, in that convenient rescue attempt, I didn't stop to ask myself or others why a Creator interested

174

in sending a savior and communicating unequivocal truth would choose to do it in the Bronze Age when the world was essentially illiterate. Why not in the modern era with the Internet, television, and countless technological means to confirm the authenticity of documents and personages?

That reasonable question aside, I came to realize the real problem was reconciling what the Bible actually said with what we can know of the Creator by just examining the created laws holding the universe together. A document authored by the Creator must mirror those laws by being true, noncontradictory, and ethical. Moreover, at the least, there should be substantial, unequivocal, and solid historical evidence for central figures such as Jesus.

Let's see if those expectations prove true.

KIDS AND THE BIBLE

- In the first book of the Bible, Guinessis, God got tired of creating the world so he took the Sabbath off.

- Adam and Eve were created from an apple tree. noah's wife was joan of ark. noah built and ark and the animals came on in pears.

- Lots wife was a pillar of salt during the day, but a ball of fire during the night.

- The Jews were a proud people and throughout history they had trouble with unsympathetic genitals.

- Sampson was a strongman who let himself be led astray by a jezebel like delilah.

- Samson slayed the philistines with the axe of the apostles.

- Moses led the jews to the red sea where they made unleavened bread which is bread without any ingredients.

- The egyptians were all drowned in the dessert. Afterwards, Moses went up to mount cyanide to get the ten commandments.

- The first commandments was when eve told adam to eat the apple.

- The seventh commandment is thou shalt not admit adultry.

- Moses died before he ever reached canada, then joshua led the hebrews in the battle of geritol.

- The greatest miricle in the Bible is when joshua told his son to stand still and he obeyed him.

- David was a hebrew king who was skilled at playing the liar. He fought the finkelsteins, a race of people who lived in Biblical times.

- Solomon, one of Davids sons, had 300 wives and 700 porcupines.

- When Mary heard she was the mother of Jesus, she sang the magna carta.

- When the three wise guys from the east side arrived they found Jesus in the manager.

- Jesus was born because Mary had an immaculate contraption.

- St. John the blacksmith dumped water on his head.

- Jesus enunciated the golden rule, which says do unto others before they do one to you he also explained a man doth not live by sweat alone.

- It was a miricle when Jesus rose from the dead and managed to get the tombstone off the entrance.

- The people who followed the Lord were called the 12 decibles.

- The epistels were the wives of the apostles.

- One of the opposums was St. Mathew who was also a taximan.

- St. Paul cavorted to christianity, he reached holy acrimony which is another name for marraige.

- Christians have only one spouse. This is called monotony.

Figure 165

26
QUESTIONABLE FOUNDATIONS
OF CHRISTIANITY

In my foray into holy book history, I learned that beliefs based upon events of the past are best derived from reliable evidence, such as eyewitness accounts, artifacts, archeology, paleontology, reliable dating, and self-written documents. That's the preferred evidence used by historians to create a credible history.

That's not the evidence available for god figures, of which there are thousands. It's noteworthy that the gods, prophets, great sages, and theologians upon which religions are based have all died out. None are around or being born into our day to interview and check credentials. Those who do appear as our contemporaries always turn out to be either frauds or far less than claimed.

Notice that it's always in the ancient past when nothing can be verified with certainty that the great religious figures existed. Religions capitalize on the human inclination to ascribe greater credit to the unfamiliar than to the familiar. People and script in the distant past, from a different country, with a different language, somehow always seem more fascinating and believable than our neighbors and contemporary writings.

A case in point is Christianity.

(The following history of Christianity threw me for a loop when I first discovered it. As I learn more, I'm more and more astonished. But, as is apparent in our dissection of evolution, materialism, and religion thus far, consensus views being out of step with reality are not only common but expected. If what follows seems too unbelievable, please delve more deeply by perusing the sources in the Resource section for this chapter or Internet search any of the terms, names, or phrases.)

Noncontemporary Hearsay Evidence

Exceptional claims, particularly related to events in the misty past, demand evidence, not uncritical acceptance.

Instead, religions are usually founded on the most unreliable support of all, namely noncontemporary hearsay evidence. That means we today are relying on the writings of someone testifying about a religious figure. But that person is reporting what they heard or read about the stories of someone else who did not even live at the same time as the religious figure upon which the religion is based.

"In summary, the witness says a friend passed him a note from someone about what was overheard at a party about someone who said they heard from their girlfriend, who can't be found, that the defendant did it. Clearly the evidence is overwhelming and you must convict."

© Wysong   Figure 179

Imagine one day being dragged into court to face an accuser who got on the stand and said under oath, "I heard from someone who heard from someone else who heard from someone else—who can't be found and was not born until the year 2000—that you were a serial killer in 1961." There's no evidence other than the accuser's word. Of course, no judge or jury in a just society would take for granted the accuser's hearsay words. A qualified judge would throw the matter out before it ever got to trial.

Tragically, throughout history, the firm belief in such sham evidence has been used to kill and torture millions.

Courts interested in truth only allow direct eyewitness evidence, logic, expert witnesses, circumstantial evidence, scientific, and other demonstrative evidence. What courts forbid is hearsay evidence, particularly if it's noncontemporary.

Reliable Evidence

People today agree that many god figures, such as Hercules and Zeus, didn't exist. Reliable evidence is lacking.

Astonishingly, I found that there is scholarly debate today about whether Jesus is a historical figure or an imagined religious playmate. As noted in the previous chapter, even many of the earliest Christians did not espouse the belief.

Scholars rely upon tenuous evidence to argue that he did exist. But that's either because they have a vested interest in their own belief or position, or because it's safe. It's safe because it's impossible to prove a negative. One cannot prove that Santa Claus, tooth fairies, or any proposed figure of the past, like Jesus, did not exist. That would require universal knowledge of all potential hiding places in the universe which, of course, no one possesses.

True history, which is not tradition, myth, opinion, belief, or hearsay, traces to the sources. Generally, accepted historical figures such as Alexander the Great, the Caesars, Napoleon, Hitler, Greek philosophers, etc., are usually supported by artifacts, busts, first-hand writings, and eyewitness accounts.

However, no bust of Jesus sculpted by a contemporary can be found. None of the Bible writers describe the physical appearance of Jesus, as was common in historical writings about noted people. There are no proven Jesus artifacts, no eyewitness testimonies, no descendants with pedigrees, and no works of carpentry, dwellings, or written documents attributable to him. Although this is also true for other figures who are thought to be valid historically, it would seem that mountains of incontestable evidence would exist for Jesus, considered to be the same as the Creator by most Christians.

No Eyewitness Accounts

Although I thought, as do most others, that the Bible is a first-hand eyewitness account, the stories are actually from authors who lived after the events happened. Christian song stories, word of mouth accounts, and writings were passed on for decades and centuries throughout the Middle East and Roman Empire. Only later were writings winnowed into the holy books upon which billions of readers, today and in the past, base beliefs.

Imagine trying to recall accurately what somebody said a month ago, let alone decades or hundreds of years ago. Even if there were first-person accounts, imagine attempting to recall and write the exact words from another person decades after the words were spoken.

All the New Testament documents turn out to be just copies of copies of copies of noncontemporary hearsay evidence, the most unreliable of all evidence.

Moreover, the early church, the holder of the copies upon which the Bible was based, was not above fabrication and prevarication. For example, Ignatius of Loyola, the theologian founder of the Jesuits, wrote: "To be right in everything, we ought always to hold that the white which I see, is black if the Hierarchical Church so decides it." The early church father and sainted John Chrysostom wrote: "And often it is necessary to deceive, and to do the greatest benefits by means of this device, whereas he who has gone by a straight course has done great mischief to the person whom he has not deceived."

Contemporary Writers

I thought there surely must be support for Jesus from contemporary Roman, Jewish, or Greek writings. That turned out not to be true either.

Josephus was ostensibly a Jewish noble, a general in wars against the Romans, and then a defector who later even assumed the emperor Vespasian's family name of Flavius. Flavius Josephus, in his Antiquities book, was the earliest historian to mention Jesus and his brother, James. But he was not born until 37CE, which was after Jesus' reported death. He didn't write Antiquities until 93 CE. The small portion of his writings, about a paragraph, called the "Testimonium Flavianum," uncharacteristically (since Josephus was a Jew and remained such) affirms Jesus as the Messiah.

A survey by Feldman found that 4 scholars regard the passage as completely genuine, 6 more as mostly genuine; 20 accept it with some interpolations (putting words in another person's mouth—meaning later editors inserted the words and ascribed them to Josephus), 9 thought there to be several interpolations; 13 regard it as being totally an interpolation. The Caesar editors and/or the Catholic Eusebius reportedly did this insertion in the third to fourth century CE.

The reference to Jesus as Messiah would create some much-needed secular evidence for an earthly Jesus. Thus, it has been enthusiastically used by Christians ever since.

Huge amounts of ink have been spilled arguing whether Josephus affirms the existence of Jesus or not. In those puddles of ink can be found compelling evidence and arguments that Josephus was, in fact, a fictional character created by the Romans who devised Christianity to quash the continuously rebellious Jews. The New Testament stories, particularly the Gospels, written, accumulated, and given imprimatur by Caesars in the second to fourth centuries, follow quite closely the Josephus writings dated at 93 CE. This would make the Gospels not original accounts of Christianity, but copies of Roman writings some sixty years after the time of Jesus.

Most scholars regard the New Testament as pro-Roman. Others take it a step further arguing that Christianity is a mere Roman political device to create a story that fulfills awaited Jewish prophesies. By blending Judaism with the new Christian religion, the Caesars created a new Roman controlled messianic Jewish religion that was inclusive of all peoples under the Roman domain.

Roman Christianity was opened to Jew and Gentile alike, abrogating the Jewish claim to being god's chosen people. This had the effect of denying their clannishness which fed their rebellious proclivities. The Roman Jesus messiah preached "turn the other cheek" anti-sedition, and kept the money flowing to Rome with Jesus' command to "give to Caesar what is Caesar's." This pacifistic and Roman obedience message served well the interests of Caesars, and later their religious heirs, the <u>Roman</u> Catholic popes, who arrogated to themselves "Christ on Earth" authority and power.

If we keep in mind that Rome was the greatest power on Earth at the time, and primarily interested in keeping that position and power, such shenanigans with religion are to be expected. Think of the covert and deceptive things governments do to this day to retain or expand their power. Nothing is beyond bounds.

More so was this true in the past when plebian ignorance was enforced and people were constantly reminded of the consequences of disobedience by public executions and impaled bodies and heads scattered strategically about like billboards. Religions were the greatest threat since they required homage to other than Roman leaders and engendered enthusiastic rebellious gumption. To deal with that, the Caesars simply adopted religious beliefs into an amalgamated state religion with them at the head.

In that regard, it is of note that the first official Christian religion is called, to this day, the Holy Roman Catholic Church. This name embraces the very purpose of the Caesars: one universal (the definition of "catholic") Roman authority.

A common Christian retort to the idea that Rome and Christianity are inextricably related are the stories of early Christian persecution and martyrdom at the hands of Romans. But historical research demonstrates that Christians assimilated well into Roman society, as was the objective of the Caesars, and were not singled out for persecution, other than in stories created hundreds of years after a person's death.

But there was utility in this theme of heroic martyrdom, which, not coincidentally, emulated Greek, Roman, and Jewish mythologies. In ancient times, death was common everywhere all the time. So, a heroic death at least gave a person longevity in legends. Moreover, the state would kill people for picayune infractions, or even reports of such. It's likely that many Christian deaths were due to matters entirely unrelated to Christianity. As it turns out though, people were venerated hundreds of years after their deaths in order to serve the purposes of those venerating them. Stories of "martyrs" banded people together in an us-against-them mentality, used in religions down to this day.

An internet search will provide you (living 2000 years since the purported events) with a lifetime of study to try to determine if the words of someone of questionable existence, Flavius Josephus, writing in 93 CE, proves the existence of people living more than 60 years before that.

Pliny the Younger, Tacitus, Suetonius, Lucian, Origen and other early religious writers mentioning Jesus were also not contemporaries of Jesus. The dates of documents and the birthdates of the writers always give the writers away as unreliable storytellers expressing beliefs, not facts, about Jesus' existence.

All their testimony is, therefore, hearsay as well.

The Bible claims great multitudes and fame followed Jesus and that Jewish high priests and Roman officials knew of him. The Bible describes a three-day eclipse, an earthquake with graves opening up at the time of Jesus. Not a single historian, philosopher, scribe, astronomer or follower who lived during the alleged time of Jesus ever mentions him or these spectacular events. This is in spite of historians, poets, orators, and travelers aplenty in the time of Jesus.

Although Pontius Pilate has been verified archeologically, there is no secular evidence of him trying Jesus. Nor is there such evidence of Herod killing all the baby boys in Bethlehem (although the historical Herod seemed capable of such atrocity). Additionally, there are many Roman records of the killing of many messiahs, but none for Jesus.

This incredible silence is particularly noteworthy since Jerusalem was a center for scribes, books, education, and record keeping.

Philo Judaeus (also known as Philo of Alexander) was born in 20 BC and died 50 CE, spanning the entire life of Jesus. He was considered the most noteworthy Jewish-Hellenistic historian of the time. He lived and traveled in Greece and Jerusalem during the alleged life of Jesus and wrote detailed accounts of the Jewish events that occurred in the surrounding area and of a pre-Christian celestial Jewish messiah. In all of his volumes of writings, there isn't one reference to an earthly Jesus.

There is also no mention of an earthly Jesus in other historical writings of the time, such as from:

Aulus Perseus (60 CE)	Plutarch (46-119 CE)
Columella (1st cent, CE)	Pomponius Mela (40 CE)
Dio Chrysostom (1st cent, CE)	Rufus Curtius (1st cent, CE)
Justus of Tiberius (1st cent, CE)	Quintilian (35-LOO CE)
Livy (59 BC-17 CE)	Quintus Curtius (1st cent, CE)
Lucanus (63 AD)	Seneca (1 BC-65 CE)
Lucius Florus (1st cent, CE)	Silius Italicus (25-101 CE)
Petronius (66 CE)	Statius Caeliaus (1st cent, CE)
Phaedrus (15 BC-50 CE)	Theon of Smyrna (70-135 CE)
Phlegon (1st cent, CE)	Valerius Flaccus (1st cent, CE)
Pliny the Elder (23-79 CE)	Valerius Maximus (20 CE)

Gospels and Letters

Although I thought the four gospels were the only ones and were written by contemporary disciples of Jesus, that cannot be established as true. For one thing, the texts of the gospels do not identify their authors. Nor have any of the originals been found. For another, Irenaeus of Lyon, who lived in the middle of the second century, primarily chose certain gospels from among many that were lost or destroyed. Some early Christians accepted one gospel, others accepted four, while others accepted more than four.

Historians date the writing of the gospels from 70 CE to 90 CE which would put them beyond the feasible age of the disciples (given the short lifespans for common people of the day). Besides, the disciples were likely illiterate peasants not capable of the sophisticated language and style in the gospels.

The gospel writers do not admit to actually seeing Jesus. They were not eyewitnesses.

Paul's and others' New Testament letters which follow the gospels, reveal that the authors never met a physical Jesus.

The gospels do cite historically verified people, events, and places which seem to give credibility to the stories. But inventing historical events that are then seeded with real places and people is common in fictional stories. Historicizing myths is done even today in fiction such as Superman and Star Trek.

There Should Be Unequivocal Evidence

The laws of nature, the things of creation, are clear, unequivocal, and universally understood by people of all cultures and languages. There is no interpretation of 2+2 or gravity. People of all rank and file understand perfectly.

Jesus is worshipped as a god-man on Earth in whom all must believe to be saved. If that be the case, it seemed to me that the Creator of the universe would be capable of making sure the evidence for the existence of Jesus on Earth was overwhelming unambiguous and crystal clear, like 2+2=4.

The question loomed as to why a pivotal and critical figure that people are required to believe in was not born in our modern era. Rather than handwritten scraps of copies of copies of unknown origin, there could be first-hand documents, photographs, recordings, interviews, videos, DNA testing, forensic technology, and other means to prove beyond any doubt existence and acts.

Nevertheless, people en masse, Christian and not, believe Jesus and his acts are certain. I did too. That's what happens when faith trumps reason and evidence, or lack thereof.

To repeat, a quick internet search will provide an almost endless array of information briefly touched upon here. Search words and names in this chapter as well as phrases such as "did Jesus exist," "pagan origins of Christianity," "origin of the Bible," etc. (truthbeknown.com is a good start.)

Why Belief

There were cultural and religious reasons for belief in a messiah. In 70 CE, under Titus, the Romans laid waste to Jerusalem. About a thousand desperate Jews later took a stand on Masada and rather than be captured or slaughtered, committed suicide. Indeed, these were times in need of a savior.

The Jews had prophesized one in the Old Testament and fervently hoped one would appear to lead them out from the oppression of the Romans and into the Promised Land. As this oppression was escalating, savior stories were being composed and written, and messiahs popped up here and there. These provided hope and served to authenticate Hebrew scripture and validate the Jewish priests. Forced fulfillment of prophecy was common.

Today many scholars (not all) agree that an unremarkable Clark Kent physical Jesus did exist. However, they do not agree that he was the Superman version walking on water, raising the dead, etc. Myths abounded in the time of Jesus, as even the Bible admits. (2Peter1:16) Scholars thus conclude, in the absence of any evidence to the contrary, and due to the shared features with prior pagan gods described in the previous chapter, that the Superman version of Jesus was a myth as well. They contend that the sensational version of Jesus, complete with a resurrection and the ability to erase sin was needed.

The Roman goal was enduring awe and dedication from the masses, so a fantastic story worthy of a god fit the bill. Once the state fostered Christianity with Caesars as god personified and the fulfillment of Jewish messiah stories (Roman popes taking over later where Caesars left off), people had little choice but to believe. Today, however, it's the sheer momentum and ubiquity of the belief in itself that is compelling. People find it hard even to imagine that a belief so prevalent, supported by so much voice and ink, and with such stature, architectural presence, religious hierarchy, scholarship, and wealth could be questionable. I had been swept along in this belief as well.

27
HOW BEST TO
MEASURE HOLY BOOKS

The history of holy books does not inspire confidence that they are anything more than human-created artifacts. With regard to the Bible, the fact that virtually all of its doctrines predate it in pagandom demolishes the claim that it is unique.

Nevertheless, religions and their scholars contend that what their books say proves they are the product of the Creator's hand. So, the common urging is for unbelievers to just read the books and the divine inspiration and truth will become apparent.

That means the books, at the least, should comport with our own reasoning sensibilities. They should match what we can know about the Creator by looking at the reality that has been created and the created laws governing it.

Vedic Holy Writings

In the Ordinances of Manu—a Vedic legal scripture (500 CE), it's said: "the king should cause his (a person of low rank who spits upon another of high rank) two lips to be cut off; and if he make water upon him, his penis; and if he break wind upon him, his buttocks . . . Anything pecked by birds, smelt by a cow . . . sneezed on or polluted by head lice becomes pure by throwing earth upon it."

This holy book goes on to describe that one becomes a heron for stealing fire or a house-wasp for stealing a house utensil. For stealing silk, linen, cotton, a cow, or molasses, one is reborn as either a partridge, frog, curlew, iguana, or bird. A Brahman who has violated his rules returns as the ghost Ulkamakhu, an eater of vomit.

Such illogical and unjust nonsense is inconsistent with natural law and conscience and thus reflects human authorship, not Creator authorship.

The Koran

The Muslim Koran says: "Prophet, make war on the unbelievers and the hypocrites and deal rigorously with them. Hell shall be their home: an evil fate." – 9:73; "Believers, make war on the infidels who dwell around you. Deal firmly with them . . ." – 9:123. Many other examples of dealing harshly with unbelievers can be found at Qu'ran:2:15; 2:89; 2:98; 2:122; 2:126; 2:168; 2:176; 2:190-93; 2:216; 2:217-18; 3:10; 3:19; 3:118; 3:140; 3:169; 4:46; 4:55-56; 5:86; 6:70; 6:125. According to the Hadith (number 2,562 in the collection known as the Sunan at-Tirmidhi), believers who blow themselves up to kill unbelievers can do so with the incentive of, "The least [reward] for the people of Heaven is 80,000 servants and 72 wives, over which stands a dome of pearls, aquamarine, and ruby."

Such injustice and unverifiable promises are not consistent with natural law nor conscience and thus reflect the authorship of humans, not the Creator.

The Bible

Martin Luther began the movement away from religious authority. He assumed the Bible was written by the Creator and was the source of redemption, not the Catholic church. But he didn't go far enough in his urgings for disintermediation between man and god. The religions that arose out of his rebellion still had intermediaries between individuals and their Creator, namely the Bible and its interpreters.

That's fine as long as the book accurately reflects what we can know about the Creator from the creation itself.

<u>The Creator's natural laws are reasonable, truthful, and consistent.</u> <u>A Creator book must be the same.</u>

However, the Bible says:

A fish swallowed a man who then lived for three days in its belly and then was spit out on dry land. (Jonah 1-2)

A boat could hold and feed breeding representatives of all land creatures on Earth for a year. (Genesis 7-8)

The Earth will remain forever (Ecclesiastes 1:4) —but that contradicts the Creator's Second Law of Thermodynamics that demands all things eventually degrade to absolute disorder.

Genesis says the creation occurred in steps, days, interpreted by some as twenty-four hours and others as thousands of years each. But that contradicts the absolute interdependency of planets, moon, stars, and sun as well as that of plant and animal creatures.

In the book of Joshua, it says the sun stood still permitting the Jews to slaughter non-believers. (Joshua 10:12) This implies that the sun rotates around the Earth and denies the catastrophic effects of a solar system in stasis. In addition, the Bible wrongly says the Earth has foundations, skirts, edges, ends, and corners.

The god of the Bible is said to do nothing without revealing it first to his prophets. (Amos 3:7) But it would be impossible for an infinite god to reveal all actions to a finite mortal, nor is there any evidence the Creator has done so.

Leprosy, venereal disease, and other ailments are said to be cured by treatments such as sprinkling the blood of two turtledoves around a house, getting rid of demons, or being dipped in water seven times. (Leviticus 13; 14; 15)

Men who lap water like a dog are claimed to be the best soldiers. (Judges 7:5-)

An entire army would flee because one soldier was killed with a stone. (1 Samuel 17:49-51)

A plague that killed 24,000 could be stopped by thrusting a spear into the genitals of a woman. (Numbers 25:8)

Jesus says only those without sin should judge, but that would mean courts would be vacant of judges and juries. (John 8: 3-11)

A dead person could come to life and sneeze seven times because a prophet laid on him. (2 Kings 4:34-36)

. . . and so on.

Given that the Creator is the epitome of reason, truth, consistency, and justice, such attributions are, therefore, slanderous and blasphemous.

The Creator's natural laws are consistent and not contradictory. Therefore, a Creator book must be the same.

However, the Bible says:

A person cannot live and see the Bible god vs god talked face to face with men, wrestled with a man and put his leg out of joint, and demanded that a camp be kept clean so he could walk through it at night. (Exodus 33:20;1Timothy 6:16 vs Exodus 33:11, Numbers 12:5,8; Numbers 14:13-20/Genesis 32:24-30 vs Leviticus 26:12; Deuteronomy 23:14;1Chronicles 17:6)

No man can hear god's voice vs he speaks and is heard. (John 5:37 vs Mark 1:11; Mark 9:7)

God does not change his mind vs he changes it. (Psalm 89:34; Malachi 3:6; Hebrews 1:10-12; James 1:17-20; vs Exodus 32:14; Numbers 14:13-20; Hebrews 7:18; 8:6-13)

Women with no hymen should be stoned to death vs there should be forgiveness for fornication. (Deuteronomy 22:20,21 vs John 8:4-11)

God cannot defeat chariots of iron vs he is all-powerful. (Judges 1:19 vs Job 37:23; Revelations 4:11, 7:12)

Wisdom, knowledge, and pride are good vs those attributes are condemned. (Acts 17:11 vs Proverbs 19:8; Matthew 10:16,19; Romans 12:2; Philippians 1:9-10;1Thessalonians 5:21;1Peter 3:15)

Animals are to be sacrificed, maimed, and given diseases vs cruelty to animals is condemned. (Leviticus, Deuteronomy vs Proverbs 12:10)

God is not all-knowing vs he is all-knowing. (Exodus 3:7-; 12:13; 33; 34-; Numbers 12:5-;1Samuel 8:21- vs Jeremiah 39; Ezekial 7:3,8; Revelations)

God promises not to get angry vs he does get angry and slaughters thousands. (Isaiah 54:9-10; Jeremiah 3:12 vs throughout the Bible)

God demands aid, love, and assisting the enemy vs commands killing and plundering them. (Exodus:23:4,5 vs Numbers 31; Deuteronomy 13)

The Bible god is perfect vs he has regrets. (Deuteronomy 32:4; Psalm 18:30 vs Genesis 6:7; Judges 2:18;1Chronicles 21:15; Jeremiah 26:19; Joel 2:13)

An eye for eye justice vs forgive and turn the other cheek. (Leviticus 24:16- 22 vs Matthew 5:38,39)

It is impossible to fall from grace vs it is possible. (John 3:16; Acts 16:31 vs Joshua 2:13;1Corinthians 5:11-13; Galatians 5:19-21;1Timothy 5:8;1Peter 1:17; Revelations 21:8)

People should be critical and prudent vs believe like children and don't question. (Proverbs 14:15; Romans 12:2;1Thessalonians 5:21 vs Matthew 18:3; Mark 10:15; Luke 18:17;1Timothy 1:4; 6:4; 2 Timothy 2:23; Titus 3:9)

Distinguishing good from bad is condemned vs exercising conscience is praised. (Genesis 3:4 vs Hebrews 5:14)

Divorce is okay vs it's sinful. (Deuteronomy 24:1,3; Isaiah 50:1 vs Matthew 19:9; Mark 10:11-12; Luke 16:18)

Jesus brings peace vs he comes to divide. (John 14:27; Acts 10:36;1Corinthians 14:33; Hebrews 12:14 vs Matthew 10:21, 22, 34-36; Mark 13:12- 13, Luke 12:51-53; 14:26; 21:16-17;1Thessalonians 5:3)

Jesus says anyone who calls another a fool is condemned vs he calls people fools. (Matthew 5:22 vs Matthew 23:17)

Jesus says commandments must be obeyed to be saved vs he disobeys them. (Mark 10:19 vs Matthew 12:46-50; 19:29; 21:1; Mark 2:24-27 [work on Sabbath]; 3:31-35; 5:13; 10:29,30, Luke 8:20-21; 9:61-62; 18:29-30 [disrespect parents] Luke 19:29-35 [theft])

Defend beliefs vs don't argue. (Proverbs 14:15; Romans 12:2;1Thessalonians 5:21;1Peter 3:15 vs1Timothy 6:20; 2 Timothy 2:14, 23-26)

Don't judge vs do judge. (John 8:15-, 12:47; Romans 14:13 vs1Corinthians 5:3, 6:2, 11-13;1Timothy 5:20; 2 Timothy 4:1,8)

The second coming will be attended by signs and miracles vs there will be no signs and miracles. (Matthew 24:29-30; Mark 13; Luke 21:10-11 vs Luke 17:20-)

Only those who believe in Jesus will have everlasting life vs those who don't will also have everlasting life—albeit in Hell. (John 3:16 vs Revelations 14:10,11)

People are saved by faith vs they are saved by works. (John 3:16; Romans 3:27; 9:32 vs Exodus 32:33; Matthew 5:48; 24:13; Mark 9:41; 10:21; Luke 10:25-37; John 8:31; Romans 1:20; 2:6; 11:21-22; 1Corinthians 9:24; 10:12; 2 Corinthians 6:3-10; Philippians 2:12; 3:13; Hebrews 6:4-8; 10:26-31; 12:1; James 2:17,24; 1John 2:3-4; 3:10; Revelations 2:6)

People must imitate Paul vs one must follow God, not men. (I Corinthians 4:16; 2 Corinthians 11:20 vs Matthew 10:38; Mark 8:34; 2 Peter 2:19)

Jesus was crucified on the third hour vs the sixth hour. (Mark 15:25 vs John 19: 14,15)

Polygamy is okay vs it's not okay. (Genesis 19, 20, 21, 29 vs Matthew 19:3-9; Ephesians 5:28-31;1Corinthians 7:2,12-16;1Timothy 3:2)

Prophecy is good vs it's bad. (Acts 19:6; 1Corinthians 14; 1Thessalonians 5:20 vs Leviticus 19:31; Leviticus 20:27)

People must follow law vs they must follow their conscience. (Romans 11:21,22; 1Timothy 1:8-10; 1John 2:3,4 vs Romans 2:15)

Bible apologists can respond to any of the above with claims about context, syntax, variable meanings in ancient languages, and so on. I once did that too. But really, people the world over are encouraged to, on their own, read the Bible and gather its truths and inspiration. Reading the verses cited above for what they clearly say proves the opposite, namely that the Bible is neither consistent with facts nor consistent with itself.

Surely the Creator would not create a book with such vulnerabilities. To make the attribution is, therefore, slanderous and blasphemous.

The final and ultimate test of holy book origination is to determine if it is a paragon of perfect justice, as it must be if it is a product of the Creator.

28
THE ULTIMATE HOLY BOOK TEST

Natural laws are perfectly ethical in that they are sure, reliable, predictable, reasonable, consistent with fact, and are just in that they exert themselves with no partiality.

Ethics, including kindness, respect for life and property, fairness, and honesty, are a reflection of those laws. Like nature's laws, which are true and consistent, not arbitrary, right and wrong are not arbitrary either. Where the distinction between right and wrong seems blurred, the created conscience within each of us is the arbiter.

Since holy books are claimed to be the source of ethics and morality, one would most certainly expect those books to reflect the highest conscience and consistency with the ethical purity of the laws of creation.

This is what the Bible god/Jesus commands or did:

Kills the firstborn humans and animals of the entire Egyptian nation and commanded that the event is celebrated yearly as Passover. (Exodus 12; 14; Romans 9:17)

Dwarfs, people with flat noses, those lame, with broken feet, unrounded corners of beards, and all people other than one race, the Jews (who, not so coincidentally wrote the Bible words), are in disfavor. (Leviticus 21; 29; Numbers 14:2)

People are condemned for ten generations if they have mutilated sex organs or are of illegitimate birth. (Deuteronomy 23:1-)

Kills people for making an ointment, burning incense, taking a census (75,000 slaughtered), for not cutting the ends of young boys' penises off, or eating fat. (Exodus 30:33; 2 Chronicles 26:19-;1Chronicles 21; Torah)

50,000 threescore and ten men are killed for looking in a box. (1Samuel 6:19)

Children were forced to wander and die in a wilderness for forty years because of the sins of the parents. (Numbers 14:33)

Killing unbelievers is commanded. (Deuteronomy 13; 2 Kings 10)

Children and their children, and a king who burned incense were condemned to leprosy. (2 Chronicles 26:19-)

Orders that young boys who disobey their parents or curse them be stoned to death. (Exodus 21:17; Deuteronomy 21:18-21)

Starved people, opened the earth to swallow them when they desired to eat, and then sent a plague to kill 14,700 more who complained about it. (Numbers 16)

Killed people for working or gathering sticks on the Sabbath, and for profaning it. (Numbers 15:32-36: Exodus 31:14,15)

Induced snakes to bite people and sent bears out of the woods to tear apart forty-two children who called a man "baldhead." (Jeremiah 8:18; 2 Kings 2:23,24)

Sent a famine that forced people to eat their children, and beheaded seventy innocent sons and put their heads in a pile as a lesson. (2 Kings 6:28-)

Tells men to kill their wives (even if pregnant), children, and friends if they disagree with them on religion, commands no mercy be given and is wrathful if lives are spared. (Deuteronomy 13:6-; Exodus 32:27)

Condoned Jael lying to a man and driving a tent peg into his temple while he slept. (Judges 4:17-21)

Is partial to one race and keeps them in good graces if they commit murder, bash babies to the ground, and rip open pregnant women. (Exodus 22:20; Hosea 13:16; Joshua 10:1-42; 1 Samuel 15:3)

Condones the practice of incest, adultery, genocide, sexism, keeping concubines (300 for Solomon), keeping and beating slaves (with the only limitation being to not injure their eyes or teeth). (Genesis 19; 20; 28; 29; Exodus 21; . . . throughout Torah)

Commands the killing of adulterers and non-virgins brought to marriage. (Deuteronomy 22:20-)

Commanded Jews to slaughter entire cities and to steal all their goods, kill and maim the animals, but keep alive the young virgin maidens to rape for their pleasure. (Deuteronomy 2:34; 3:6; 13; Judges 21; Numbers 31)

Equates love with having himself in the form of Jesus sacrificially tortured to death. Guilt for this is collectivized by demanding that all people be responsible for the torture that was necessary to make amends for an original sin for which all humans but Adam and Eve had no part, but for which all of humanity is condemned to eternal torture in hell if they don't agree. (Genesis 3; Romans 5:12,14;1John 1:8-10).

Christians, when confronted by such Bible atrocity, disassociate themselves by arguing that the Old Testament is figurative, or "old law," and not relevant to them. But the Bible itself says adding to or taking away from it is punishable by death. Also, Christians consider the god of the Old Testament to be the same as Jesus as part of the Trinity. No Christian would argue that their god and Jesus disagree on anything. So, what is attributable to god in the Old Testament is attributable to Jesus.

None of this is to say Jews and Christians have been uniquely cruel and barbaric. They simply reflected the moral landscape of their eras. The Jews lived amongst Persians, Babylonians, Assyrians, Greeks, Egyptians, and other ancient cultures; Christians lived among Romans and others in which beheadings, rape, pillaging, ripping tongues out, impaling, skinning alive . . . were common. It's important to note it was all done in the name of the respective gods. But this context does not excuse the immorality. Nor does it show the Bible god uniquely benevolent as commonly thought, much less consistent with the pure ethics and justice of the Creator.

Either the justice, ethics, and truth we see in the creation do not reflect its Creator, or the Bible is not of the Creator's hand.

As an aside, consider that Bible-based religions condemn the Muslim atrocities done in the name of Allah and the Koran. Yet the Bible god commands and does many of the very things Islamic statists do. That's because Islam is derived primarily from the Bible. If the Bible were practiced as commanded by its god/Jesus, all Jews and Christians would be committing the unspeakable injustice and barbarity of not only jihadists but the Bible itself.

Thomas Paine said he could believe no religion that would "shock the mind of a child," that "it is not a God, just and good, but a devil, under the name of God, that the Bible describes," and "there are matters in the Bible said to be done by the express commandment of God that are shocking to humanity and to every idea we have of moral justice."

George Carlin, the comedian, said in referencing the Bible: "Religion has actually convinced people that there's an invisible man – living in the sky – who watches everything you do, every minute of every day. And the invisible man has a special list of ten things he does not want you to do. And if you do any of these ten things, he has a special place, full of fire and smoke and burning and torture and anguish, where he will send you to live and suffer and burn and choke and scream and cry forever and ever 'til the end of time . . . But He loves you!"

Unfortunately, he, like about everyone else, and me for a time, mistakenly and unfairly equate holy books and religions with the Creator of the universe. I found no holy book that could live up to the truthful, logical, consistent, and just qualities evident in the creation and within conscience. I had to come to the inevitable conclusion that by failing those attributes, all human-made holy books prove themselves to be exactly what they appear to be, human-made, not Creator-made.

29
RELIGION UNLEASHED

When I was immersed in religion, the Bible god's atrocities, like killing the first-born of an entire nation, were just excused as moral lessons about obedience to god. It's amazing what the mind can justify in service to a belief.

Today, Muslims following the god of the Qu'ran and Hadith can kill women for speaking to a man without permission. That can be done by having her throat cut, drenching her with gasoline and setting her aflame, and stoning or shooting her. If a woman is raped and she doesn't have male witnesses who will testify on her behalf, she may be accused of fornication or adultery and then be either killed or imprisoned.

The Qur'an's god says people who do not accept Islam are to be killed. Islamists who convert to another religion are to be killed. Those who question doctrine are to be killed. The Afghan Taliban amputated limbs and executed accused Qur'an violators in front of soccer stadium crowds shouting "Allahu Akbar" (god is great). The blood-soaked fields had to be excavated and restored to prevent players slipping. The majority of Muslims (by some reports, 70% or more) believe suicide bombings are holy acts that efficiently transport martyrs to paradise where a bounty of virgins awaits men and virile men await women.

The Bible, which was the template for the Qur'an, states that any who worship gods other than Yahweh are to be slaughtered: "Thou shalt surely smite the inhabitants . . . with the edge of the sword . . .

and all that is therein, and the cattle thereof, with the edge of the sword." (Deut. 13:15,16) "All therein" includes women, children, old folk, and the poor. Those who don't do the killing in the name of the Bible god are also to be put to death.

The Old Testament Bible god also demands death for numerous other transgressions, such as taking the Lord's name in vain, homosexuality, working on the Sabbath, cursing one's father or mother, adultery, being a non-virgin when married, etc. (Lev. 24:16; Ex. 31:15, 21:17; Lev. 20:10) Today, Judaism and Christianity put such Bible commands aside. However, the Bible presents no real choice since those who "add to or take away from" it (do not follow all of it to a tee) are worthy of death. (Deuteronomy 4:2; 12:32; 13; Proverbs 30:6; Matthew 5:17; Revelation 22:18-19)

The New Testament, today thought to advocate only love and peace, has been interpreted differently through the ages. Jesus exclaimed that he came to divide and likens heretics to branches to be burned: "Think not that I am come to send peace on earth: I came not to send peace, but a sword." (John 15:6; Matthew 10:34) Christian verses can also be found to lay the groundwork for persecution of nonbelievers. (1Corinthians 1:10-13, 3:3, 11:19, 14:33; Galatians 5:19-21; 2Peter 2:1; Romans 16:17; Philippians 4:2; Jude 19)

Acting out such admonition, the Catholic Church did not withdraw its judgment of deicide (killing Jesus) against the Jews until after World War II. This stance justified the killing of millions of Jews up to that time.

In 1348, King Philip of France consulted Bible clerics about how to fix a pestilence. They told him it was due to blasphemy among the populace. To fix that he made the penalty for one blasphemy the loss of one lip, the second infraction would result in slicing off the other lip, and with the third infraction, the tongue would be removed.

To make sure the disease disappeared, the Christian clerics also told Philip to forbid black clothes, showing any grief (which could be interpreted by god as not being happy about the punishment he was visiting on people), working after noon on Saturday, swearing, living in sin, or gambling. (The dice makers quickly turned to rosary making.) Nevertheless, Philip was evidently not hard enough on the folks. Twenty-five thousand died anyway.

In 1095 CE, Pope Urban II ordered the first Crusade in order to reclaim the Holy Land. Muslims, Jews, heretics, pagans, and atheists were targets. The rallying cry was "Deus vult," meaning "God wills it" As an incentive, the pope promised salvation by way of indulgences. These, he promised, would reduce the amount of punishment the Bible god would exact for sins. Since everyone knew they had sinned, avoiding hell and purgatory was motivating. Additional bonuses were earthly rewards, including plunder from conquest, the forgiveness of debts, freedom from taxes, fame, property, and political power.

From Europe, the tens of thousands of Crusading pilgrims and knights traveled by sea or by foot more than 2000 miles over snowy mountains and across deserts. About one in twenty survived.

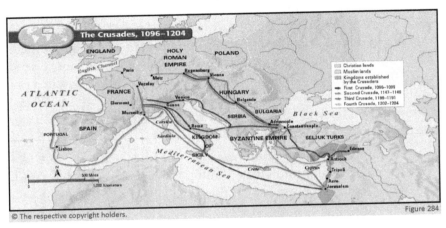
Figure 284

They had to carry food, water, hard money, armor, siege equipment, tents, and drive thousands of animals. The consequences of sieges lasting months and years were underestimated. Starving and dehydrated soldiers were called upon to engage in brutal hand-to-hand combat. Rotting bodies, waste, and feces piled up. People were reduced to drinking urine, eating grass and leather, and cannibalism. Disease flourished.

Godly plundering the countryside for supplies and loot left resident peasants to starve. People in cities who would not give over control were subject to siege and then slaughtered, raped, pillaged, enslaved, and tortured in every imaginable way. Human heads and putrefying horses and cattle were catapulted over walls into cities under siege.

The vanquished may be blinded, and noses, lips, tongues, and ears sliced off as punishments for resistance. The slaughter by Crusaders created rivers of blood in the cities they entered. In the Albigensian Crusade, the battle cry of the papal legate was: "Kill them all, surely the Lord discerns which ones are His." Irreplaceable art and monuments were desecrated and melted for coin. Ancient libraries were destroyed. Muslims, tit for tat, did likewise. Both sides justified it in the name of their gods and holy books.

An estimated nine million people and countless animals died miserable deaths during the 200 years of the Crusades.

Vanity, greed, corruption, factionalism, power mongering, and internecine battles occurred within each religion. It seems their gods were fickle, wavering between which enemy or faction to starve, mutilate, torture, and slaughter.

The perfectly just Creator of the universe can't be found anywhere in these acts. Only people doing the evil they can do, particularly when the state merges with religion and people abandon conscience in favor of man-made religions. Where Muslim and Christian communities merged after a conquest or treaty and followed common decency toward one another, bishops would be sent to put an end to such devil's play. Christians who were enjoying the ungodly Mideastern custom of bathing were also set straight.

Battle of Ascalon engraving during the first Crusade

Figure 285

Cycles of religious revenge continue to this day with no denoument. The Crusades are thought to be the beginning of east gods meeting west gods and the current Mideast animosity. However, godly Persians, Greeks, Huns, Goths, Avars, Romans, and Byzantines warred and mutilated one another back and forth for thousands of years prior. Who struck the first blow thousands of years prior to the Crusades is unknown. But religious justification was always there.

The Inquisition was begun in 1184 by Pope Lucius III and continued into the nineteenth century. Truth became whatever could be elicited by a tortured confession (trial by ordeal), not what the truth naturally was. Even young children were tried and any accusation by anyone was permitted. Defenses were not tolerated. Crimes included changing bedding on a Friday, not eating pork, dressing in certain ways, wearing earrings, speaking in foreign languages, owning foreign books, casual swearing, criticizing a priest, and failing to show due reverence to the Inquisitors. The accused had to confess to sins even though they were not told what they were accused of. Torture continued until they guessed the right sin, went mad, died, or committed suicide.

The accused had to pay for all trial and torture expenses, including wine, meals, travel expenses, and fees for guards, judges, torturers, and executioners. What remained of the accused's estate usually went to the Catholic church. Children of accused rich people were left to beg and starve in the streets. This was so profitable that dead people were dug up, tried, and their heirs disinherited of possessions.

The shedding of blood was proscribed, but that made any other macabre and sadistic torture fair game. Disemboweling innocent people in front of their families could be done with little bloodletting. Squassation was also bloodless. In this godly torture, the accused's hands were tied behind the back, and then the victim was hoisted into the air by the wrists. Weights could be tied to the feet so that when the victim was released and then jolted to a stop before reaching the ground, the shoulders would be completely disarticulated.

Devices were invented that could be used to crush bones and heads and stretch mouths and joints to create as much pain as possible—without blood. Death and unconsciousness were the only things that limited pain.

HOLY TOOLS OF THE INQUISITION

Spanish Spider

Spanish Spider: Abiuro - "I recant" – was the Latin engraved into the side of this double-ended two-pronged fork, the only words that the victim was allowed to speak. The head was tilted back and the top two prongs embedded deeply under the chin; the bottom prongs were embedded into the flesh above the sternum. The leather strap was fastened tightly behind the neck.

Heretic's Fork: Suspended from the ceiling, the cold or hot pincers could be used to lift a person into the air, using the soft flesh of the buttocks, belly or breasts—or the eyes and ears, much like a bowling ball would be held.

Heretic's Fork

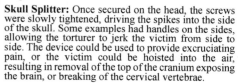

Tongue Tearer: This iron device was used to grab the tongue within its rough grippers. Once a firm hold was maintained, the screw could be firmly tightened and the tongue was roughly torn from the head. Some versions contained staggered teeth which shredded the tongue into ribbons.

Tongue Tearer

Skull Splitter: Once secured on the head, the screws were slowly tightened, driving the spikes into the side of the skull. Some examples had handles on the sides, allowing the torturer to jerk the victim from side to side. The device could be used to provide excruciating pain, or the victim could be hoisted into the air, resulting in removal of the top of the cranium exposing the brain, or breaking of the cervical vertebrae.

Skull Splitter

Breast Ripper

Breast Ripper: Used red-hot to mark the breast of unmarried mothers. For interrogation it was used on women accused of heresy, blasphemy, adultery, self-induced abortion, erotic white magic, and any other crime that the Inquisitors selected. The claws were used, either cold or heated, on a female's exposed breasts—rendering them into bloody pulps. A variation was called the Spider. This consisted of clawed bars which protruded from the wall. A woman was pulled alongside the bars until her breasts were torn away.

Spanish Crusher

Spanish Crusher: This nutcracker-like device could be used to crush anything that could fit between the jaws—fingers, thumbs, toes, ears, etc.

Knee Splitter: This device permanently destroyed the knee and elbow joints by placing the limb between the teeth and then slowly tightening the screws.

Thumb Screws: These screws would either crush the thumb between two hard surfaces, or the screw would be forced through the skin surrounding the thumb attaching it to a piece of wood.

Knee Splitter

Thumb Screws

The Pear: The vaginal pear (along with its infamous cousins, the anal pear and the oral pear) was inserted into the appropriate orifice. Upon insertion, a key was turned, causing spikes to emerge from the pear and wedge it in the victim, ensuring it could not be removed. Because it damaged the body only inside body cavities, it could be used to extract confessions and pass them off as freely given. A man accused of homosexual acts would be tortured anally. A woman accused of carnality with the Devil or his familiars would get the vaginal version. A blasphemer or heretic would get the oral pear. The pointed prongs at the end of the segments ripped into the throat, the intestines, or the cervix and proved almost always eventually fatal.

Impalement: A post was forced through the entire body of the victim, entering the rectum and exiting through the mouth or neck.

The Pear

Impalement

Figure 184

Anyone could be accused of heresy, such as denying that god took the stars out of his treasure chest each evening to hang them from the dome of the heavens (Saint Philastrius). To make sure a person was telling the truth, they would be "put to the question." If under torture the contumacious heretic still denied the charge and refused to repent, and there was any evidence (like the word of an accuser) that they were guilty, they could then be put to death. For those who later withdrew their confession, they would be put to death at the stake as a relapsed heretic. Putting them high above the fire to slow roast was preferred.

If the persecutors could have found a way to torture someone forever, imagining they were emulating the Bible god's eternal hell, they would have gladly cranked the screws or stoked the fire endlessly.

Having gathered the always sure confession, the clerics would set the innocent and pathetic victims—no longer able to walk or even close their mouths from the fractures and disarticulations—in a collapsed heap on the street to succumb to disease and starvation.

Even the more reasonable philosopher, Thomas Aquinas, fulminated about heresy and sanctioned burning witches at the stake. He was sainted. What else could Aquinas preach, since the Bible god said, "Thou shalt not suffer a witch to live." (Exodus 22:18; Deuteronomy 18:10-12) Most everyone who was accused and then tortured admitted to the crime. As for the argument that torture can cause people to confess anything, the holy clerics had a perfectly logical reply: If people were telling the truth, god would give them the strength to not admit to a lie.

Some estimate eleven million women were killed as witches. The old, widowed, ugly, mentally disturbed and epileptics were fitting suspects. Burning witches saved the rest of the population from these mortal demons who shapeshifted into cats, and molded candles out of human fat to make themselves invisible. Besides, witches were going to end up being burned forever anyway, so why not help the Bible god by giving them a head start?

Other participants in this incredible brutality included the protestant, John Calvin, the founder of the Presbyterian Church, and Martin Luther.

The inquisitors reasoned that it was the evil, the sin they were punishing, not the person. How could one be too cruel to evil, sin, or the devil? Besides, what's a little torture and murder if you are saving a soul for eternity? A torturer didn't even need a thick skin since any cries of pain were just a ruse by victims to elicit sympathy, a mere ploy to free them so they could continue to do the devil's work. The impassible Inquisitors were never fooled. They knew better since all of the devil's minions were immune to pain.

One woman was thought possessed because she didn't make the sign of the cross before eating a head of lettuce. She explained that she did not know the devil was sitting on the lettuce. A priest took care of that by exorcizing the evil spirit off the head of lettuce, thus absolving the woman. Since the Bible says Jesus once put evil spirits in some pigs, then obviously creatures could be home to demons. A rooster was unaccountably found with an egg. He was tried in a solemn court of justice and burnt as a sorcerer. St. Bernard excommunicated a swarm of flies that irreverently interrupted his sermon.

Cats were viewed as agents of the devil and killed with impunity. An unintended consequence was the proliferation of rats carrying the Black Death that killed almost half of Europe's population in the Middle Ages.

The ill were persecuted for the impiety of seeking medical relief rather than paying for holy relics and using saints' bones. Illness and disease were thought of as divine providence, and trying to interfere with it would surely make the Bible god even angrier. Surgery was forbidden and believed unnecessary because the savior, not a knife, was the way to cast out demons. There was also the danger of fiddling with a bone residing somewhere in the torso that was the nucleus of the resurrection body. Imagine the disaster if a surgeon removed that by accident or shifted it out of place such that a patient might head off in the wrong direction after death. Anesthetics for childbirth were disallowed because experiencing Eve's curse of the pain of childbirth was a divine duty.

Railroads and telegraphs were pronounced as heralds of the antichrist. Natural gas was opposed because it was the noxious emanation from the bowels of the Earth where evil spirits resided.

A petition presented to the American Congress in 1864 condemned the extraction of petroleum from the Earth since the Bible god was obviously storing it there as fuel for the conflagration of Armageddon. Life insurance was seen as an evil attempt to thwart the will of god.

Mennonite, Amish, Mormon, Jewish and other clannish religious groups suffer terribly due to the inbreeding that is encouraged (if not mandated) by their Bible god. There are some fifty genetic diseases endemic in these groups so far identified. The misery this misguided attempt at Biblical homogenous purity, racism, and supremacism has visited on families is incalculable.

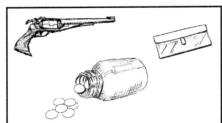

Suicide and Torture – Shunning, excommunication, and disfellowshipping are practiced by many religions to this day. The social torture from this practice has caused an extraordinarily high rate of suicide among those who are ostracized in this way.

© Wysong   Figure 185

There is a verse in the Bible that says "By their works you will know them." When this is applied inwardly to religious institutions and their history, the conclusion that they are human-made is unavoidable.

Modern religions set aside their past evils. You know, those folks way back then just didn't have the spiritual insight modern religions have. So, citing scripture, forgive and forget. Infallibility marches on.

However, a thinking person cannot forgive and forget an immoral tradition. Particularly is this so when the underlying sin and hubris of attributing holy book cruelty and injustice to the Creator persists.

Today, children are sent off to holy book classes that celebrate a god who takes joy in killing babies and commanding parents to stone to death children who backtalk. Religions create an ominous lingering potential for the resurgence of atrocities should the state ever unleash them to do as their holy books demand.

30
END(S) OF THE WORLD

The ace in the hole for many Bible believers is prophecy. For example, one Internet Bible apologist proclaims that "2,500 prophecies appear in the pages of the Bible, about 2,000 of which already have been fulfilled to the letter—no errors."

I was led along by this as well. It works if you confine yourself to limited information. However, in no case is there a documented example of people reading a holy book prophecy at a certain date, then taking action based upon it, then having it come true at a later date.

Even if a prophecy happens to predict accurately, that would not single a holy book out as being unique or divinely written. Quantum reality (discussed in the coming chapters) permits clairvoyance and there is substantial evidence, in real time, today, that people not claiming to be inspired by god can make accurate predictions (prophesies).

Foreknowledge has allegedly also been discovered in ancient cultures predating the Bible. For example, the Dogon tribe in West Africa has lore dating to 3200 BC about a companion star to Sirius. They say it has a 50-year elliptical orbit, is super dense, and rotates on its axis. This lore has been confirmed and the star is called Sirius B. It's smaller than Earth, invisible to the naked eye, not discovered by astronomers until 1862, and not photographed until 1970. The Dogon also described a third Sirius star (C), not discovered until 1995 with .05 the mass of Sirius B. Many Dogon details are said to have been found in 400-year-old artifacts.

Long before Galileo invented the telescope, the Dogon are reported to have explained that Jupiter has four major moons, Saturn has rings, and that the planets orbit the sun. Does this mean the Dogon are inspired by god? Using Bible inspiration logic, that would have to be so. Yes, the Dogon lore is disputed by scientists. So too the Bible's. Such is the way of things made of men.

People can, after the fact, retrodict and reverse engineer to show all sorts of proofs of prophecy. For example, the 911 Trade Center destruction has been shown to be predicted in Star Wars, and by reading certain texts upside down, diagonally, and backward. Consider how words and numbers can be used to show extraordinary things, whether or not they are found in a holy book: 9/11 is the date of the Trade Center terrorist attack and 911 is the emergency number; 9+1+1=11; 9-11(September 11) is the 254th day of the year, 2+5+4=11; After 9-11 there are one hundred and 11 days left in the year; The twin towers look like an 11; The first flight to hit the towers was 11; There were 92 people on board: 9+2=11; New York is the 11th state added to the union; New York City has 11 letters; The winning lottery number on that day was 911. All of this was elaborated after the event.

Such coincidences surrounding various events and written words provide fuel for endless conspiracy, prophetic, and inspirational theories.

The Apollo 13 mission, launched on April 11, 1970 (the sum of 4, 11 and 70 equals 85 - which when added together comes to 13), from Pad 39 (three times 13) at 13:13 local time, and exploded on April 13. All elaborated after the explosion.

PALINDROMES

-Words or sentences that read the same backward

Madam, I'm Adam.

A man, a plan, a canal—Panama.

Able was I ere I saw Elba. (Napoleon's lament.)

Step on no pets.

Never odd or even.

Anna: "Did Otto peep?" Otto: "Did Anna?" (Each word is a palindrome.)

Dennis, Nell, Edna, Leon, Nedra, Anita, Rolf, Nora, Alice, Carol, Leo, Jane, Reed, Dena, Dale, Basil, Rae, Penny, Lana, Dave, Denny, Lena, Ida, Bernadette, Ben, Ray, Lila, Nina, Jo, Ira, Mara, Sara, Mario, Jan, Ina, Lily, Arne, Bette, Dan, Reba, Diane, Lynn, Ed, Eva, Dana, Lynne, Pearl, Isabel, Ada, Ned, Dee, Rena, Joel, Lora, Cecil, Aaron, Flora, Tina, Arden, Noel, and Ellen sinned.

Palindromes – Palindromes demonstrate the unusual, seemingly impossible, things that can done with words. It is little wonder esoteric meanings and prophesies can be extracted from texts with tens of thousands of words if one searches hard enough.

Figure 186

Some Kabbalistic Jews go so far as to attach meaning to the spacing between words.

A favorite evangelistic tactic is to prophesize the end of the world. The message is simple: Believe what my religion says, or be doomed in a coming apocalypse. That message certainly caught my attention at one time. If the end was coming, I wanted my family and me on the boat. It led me through all sorts of hermeneutical exercises cross-referencing passages all over the Bible to verify the date Bible scholars said was certain.

We are vulnerable to a doomsday message because people throughout time have thought that the world revolves around them and that they and their special generation have been singled out. It is human to think that our time is the best of times and the worst of times.

Consider the words from an Assyrian tablet, 2800 B.C. (notice that's BC): "The Earth is degenerating today. Bribery and corruption abound. Children no longer obey their parents, every man wants to write a book, and it is evident that the end of the world is fast approaching."

Writers of holy books were like all other people and were dramatically influenced by the political events of their times, surrounding religious beliefs, and natural disasters thought to be acts of their gods.

At the very time that Christian Biblical stories were being composed, Pompeii and its sister Roman city, Herculaneum, were turned to ashes by the eruption of Mt. Vesuvius (79 CE). A memory was embedded that echoed through centuries. It and the destruction of Jerusalem in 70 CE created the language and metaphors for Biblical eschatology (final prophetic events) that have inspired prophetic doom for the past 2000 years.

When Vesuvius erupted, an estimated 4,000 feet of the 8,000-foot mountain exploded into the sky and across land and sea. The sun darkened as far away as Rome. But people closer to ground zero were blinded. When they attempted a breath, they inhaled volcanic cinders that were more than a thousand degrees. The pyroclastic flow was so fast and lethal that it would disintegrate a person before nerves could transmit to the brain that anything was even happening.

Food and water were decimated. Disease became rampant. The volcano's impact on life and survival created a memory burnt into minds for centuries.

Vesuvius Ruins and Stone Bodies

© 1998 Morn the Gorn (left) | © Lancevortex (right)   Figure 187

The "world," to the Italians, was Rome and its provinces. For Pompeii and Herculaneum, the Vesuvian cataclysm was interpreted as an act of gods to end the world.

The Vesuvian end of the world and the destruction of Jerusalem by the Romans in 70 A.D. provided fodder for religious stories. It was not enough to simply experience or observe such events. The survivors perceived deeper meaning and a cause other than blind nature.

Dio Cassius, some 130 years after the eruption, wrote in his History of Rome:

". . . giants (black volcanic dust clouds) appeared, now, on the mountain, now in the surrounding country, and again in the cities, wandering over the Earth day and night, and also flitting through the air . . . day was turned into night and light into darkness . . . a sound of trumpets was heard . . . others believed the whole universe was being resolved into chaos and fire . . . it destroyed all fish and birds . . . believed the whole world was being turned upside down, that the sun was disappearing into the Earth, and the Earth was being lifted into the sky . . . a terrible pestilence upon them."

Out of the mix of the Vesuvius disaster, the destruction of Jerusalem, and the desire for an end to Roman persecution, the apocalyptic narrative in the New Testament was created.

Dio's account of the Vesuvius eruption contains language practically identical to the Bible's apocalyptic verses written at a similar time:

"There shall not be left here one stone upon another, that shall not be thrown down . . . there should no flesh be saved; but for the elect's sake those days will be shortened . . . and lightning will come out of the east and shine even into the west . . . the sun will be darkened and the moon will not give light, and the stars shall fall from heaven . . . and great earthquakes, and famines and pestilences and fearful sights and great signs will there be from heaven – the sea and the waves roaring and men's hearts filling with fear . . . the angel took the censer and filled it with fire and cast it to Earth and there were voices, thunderings, lightnings and earthquakes . . . followed hail mingled with fire and blood . . . and a third of the trees were burnt up. And the second angel sounded and a great mountain burning with fire was cast into the sea, and a third part of the sea became blood and a third of the creatures in the sea died . . . and he opened the bottomless pit and there arose smoke out of the pit, as the smoke of a great furnace, and the sun and the air were darkened . . . and I saw the three horses of the apocalypse and these three were the third part of the men killed by the smoke and brimstone." (Revelation)

Now, some 1700 years later, Bible readers ignore the political, religious, volcanic, and historical context of the writings. Anti-typical, modern-day, end-of-our-world meaning is attached to those ancient words with author attribution given to the Creator of the universe.

End time musings by apocalyptic religionists can fuel unspeakable hatred. If we become convinced that the end is imminent, that our group has been singled out as superior to all others by the authority of god and our special belief, and that our actions can hasten the end and speed us to our great reward (such as stature in heaven or a bounty of virgins), then almost any atrocity can be justified. Millions have been butchered in holy wars fomented by holy book end-time prophesies.

The president of Iran, Mahmoud Ahmadinejad, spent millions renovating Tehran in preparation for the imminent return of the Mahdi, a ninth-century figure who will emerge from a well, partner with Jesus, and violently convert the world to Islam.

At the same time, messianic Jews are trying to get the cornerstones for a new temple in place to ready for the coming of their Messiah and the end to Islam. Clyde Lott, a Mississippi preacher, is attempting to breed blemish-free red heifers (red hairs only) for export to Jerusalem. The Bible says (Numbers 19:2-10) their sacrifice and ashes are necessary to purify the Jews to build the temple. Muslims specify a yellow heifer.

For many Bible believers, the end times started clicking on May 15, 1948, when the United Nations recognized Israel. So, there is no time to spare in making prophecy fit world events. Every disaster, every conflict in the world gladdens a prophet of doom somewhere.

End of the world religious predictions fuel fear, false hope, and satisfy our it's-all-about-me obsession. They serve to keep a lot of people industriously calculating dates and watching the newspapers hoping they read more and more like the events presaging Revelation's Armageddon, or Islam's coming of al-Mahdi and "The Hour." Almost fifty percent of the population believes their god will bring an end to the world within the next fifty years, rewarding the believers and slaughtering the unbelievers.

Humans have a habit of making their small interpretation of their sphere apply to the whole world.

© Wysong   Figure 188

If there is a divine plan that the Creator wants us to know, and it includes the end of the world, why would it be made a mystery? Certainly, if there is honesty, justice, and truth (which there is), all of us should have equal access. We should not be faced with the impossible task of trying to find out which modern or ancient "prophet" (among the tens of thousands) has the right prediction.

Holiness, purity, grace, or ethics have nothing to do with making presumptuous predictions in the name of the Creator of the universe. Life is about getting out there and doing and being good, not attempting to discern ancient manuscripts to calculate end-time prophecies.

Perhaps the healthiest perspective is to not worry about the end of the world today when it is already tomorrow on the other side of the world.

31
DEFENDING HOLY BOOKS

Given that nobody likes to have their sure religious beliefs overturned, defenses against challenge are usually ready and waiting. Although faith, not reason, is the mainstay of religious defense, reason is attempted at every opportunity. Using all the presuppositions inherent in the Bible-based religion I attached to, I became pretty good at defending my beliefs and, sadly, convincing others. That is until I opened my mind. Then, the full array of facts and unbridled reason made my clever arguments seem silly. I had fallen victim to confirmation bias, that is, entertaining only those facts and ideas which comported with my preexisting beliefs.

Here are some of the defensive arguments commonly used.

The Waiting for "New Light" Argument

To those who, in effect, worship a holy book, contradictions, conflicts with ethics, injustice, absurdities, and obscure passages are attributed to "spiritual blindness." "Divine mysteries" veiled in the mysterious sacred words must wait for "new light" to be shed through special anointed human religious agents.

However, the ever-present prospect of "new light" effectively inoculates holy books against any possible disproof. Making a holy book unfalsifiable also makes it unverifiable.

> *I was walking across a bridge one day, and I saw a man standing on the edge, about to jump off. So I ran over and said "Stop! Don't do it!" "Why shouldn't I?" he said. "Well, there's so much to live for!" "Like what?" "Well... are you religious?" He said yes. I said, "Me too! Are you Christian or Buddhist?" "Christian." "Me too! Are you Catholic or Protestant? "Protestant." "Me too! Are you Episcopalian or Baptist?" "Baptist." "Wow! Me too! Are you Baptist Church of God or Baptist Church of the Lord?" "Baptist Church of God!" "Me too! Are you original Baptist Church of God, or are you Reformed Baptist Church of God?" "Reformed Baptist Church of God!" "Me too! Are you Reformed Baptist Church of God, reformation of 1879, or Reformed Baptist Church of God, reformation of 1915?" He said, "Reformed Baptist Church of God, reformation of 1915!" I said, "Die, heretic scum," and pushed him off. (Emo Philips)*

© Emo Philips   Figure 189

The "Out of Date" Argument

The previous chapters outlining how the Bible conflicts with reason, facts, consistency, and ethics create a terrible dilemma for believers. In defense, they (and I for a time) say the "Old Testament law" is out of date and replaced by the "new law" of Jesus and Paul. (Romans 10; 2; Corinthians 3) Those guys of the past, well, you know, boys will be boys. (Similarly, Islamic scholars solve such problems in their holy book by what they call abrogation, meaning the more recent texts trump the older ones. Jihadists disagree.)

The Bible itself, however, says all of it must be embraced and specifically forbids selective cherry-picking. As detailed previously, but worth repeating, the New Testament refers to the Hebrew (old) books and says: "All scripture is God-breathed and useful for teaching, rebuking, correcting and training in righteousness." (2 Timothy 3:16) "You received the word of God, which you heard from us, you accepted it not as the word of men, but as it actually is, the word of God." (1 Thessalonians 2:13).

Everything in the Bible is to be exactly obeyed upon penalty of death or worse: "See that you do all I command you; do not add to it or take away from it." (Deuteronomy 12:32; also note: Joshua 1:8; Isaiah 40:8: Leviticus 19:37, Matthew 5:17; Luke 16:17; John 7:23; 10:17-19,35; 1 Corinthians 4:6; Hebrews 11; 1 Peter 1:20,21). "The word of our God stands forever" (Isaiah 40:8); "The scripture cannot be broken." (John 10:35; see also Hebrews 11:1-39; Matthew 5:17)

The Allegory, Metaphor, Symbolism, and Context Argument

As I look back, I was able to set aside virtually every criticism of the Bible because I had allowed myself to be convinced by superficial proofs that it was inerrant. Once you do that you're bulletproof.

For example, the literal meaning of words is taken until there is a conflict with fact, science, or other words in the book. Then the interpretation is groomed with arguments about symbolism and context to make the problem disappear. It's like making a doctrinal smoothie—a little of this, a little of that, a lot of the most delicious, and something to mask the bitter taste of contradictions and nonsense.

All words permit multiple meanings, particularly when parsing ancient languages. This can result in obvious virtue (like not slaughtering unbelievers) being a crime, and obvious crime (like stoning to death a disobedient son, offering a daughter to be raped, etc.) being a virtue.

But this means the books have no certainty or ethical standard. And certainty, unlike human-created words, is what the Creator is, as evidenced by the natural laws governing us and the universe.

THE UNCERTAINTY OF WORDS

Last night a man went to a 24-hour grocery. When he got there, the guy was locking the front door. The man said, "Hey, the sign says you're open 24 hours." The proprietor says: "Not in a row!"

A car hits a man. The paramedic rushes over and says, "Are you comfortable?" The guy says, "I make a good living."

A lady was on the subway, sitting on a newspaper, and a guy comes over and asks "Are you reading that?" She said yes, stood up, turned the page, and sat down again.

I went to the psychiatrist and he says "You're crazy." I tell him I want a second opinion. He says, "Okay, you're ugly too!"

I went to a restaurant with a sign that said they served breakfast at any time. So I ordered French toast during the Renaissance.

A guy shows up late for work. The boss yells, "You should have been here at 8:30!" He replies: "Why? What happened at 8:30?"

Figure 190

The Religious Experience Argument

Many believe their religion is affirmed by the feeling of holiness and connection to god when reading their holy book, the joy of conversion, the results of prayer, or being transformed from a wayward life when "born again." Such feelings, and then any benefit that coincidentally may come to life, are considered all the proof needed that holy providence is at play.

But feel-good personal experiences are not a compelling reason for committed belief. After all, people can experience transformation by getting a new job, being in love, having children, or having quarters gush out of a slot machine. Some never feel closer to god than when their children martyr themselves blowing themselves up in a shopping mall, guaranteeing the family a certain seat in heaven and a paycheck from sponsors of terrorism.

If you feel good, saved, excited, or fulfilled, that's true to you. But it has nothing to do with the rest of reality—where the real world and Creator of the universe reside.

Arguments from Authority, Name Dropping, and History

Many believers cite religious authorities as proof. There are religious scholars, departments in universities, and countless books that defend human-made religions. Famous people, scientists, Ph.D.'s, and rulers can be quoted who espouse belief. Then there are thousands of years of religious history, Cathedrals, traditions, beautiful music, and community. The Bible is the best-selling book in history, with over five billion sold and distributed. The Koran has sold about 800 million.

But, of course, none of that proves anything other than the ability of humans to create ideas and institutions that other humans follow. Truth, on the other hand, is revealed by reason, evidence, natural law, experience, and conscience which have nothing to do with following other people's ideas or commands.

"He knocked him out in the first round and didn't even thank me. Make sure he gets decked next time"

© Wysong · Figure 183

214

32
FAITH

Most religious believers don't bother with the nitty-gritty details and work required to argue their beliefs intelligently. Instead, they claim faith, which, by definition, requires no defense. Even highly intelligent people working in the sciences and applied fields where strict proof and evidence are required will proudly proclaim religious faith. (While, if they are theistic evolutionists, denying that faith has anything to do with evolution.)

Faith is never something I could feel comfortable with. It's like saying I can believe in any stupid thing I want and that's as legitimate as the laws of geometry or the wrongness of murder.

If we are ever to have a chance at a better world, we must agree that it is always wrong to believe anything on insufficient evidence. Faith without fact is unreasonable. (Hell is best described as a world without reason.) Far better it would be if we simply said we don't know when we don't.

Thomas Jefferson admonished: "Ignorance is preferable to error, and he is less remote from the truth who believes nothing than he who believes what is wrong . . . you must recur to the pretensions of the (Bible) writer to inspiration from God. Examine upon what evidence his pretensions are founded, and whether that evidence is so strong, as that its falsehood would be more improbable than a change in the laws of nature."

During my Bible-believing days I tried to apply reason as best I could and cited scriptures in support, such as: ". . . do not believe every inspired expression,

How Materialists and Religionists Reason
1. I have faith that A is true.
2. Therefore, fact B, which contradicts A, cannot be true.

© Wysong   Figure 195

but test the inspired expressions . . ." (1 John 4:1) Also: "always be ready to make a defense before everyone . . ." (1 Peter 3:15; see also Proverbs 14:15; Romans 12:2; 1 Thessalonians 5:21) My opponents could, of course, site completely contradictory passages hailing the virtues of blind faith: "Now faith is confidence in what we hope for and assurance about what we do not see." (Hebrews 11:1; etc.)

Well into the nineteenth-century American citizens could be jailed for the blasphemy of Bible criticism. The famous evangelist, Spurgeon, summed up the obligation of the dutiful flock by saying, "If the whole of all evil and wickedness were rolled up into one gigantic black ball of corruption it would be less than the sin of unbelief." To this day there remains a lingering paranoia about being critical of holy books and religions. (Which I must admit to in writing these chapters.)

Belief in belief has the bonus of being politically correct. Somehow, the mere proclamation, "I believe and have faith . . ." is supposed to garner respect and end any dispute. Everything is open to question, just not faith.

But forgotten in this zeal to protect and justify faith is the fact that it is belief that starts the evil. The body merely repeats the impressions that have been made upon it by the mind's beliefs.

Faith and Belief in Search of Facts

Although holy book believers will proudly proclaim their faith-based belief, they inwardly crave facts and evidence to counter criticism and quiet their own suppressed doubts. That's why so much current energy and hope is invested in holy book archeology and scientific creationism.

It's a human failing, called confirmation bias, that we consider and remember evidence that is consistent with our beliefs and ignore evidence that might disconfirm them. It's like looking at a crowd and picking out only our friends.

Why the World Can't Get Along

© Wysong   Figure 196

Consider how reason has been used by Bible believers to chase belief about the shape of the Earth. Isaiah (written about 600-700 B.C.) speaks of the "circle" of the Earth (Isaiah 40:22). That is taken as proof of Bible inspiration since the Earth was not proven to be a circle until it was circumnavigated in the sixteenth century. But even that Bible proof is wrong since the Earth is actually an ellipsoid.

Although the interpretation of that scripture is now taken to be obvious, the round Earth interpretation only came after the sixteenth-century discovery. This is true to form since never do holy books forecast a scientific discovery. Rather, verses are found post hoc—after a scientific discovery— to make the holy book seem like it was accurate science all along, but we were just too sinful or spiritually dumb to get it.

In fact, prior to the discovery of a round Earth and long after Isaiah was written, Bible texts were used to persecute anyone who did not believe the Earth was flat, a disc, had corners, was geometrical, stationary, floated on water, rested on foundations, and, like the Jewish Tabernacle, was the center of the universe.

Moreover, consider that in the above Isaiah 40 verse, the Hebrew word for circle is hwg (chûgh). This is a different word than the Hebrew word for ball or sphere, which is duwr, as used in Isaiah 22:18 (not referring to the shape of the Earth).

It would, therefore, seem that in Isaiah 40 the circle referred to is like a disc that can be seen by standing in an area where one can look to the horizon without obstruction for 360 degrees. As one turns in a circle to view the horizon, there appears to be a perfect circle.

This corresponds to other verses implying that the Earth is a circular disc. For example, in Revelation 1:7 Jesus is said to be coming on a cloud and that "every eye will see him," which, of course, would not be possible for the people on the other side of a round Earth.

During the Dark Ages when the clergy used the Bible to wield absolute power and dictate finality on all matters, the idea of a flat Earth was law. Even today, a twentieth-century Bible-based religion, the Christian Catholic Apostolic Church, fervently holds to a flat Earth cosmology and cites numerous scriptures as proof. (Job 38:12-14; Matthew 4:1-12; Daniel 4: 10,11; etc.) Samuel Rowbotham, a modern-day flat-Earther cites 76 different Bible verses that deny a round Earth.

Even if the Bible taught a spherical Earth, or, more accurately an ellipsoid, that would not be a reason to attribute the book to the Creator. Belief in a round Earth predates the Bible by thousands of years. It was an inference from observation by ancients like Aristotle, Eratosthenes, and Ptolemy observing how the stars and moon circled the Earth, the outline of the Earth on the moon during the lunar cycle, and the disappearance and reappearance of ships on the horizon.

For Bible believers, however, the Earth remained flat. Only with the explorations of Columbus and Magellan in the fifteenth and sixteenth centuries was the round Earth given religious standing.

Moreover, it was even pronounced that questions about the exact nature of the heavens were wasted effort since the Bible said there was going to be a "new heavens and new Earth." In the meantime, St. Philastrius pronounced that it was heresy not to believe that god hung the stars in the sky each evening and took them down in the morning.

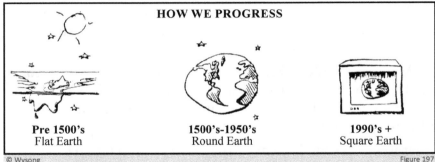

HOW WE PROGRESS

Pre 1500's	1500's-1950's	1990's +
Flat Earth	Round Earth	Square Earth

© Wysong   Figure 197

And religions are not quick to come around to the astronomical facts. Galileo, persecuted for claiming the Earth orbited the sun, rather than vice versa, was not absolved by the Catholic Church until 1992. And even today, defenders of the Bible's geocentric view are putting forth selective facts and arguments that the Earth is the focal point of the entire universe. (see: theprinciplemovie.com)

To explain contradictions between the Bible and facts, people of faith say those who read the Bible and believed in a flat and geocentric Earth, and stars hung each evening, just didn't know how to read the text correctly. One gets the sneaking suspicion, however, if discovery had revealed that the Earth was flat and supported by pillars, that the "circle" scripture would be read to mean other than sphere, and the "foundation" scriptures would be heralded as proof of the Bible's science.

Faith is like a talisman that can change any contrary word or fact into support.

The Source of Faith and Belief

Faith and belief are so handy because they are immune to disproof. By definition, faith and belief do not need to be tied to reality, and reality is the only thing that can disprove anything.

We hate the confusion and heavy lifting of self-responsibility, foresight-driven thinking, reflecting upon what is within, sorting through evidence, evaluating all options, and making decisions for ourselves. We hate doubt and like the ease of being told what to do to be safe now and in the hereafter. We want, like fast food, answers in an easy-open package. A book, a material idol that materializes (anthropomorphizes) the Creator, and religion experts to explain what the rules of the biggest dad of all are, fills the bill.

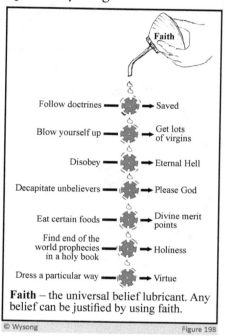

Follow doctrines → Saved

Blow yourself up → Get lots of virgins

Disobey → Eternal Hell

Decapitate unbelievers → Please God

Eat certain foods → Divine merit points

Find end of the world prophecies in a holy book → Holiness

Dress a particular way → Virtue

Faith – the universal belief lubricant. Any belief can be justified by using faith.

© Wysong   Figure 198

Truth is Anti-Faith and Anti-Belief

Accountants, lawyers, factory workers, taxi drivers, carpenters, doctors, moms, dads, and kids use facts and reason in going about daily life and business. We unscrew caps counter-clockwise, place food in the mouth and not the ears, add and subtract in checkbooks, don't walk into traffic, and push the brakes when we want to stop. What is it that comes over us such that once the topic of religion is brought up a lever is switched in the brain so that rational discourse ends, logical action stops, eyes glaze over, ears seal off, and the mouth spews only unctuous pre-learned incantations?

No, faith and belief are not badges of honor. Any belief not honestly derived, as well as being constantly available for dismissal by open inquiry, is one long sin.

© Wysong   Figure 199

Brain Gauge – Faith and intelligence are inversely related. The more faith we have the less room there is for intelligence.

© Wysong   Figure 200

Life is supposed to be an adaptable, dynamic process. Not a living death where we select a belief state (always put forth by authority figures) to shelter us from the tides of inquiry and criticism. Bertrand Russell said, "Have no respect for the authority of others, for there are always contrary authorities to be found."

Contrary to faith, things of the Creator are clear, obvious, and unerring. Faith, on the other hand, is the uncoupling of our brains and conscience from the regularity and reality of the world. In other words, faith is credulity.

As such, faith is opposed to the Creator, the epitome of reason and truth. Embracing it is therefore in opposition to the very Creator people think they are confirming.

HOW TO RETAIN YOUR BELIEF AND FAITH IN THE FACE OF REASON AND FACTS

1. Avow that the matter is too deep and over our heads, but you know there are experts that have it all figured out and could easily explain it.

2. When an argument is unanswerable or a fact not consistent with your belief, make it one of those things you forget.

3. Claim the opponent is confused by too much learning.

4. Say he is being heretical, bullheaded, or stupid.

5. Claim the person is sick, immoral, demonized, unscholarly, or uneducated.

6. Change the subject to something you are sure you can win.

7. Claim that the person actually believes as you do but is too proud and arrogant to admit it and is just showing off.

8. Use strong-arm tactics and threaten the opponent with hell or ostracism.

9. Say, "Even though I can't defend my belief it is unshakable."

10. Explain that the answer will be forthcoming as new light is shed.

11. Become busy, tired, or ill and put off the discussion until later, but make sure later never comes.

12. Ask for time to do some research that will surely prove your point, then make the date far enough away that hopefully your opponent will forget to bring it up again.

13. Say, "There's a call I have to make, family crisis, roof is leaking…"

14. Say the person has an impure motive like money, fame, fear of death, fear of life, lust, or whatever else your belief labels as bad.

15. Say that any honest or enlightened person believes as you do.

16. Claim your belief is faith-based and thus does not have to be reasonable.

17. Tell the opponent that they have to look at the big picture, not facts.

18. Changing your position would mean quitting your club, church, organization, or job and so there is no point discussing it.

19. Ignore intelligent arguments; people of good heart must believe like a child.

20. Excuse yourself then later send them a book supposedly proving you were right.

21. Say everyone is entitled to their own opinion.

22. Say, "Those are old arguments that have long ago been defeated."

23. Nod in agreement, keep your belief, and then send them a joke or a pie or some other gift to make them feel guilty.

24. Tell them about your credentials, high IQ, or famous people you know or whose books you have read.

25. Remember that Satan is capable of transforming himself into an angel of light and thus the better the argument of the opponent the more likely he is doing the devil's handiwork.

26. Any combination of the above.

Figure 194

33
THE SOURCE OF GOODNESS

Religions and holy books are commonly assumed to be the path to goodness.

However, all the basic ideas of morality, such as rights of property, the sanctity of life, and honesty can be determined by simply looking within. A person no more needs a book to tell them that cruelty, killing, stealing, and lying are wrong than they need a book to tell them 2+2=4.

In fact, if any religionist is asked to describe an ethical precept that is unknown without their religion, they will be incapable of doing so. The only thing unique to religions are human-made stories, doctrines, rituals, and equating, murder, torture, animal cruelty, ritualistic sacrifice, maiming, genocide, racism, sexism, slavery, and ignorance with morality and the will of the Creator.

Goodness Exists Everywhere

Spiritual movements and leaders such as Lao-tze, Zoroaster, Confucius, Hinayana, Zen Buddhism, Jainism, Shankara, Padmasambhava, Nagarjuna, Epictetus, and Longchenpa claim no Western-style god or inspired holy book, and yet represent highly moral systems. Even diehard atheists and agnostics feel an ethical pull.

The fact of the matter is that bad, as well as good people, emerge out of every religion and every society.

The poor farmer in a third-world country tied to the plow from sunup to sundown eking out a living for his family, and the primitive in the middle of the bush without any reading skills, must still be capable of discerning right from wrong.

And that is the case. The Senoi of the Malay jungle live a highly ethical and benevolent life where unconditional love is just a fact. The Yequana aborigines of the upper Cuara River basin in Venezuela demonstrate similar wisdom without compulsion. These remote people have no formal religions, codes, holy books, prophets, priests, or other such trappings.

In the famous Christian "good Samaritan" Bible story, a man was robbed, beaten, stripped of his clothes, and left for dead by the side of the road. Both a priest and a religious Levite ignored him and passed him by. A Samaritan came upon him, took pity, and saved him. Although the story is used by Christians to teach an ethical lesson, the Samaritan was not a Christian and thus not motivated by Jesus. Rather, the story highlights the hypocrisy of religion and the ability and duty of ordinary people to activate conscience and do the right thing.

Ethics Predates the Bible and Its Impossible Rules

Concerning the Bible, Adam and Eve had no such holy book, nor did Noah, Abraham, or any of the people mentioned therein. People were not without ethical direction before Moses descended from the mountain with the Ten Commandments. Moreover, only three of the Ten Commandments—shalt not steal, kill, or lie—qualifies as ethics. But that doesn't single out the Bible as unique since no society has existed or could exist without these prohibitions.

Some of the Commandments are impossible to comply with, such as not coveting (desiring) things. That's condemning people for thoughts that pop into their heads. Other Commandments about the name of god, a sabbath, graven images(idols), and swearing, have nothing at all to do with ethics.

The two principle rules of Jesus are impossible to follow. The paramount one is, "'Love the Lord your God with all your heart and with all your soul and with all your mind." That is an impossible abstraction. The second is, "Love your neighbor as yourself."

(Mathew 22:37-) Attempting to obey this command would make functioning, even survival, impossible. Imagine trying to love and care about every aspect of all your neighbors' lives like you care about yours.

Religions and Holy Books Have a Bad Ethical Record

Contrary to the refrain that religion is where to learn right from wrong, throughout history, slitting throats, warring, and denial of basic human rights are the signatures of human-made holy book religions. Today, in seemingly benign religions, children are taught to celebrate in song the slaughter of non-Jews at Jericho, the annihilation of humans and creatures by a world flood, the killing of innocent first-born children, and to look forward to an Armageddon where everyone who does not believe as they do is slaughtered.

The Bible justifies killing whole populations in unbelieving cities, brides who are not virgin, adulterers, those who take the Lord's name in vain, those who disobey a mother or father, and young boys who aren't circumcised— and done so "correctly" by a Jewish mohel biting the foreskin off so blood is let.

Slavery is a Bible practice. In large part, it's justified by Bible racism. The granddaddy of all racisms is Jews writing a Bible, claiming god wrote it, and then having that god say he chose them over all other races. The "mark of Cain" and "Curse of Ham" are also Biblical justifications for racism. Then there's the story of Noah and his family being the only people to survive the worldwide flood. They are thought to be white. Therefore, it's reasoned, black, yellow, and brown races must have been on board, but way back with the animals! Yes, there are passages contrary to slavery. But that makes the point that any form of morality can be derived from the Bible.

Muslims and Hindus war in Pakistan and India. Jonestown cultists committed suicide following their Bible-thumping leader. Protestants and Catholics kill one another in the British-Irish conflict. Catholic priests (including modern-day), supposedly obedient to the Biblical doctrine of celibacy, have sexually abused and scarred for life innumerable children. Meanwhile, the church hierarchy and many parishioners turn a blind eye. (See the documentary movie, The Spotlight.)

Believers justify all such horrors as moral lessons. But morality is not taught by unjust horror. Such horror only teaches how unethical people can become by assigning their conscience to religions.

Go through the inspection at an airport to be reminded of the horrendous deeds perpetrated by human-made religions. The Qur'an can be read to make it moral to fly planes into office buildings, behead nonbelievers, kill women who are raped, marry nine-year-old little girls, cut the clitoris and labia off girls (circumcision/infibulation) and sew the vagina all but closed, only to be broken open on the wedding night.

If the literal words in the Qu'ran or Bible were followed—as the books demand— one would find far more reason to kill neighbors than to turn the other cheek. There should be no tolerance or liberty. Unbelief should be the highest of all crimes and deserving of the most brutal death. Female bondage should be the norm, and if a wife misbehaves, she should be sent out on the streets penniless. Homosexuality and sex acts other than intercourse should be punishable by death. Children of our killed enemies should be our bound servants forever. We would be free to sell our children.

When the Spaniards conquered Mexico and Peru, they would baptize Indian infants and then immediately bash their heads. This was to assure that they went to heaven. Otherwise, it was believed that they would grow up in a pagan world and be condemned to hell.

That leaves the ethical question of whether one should support, much less defend, religions using guidebooks advocating this potential and with a history of actually performing acts no person engaging conscience would even contemplate.

Religion, ostensibly speaking for a god, can supplant normal human ethical sensibilities. Muslim children are indoctrinated to equate goodness with suicide bombings. Jewish and Christian children celebrate a "vengeful god" who kills a whole world with a flood other than one family, the firstborn of an entire nation, and tells his "chosen" people to stone to death disobedient sons, and slaughter entire "unbelieving" nations but keep the young maidens for their pleasure. When such things pass as lessons about morality all bets are off.

Little wonder that war and inhumanity justified by various religions occur constantly and worldwide.

Consider the current war on infidels by Islamists.

The following is small small excerpt from the list of Islamic terror attacks maintained by **The Religion of Peace.** thereligionofpeace.com					
Date	**Country**	**City**	**Killed**	**Injured**	**Description**
2020 05/31	Somalia	Hawa Abdi	10	13	Ten civilians are blown to bits by Religion of Peace bombers.
2020 05/31	Burkina Faso	Kompienbiga	30	0	Islamic Supremacists fire into a livestock market, slaughtering thirty patrons.
2020 05/30	Egypt	Sheikh Zuweid	2	2	Two security personnel are vaporized by an Islamic landmine.
2020 05/30	Burkina Faso	Loroum	15	15	Children are among at least fifteen innocents murdered by Islamic extremists targeting traders.
2020 05/30	Afghanistan	Kabul	2	4	A television van is bombed by the Islamic Emirate, killing two employees.
2020 05/30	Kenya	Diana	2	4	Two children are killed when a terrorist uses them as a human shield.
2020 05/30	Afghanistan	Parwan	3	0	Three children are disassembled by an 'insurgent' mortar round through their roof.
2020 05/29	Egypt	al-Ajra	2	0	Two tribesmen lose their lives to a fundamentalist attack.
2020 05/29	Afghanistan	Dande Patan	14	5	Fourteen security force members are killed during an attack by Mujahideen.

This list continues on for several pages on the thereligionofpeace.com website.
(TROP does not catch all attacks. Not all attacks are immediately posted.)

© TheReligionofPeace.com   Figure 201

37002

Deadly Terror Attacks since 9/11/2001 - 6/2/2019

© TheReligionofPeace.com   Figure 202

Other religions condemn these horrors, but the underlying cause is largely ignored: Islamists are simply acting on belief and faith in a holy book.

If today's Jews and Christians followed their holy books (as they have in the past and are commanded to by the books), they would be engaged in similar horrors.

True, many now put a liberal patina on holy books, but literate people without coaches read scriptural urgings that clearly encourage the killing of unbelievers and those who commit the sin of reason.

In other words, morality is not a reason to embrace religion, it's a reason to flee from it.

Religions Are Ethically Tamed by Secular Governments

Religious atrocities are held in check today because the secular state has stepped in to forbid it. Where religion can dictate its own terms, fuse eschatology (end-time guessing) with the state, and make demands people cannot refuse, heads getting lopped off and religious war and torture of heretics are still a part of life.

Even in modern societies, religions bless troops and condemn those being blessed on the other side. Nations that do not benefit from such helpful guidance could fare at least as well.

All soldiers have their special God.

© Wysong   Figure 203

It's a sad fact of history that the words that divide people and then unite them in butchering one another are often traceable to the religious institutions and holy books humans create.

America's Virtue Is Not Due to Religion

Christians and Jews brag that America's greatness is the result of Judeo-Christian principles. The fact is, the unsavory history of Judeo-Christian religions led America's founders to write a Constitution that separated church and state. It doesn't even once cite or refer to any holy book. Moreover, the very first thing mentioned in the Bill of Rights is: "Congress shall make no law respecting an establishment of religion."

People were fleeing to the New World in search of both freedom of religion and freedom from it. Most Founding Fathers understood this and created a secular (meaning nonreligious, not godless) nation based on freedom and the inherent "God-given" morality within each individual. "God," for most of the founders, was a secular Creator.

The Good Religions Do Does Not Excuse the Bad

This does not deny that religions can do good. For example, even in Islamic states that promote terrorism and brutal punishment for disobedience, social services, and charitable giving rivals that of any other religion or nation. The same is true for Christianity and Judaism even before the secular state tamed them. However, religions and holy books that justify both atrocity and benevolence provide no clear ethical guidance that should supersede one's conscience, nor are they reflective of the pure unequivocal justice of the Creator.

Nevertheless, nobody likes uncertainty. Thus, there is a natural inclination to follow systematized and formalized morality. People want clear and easy, right and wrong, black and white. We don't want to have to think and probe our consciences: "Somebody just tell me what to do so I can check off my moral chores, avoid god's ire, and get on with my life."

God Running Lives - "John Morgan in Topeka, 20 cent raise. Jane Reid in Boston, alarm doesn't go off. Rocky 'the Hammer' in Philadelphia, wins with a TKO in the fifth. Paul Wilson in Chicago, wins Bulls tickets. Ed Black in Miami, gets a sunburn. Ted Miller in Cheyenne, steps in horse poo..."

© Wysong

Figure 193

Religions come to the rescue by providing grocery lists of dos and don'ts to check off each day. But does it fit any semblance of rationality that guidance from the Creator of the universe as to right and wrong should come from such stories as an angel Gabriel reciting text to the illiterate Mohammed in a cave in 610 CE, or Joseph Smith burying his face in a white top hat in the 1800s to read god's Mormon messages from a "seer" stone, or Moses climbing a cloud-covered mountain and remaining there for forty days to obtain the Ten Commandments written on stone by the finger of god?

Such untenable stories serve only to create huge worldwide religious institutions with immense power over people's minds. Dutiful believers can then employ the Nuremberg defense, regardless of the damage done by following religious rules: "I was only following god's orders."

Goodness Comes From Free Will and Conscience, Not Following Others

It's human to seek to be good. That's a consequence of free will, not an original sin putting us in need of salvation. The struggle between right and wrong, good and bad, underlies and pervades every religious, political, legal, and social institution, and has from time immemorial. Equity, justice, propriety, social graces, respect, honesty, and so on weigh on each of us personally every day because we have been given the gifts of conscience and free choice.

On the other hand, thousands of years of cathedrals, temples, churches, mosques, pyramids, Inquisitions, mummification, animal sacrifices, self-mutilation, witch trials, holy book reading, wall wailing, breast-beating, flagellation, jihads, fatwas, idolatry, sacrifices, converting savages, witch trials, celibacy, polygamy, circumcision, infibulation, not sparing the rod, stonings, suttees, ecumenism, parochial schools, catechisms, beheadings, conquistadors, pilgrimages, holy books in motel room drawers, drawing and quartering, eye and tongue removals, forbidden foods, special clothing, tithing, speaking in tongues, poison drinking, dancing with snakes, indulgences, evangelizing, chants, excommunications, hymn singing, hermeneutics (deciphering holy books written in arcane languages), eschatology (attempting to figure out from holy books when the world will end), missions, confessions, wafer eating, wine drinking, prayer in the right direction, penance, and heretic burning have not brought us closer to truth, made us better people, nor improved our lot.

Religions impose the impossible task of eliminating uncontrollable thoughts ("thou shalt not covet") and leaving people forever guilty and condemned for having them. Our measure should be what we choose to do, not by thoughts we have no control over.

Note how the religious leaders writing the Bible, from the get-go, attempt to deny free choice and conscience. Eve's "original sin" was to eat an apple from the "tree of knowledge of good and evil." (Gen 2:17) To know good and evil is to exercise one's own conscience. This was painted by the Bible writers as so egregiously criminal that all humans, billions and billions of us, supposedly inherit it as an "original sin" and the cause of all depravity and death.

This mysterious passage becomes crystal clear when the true authors are recognized, namely human religious leaders. These leaders didn't want people to decide for themselves. Their goal was power and control, meaning they alone, not the people, were to have the "knowledge of good and evil." Proof that is the case is the supposed knowledge of good and evil laid out as rules and regulations in their holy book.

Actually, the ultimate sin is not to eat the apple, meaning to follow other humans (and their human-made religious "knowledge of good and evil") rather than one's own Creator-given conscience.

When people come to believe that following the rules of others constitutes their duty to ethics, they abandon the best moral governor of all, conscience. We must freely author our actions.

Figure 204

Yes, we all struggle with nasty thoughts and imperfect actions, but we almost always intuitively know how we should behave. If we don't know and act improperly, consequences always follow and we make better choices next time. Such experience is the best teacher of all. And Earth life gives us plenty of that.

Up to a certain age, children have little empathy or ethics. They simply follow the commands of elders for fear of punishment. Adulthood brings with it free choice and an active conscience.

However, unlike a hairy chest or breasts that come automatically with maturity, activating free choice and conscience is a choice. We can remain like children and look to other humans and institutions (surrogate moms and dads) for rules to live by, or listen to the voice of conscience—eat the apple—implanted by the Creator.

We are also given reason and logic. Engaging those truth-deciphering skills is as much a matter of ethics as not lying, stealing, or harming others. Without truth, we live in a lie and contribute to a false world that ultimately brings harm.

We may be diamonds in the rough and struggle with making goodness manifest. But it's always there, urging if we will only listen to the voice within.

Thinking about . . .

THE REAL REALITY

In This Section: Although it seems that our world is the extent of reality, it isn't. Reason and modern physics prove that matter is an illusion. Real reality provides boundless possibilities beyond the constraints of time and physicality.

34
MATTER IS AN ILLUSION

Once I realized that materialism, evolution, and religions were false concepts, it seemed there was nowhere to turn. Even though it was exhilarating to discover what was not true, the comfort of having everything all figured out was hard to leave behind.

Once we reach that point of unknowing, we are left where we should have begun in the first place. Namely, the reality we can know, experience directly, and reason upon, rather than beliefs pushed on us by others.

The Smallest Thing

At first glance, it would seem that if we are just matter, we must go the way of matter—from dust we come to dust we return. However, if way down underneath we are actually something other than matter, then we would have a different destiny.

Let's probe our smallest parts.

Atom is a word invented by the Greeks to describe the smallest thing. But now we know atoms are comprised of smaller parts called protons, neutrons, and electrons. But reason tells us that even those parts have to be composed of parts, those parts composed of parts, and on and on. Taken infinitely downward, matter must boil down to nothing—in the physical particle sense.

That's where just doing a thought experiment takes us.

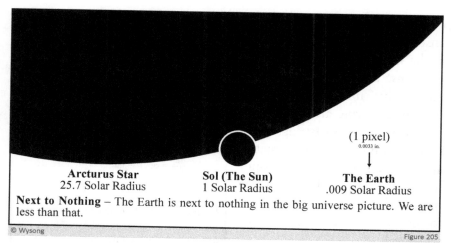

Arcturus Star	**Sol (The Sun)**	**The Earth**
25.7 Solar Radius	1 Solar Radius	.009 Solar Radius

(1 pixel)
0.0033 in.

Next to Nothing – The Earth is next to nothing in the big universe picture. We are less than that.

© Wysong

Figure 205

Then we can consider the implication of Einstein's famous equation, $E=MC^2$, where E is energy, M is mass (matter), and C is the velocity of light. Using simple algebra, the equation can be rearranged like this: $M=E/C^2$. Since both things on the right side of the equation, the speed of light and energy, are nothing in the touchy-feely material sense, and they equal matter, then matter must be nothing as well.

That jibes with modern quantum physics. Beneath the billiard ball atom models with nuclei, electrons, protons, and neutrons that look like tiny solar systems, are subatomic particles known as quanta. Quanta is a growing family with names such as quarks, leptons, bosons, baryons, mesons, fermions, gravitons, and superstrings. Over 200 quanta are now known to reside within the nucleus.

These subatomic particles are not just clustered together like a bunch of grapes. They're traveling about in the nucleus at 40,000 miles per second. Physicists can't get matter to stand still long enough to have a good look at it. Even if they did, they wouldn't see anything any more than they could see a thought.

Proposed actual size of the universe a fraction of a second after the Big Bang.

© Wysong

Figure 206

A superstring, believed to perhaps be the smallest unit, is 100 billion, billion times smaller than a proton. It's not actually a particle, but more like a vibration. Physicists arrived at this idea by exploring the results from supercollider machines that explode atoms into pieces, and with mathematical calculations that give me a headache just to look at them.

As superstrings vibrate, they create the harmony that manifests as the subatomic particles, nuclei, electrons, atoms, and molecular matter that makes up you and the goulash you are having for dinner tonight. Superstrings mean that the various forms of matter are—way down underneath—not matter, but more like different tunes. In other words, we're back to nothingness in the material sense again.

$$(\lambda f.[f(fx)])g = g(gx)$$

$$\oint (E\delta t - \mathbf{p}\delta \mathbf{x}) = 2\pi \frac{m_0 c^2}{\omega_0} \quad n = nSh = nh;$$

$$U = -\frac{\hbar^2}{2m} \sum_{i=1}^{N} \frac{\nabla_i^2 R}{R}$$

$$I_c = \sum_k \oint Cp_k \delta q_k$$

$$\sim \exists x[R(x)] \Leftrightarrow \forall x[\sim R(x)]$$

$$\pi_i^1 = \sum_n \beta_{in} q_n = 2 \sum_n \beta_{in} \sqrt{J_n} \sin\phi_n$$

$$\delta\pi_k = \frac{a}{\Delta t} \cdot \frac{|\delta\phi_k|}{\Delta t} = \frac{ab^{1/2}}{(\Delta t)^{1/2}}$$

$$i\hbar \frac{\partial}{\partial t}|\psi\rangle = H|\psi\rangle.$$

$$S_{bh} = m^2 \times 2\pi(kG/\hbar c)$$

$$\frac{1}{c^2} \cdot \frac{\partial E}{\partial t} = \text{curl } B - 4\pi j, \qquad \frac{\partial B}{\partial t} = -\text{curl } E,$$

$$\text{div } E = 4\pi\varrho, \qquad \text{div } B = 0.$$

Quantum Calculations – Examples of the mathematical equations used to explore the universe and subatomic realm.

© Wysong   Figure 207

Matter Is Mostly Space

Even before we dismantle matter into the nothingness of vibrations by using our thought experiment and quantum physics, the basic structure of an atom is already primarily the nothingness of space.

Take one atom and expand the nucleus to the size of a pea and place it on the 50-yard line of a football stadium. The outer walls of the stadium and parking lot would be where the electrons are. Everything in between is space and forces. If the nucleus were the size of a soccer ball, the electrons would be ten miles away. If all the space within the atoms that make up your body were removed, and all the atomic parts compressed to the density found in an atomic nucleus, you would fit on the head of a pin.

The point being, atoms that comprise us and the physical world we perceive as solid, are essentially all empty space. The atomic and quantum parts are also immaterial. Matter is, in effect, an illusion, a perception created by material brains that have the ability to perceive something from nothing.

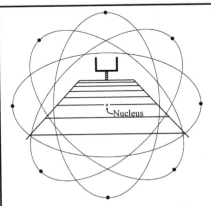

Atoms Are Primarily Space – If an atom is expanded to the size of a football stadium, the nucleus would be the size of a pea in the middle of the 50-yard line.

© Wysong   Figure 208

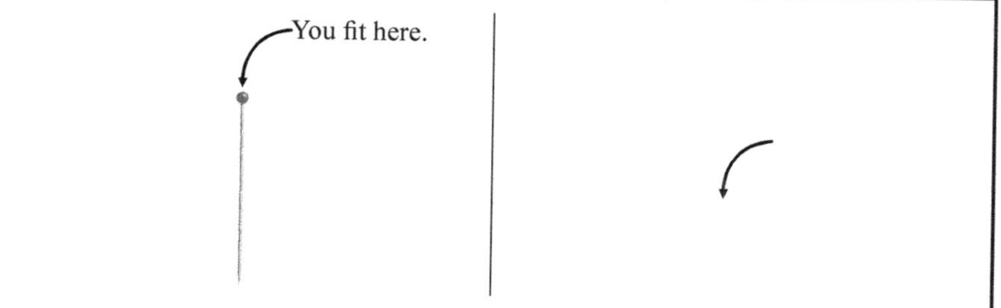

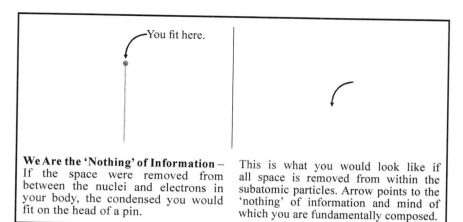

We Are the 'Nothing' of Information – If the space were removed from between the nuclei and electrons in your body, the condensed you would fit on the head of a pin.

This is what you would look like if all space is removed from within the subatomic particles. Arrow points to the 'nothing' of information and mind of which you are fundamentally composed.

© Wysong

Figure 209

All Is One

In classical physics, beginning in the seventeenth century and still embraced by most everyone to this day, things are thought to exist only if they can be perceived in a materialistic sense. It's all about weights, measures, levers, pulleys, speed, distance, timing and so on. This serves us well in the material world. But human-centered physics is naïve in that it is constrained by matter, our four dimensions, and the senses.

In order to function day to day in our material world, with beginnings and ends, and under the constraints of time, we require material bodies, brains, senses, and material things to sustain us. However, the true underlying quantum reality is timeless, connected, and nonmaterial.

This is very difficult to comprehend since we tend to think in terms of parts and pieces, beginnings and ends. We also think our four dimensions are all-inclusive. But in the quantum understanding, our dimensions are but an infinitesimal blip on a spectrum of reality that's not only connected but limitless.

Consider light. The visible portion of it is just a minuscule part of an electromagnetic spectrum that apparently extends both ways endlessly. Just because we can only perceive the narrow visible light part of the spectrum, does not deny the existence of other realities that exist in different parts of the spectrum.

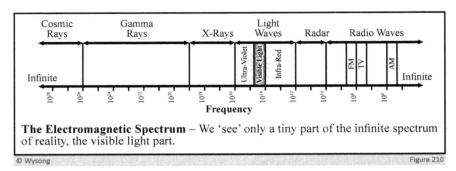

The Electromagnetic Spectrum – We 'see' only a tiny part of the infinite spectrum of reality, the visible light part.

© Wysong   Figure 210

For example, insects see a different world than we do since their eyes are tuned to less of the long wave infrared part of the spectrum, and more to the short wave invisible (to us) ultraviolet portion.

Similarly, the sound we can hear occupies only a narrow range in the sound spectrum. The high-frequency sound from a dog whistle does not exist to our ears but does to a dog's. The low-frequency sounds that are part of elephant language don't exist to our ears, but they use it to communicate over miles.

We are only privy to our one reality. Our brain just keeps dialing this four-dimensional material world and then our brain receiver concludes that's all there is.

In our physical world, distance is thought to separate things. However, at the quantum level, all points in space and time are best understood as being the same. Future and history are both accessible.

How Humans Always See the Universe

Edge of the Map Syndrome – Ancient cartographers wrote on the blurred edges of their maps, "there be dragons." The maps of today's evolutionary, materialistic, and religious cartographers by no means define the scope of our underlying reality.

© Wysong   Figure 211

Time is not the coming-here-gone linear phenomenon we think it to be. It's a perception of beginnings and ends created by our brains to cope with the dimensional world within which we're imprisoned. Einstein wrote of this, ". . . the distinction between past, present, and future is only a stubbornly persistent illusion."

A point in time is not gone; it is just elsewhere. Nothing begins and ends; everything just is—including us.

Quantum physics not only proves that touchy-feely matter is an illusion, but also that all things are interconnected and not even subject to time or distance. A butterfly cannot flap its wings in Hong Kong without a breeze occurring in Chicago. Quantum reality is like an infinite ocean where every single molecule is connected to every other one. Events we perceive are like waves—unique but inseparable manifestations of the same underlying ocean.

This interconnectedness is like a holographic film. Holograms are three-dimensional images in mid-air. If the film is broken into fragments and a laser beam directed at any one of the fragments, a complete holographic image will emerge. The image is stored everywhere on the film at the same time.

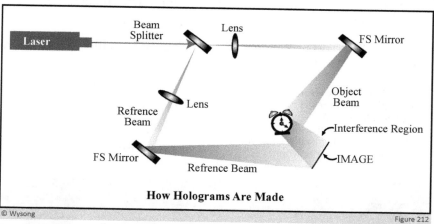

How Holograms Are Made

© Wysong

Figure 212

The holographic phenomenon of the whole containing all the parts, and any part containing the entire whole, is what our universe is unveiling itself to be at its fundamental implicit level.

That is why a starfish broken in pieces will regenerate the whole starfish. If the tip of a human finger is cut off, it will regenerate the lost tip of the finger if bandaged. If the lens of the eye of a newt is lost, the iris will regenerate it.

As early as 1935, physicists Einstein, Polosky, and Rosen proposed interconnectedness (nonlocality) which is the idea that at the quantum level things are not detached at all. For example, if two twin photons of light take off from the same point in opposite directions at 186,000 miles per second (the speed of light), what happens to one instantaneously affects the twin thousands of miles away. Though separate, they remain connected. Time and distance are not even relevant to them.

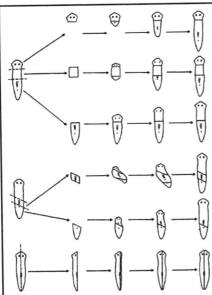

Living Things Are Holograms – The regeneration of complete flatworms (of the genus Planaria) from pieces of worm, cut as indicated on the left. Each piece of flatworm holographically contains the information for the entire worm.

© 1901 Morgan, T. H.   Figure 213

As strange as these ideas may sound, they reflect our true underlying reality. Consider these quotes from noted scientists:

Max Planck—". . . each individual particle in the system, in a certain sense, at any one time, exists simultaneously in every part of the space occupied by the system . . . We see that nothing less is at stake here than the concept of the particle."

Henry Stapp—"Quantum theory indicates that there are no such things as separate parts in reality, but instead only intimately related phenomena so bound up with each other as to be inseparable . . ."

Phantom Leaf Effect – If a piece of a leaf is cut off, (left) and the remaining leaf is energized with electricity and photographed with Kirlian photography, the missing part appears. (right) This demonstrates the holistic nature of matter in that a part contains a memory of the whole. Such "memory" has nothing to do with brain cells, rather it is a reflection of the implicit interconnectedness of all things in dimensions not yet explored.

© 1975 Robert M. Wagner   Figure 215

Werner Heisenberg—Reality is divided " . . . not into groups of objects, but into different groups of connections . . . An elementary particle is not an independently existing analyzable entity. It is, in essence, a set of relationships that reach outward to other things."

Alfred North Whitehead—"Nature is a theatre for the interrelations of activities . . . there is no possibility of a detached, self-contained existence."

Albert Einstein—"Physical reality as represented by continuous fields, is not mechanically explicable . . . Physical reality must be described in terms of continuous functions in space. The material point, therefore, can hardly be conceived any more as the basic concept of the theory . . . This change in the conception of reality is the most profound and truthful one that has come to physics since Newton."

Niels Bohr—"At the quantum level there is no objective picture at all."

The way it really is.

Two-dimensional plane.

What we think reality is if we are two-dimensional beings.

Multiple Dimensions – There are likely many other dimensional realities. Moving from one to the other will not be possible with metal ships but with thought.

© Wysong
Figure 247

Mental Feats Prove Holographic Connection

Some mentally disabled people can do amazing feats. Without seeing or understanding the parts, they can see the whole.

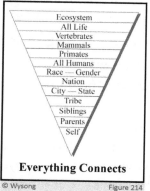

Everything Connects

© Wysong   Figure 214

The identical twins, George and Charles, can calculate in their heads the day of the week on which a date will fall 40,000 years forward or backward and give the answer in a few seconds. Neither of them can add simple numbers, nor do they know what a formula is, much less how to write one out. They can also describe the weather conditions of any day in their lives and repeat 300 digits in order from memory.

239

In 1920, Kenneth, a 38-year-old with the mental age of 11, and a day-to-day working vocabulary of 58 words could recall the population of every city in the United States over 5,000, identify any city by population alone, and quote the distances of each city from New York or Chicago. He knew all county seats; the names, number of rooms, and locations of 2,000 hotels, statistics on 3,000 mountains and rivers, and details on 2,000 inventions and discoveries.

Jedediah Buxton (1700s), with a mental age of 10 and inability to write his name, could make lightning-fast calculations. For example, he could give a 28-digit answer to the question: How many cubic 1/8ths of an inch are in a body with three sides of 23,145,789 X 5,642,732 X 54,965 yards?

Leslie Lemke is blind, mentally disabled, and has cerebral palsy. He cannot hold a utensil to eat with, but upon hearing Tchaikovsky's Piano Concerto No. 1 when a teen, he played it back flawlessly. He can playback any music regardless of its length, note for note, after hearing it only once.

Ellen is another musical savant who is blind and has an I.Q. of less than 50. She sang the entire Evita Broadway musical after hearing the album only once.

David, although mentally disabled, can tell you on what corner you are standing anywhere in Milwaukee, Wisconsin if you tell him the number of the bus pulling up in front of you and the time of day.

Alonzo has an I.Q. of 50 and a minimal vocabulary but can sculpt anything he sees with amazing speed and perfect accuracy.

Tony was considered mentally disabled but had an almanac-like ability to detail historical events that occurred on any day of the year.

Macaulay, an English historian with an amazing eidetic (photographic) memory, on a bet memorized Paradise Lost in a single night.

Bhandanta Vicitasara could recite from memory 16,000 pages of Buddhist canonical texts.

In Japan, Akira Haraguchi recites pi from memory out to 83,431 decimal places, a feat that takes hours and hours to do. He has a tough time proving this ability since radio and television programs always close up shop while he is still reciting the answer.

Alonzo Clemons – As a toddler, Alonzo suffered a head injury in an accident leaving him with developmental disabilities. At the same time he developed an amazing ability to sculpt with incredible speed and beauty. How could an accident to a delicate machine such as the brain create such extraordinary ability?

© Alonzo Clemons

Figure 216

Such feats escape the smartest among us. That's because intelligence in the worldly sense is not at play, but rather the special ability of some to perceive aspects of reality holographically.

```
3.1415926535897932384626433
0193852110555964462294895
2925409171536436789259036
3367336244065664308602139
4654958537105079227968925
3526193118817101000313783
5720106548586327886593615
0092770167113900984882401
5019351125338243003558764
8720275596023648066549911
6843852332390739414333454
0511739298489608412848862
6946839835255957098258226
```

Daniel Tammet – In his mind each integer up to 10,000 has its own unique shape, color, texture and feel. He can intuitively "see" results of calculations as synaesthetic landscapes without using conscious mental effort. Tammet holds the European record for reciting pi accurately from memory to 22,514 digits in five hours and nine minutes. He also speaks eleven languages and when challenged to learn Icelandic in one week, appeared on television conversing in Icelandic.

© Daniel Tammet

Figure 217

The Something of Nothing

Scientists tear apart the atom and probe deep space for answers to the Big Questions. They've searched high and low for a nice neat equation, force, or particle that is sufficient to explain all of existence. Instead, the underpinning of reality reflects mind, not matter. That's the same conclusion forced by the laws and design in nature.

Not only is the quantum world invisible and nonmaterial, but it is also unpredictable. These features are also characteristic of mind and free will.

Daniel Tammet – This is how this savant pictures in his mind the 22,514 digits of pi he has memorized. It is not a series of numbers, but one colorful image in his brain from which he extracts the particulars.

© Daniel Tammet Figure 218

With regard to unpredictability, if an electron is shot at a pane of glass, it might penetrate the glass and continue on, it might stop and reverse its course, it may vanish in front of the glass only to reappear on the other side and then continue, or may take route in any number of counterintuitive trajectories. Its behavior may also change based upon whether it is observed or not. Such behavior is characteristic of mind, not mere matter.

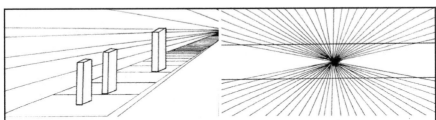

The Unreliability of the Senses – Superficial impressions can often be misleading. Does the highest block in the left drawing appear larger than the other two blocks? Do the two lines in the right drawing appear bowed? Close examination may be needed to give the correct answer to these questions. Would it not also be wise to closely scrutinize all ideas, regardless of how they may appear at first glance, to be sure we determine truth?

© Wysong Figure 219

At the larger physical level, our reality is like a painting that can only be explained by the creative choices of the painter, not an analysis of its atoms. Or consider a beautiful flower. If it is burned, its mass and energy remain quantitatively the same. But what about the qualitative aspect of beauty? If we capture all the atoms and heat of combustion from the fire, the form and beauty of the original flower is not retained therein.

That's because beauty is information, nothing in the material sense but everything in the mind sense. Beauty simply uses the flower's atoms and energy for expression. Since the ashes and energy from the flower no longer possess beauty, that would mean that they were not responsible for it in the first place. The flower's beauty must have preexisted, expressed itself when the flower blossomed, and will continue to exist in a non-physical realm even if the flower is burned to random ashes.

All of the qualities of our world are similarly emergent; they are gestalts and not reducible to an examination of the parts and pieces as materialism demands. The choices of a creative mind are the only explanation for functional complexity and beauty.

Humans once filled the heavens with gods to explain the world. Most gods were thrown out when atomism, Newtonian science, and Darwinism joined hands to form the beliefs of materialism and evolution. Mind became the product of matter, not matter the product of mind. Materialists, including most quantum physicists, stop short of crediting mind with the existence of our reality. They are either blinded by evolutionary bias or equate mind with humans and cannot understand why, if there is a Creator, he/she does not talk to them or remove all adversity from the world.

This brings to mind the musing of Woody Allen: "If only God would give me some clear sign! Like making a large deposit in my name at a Swiss bank." Clearly, an anthropomorphized god is not the same as the incomprehensible cause of our reality.

Materialism and evolution have not lived up to their promise of providing answers to the Big Questions. Matter, physical laws, functional complexity, free will, and beauty cannot explain themselves nor the indeterminate nature of the quantum world.

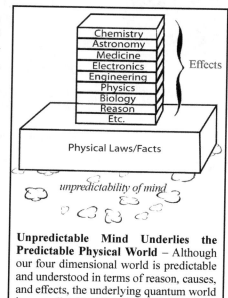

Unpredictable Mind Underlies the Predictable Physical World – Although our four dimensional world is predictable and understood in terms of reason, causes, and effects, the underlying quantum world is unpredictable, like mind and thought.

© Wysong   Figure 220

243

Advancing technology permits peering deeper and deeper into atoms, and further and further out into space. But all that is ever learned is what is there, not how it came to be or why it's there. The Big Bang no more answers the Big Questions than did the gigantic turtle once thought to balance the world on its back.

The invisible, timeless, interconnected, and unpredictable world underlying our four dimensions and the laws governing them, points to mind. This, in turn, points to humans not only being the product of mind, but fundamentally being invisible, timeless, interconnected, and unpredictable minds as well.

"Men become the tools of their tools."
—Thoreau

Figure 221

35
WEIRD THINGS
DISPROVE MATERIALISM

The most compelling evidence any of us will ever be faced with is personal observation and experience. No argument, no matter how erudite or authoritative, ever defeats direct experience. So, it is wise to keep an open mind and not take the position of the anonymous person who said to Margaret Mead, "This is the kind of phenomena I wouldn't believe even if it were true."

Let's explore evidence that reality extends beyond the physical world with something you can experience right now.

At one time I was faced with the problem of locating a drain line under a cement floor in the warehouse at my office. The original construction drawings were lost and we needed to plumb into a drain for an expansion. After calling everyone we could think of to see if there was some instrument that could detect pipes under cement, nobody had any better idea than to start randomly breaking out the concrete floor. That was a daunting and depressing prospect, to say the least.

A fellow worker suggested that he try to "witch" the drain line. He proceeded to bend some coat hangers (see drawing) and walked about the warehouse until he had mapped out what he claimed was the entire drainage system, hidden under 6 inches of solid concrete! I watched him walkabout as the wires mysteriously crossed as he passed over certain spots. He then chalked an X on the floor everywhere they did.

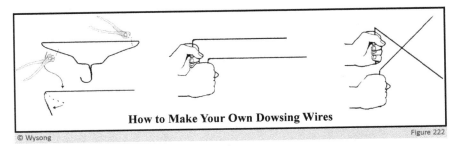

How to Make Your Own Dowsing Wires

© Wysong   Figure 222

Intrigued, but thinking he was probably moving the wires voluntarily, I decided to try it. To my amazement, the wires crossed in every spot he had chalked an X. No visuals were at play since I even repeated it closing my eyes.

We broke through the concrete in line with the X's and dug down. There was the line, three feet down.

Drain pipe 3½ feet under floor

Dowsing wires crossed

Concrete

How We Found a Drain Pipe – "X's" on the floor mark where our dowsing wires crossed. When we broke through six inches of concrete reinforced with wire mesh and dug another three feet down we found the plastic drain pipes.

© Wysong   Figure 223

On another occasion, after digging for an hour in my yard to find plugged drain pipes leading from my eavestroughs, I remembered dowsing. I bent some coat hangers and walked about the yard. In about two minutes I found the pipe.

I had the same experience trying to find a buried electrical line going to an outside light that had become dead. I found some scrap electrical cord and stripped out a small piece of the copper wire in it. Holding this in my hand while I held the dowsing wires, I again amazed myself as I was able to track the line two feet underground.

For centuries, dowsing has been used to find underground water; for centuries it has been pooh-poohed by the scientific community. What happens between the wire and the water (or other buried objects) and why the wires turn toward one another is totally mysterious. (Some dowsers use a y-shaped stick that points down over the target.) There is some form of communication going on, but it hasn't been measured, harnessed, defined, or explained.

Here is how you can experience this yourself to help open your mind to the mysterious and unseen world. Just lay a hose on the ground and let water trickle through it. Slowly walk across it perpendicularly, very lightly holding your dowsing wires so they can easily swivel back and forth. Hold them body width apart, parallel to the ground, and pointing forward. Keep your elbows tight to your sides to help your hands steady. Feel for the wires' desire to turn toward one another and let them do it. They will do this as you pass over the hose. When you feel them start to turn, slow way down or stop to let them finish their swing inward toward one another.

You can also experience coins communicating with one another by putting one coin on the ground and another in your hand as you hold the wires. Then walk over the coin and the wires will cross.

If it doesn't work for you, retry by moving very slow and steady, making sure the wires are held VERY loosely so they can do their own thing. Have friends or family give it a try if you can't make it work.

On the other hand, if you prefer to not try this for yourself and just doubt, you can do that too and have plenty of support. For example, in a debunking book entitled: Why People Believe Weird Things, the author, the founder of Skeptic Magazine, states, "Some things such as water dowsing . . . have been tested and have failed the tests often enough that we can provisionally conclude that they are false." (Thanks for "provisionally.")

Another author, in the book, Quantum Leaps in the Wrong Direction – Where Real Science Ends . . . and Pseudoscience Begins, remarks: "Alleged psychic ability of dowsing . . . Do these events support the hypothesis that dowsers can detect hidden substances better than with chance guessing and without the use of clues in the environment? No . . . Controlled experiments set up to test the abilities of dowsers have shown that dowsers are no better at finding hidden substances than chance would predict . . .

What does cause the muscle contractions that move the dowser's rod . . . The movement is caused by suggestion and unconscious muscular activity in the dowser. It has been demonstrated that just thinking about a certain physical action (like a dowsing rod tilting . . .) causes minute reactions in the muscles that would be used for such actions. And, the slightest movement in the wrists or hands will be magnified in the movement of the rod . . ."

Reading that, after experiencing what I did in the warehouse and in my yard, gave me the same feeling you would have if you walked into a building after being drenched in the rain, shoes sloshing as you walked, and were met by people who insisted that it couldn't be raining because the meteorologist on the weather station said it wasn't forecast for the day. To believe the Quantum Leaps author, I would have to believe that the results I and everyone at the office had, even blindfolded, were just imagined or we were all delusional that particular day. His take on dowsing and the results of "controlled experiments" would mean everyone at the office happened to agree by just guessing where pipelines were buried three-and-a-half feet under 15,000 square feet of six-inch thick concrete.

Decide for yourself. When you do it, you will feel the wires moving on their own. They are loose in the hands and cannot, therefore, be moved by "muscles." It is only if they are totally loose and free to swing on their own that it will work.

Notice in the above skeptic's quote the allusion to "thinking about" a particular result making it happen. He may be on to something there, but not for the muscle reactions he speculates. As we have learned, mind underlies reality. It may be that our mind's desire to find water pipes or copper wire is the force that makes the wires move. But it is not your "muscles," it's the wires themselves that move, as you will experience.

Please go bend the hangers and create the ultimate proof, personal experience. Do it right now before you venture on through these next chapters. It will help make them seem not quite so unbelievable.

36
EVEN WEIRDER THINGS

I hope you were successful with your dowsing experiment. If you were, nobody is going to convince you that what you experienced did not happen, correct? It doesn't matter that there is no explanation, that conventional science has no clue as to what the forces are that cause the wires to move, or that your friends won't believe you if you tell them.

Keep this conviction you have with regard to your own experience in mind as we survey many other weird things that people experience. Others are as convinced of their experiences as you are convinced of yours. Just because standard science and materialism don't have sufficient scope to explain phenomena beyond the edges of their map, is no reason to reject them out of hand.

Since most of what follows will seem unbelievable, you must measure it in the context of the preceding chapters, the resource section at the end of this book, and pro and con information you can retrieve by searching names or terms on the Internet.

If you find evidence that seems to discredit some of what follows, that's okay. But also allow that any extraordinary event is going to be met with vigorous criticism. This is particularly so when such evidence challenges cherished beliefs, such as evolution, materialism, atheism, and human-made religions. Weigh the evidence, all of it, and decide from there.

Remote Dowsing

In remote dowsing, lines, figures, and shapes created in the mind of a sender are dowsed (received) by another person in the next room or thousands of miles away. Dowsing wires such as we described in the previous chapter aren't used; rather, the dowser receives the information mentally and writes it down on paper. The sender can be on the ground, in a cave, flying in an airplane, or closed in a Faraday cage (electromagnetic shield). The speed of information transfer is instantaneous, and the figures, lines, or shapes created by the sender linger in the 'dowsing realm' for years permitting them to be dowsed long after the sender has sent them. Such experiments are conducted by many researchers, including the engineers at the Dowsing Research Group in Britain.

Evidence That Supports Mind Influencing Matter

- Controlled scientific studies demonstrate healing using thought, touch, and prayer.

- Imagery alone can affect immune cell counts.

- Visualizing athletic training can improve performance better than actual training.

- Staring at one side of a person's face can increase the blood flow on that side of the face.

- Placebos can cure cancer and cause addiction. Thirty percent of a noncancer control group receiving a placebo ("sugar pill") in a cancer study lost hair.

- Caffeine didn't keep caffeine-sensitive people awake if they believed they were receiving a sedative.

- Some people can put needles through their body without bleeding, a fencing foil through vital organs without harm or pain, burn cigarettes against the flesh, handle live coals, and place hooks through the skin and then hang or drag heavy loads by lines attached to them.

- People have been reported to levitate, such as St. Joseph of Cupertino rising 20-30 feet in the air.

"The placebo is more effective than the product. Let's market the placebo."

© Wysong   Figure 224

Nonlocal Biocommunication

Leukocytes (immune cells) extracted from a person are kept alive in a test tube to which electrodes are attached. A tracing of the cell's electrical activity is made similar to the way a polygraph works. The person from whom the cells are taken goes <u>miles</u> away and is shown a movie that will have a disturbing personal scene. At the instant the person is shocked by the scene, the polygraph tracing of the leukocytes—miles away—shows a dramatic deflection from the flat line.

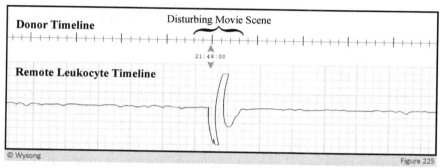

Figure 225

Cells, bacteria, plants, and chicken eggs show similar capabilities. In an experiment, six people were introduced to two philodendrons. One of the people proceeded to murder one of the plants by tearing it out by the roots and then shredding and stomping on it. The remaining plant was attached to electrodes, and the six people left the room. Then, one by one they were reintroduced to the remaining plant. The electrode tracing remained flat but then spiked when the murderer came into the room.

In another case, a woman who cared for a philodendron was asked questions while the plant was hooked to a polygraph. When the woman lied, the recording spiked.

Fresh beef meat was hooked to electrodes. When trimmed pieces were fed to a cat, the recording spiked. When the cutting board with blood on it was washed with Ajax cleanser, the recording spiked.

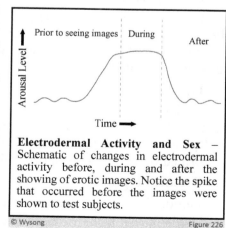

Electrodermal Activity and Sex – Schematic of changes in electrodermal activity before, during and after the showing of erotic images. Notice the spike that occurred before the images were shown to test subjects.

Figure 226

Such action-at-a-distance, or nonlocality in response to a host's conscious state of mind, has been demonstrated repeatedly. This provides evidence that the implicit reality of which we and all other living and nonliving things are a part is one and unaffected by time or distance.

Group Intention

People joined in common thought and intention can affect health and even world events.

Acupuncture

This proven medical modality is not explicable in traditional materialistic terms. It relieves pain, heals, and permits painless surgery by creating anesthesia. Something besides material organs, tissues, and cells resides in the body.

Homeopathy

This medical approach was the prevailing healing system into the twentieth century. It has been largely displaced by more profitable patented pharmaceutics and allopathy (treating illness by removing symptoms). Homeopaths create remedies based upon like healing like: if a substance can cause illness, in minuscule dosage it can stimulate the body to heal. It works similarly to vaccines where a modified disease agent is used to create immunity against the disease caused by that agent. Remarkably, homeopathic remedies can cure illness even when the dose is diluted so much that the starting material cannot even be found in the end product. The remedy somehow mysteriously imprints on the inert carrier. Homeopathy has been proven in controlled studies and remains a predominant form of medicine in many parts of the world.

Healing by Touch

In repeated controlled scientific studies, mice that would normally die from induced mammary cancer within about seventeen days were cured by non-religious healing by touch. Attempts to induce the cancer subsequently failed. bengstonresearch.com

Hypnosis

Under hypnosis, people can see through people and identify objects held behind the back. Subjects can also experience taste, sounds, and pain experienced by another. Thousands of surgeries have been performed on people anesthetized with nothing but hypnosis.

Remote Hypnosis

Hundreds of cases have been reported of subjects hypnotized in a location removed from the hypnotist.

Magnetic Field Perception

Karl Reichenbach (1844), the German chemist who discovered paraffin, was the first modern-age person to study and verify the ability of a person to perceive the field surrounding a magnet.

Psychic Detectives

Psychics are employed by police agencies around the globe to help solve difficult cases. A television program series (on cable Court TV) demonstrates the usefulness of the ability of psychics to give detailed information about crime scenes, victims, locations, and perpetrators.

"I almost had a psychic girlfriend, but she dumped me before we met."

© Wysong   Figure 227

Reverse Speech

If a person's speech is reversed on a recorder, they will say things either confirming that what they have said is true, false, or what they are really thinking. The forward voice is the conscious; the backward voice is the unconscious revealing itself. A website, reversespeech.com, has numerous examples. The political speech examples are particularly telling. Although called a "pseudoscience" by skeptics, it has been proven to be reliable to the extent that the CIA and FBI use it.

Neimology

The placement of letters in a name can foretell a person's characteristics. Scientific studies prove the predictive value in human resource departments, understanding friends, parents, and siblings, selecting mates, understanding life's purpose, and in litigation to learn the leanings of judges and jurors.

Diagnosis/Healing

Some people can diagnose and heal disease from a remote distance without ever seeing the patient (called DMILS— distant mental influence of living systems).

X-Ray Vision

At the age of ten, Natasha, a young girl in Saransk, discovered that she could see inside of bodies. Since then, she has had people from near and far line up for diagnoses that have proven to be remarkably accurate. (Type "Natasha Saransk" in an internet search engine for interesting pro and con discussions of Natasha's abilities and the attempts to discredit her.)

Twins Connection

Twins raised apart from birth and with no communication between them were both named Jim by their adoptive parents. Both married a Betty, divorced, and remarried women named Linda. Both named their firstborn James. In childhood, each twin had owned a dog named Toy. They had enjoyed family vacations on the same beach in Florida and had worked part-time in law enforcement. They shared a taste for Miller Lite beer and Salem cigarettes. Just before their first meeting at the University of Minnesota, after having been separated for 39 years, each of them built a circular white bench around a tree in the back yard.

Pain experienced by one twin is often felt by the other. More than 30% of twins experience telepathic interconnection.

Absurd Coincidences

In Detroit, in the 1930s, a young man named Joseph Figlock was walking down the street. A young mother's baby fell from a high window onto Figlock. The baby's fall was broken by Figlock and both man and baby were unharmed. A year later, the very same baby fell from the very same window onto poor, unsuspecting Joseph Figlock as he was again passing beneath. And again, they both survived the event.

In 1883, Henry Ziegland broke off a relationship with his girlfriend who then committed suicide. The girl's brother was so enraged that he hunted down Ziegland, shot him, and then turned the gun on himself. But Ziegland had not been killed. The bullet had only grazed his face and then lodged in a tree. Years later, Ziegland decided to cut down the large tree, which still had the bullet in it. The task seemed so formidable that he decided to use a few sticks of dynamite. The explosion propelled the bullet into Ziegland's head, killing him.

Mark Twain was born in the year of the appearance of Halley's Comet in 1835. In 1909 he predicted he would die upon its return in 1910. He did.

In 1975, a man riding a moped in Bermuda was accidentally struck and killed by a taxi. One year later, the man's brother, riding the very same moped, was killed in the very same way by the very same taxi driven by the very same driver—and carrying the very same passenger.

In Monza, Italy, King Umberto went to a small restaurant for dinner. When the owner took King Umberto's order, the King noticed that he and the restaurant owner were virtual doubles, in the face and build. Both men began discussing the striking resemblance between each other and found many more similarities:

1. Both men were born on the same day, of the same year (March 14, 1844).

2. Both men had been born in the same town.

3. Both men married a woman with the same name, Margherita.

4. The restaurateur opened his restaurant on the same day that King Umberto was crowned King of Italy.

5. On July 29, 1900, King Umberto was informed that the restaurateur had died that day in a mysterious shooting accident. As he expressed his regret, an anarchist in the crowd assassinated him.

This chain of coincidences all happened in just two days: on the 28th of July the King met the restaurateur, and on the 29th both were dead.

Projections

Mind images have been reported to create physical effects. For example, projecting a crown of thorns, three nails, a cross, and a sword that was found imprinted on the heart upon autopsy. A person envisioning an angel piercing the heart resulted in a deep fissure in the heart. Another individual could consciously command images such as of dogs, horses, and words to appear on the arms, legs, and shoulders.

Multiple Personality Syndrome

When a new personality takes over, a drunk person can become sober, an adult drug dosage can cause over-dosage in the child personality, and an anesthetized person will awaken. Conditions that can vary from personality to personality include scars, birthmarks, cysts, right- and left-handedness, visual acuity (requiring the person to carry two or three sets of different glasses), eye color, color blindness, menstrual cycles to match each "new lady," voice pattern, diabetes, epilepsy, and tumors.

Psychokinesis(PK)

There are many documented cases of the ability to move physical objects with thought, as well as dematerialize objects and rematerialize them in another location. The Princeton University Engineering Anomalies Research lab (PEAR), founded in 1979, has demonstrated compelling evidence for PK. In experiments with random number generators, subjects were able to increase the machine's generation of ones or zeros using mental efforts alone.

Uri Geller fixes broken clocks with his mind. He even has listeners and viewers bring their broken clocks to the television or radio when he is broadcasting. He then proceeds to help the viewers fix their clocks using only their minds. (See urigeller.com)

Everyone who believes in psychokinesis, raise my hand.

© Wysong   Figure 229

Creating Radiation, Gravity, and Magnetism

Geller reportedly willed a Geiger Counter to read radiation levels 500 times that of the background radiation. He could also change the weight of an object while it rested on a precision weighing machine. By placing his hand over a magnetic field gauss meter, it would read a level half the strength of Earth's magnetic field.

Metal Bending

Metal bending is a form of psychokinesis. Uri Geller routinely teaches people via television how to bend spoons with the mind. A twelve-year-old boy twisted a large piece of metal out of shape at a distance of thirty feet. Jean-Pierre Girard in France bent pieces of metal sealed in glass tubes. Some subjects have bent metal that is beyond the strength of any human to bend, while others have turned a spoon "as soft as chewing gum." Others with these skills include Nicholas Williams, Stephen North, Julie Knowles, Masuaki Kiyota, Nina Kulagina, and many juveniles in England.

Sympathetic Magic (Telesomatic Effects)

Shamans, witch doctors, and spiritual healers are reported to impact the health and wellbeing of someone remote from them. This is done by just "sending" the signal or creating an effigy of a person.

Transpersonal Dreaming Experiments

A group of empathetic people chooses to dream help for a target person in need. The target does not reveal the problem to the group but loans each person a personal item to sleep with, such as comb, bracelet, key, etc. In the morning the group reveals the content of their dreams, only to find common themes and helpful guidance and remedies for the target. (Internet search this Ph.D. researcher: henryreed.com)

Eyeless Sight

One person sees well enough with the skin in the armpits to read notes and discern colors placed there. Another sees by clicking his tongue and echolocating.

Blind people discern colors. An autistic savant child who cannot read or write, correctly reveals five-digit numbers an out-of-sight mother views. (see: youtu.be/TRAPuMEpk4A)

Energy Fields

A woman could walk blindfolded through the woods and avoid trees by sensing their "energy fields." Some 97 different cultures have words to describe auras. Even famous surgeons, professors, and heads of departments in medical facilities, such as Cornell and Mayo, report seeing auras surrounding patients.

Time Slips

While at a location where a certain historical event occurred, many people have reported observing and experiencing the event. For example, one might be walking down a country road in Georgia, and all of a sudden be viewing a civil war battle exactly as it occurred in that location.

Astrology

French researchers have shown a correlation between the position of Mars and the birth times of exceptional athletes. Scientists elsewhere have duplicated the results. Other studies have verified astrological correlations to human behavior and traits.

Yawns

Out of vision and hearing, yawns (pandiculating) can be contagious. Human yawns can also induce yawning in animals.

Mind Changing Matter

The mere observation of quanta by scientists can change their behavior.

Telepathy

Transmitting and receiving thought has been well studied. In an American survey, 58% of respondents claimed to have experienced telepathy. Unlike other energies, telepathy does not fall off with distance. It is instant, exceeding even the speed of light barrier.

Psychometry

Psychometry is the ability to hold an object previously unknown and describe details of its history that could not possibly be deduced from the object.

Wraiths

Apparitions that serve as a premonition of a person's imminent death have been observed for centuries.

Remote Viewing

For twenty-three years, during the height of the cold war, people with the ability to perceive and describe distant locations were employed by the U.S. government (a 20 million dollar budget). This is known as remote viewing and is a natural ability of some and can be learned by others. (There are over 365,000 websites from around the world on the subject of remote viewing.) Distance from the target is not a factor. Former government remote viewers are for hire through the Monroe Institute in Ohio.

The CIA and other intelligence agencies around the world continue to use remote viewers for spying. The CIA's Stargate Project was recently declassified (January 2017) resulting in thirteen million pages of evidence of psychic phenomena and remote viewing.

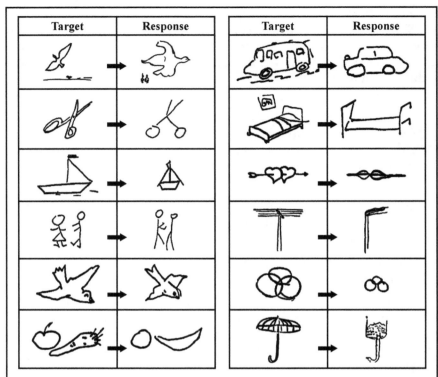

Target	Response	Target	Response

Remote Viewing – Examples of remote viewing where 'sender' and 'receiver' were in completely separated locales. The 'sender' would draw or look at an item, or open a random envelope with a picture of a target. The 'receiver' responses are the drawings to the right.

Figure 230

Clairvoyance, Pre-Cognition, Premonitions, Presentiment

Participants in some studies successfully dream about a picture that would be chosen by others the next day. Others can describe locations experimenters would visit before the locations had even been decided upon.

Thousands of controlled laboratory tests prove mind is not tied to time or confined to matter. For example, study participants monitored similarly to lie detector testing will show an excitatory response <u>prior</u> to an exciting image shown on a screen. Scenes are randomly altered with peaceful scenes where no prior response is seen. (See Dr. Radin in Resources)

The famous 16th-century French seer, Nostradamus, wrote a letter to Henry II that was published in 1555. Therein he predicted the precise year of the French Revolution (200 years in the future), and other details related to it.

In 1625, the German, John Englebrecht, described the storming of the Bastille some 154 years in the future.

The American Civil War soldier, John Davis, foresaw war events that only came to pass after he had died. Jacob Burkhardt, Stormberger, Edgar Cayce, Heinrich Heine, Madame Blavatsky, Lanz von Liebenfels, and others made remarkable predictions about world wars.

Go to the Amazing Kreskin's website and review a whole series of prophecies he has made over the years.

Take the case of the young teenage boy that came up missing in the early '70s. Detectives were stymied, so they reluctantly decided to try a psychic. She identified John Wayne Gacy as the murderer and said she could see corpses buried in a semicircle. The officers got a search warrant and found the bodies buried in the crawl space exactly as described. They had stopped this serial torturer and murderer who had made victims of at least 33 men. But the young boy was not one of the bodies found. Another psychic drove around the city with an officer until she sensed where the boy was. They were by the Des Plaines River and she said the boy was under the ice and snow at the bottom of the embankment. The police were unable to access the area due to the winter conditions. In parting, the psychic handed the officer a piece of paper upon which she wrote the date, "April 19." She explained that on that date they would find the boy where she said he was. Months later in the spring, the station got a call that someone had found a body. It was the boy. He was where the psychic said and the date was April 19. Millions, along with me, watched this documentary broadcast on the cable Learning Channel, October 28, 2005.

Predictions, prophecy, and presentiment are to be expected since our underlying reality is timeless and holographically entangled with mind.

Everyday Occurrences

If the above extraordinary things seem doubtful to you, I get it, me too. Other than witnessing the events there's no way to be sure. But we must admit, given that mind underlies our reality, that virtually all things are possible, not just physical causes and effects.

The following more common things most people have experienced are just as fantastic as the above. If they are real, so too could be the preceding extraordinary phenomena.

- Knowing what someone else is about to say
- Guessing the correct time
- Singing or humming a tune somebody else is thinking about
- Thinking what others are thinking
- Think a question and someone else answers it
- Silent transference between therapists and patients
- Anticipating opponent's moves telepathically in competitive sports
- Transmission of thoughts to another person who is dreaming
- Transmission of images to another person by mental focus
- Milk leakage from mothers remote from a hungry baby
- Mothers awakening just before babies do
- Sensing when visitors are about to arrive
- Knowledge of another's sexual desire or infidelities
- Thinking of someone and their letter arrives
- Inducing people to call by only using thought
- Anticipating when an e-mail arrives
- Telephoning someone and they are on the line calling you
- Sensing what part of the body another is staring at
- Transference of feelings to the one being stared at
- Sense of being stared at by professional surveillance equipment
- Sense of being stared at through telescopes and binoculars
- Sense of danger if being stalked as prey
- Evil eye transference of bad fate to others
- Foreboding of death and disaster
- Waking just before the alarm is to go off or at a time desired
- Thirty-eight people reported seeing the 9-11 disaster in dreams
- Five people reported having 9-11 premonitions and presentiments

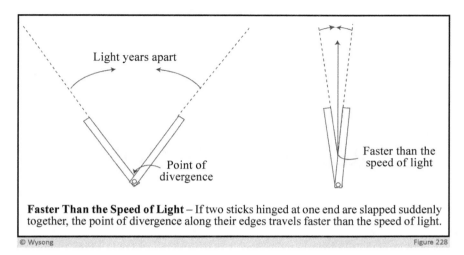

Faster Than the Speed of Light – If two sticks hinged at one end are slapped suddenly together, the point of divergence along their edges travels faster than the speed of light.

© Wysong   Figure 228

Life Itself

Life is an anachronism, a paradox, actually more like a miracle. Not only is the existence of its order, complexity, and information out of sync with the natural entropic flow of things (downhill towards disorder), but its moment-by-moment sustenance is miraculous. Something other than known physical forces must explain whatever it is that keeps life going. That something eludes our measure or comprehension, so we ignore it and proceed as if life is nothing but a clever engine requiring fuel. To do so requires that we gloss over the fact that this particular engine is self-aware, has free will, grows, reproduces, self-repairs, and self-feeds with no intervention.

For life to continue, there must be instantaneous (faster than the speed of light) and continuous communication between all of its trillions of elements and processes.

Metabolism is described in textbooks as if it were sequential, occurring a step at a time. Although there is linear and cyclic activity, all living processes are entangled incomprehensibly with all other activity such that nothing proceeds in isolation. Life is better understood as being one gigantic dynamic, rather than a summation of individual events. It is irreducibly complex.

We need no evidence outside of ourselves. With every breath we take, life cries out that there is more at play in the universe than blind matter and energy.

37
CREATURE TESTIMONY

Plants and animals provide a rich field of study proving that reality extends beyond the material.

Beyond Five Senses

For example, new animal senses are being discovered that are poorly understood and for which no sense organs have even been identified. Examples include the electrical fields generated by eels to sense their environment, the ability of sharks and rays to sense the electrical fields generated by prey, the thermographic heat-sensing ability of some snakes, and the magnetic compass in migratory birds, turtles, and fish. Termites in a colony separated by plates will build tunnels that meet precisely on each side of the plate.

Thought and Bacteria

Thought can impact the growth of bacteria and fungi in laboratory cultures. For example, the bacterium, E. coli, can metabolize lactose sugar. This can be influenced by human thought resulting not only in altered growth but altered genetic structure. In one experiment, bacteria were subjected to paralyzing phenol. All in the control group were paralyzed, except for 7% of those that were willed by experimenters not to be paralyzed.

Animal Psychics

Some people can telepathically communicate with both living and dead animals.

Animals as Psychics

The biologist, Dr. Rupert Sheldrake, has accumulated hundreds of case studies and performed extensive controlled research on both humans and animals:

- Dogs secluded and observed by video in a building away from the owner will form a semicircle around the door and wag their tails when the owner thinks about coming to let them out.
- Horses anticipate the desires of riders.
- People call pets and pets call people telepathically.
- Animals and people sense distant accidents and deaths.
- Pets knowing who is telephoning.
- Prey will sense being stared at by hungry predators but not by those predators that are not in the hunting mode.
- Animals show premonition of earthquakes, avalanches. and air raids days before the events. The Chinese have used animals in this way to save tens of thousands of lives. Animals in Indonesia alerted people and broke restraining chains to escape the impending tsunami disaster of 2005.
- Animals warn of people's seizures and comas.

Sheldrake has carefully analyzed 585 reports of dogs knowing when their owners are coming home. For example, whenever Peter Edwards returns to his farm in Essex, England, his Irish Setters are at the gate to greet him. He works irregular hours and usually doesn't even let his wife know when he is returning. But the dogs know.

Jackson, the family dog, always anticipated the return of the kids on the bus. He also got excited, wanted out, and went to the end of the sidewalk to wait for the father who, it just so happens, had just arrived in port some 20 miles away. His schedule was not at all regular. The mother, observing the dependability of Jackson, even prepared a meal and primped timed with his behavior.

Similar accounts come from other dog owners who have irregular schedules, such as lawyers, taxi drivers, military personnel, midwives, and airline workers. Distance is not a factor, nor is sound, wind direction, time spent away, nor schedule.

In carefully tracking the simultaneous actions of the animal and those of the owner, the trigger was found to be when the person decided to come home. It was the thought-action that the bonded animal perceived and responded to. If an owner changes his/her mind, the pet settles back into its pre-alerted demeanor.

Gould, another researcher, found that when he decided to move the food source of a hive of honeybees, they would be found circling the new location before he ever got there. The bees did this possessing only 1/10,000 of an ounce brain. When asked if he could explain how they did it, Gould replied, "I can't. I wish they'd never done it!"

Oscar

© Stew Milne Figure 232

In Providence, Rhode Island, a nursing home is also home to a cat named Oscar. He is revered for his compassionate care. Again and again, he can predict who in the home is about to die. About four hours before a person's death, he will curl up and nuzzle next to them, purring until they pass. Staff trusts his anticipation so much that they call family members when he takes up his post.

Incredible Parrots

African Grey Parrots have shown remarkable speech and telepathic abilities. Over the course of twenty years, a parrot named Alex acquired a vocabulary of 200 words. This little birdbrain rivaled the

African Grey Parrot

© Miguel Bugallo Sánchez Figure 231

abilities of primates and was capable of abstractions, recognizing colors, articulating concepts about present and absent, and communicating far beyond parroting.

In 1997, inspired by seeing Alex on television, the owner of an African Grey parrot named N'kisi began teaching him to speak as if he were a child. In a little over 5 years, he developed a vocabulary of almost 1000 words (about 100 words are necessary for half of all writing in English), over 7,000 original sentences (which have been recorded), and he invents his own words for things his repertoire does not cover, like "flied" for flew. He also uses words in context, knows past, present, and future tenses, is inventive, and has an excellent memory.

After seeing a picture of Dr. Jane Goodall with apes, N'kisi remarked when he met her for the first time, "Got a chimp?" He also has quite a sense of humor. When he saw another parrot hang upside down from a perch he said, "You got to put this bird on the camera."

N'kisi also has remarkable telepathic abilities. Over 600 instances were recorded in just his first five years. For example, when the owner decided to call Rob, N'kisi said, "Hi Rob," as the owner was scrolling through the Rolodex looking for the number. In another instance, N'kisi was behind the television while a movie was playing in which Jackie Chan was precariously lying on his back high on a girder. N'kisi said, "Don't fall down." When the movie cut to a car commercial N'kisi said, "There's my car" even though all that was audible was the music soundtrack.

In a controlled experiment, N'kisi was put in one room while the owner viewed cards in the other. N'kisi identified what the owner was looking at with odds three times greater than chance.

Morphic Resonance

Reminiscent of the underlying holographic nature of reality previously discussed, Sheldrake describes morphic resonance as an interconnection between all living things in the collective consciousness. There have been over 500 case histories and more than 20,000 people participating in experimental tests.

For example:

In 1984 the BBC cooperated with Dr. Sheldrake in an experiment in which 80 million people were shown solutions to puzzle pictures. After the airing, 6,500 people who did not see the airing were tested to see how fast they could solve the puzzle. The time for them to solve the puzzle was less than the time for those who tried to solve the puzzle before the program was aired.

New ideas, inventions, ideologies, awakenings, fads, skills, infirmities, and premonitions can seem to inexplicably sweep through a community or the entire world.

Rats taught to run a maze kept reducing the time to get to the target with each generation. The 22nd generation of rats was completing it ten times faster than the first generation. This improvement in maze time occurred en masse among the entire generation.

The length of time to train pigeons to peck at lighted "Skinner boxes" keeps decreasing with each generation.

Such phenomena certainly take conventional materialistic science outside of its explanatory capabilities. Evidence either has to be dismissed or the mind opened to accommodate an extradimensional biology.

38
PERSONAL WEIRDNESS

If you think back through life, you will probably recollect experiences that are in keeping with some of the examples cited in the previous chapters. I can lay claim to none of the extraordinary abilities. But I have experienced déjà vu, contagious yawns, anticipating phone calls, guessing the time, dowsing, and witnessing some unusual animal capabilities.

I recently listened to a program on the radio about the development of rocketry. Werner von Braun was being discussed, and just before the speaker was going to state the year of his death, I tried to guess it. I thought 1977. The commentator then said "1977." I knew nothing about his life. I impressed me very much.

Here's another example of my amateur "psychic" abilities. My wife had been setting the alarm so she could get up early to see our daughter off to school. On this particular morning there was no school and thus no need for the alarm to go off. At about 4 AM I was lying awake going through the work I was going to try to accomplish for the day. I didn't want to get up because that would awaken her. She wasn't getting a lot of rest, and I wanted her to sleep in.

Then I remembered that she probably had the alarm set. So, I slowly rolled out of bed and crept around to her side where the alarm clock rested on a nightstand within her reach. I moved quietly and listened to make sure her deep sleep breathing continued.

When I got to the stand, I crouched, so she could not see my silhouette if she were to wake up. I then reached for the clock to press in the little alarm-off button. I hadn't made a sound. Everything was perfect. I was so clever.

But as my hand was on the clock silently searching in the dark for the button, I heard stirring. The deep breathing stopped. I froze with my hand on the clock. Then, to my amazement, I felt her hand probing the top of my hand searching for the alarm-off button. She was going to get up and didn't want the alarm to awaken me.

After surveying my hand for a moment, she slowly pulled her's back. I held my position with my hand still on the clock hoping she would just fall back asleep. No such luck. Her hand returned, this time timidly feeling and squeezing this strange fleshy protuberance growing out of the top of her clock in the pitch black.

I thought by then that she was fully awake and knew it was my hand, so I grabbed hers in fun. Then all hell broke loose as she yanked her hand back and began screaming, kicking and swinging. I got up and tried to quiet her, but she would have nothing to do with that. She jumped out of bed yelling expletives. Out the door she went leaving me thankful that I had missed the full force of at least some of her swings. Talk about good intentions gone bad!

She returned in a few minutes after she had gathered herself, realized she was awake and that it was not an alien she had just encountered. I explained and then we began to laugh ourselves silly. What an incredible nightmare for her to have experienced. We still laugh about it to this day and I can't help but chuckle as I write this.

Anyway, the point is that something went on between her mind and mine, unspoken, unheard, that made her hand meet mine in that particular instant on that fateful morning on top of the alarm clock. The probability of it happening by chance was just far too remote.

Here's another instance of the two of us being on the same wavelength. One winter we made a snowboarding trip with the kids and their friends to the Rockies. We were staying in a small apartment in a rather remote area. On an afternoon when the rest of the clan was away, I decided to walk into the mountains and find a place to lie down in the warm sun. I took no established path and set out up a hill facing south where the sun had melted all the snow. Several hundred yards away from the apartment I found a nice secluded spot to soak up the wonderful sun on what was otherwise a pretty cold day.

I drifted off into a little nap only to be awakened by the cracking of brush nearby. With the prospect of a bear, I was quickly at full alert. Watching through the brush, I heard my name called. It was my wife within 20 feet of me!

I have no idea how she found me and neither does she. She just says she went in the direction she thought I would be. She had 360 degrees of options, and she chose the precise one.

Figure 233

Just before this book was going to press, another remarkable event happened to me. On and off for several days, John, an old grade school and sports buddy came to mind. While in the middle of work one afternoon, the thought came to me to phone him, even though I had not seen nor heard from him in over thirty years. At first, I put it aside. I was busy. Besides, I wasn't sure if he still lived in the city where we grew up. But the urge persisted and welled up in me like a duty. So, I put my work aside and searched his number. I called, somewhat nervous about what to say after all this time. His wife answered and we briefly exchanged some pleasantries. Then I asked if I might speak to John. Silence. Then, "John just died a few days ago." I was shocked. I expressed my condolences and got the details of the illness that had consumed him over the last week or so. I felt terrible that I had not made contact with him when I first felt the urge, which coincided with his death. This extraordinary "coincidence" seems best explained—given the evidence in these and the following chapters—by assuming he had brought me to mind during the time of his dire illness.

It doesn't stop there. I worked on this book for close to fifteen years. During that time hundreds of graphics were accumulated, and some got lost. When the book was about ready for press, I was told that the below comparison could not be found. The next morning I received an email from my daughter who is grown, living apart from me and has no idea what I am working on. In that email was a link to the Lincoln-Kennedy similarities. She sent it to her friends and me because she thought it was interesting. The odds of that are so remote that there are no odds for it.

Abraham Lincoln 	John F. Kennedy 
Lincoln was elected to Congress in 1846	Kennedy was elected to Congress in 1946
He was elected President in 1860	He was elected President in 1960
His wife lost a child while living in the White House	His wife lost a child while living in the White House
He was directly concerned with Civil Rights	He was directly concerned with Civil Rights
Lincoln defeated Stephen Douglas who was born in 1813	Kennedy defeated Richard Nixon who was born in 1913
Lincoln failed to win the Vice Presidential nomination in 1856	Kennedy failed to win the Vice Presidential nomination in 1956
Lincoln had a secretary named Kennedy who told him not to go to the theater	Kennedy had a secretary named Lincoln who told him not to go to Dallas
A week before Lincoln was shot, he was in Monroe, Maryland	A week before Kennedy was shot, he was with Marilyn Monroe
Lincoln was shot in the back of the head in the presence of his wife	Kennedy was shot in the back of the head in the presence of his wife
Lincoln was shot in the Ford Theatre	Kennedy shot in a Lincoln, made by Ford
Shot on a Friday	Shot on a Friday
Booth shot Lincoln in a theater and fled to a warehouse	Oswald shot Kennedy from a warehouse and fled to a theater
Booth was killed before being brought to trial	Oswald was killed before being brought to trial
There were theories that Booth was part of a greater conspiracy	There were theories that Oswald was part of a greater conspiracy
Lincoln's successor was Andrew Johnson, born in 1808	Kennedy's successor was Lyndon Johnson, born in 1908

Figure 234

39
PROVING WEIRD THINGS

For those who have experienced the paranormal, no further proof is needed. No argument ever defeats direct experience.

Nevertheless, self-doubt and fear of ridicule can arise in experiencers since the paranormal is contrary to popular religious, academic, and scientific beliefs. However, as shown in the preceding chapters, these beliefs do not represent truth or reality. Coming to understand that emboldens experiencers and opens the mind of anyone willing to explore the vistas that paranormal abilities and events reveal.

Also lending credibility is the fact that paranormal abilities are utilized by people and organizations with the goal of obtaining objective, tangible, and pragmatic results. This also lends credibility to the phenomena.

For example, governments have set up special intelligence-gathering branches using individuals gifted with paranormal abilities. For-profit companies also employ dowsers and psychics to help them find water, oil, mineral deposits, sunken ships, archeological sites, and to read the minds of competitors. Remote viewers even create profits for clients by predicting commodity futures markets and S&P 500 Index funds. Police departments have used psychics and remote viewers to solve crimes.

Such things would not be done and money spent on them if they did not create results.

Addressing the scientific pedigree of many studies on extrasensory perception and mediumship, Professor Eysenck of London University remarked: "Unless there is a gigantic conspiracy involving some thirty university departments all over the world and several hundred highly respected scientists in various fields, many of them originally skeptical of the claims of the psychical researchers, the only conclusion that the unbiased researcher can come to is that there does exist a small number of people who obtain knowledge existing in other people's mind, or in the outer world, by means as yet unknown to science."

Researchers at the Princeton University's Engineering Anomalies Research (PEAR) Center tested the ability of people to will higher or lower numbers produced by an electronic random number generator. They also found that people could will the fall of cascading balls that can go either right or left into bins. A meta-analysis revealed that the odds that the positive results obtained were due to chance was one in 1,000,000,000,000,000,000,000,000,000,000,000,000. That's equivalent to a virtual certainty that the machines were influenced by mind.

Figure 235

The Global Consciousness Project (GCP) is an international effort involving researchers from several countries conducting experiments since 1998. They conclude that human consciousness interacts with random event generators (REGs), apparently "causing" them to produce non-random patterns.

If we and the world around us are something different from what things on the surface appear to be, then we would expect this idea to emerge in human consciousness and persist in human experience. It does.

The belief that this world is but an illusion and that there are other realities is a thought thread throughout time. The witch doctors, seers, medicine men, death rituals, and meditative experiences of the most primitive of people around the world may not be just ignorance, manifestations of the fear of death, or wishful thinking. It is most likely enlightened knowledge from first-hand experience.

Many notable people, even hard-core skeptics and scientists, have been impressed with the scientific and experiential evidence. This would include Margaret Mead, Pierre and Marie Curie, Edgar Mitchell (astronaut), several Nobel laureates including the Curies, Richet, Townes, Crookes, and Josephson. There are countless others (see Resource Section).

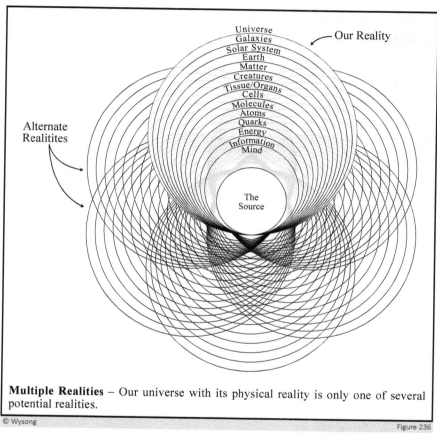

Multiple Realities – Our universe with its physical reality is only one of several potential realities.

© Wysong   Figure 236

It's noteworthy that those with metaphysical skills or who do paranormal research are not doctrinaire, but simply encourage consideration of the evidence. (This is not to suggest that there aren't charlatans, as there are in every field of endeavor, including science.) The objective in the paranormal field is not to get people to join, swear allegiance, honor leaders, or tithe. Instead, the underlying takeaway is love, unity, openness, reason, self-responsibility, and a better world.

This is in contrast to the meaninglessness, hopelessness, and amorality that can logically spring from the belief that we are nothing more than a probability event emerging from exploding stardust. It also contrasts with following human-made holy books or religious doctrines that can bring horrendous harm and rob people of money, conscience, and open-minded truth-seeking.

The more objective and altruistic nature of the metaphysical and paranormal field, in itself, speaks to its truthfulness.

40
SKEPTICS AND DEBUNKERS

Although debunkers of the paranormal fancy themselves as rational and scientific, their fixed notions of materialism, evolution, and atheism are the exact opposite.

Not only are those beliefs not proven by reason or science, science isn't a noun, a dogma to defend. It's a process, a verb. Rather than just affirming beliefs by seeking only friendly faces in an infinite universe of facts, true science, and basic honesty for that matter, is about making every effort to disprove the ideas and beliefs we hold dear.

Unfortunately, debunkers, like most people, don't do that. Instead, people identify with a fixed dogma, e.g., "I am an evolutionist, materialist, atheist, agnostic, Christian, Muslim, Buddhist . . ." or whatever. That's a sure way to fix the brain in place, insulating it from the unfolding of advancing knowledge that brings us closer to the truth.

With regard to paranormal and preternatural phenomena, reason, experience, and science (quantum physics in particular) permit their possibility. They should not be cast aside as "woo woo" out of hand. They are a gateway to exploration and enlightenment.

It's Impossible and Ridiculous

In the early 1900s when Wilbur and Orville Wright flew their plane, Scientific American dismissed the event as a hoax. Simon Newcomb, a professor of mathematics and astronomy at Johns Hopkins University showed scientifically that powered human flight was "utterly impossible." For five years people looked up at the plane flying overhead, but there was a general denial that it ever left the ground.

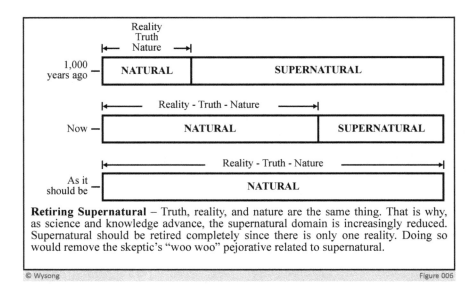

Retiring Supernatural – Truth, reality, and nature are the same thing. That is why, as science and knowledge advance, the supernatural domain is increasingly reduced. Supernatural should be retired completely since there is only one reality. Doing so would remove the skeptic's "woo woo" pejorative related to supernatural.

© Wysong   Figure 006

Even after Edison lit up Menlo Park around his laboratory with incandescent lights, scientists protested that Edison had "a positive want of knowledge of the electric circuit" and that the whole thing was "a completely idiotic idea." He was called the sorcerer of Menlo Park and told that what he was attempting would never be technically feasible.

When Charles Parsons invented the turbine and claimed it would greatly increase the speed of ships, the Admiralty told him that such a feat was impossible. The turbojet was also labeled "an impossibility."

When Baird developed a television, those who observed it were convinced "it was all a trick or something equally disreputable." Even the discoverer of radio waves, Heinrich Hertz, warned Guglielmo Marconi that he was "wasting his time" with experiments on wireless broadcasting.

When Wilhelm Roentgen announced his discovery of x-rays, Lord Kelvin—author of almost 700 scientific papers, 70 inventions, creator of the absolute zero Kelvin temperature scale, and perhaps the greatest physicist of the 1800s—remarked that x-rays were nothing but an "elaborate hoax."

Immanuel Velikovsky's ideas (1950) about the violent history of Earth contradicted the vogue slow and steady uniformitarian view of Earth history that fit the evolution hypothesis. His various predictions, such as the high temperature of Venus and the projected magnetic field of the Earth, were called by scientists "intellectually fraudulent," "dynamically impossible," and "too ridiculous to merit serious rebuttal." Macmillan, the publisher of his book, Worlds in Collision, was forced to stop printing it due to pressure from their academic textbook buyers even though Velikovsky's book was their biggest moneymaker.

Figure 237

The noted British astronomer, Sir Harold Spencer Jones, pronounced that "space travel is bunk" two weeks before Sputnik 1 was launched into orbit.

This only begins the shameful and dispiriting catalog of intolerance by supposedly rational and dispassionate scientists and their vassals. Advance seems to only ever occur by struggling against a tide of opposition, not because of cool, principled devotion to reason and science.

Debunkers

Since protecting the status quo is the status quo, it's little wonder that the paranormal and metaphysical have not been embraced by materialists and evolutionists, and even many religionists.

The primary journal in the paranormal field is the Journal of Parapsychology. It contains peer-reviewed research that's primarily privately funded and has a readership in the hundreds. On the other hand, The Skeptical Inquirer, a publication of the Committee for the Scientific Investigation of Claims of the Paranormal (CSICOP), does not conduct research relevant to discovery, but rather is in the business of debunking. It has a circulation of about 25,000. People are much more given to protecting biases than venturing into the realm of new ideas.

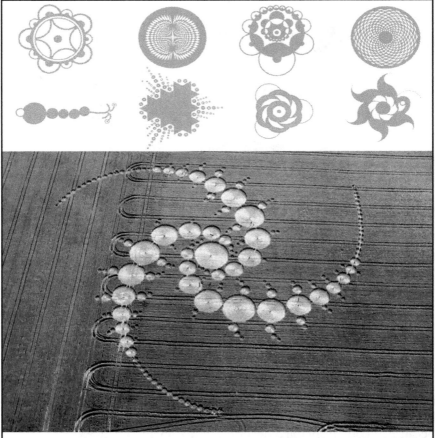

Crop Circle Art – The picture on the bottom represents a configuration seen in a field. The drawings on top display some of the dozens of others. In the cases shown here no natural explanation exists. The intricacy of some of the designs would be difficult enough to draw on a sheet of paper, let alone in the middle of a field where there are no good coordinates, no ability to erase and the accuracy and symmetry can only be seen from an airplane.

Figure 238

When trying to prove that there is no correlation between the position of Mars and the birth of gifted athletes (such scientific evidence exists) the debunkers reportedly fudged data. In another instance, to disprove ESP experiments at Duke University where a subject in one building guessed the cards in another, a CSICOP debunker proposed that the subject only pretended not to be in the building where the cards were. The debunker claimed that the subject surreptitiously gained access to the building where the cards were and crawled through the attic to view the cards through a hole in the ceiling. That the blueprints of the building showed such a scenario impossible didn't matter. This proof of ESP fraud remained in CSICOP's publications long after it was proven that the fraud was on CSICOP's part.

Consider crop circles. When some circles were traced to hoaxers traipsing on boards held by ropes in their hands, scientists around the world who had been unable to explain the phenomena rationally heaved a great sigh of relief. Die-hard believers then appeared genuinely foolish. But as the phenomenon has continued around the world and has been traced to dates before the identified hoaxers, it's again reemerging as a genuine mystery. But the thought police will forever cite the hoaxes as a reason for carte blanche dismissal regardless of what evidence comes forward.

On the other hand, materialists and religionists critical of the paranormal would never even consider dismissing their beliefs regardless of how many frauds have been found in their camps, how dangerous their doctrines may be, or why their ideas have not created a utopia.

Any failures, frauds, or adverse consequences that result from consensus beliefs are merely taken to mean more research money is needed to winnow the truth from the corruption. So long as the sacrosanct creeds are kept hallowed, no amount of adverse or contrary data and evidence matters.

In the meantime, any supplemental view of reality, such as metaphysics and consciousness surviving death, or evidence in support of it such as paranormal events, is summarily dismissed if there can be found the slightest hint of fraud.

Professional Witch-Hunting

It's supposed to be the very nature of science to look for and embrace the exception, the extraordinary, the weird. Mere vexation is not a reason to reject an idea.

Nevertheless, from the ranks of materialistic apologists claiming to be scientific come contract debunkers such as CSICOP, the "Amazing Randi," and the Penn and Teller television program called "Bull Shit." Thought policing literature and internet sites abound to protect us from the encroachment of those who would dare to tread on materialistic hallowed ground. Their advertised purpose is to protect the public from charlatans who would fleece people of their hard-earned cash.

Certainly, there's no reason for tolerance of fraud. But if Mrs. Jones spent 25 dollars for a séance where a thumping and jumping table had been rigged with invisible wires operated by a huckster who moaned like a ghost from behind a curtain, does that merit the hysteria and call to arms we see from the ranks of the debunkers? Belief in ESP, metal bending, intelligent design, and psychic abilities doesn't threaten civilization. On the other hand, the materialistic dogma at the helm of today's science, religion, and politics threatens the very existence of life on the planet.

A similar situation is the clash between conventional materialistic medicine and holistic alternative medicine. The medical profession en masse, the FDA, licensing boards, journals, research institutions, and the media are quick to point to any evidence that alternative medical care may not work or is harmful. Heaven forbid there's a report of somebody somewhere getting sick from taking vitamins (usually synthetic versions, if there is ever an incident) or an herb at 100 times the dose for an elephant. When that happens, everybody piles on and the alternative movement is cast as a scam to part people from their money. At the same time, right under our noses, trillions of dollars per year are spent on conventional allopathic materialistic medical care that is killing more people than any other single cause. There isn't a peep of protest from the mainstream.

It's supposed to be the very nature of science to look for and embrace the exception, the extraordinary, the weird. Mere vexation is not a reason to reject an idea.

Miracles Are Normal

Debunkers reject the metaphysical claiming they take no stock in miracles. Yet they do.

For example, life itself is a miracle and inexplicable. An egg the size of the period at the end of this sentence developing into a self-aware human with a body that becomes alive and marshals trillions of synchronized speed-of-light biochemical events every second is miraculous. It's a miracle that we safely travel at a million-and-a-half miles per hour on the Earth spaceship. The natural laws of gravity, motion, electricity, thermodynamics, and so on that make each moment possible are inexplicable and miraculous.

Our entire world of existence is miraculous since it cannot be explained, accounted for, or duplicated.

An immortal soul, a spirit realm, and a Creator are just as believable as earthly life and the miracles that make it possible.

It's science and reason, not malarkey, that leads to the conclusion that reality is timeless, holistic, conscious, and intelligent. This, not materialism, easily accommodates all the "quirky" and "lunatic" weird phenomena. It's all perfectly plausible as long as one doesn't get hoodwinked by the simplistic faith that puny human senses and touchy-feely matter define the universe.

Thinking about . . .

OUR TRUE NATURE AND DESTINY

In This Section: Matter cannot account for our complexity, consciousness, and free will. We are, therefore, something other than the body we occupy.

41
FREE WILL PROVES
WE ARE OTHER

Everything has a cause. That includes why we do what we do. Our choices are either caused by brain- matter and the laws governing it (materialistic determinism), or by something extraneous to matter. Since there is no natural law that can predict and account for exactly what a creature will do moment by moment, free will must lie outside the bounds of natural law.

Nevertheless, materialists contend that our entire being could be duplicated if all of our physical details were known. That's the dream of strong artificial intelligence (AI). Since every atom in the human body is the same everywhere in the universe, the only difference between you and me would be quantities, ratios, and placement of these chemicals.

With the correct percentages of atoms, algorithmic software, and a big enough computer to hold every detail of how the quantities are arranged, you supposedly could be duplicated.

In the future strong artificial intelligence Land of Oz, you could be scanned, a duplicate file of you e-mailed to the neighbor, downloaded on their computer, and then reassembled into a copy of you with a sort of upgraded 3-D printing (organic synthesis) machine.

Bird Will – The window sills show various tries at nest building by our visiting Robin. She decided on just the right ledge to build her nest and lay her eggs. Such will cannot come from mere atoms. (The stone work you see there is by me and my son, which we had the will to do.)

Figure 239

Not one experiment has ever been done demonstrating that atoms mixing on their own, or assembled in the laboratory, can create free will and the qualities characteristic of life. It can't be proven that scientists can't do it (because, logically, negatives cannot be proven), only that they haven't and that

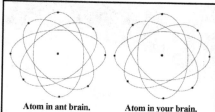

Atom in ant brain.   Atom in your brain.

Atoms Are Alike – No matter where atoms of a certain element are found, they are the same. They're also locked in to natural laws and thus display no free will no matter how they are combined.

© Wysong   Figure 240

it's unreasonable to think that they ever will. We can't prove that a cow can't jump over the moon either. But we can use common sense.

Atomic agglomerations and ratios don't create self-identity, personality, conscience, consciousness, empathy, appreciation for beauty, poetry, music, love, hate, hope, ethics, despair, compassion, creativity, curiosity, and most importantly, free will.

At death, creatures have all their physical components, yet no longer have the qualitative attributes they had while living. Moreover, identical twins and cloned animals made of identical nucleic acids, don't think, move, and behave exactly alike at all times. If materialism and determinism are true, they would even need to occupy the same space. But they don't. They are individually unique due to the nonmaterial other that has free will and unique qualities.

This forces the conclusion that we are other than the matter comprising our bodies, an other that is conscious and timeless.

Strong AI World – If we are nothing but an arrangement of atoms, one day we could be stored on a disc and reassembled from atoms. But there is no evidence that this reductionistic myth is true.

Figure 241

42
MIND OUTSIDE MATTER

Although neuroscientists believe all thought can be reduced to chemicals, they have never been able to combine chemicals in any way to produce a spontaneous thought, much less the 60,000 that spontaneously appear each day in the average human.

That's because we are not just a physical stimulus-response mechanism controlled and directed by an electrochemical computer made of meat—the brain. Consciousness is not an epiphenomenon, a by-product of cascading molecular interactions confined inside the skull.

By not possessing a precise location, consciousness can be likened to the quantum. It is best thought of as indeterminate and being everywhere at once.

Consider how the internet, man's most complex invention ever, can be likened to the brain. It consists of billions of computers electromagnetically linked together. One Intel processor measuring less than a square inch in just one computer has well over 1.5 billion transistors on it. All told, the Internet has about 1019 transistors interacting with one another like axons and dendrites in the brain. That's equal to the number of brain synapses (neural connections) in 10,000 people. Thus, the internet exceeds a single human brain by a factor of 10,000. For all its complexity, it's not conscious, nor does it have free will. It's robotically bound to and limited by the commands from human brains and physical laws.

On the other hand, our essence, our self-aware volitional identity, is holistic and extrinsic to the bounds of matter. This understanding helps us to better grasp many puzzling things, such as:

- Knowing fantastic detail in huge mathematical pictures, such as the ability of Akira Haraguchi to recite a number for pi out to 83,431 decimal places. (Also see the other fantastic abilities of people mentioned in chapter 34.)

- The transference of learned skills. For example, trace your name in the air with your left elbow, something you have never done before. The fact that you can do it suggests that skills are learned holographically and are not restricted to a particular spot in the brain.

- Recognition of a familiar face regardless of angle or part of the face viewed.

- Learning to ride a bicycle without memorizing every intricate detail of movement. We connect with things holistically, not by pieces.

- Seeing what is not there by constructing images, words and thoughts out of fragments—for example:

> fi yuo cna raed tihs, yuo dnot hvae a sgtrane mnid. Cna yuo raed tihs? msot polelpe cnoat blveiee taht tehy cluod aulaclty uesdnatnrd waht tehy weer rdanieg. The phaonmneal pweor of the hmuan mnid, aoccdrnig to a rscheearch at Cmabrigde Uinervtisy, sohws it dseno't mtaetr in waht oerdr the ltteres in a wrod are, the olny iproamtnt tihng is taht for the msot prat the frsit and lsat ltteer be in the rghit pclae. The rset can be taotl mses and you can sitll raed it whotuit a pboerlm. Tihs is bcuseae the huamn mnid deos not raed ervey lteter by istlef, but the wrod as a wlohe.

Figure 242

The mind also projects itself like a magnetic field out to where the thing is which we perceive.

Jean Piaget, a Swiss researcher, discovered that it's only with modern indoctrination that people come to believe their minds are in their heads. Primitive people and children under the age of about ten think that their minds extend out into the world around them.

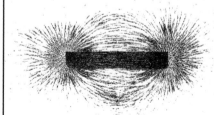

Magnetic Fields – This bar magnet that has had iron filings scattered about it shows the existence of powerful magnetic fields that invisibly stretch into space.

Figure 244

TENDJEWBERRYMUD

(You will understand the above word by the end of the conversation. Read aloud for best results.)

The following is a purported telephone exchange between a hotel guest and room-service at a hotel in Asia. It was recorded and published in the Far Eastern Economic Review.

Room Service (RS): "Morny. Ruin sorbees."

Guest (G): "Sorry, I thought I dialed room-service."

RS: "Rye .. Ruin sorbees .. morny! Djewish to odor sunteen??"

G: "Uh .. yes .. I'd like some bacon and eggs."

RS: "Ow July den?"

G: "What??"

RS: "Ow July den? ... pry , boy, pooch?"

G: "Oh, the eggs! How do I like them? Sorry, scrambled please."

RS: "Ow July dee bayhcem ... crease?"

G: "Crisp will be fine."

RS: "Hokay. An San tos?"

G: "What?"

RS: "San tos. July San tos?"

G: "I don't think so."

RS: "No? Judo one toes??"

G: "I feel really bad about this, but I don't know what 'judo one toes' means."

RS: "Toes! Toes!...Why djew Don Juan toes? Ow bow singlish mopping we bother?"

G: "English muffin!! I've got it! You were saying 'Toast.' Fine. Yes, an English muffin will be fine."

RS: "We bother?"

G: "No .. just put the bother on the side."

RS: "Wad?"

G: "I mean butter ... just put it on the side."

RS: "Copy?"

G: "Sorry?"

RS: "Copy ... tea ... mill?"

G: "Yes. Coffee please, and that's all."

RS: "One Minnie. Ass ruin tori no fee, strangle ache, crease baychem, tossy singlish mopping we bother honey sigh, and copy .... rye??"

G: "Whatever you say"

RS: "Tendjewberrymud."

G: "You're welcome."

The Brain – is not so much a producer of mind, as a product of it. In the exchange above, notice how you will slowly be able to read what is not even there. Such a complex feat by the machinery in your brain points to brain engineering, not a mere coming together of organic chemicals guided by natural law.

Adapted from an Internet circulated e-mail.   Figure 243

Penfield concluded from his research that patients thought of themselves as having an existence separate from the body. The Egyptians thought the brain was a cooling organ and unceremoniously dug it out of the skull through the nose in preparation for mummification. To them, the heart was considered a far more important organ for housing consciousness.

From first awareness, we have a sense of self. That identity does not change no matter how long we live or what food we eat to make our continuously regenerating brain. The inner person does not grow old, nor does it begin young. The inner person is not something that results from the growth of a brain.

In fact, everyday language reflects the sense that we are other than body when we say "my foot," "my heart," "my brain," "my thoughts,". . . The "my" is the real conscious self-aware "us;" the body is a physical machine "we" utilize for the physical realm.

The Source of Thought

Thoughts arrive unannounced through the course of every day and steal us away. Yet nobody has any idea what the source is of those 60,000+ thoughts each day.

No piece of matter can explain why thoughts spring to consciousness in the order they do and stay organized. We don't have several thoughts coming forth all at once or lapses with no thought at all. (With the exception of some meditative practices.) If the brain is just a repository of data, that would not explain how that data creates new ideas or what prevents it from spilling out randomly, making us quite crazy and functionless.

All of the millions of inventions throughout history that add up to the marvels of technology came from human thought. It's rationally and scientifically impossible that such incredible complexity, novelty, and creativity could spontaneously emerge from a soup of mechanical and robotic brain atoms. Mathematics, for example, fundamental to all these advances, is a purely intellectual phenomenon that cannot be tied in any way to the neurophysiologist's stimulus-response model of the brain.

We are dynamic, creative, adaptable, volitional, and spontaneous. Such elusive qualities of personality are not reducible to the data our brains can amass. Trying to localize these qualities and free will is like trying to find the structure of ambition.

Brain as Receiver

Unusual abilities, such as ESP, psychokinesis, clairvoyance, and remote viewing can best be explained by the understanding that consciousness exists extraneous to our material world. When engaged with the brain, this consciousness, which is connected to everything, uses the material brain in much the same way a garage door opener controller directs the motor to lift the door. The relationship between consciousness and brain is like that between a programmer and a computer, or a farmer and his tractor. Extraneous consciousness is the cause, not the result of thinking phenomena using the matter in the brain.

The brain can also be likened to a television (receiver). When we turn the channel and see an elephant, that elephant is not actually in the television. The image of the elephant is sent to the television via invisible waves from a production company somewhere else on the globe. We can point stimulate the set (change the channel) and get innumerable messages and images, but not one of them originates from the television itself.

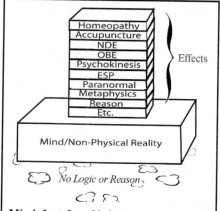

Mind Just Is – Various paranormal and meta-physical events are effects best explained by mind in a non-physical reality. Nobody can explain the origins of that mind or why it is as it is. It just is.

© Wysong   Figure 245

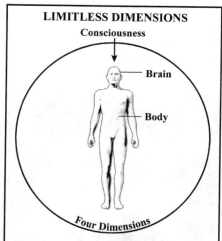

Consciousness in Quantum Hologram – Our bodies and brains are locked into our material four dimensions. The I, however, is a part of the quantum hologram that is not constrained by this physical universe.

© Wysong   Figure 246

Similarly, choices and initiation (other than reflexes) do not originate within the brain matrix. They come from elsewhere. The brain processes them and directs the body to obey them. Causation is downward from a nonmaterial consciousness, not upward out of the material brain.

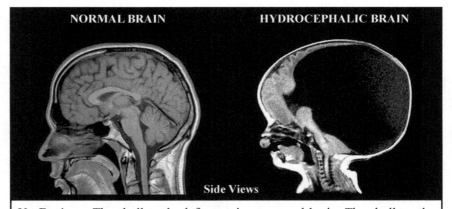

Domestic Propensities
1. Amativeness
A. Union For Life
2. Philoprogenitiveness
3. Adhesiveness.
4. Inhabitiveness
5. Continuity

Selfish Propensities
E. Vitativeness
6. Combativeness
7. Destructiveness
8. Alimenitiveness
9. Acquisitiveness
10. Secretiveness
11. Cautiousness

Aspiring & Governing Organs
12. Approbativeness
13. Self-Esteem
14. Firmness

Moral Sentiments
15. Conscientiousness
16. Hope
17. Spirituality
18. Veneration
19. Benevolence

Perfective Faculties
20. Constructiveness
21. Ideality
B. Sublimity
22. Imitation
D. Agreeableness
23. Mirthfulness

Perceptive Faculties
24. Individuality
25. Form
26. Size
27. Weight
28. Color
29. Order
30. Calculation
31. Locality

Literary Faculties
32. Eventuality
33. Time
34. Tune
35. Language

Reasoning Faculties
36. Causality
37. Comparison
C. Human Nature

Phrenology – In the late 1700s, Franz Joseph Gall attempted to reduce all human faculties to a topographical brain map. His science of phrenology, as it was called, described 27 organs in the brain. These were evidenced by bumps or other physical features of the head. Nineteen of the organs were shared with animals. He identified locales for the organs of metaphysics, property owning, desire to store food, carnivorism, love of glory (considered a beneficent trait for the individual and society), and belief in God, to name a few of the more interesting ones. Other than being scientifically wrong, his ideas became interpreted as a threat to religion and fell into disfavor.

Figure 248

NORMAL BRAIN   **HYDROCEPHALIC BRAIN**

Side Views

No Brains – The skull to the left contains a normal brain. The skull on the right is an example of the dramatic effect hydrocephalus can have on the brain. In some cases the brain is virtually obliterated. Cerebrospinal fluid builds up in the interior ventricles (cavities) and presses the brain tissue against the cranial vault. The black area represents fluid, the light area represents brain and bone. Surprisingly, some people with brains squeezed to 'nothing' can function with full mental capacity.

Figure 249

Mind Is Not Brain

Mind function can occur in the virtual absence of brains.

No Brain—In children with hydrocephalus, the fluid buildup can squeeze the cortex (the outer "smart" layer of the brain) to the point that there is almost no evidence of cortex at all. But most of these individuals do not lose self-awareness or choice. Although hydrocephalus can result in various problems, mental development may be normal. In one case, a 26-year-old student with hydrocephalus had an IQ of 126 and received honors in mathematics. He had virtually no brain other than a thin layer less than a millimeter thick. (Search boy with no brain, on the internet and YouTube.)

Brain Attrition—Each day a human loses about a thousand brain neurons. Some 80% of the neural mass is dissolved by age 14. In spite of this considerable disruption and wasting, consciousness maintains its integrity. Not only that, great intellect can be developed in the adult years as the brain mass continues to shrink.

Body Turnover—If a person is mere matter, that would mean we come from our food and leave via the toilet. Parts of the body turnover in a few days, while the skeleton takes a decade to refresh itself. The consistency of a person, through several atomic changeovers during a lifetime, speaks to something outside of matter that's the source of that constancy.

Animal Experiments—Rats with massive portions of their brains removed continued to run a previously learned maze efficiently. Salamanders that have had their brains sliced, flipped, shuffled, and with parts deleted and even minced retained certain behaviors.

Brain Excision—Patients who have a part of their brain removed due to tumors may suffer no loss of self-awareness.

Head Injury—Victims of accidents with large portions of their brains damaged may still perform functions believed to be controlled by the damaged or missing parts.

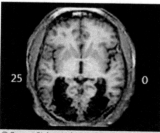

Blind Sight – This MRI is of a patient who suffered two strokes in succession uniquely destroying each visual cortex (dark areas). Although lacking any functional vision, he could navigate down a long corridor in which a number of random barriers were placed. Similarly, "Helen," a monkey with blinding brain damage, successfully navigated an open field with obstacles.

© Current Biology Vol 18 No 24 R1128

Figure 250

Blind Sight—People who have had a part of their visual cortex surgically removed or damaged, lose sight in a portion of a visual field. One patient was tested with things placed in the blind field and asked to guess what they were. Accuracy was near 100%. The mind can see when there is no visual portion of the brain to permit vision.

Inferred Sight—Some individuals who are blind insist that they can see quite well, apparently visually conscious of the inferred surroundings. You can test your own ability to see by inference. In this drawing note that you will see a white triangle even though most of the borders are not drawn.

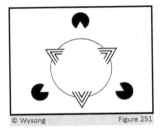

Figure 251

Phantom Limbs—People who have had limbs removed, are born without them, or have a section of the body anesthetized, can experience the motor and sensory sensations of the part missing or anesthetically blocked. Research has shown that these sensations don't originate in the brain or in severed nerve endings at the point of amputation. Out of body and near-death experiences (discussed in the next chapter) are, in effect, whole body phantoms.

Mind Outside Animals

In the absence of a controlling physical brain, the characteristics of mind and intelligence are displayed throughout nature.

Compass termites build huge stone-like monoliths. The mound is a few inches thick, about 12 feet square, and perfectly oriented north-south. This permits the knife-like edge of the mound to decrease exposure to the overhead hot noon sun, while its broad faces capture the heat from the rising and declining sun. Its elaborate internal honeycomb structure has thousands of shaft valves to facilitate air conditioning so that the internal temperature and humidity remain constant. A single termite has no idea how to build such a thing. As a group, they have the mind—X that out—genius, to do it perfectly. Since that genius of the colony mind does not reside in any single termite, it must lie outside of them.

Similarly, with outside temperatures dropping to well below freezing, and humidity at 30%, the inside of a beehive remains at 70 degrees and 90% humidity. No single bee has any idea how to do this. Bee genius comes from elsewhere.

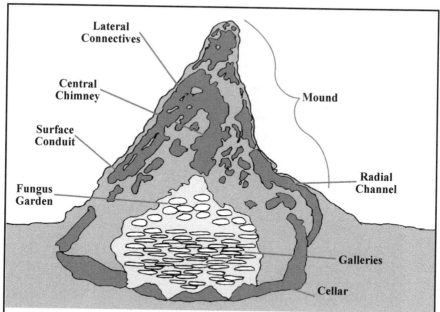

Lateral Connectives

Central Chimney

Surface Conduit

Fungus Garden

Mound

Radial Channel

Galleries

Cellar

Architecture of the Termite Mound (Macrotermes Michaelseni) in Northern Namibia – All species locate their colonies underground where they cultivate fungi that aid in cellulose digestion. The mounds enclose a ramifying network of tunnels that forms a ventilation system for the nest. Some species may build open chimneys or vent holes into their mounds, while others build completely enclosed mounds that exchange gas through porous thin-walled tunnels. The variation of structure is prodigious. The basic problem for understanding these structures is this: how can the millions of individuals in a colony work together to build a structure many times larger than themselves that has a characteristic architecture? A mind extraneous to the individuals seems to be guiding the whole.

© Scott Turner

Figure 252

African driver ants can number over 22 million in a colony. All of them are blind. There are specialized hunters, nest tenders, and fighter sentries that guard the river of ants as it flows through the jungle. Although these blind creatures can communicate to a degree by chemical pheromones, only an extrinsic colony mind could orchestrate all the ants to one unified colony purpose.

Driver Ant

© Martin Dohrn

Figure 253

Sea Anemone – The fingers of a sea anemone have no nervous system or brains yet learn, remember, and express behavior. Intelligence is not the sole domain of nerves and brains.

© The respective copyright holders.   Figure 254

A sea anemone has no brain, ganglia (nests of intermingled nerves), or even concentrated neurons, yet all its parts coordinate. Each tentacle also has a memory. If offered a trick non-food object, the tentacle will remember and reject it the next time it's offered. Only that one brainless tentacle, and none of the others remembers the trick. Intelligent feats are obviously not dependent upon a material brain.

Mixotricha paradoxa are protozoa that digest the wood in a termite's gut. They have no nervous system and move with cilia that are themselves individual rod-like bacteria. There is no physical mind-controlling that hodgepodge. Other protozoa with no nervous system have been found to both learn and remember.

E. coli bacteria can evaluate 20 different chemicals at the same time, swim to the area where food concentration is increasing the fastest, reevaluate the environment every 4 seconds, and communicate with one another. Pretty smart for being one-celled and brainless.

When food becomes scarce, the tiny brainless underground slime mold, Dictostylium, will gather in a group of about 100,000. They then decide to form into one organism, a tiny slug that wriggles its way up through the ground mulch. Some of these slugs then become a stalk, others at the top become spores so they can spread with the wind to new food sources. That process is orchestrated with no nerves and no brains.

Shoals, flocks, and swarms of fish, birds, and insects will move like one gigantic organism with no crashes and no clear leader. Millions of Indonesian fireflies spread over miles will synchronize their flash. There is no identified material seat of intelligence that directs these multitudes.

Plants, without brains, communicate and have memory. For example, trees being foraged or invaded by insects will send a message of warning to fellow trees miles away. In response, the trees receiving the message will increase the production of tannins and other chemicals that are noxious and toxic to the attackers. Roots of plants also communicate back and forth with brainless soil fungi and other microorganisms.

Mind Outside the Human Body

The human body doesn't consciously control whatever it is that keeps it alive. Something immensely intelligent must govern, coordinate, and direct the trillions of functions performed by trillions of cells (we're like a moving ant colony) going on at any given second in the body. No physical command center can be found anywhere in the body.

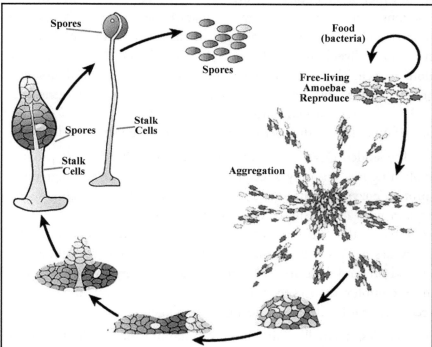

Life Cycle of Dictostylium – Free living, single-celled organisms decide to come together, divide duties and form a complex multi-celled creature that reproduces. Nothing within any of the single cells can be identified to account for this behavior. It appears that there is an intelligence, a mind that lies outside of the physical realm that provides the information that coordinates this phenomenon. Similarly the cells of a human body (protozoa, if you will), each with the same genetic material, come together to form the tissues and organs that make up a fully functioning person. There is no physical explanation for that either.

© Richard H. Kessin   Figure 255

The human brain and nervous system can be thought of as a colony of worker neurons, communicator neurons, interconnecting and supporting glial cells (microglia, astrocytes, oligodendrocytes, etc.), and a variety of other specialized cells (Schwann, ependymal, satellite, etc.). The command center of the nervous system "colony" apparently lies outside of the body since no specific material locus can be identified as the leader.

Human organs are also like colonies. There are billions of liver cells, but no identifiable controller of which liver cell will do which function, how the shape of the three pounds of liver is maintained, and what liver cell goes to which exact spot on which lobe during embryological development. The intricately coordinated mass of liver cells process about a liter of blood each minute, performs over 500 different chemical reactions, converts food to chemicals that can be used by body cells, and clears the blood of toxins—to begin the list of functions. Nobody has ever found a liver brain, nor have they explained how all the liver cells get along so well. There are no wars, insurrections, slackers, social programs, or revolutions, just harmony and peace generation after generation (unless we assault it with improper living, eating, or drugs). On top of that, if up to half of the liver is damaged, it will regenerate itself.

The lauded DNA turns out not to be some self-actuating program explaining life, but only a recipe for the use of amino acid ingredients (protein/enzyme components). DNA or other nucleic acids do not explain why all the ingredients in the trillions of creatures on Earth assemble as they do into whole functioning organisms. No physical entity has been identified that controls life's components, turns them on and off, and measures their dose. Since these machinations are far more complex than even our brains can comprehend, they are best accounted for by a super-, and supra- intelligence.

Brainless (actually half-witted—containing only half the genetic material of a body cell) spermatozoa swim miles (on human scale) to find a brainless (half-witted) egg to form a fertilized whole-witted, but brainless zygote the size of this period. This in turn divides trillions of times and some of the brainless cells become livers, some tongues, some fingers, and some brains that proceed to reason that their intelligence comes from non-intelligence.

The heart has qualities that are often ascribed to the brain, such as emotion, love, and intelligence. Dr. Gary Schwartz, at the University of Arizona, reports that there are over 70 documented cases of individuals receiving heart transplants getting far more than they bargained for. Sonny Graham received a heart from Terry Cottle who had shot himself. Sonny became infatuated with Terry's widow and married her.

Twelve years later he shot himself. A young boy who wrote poetry and songs died in a car crash. His heart was donated to a girl named Danielle, who, upon hearing a song the young boy had written, immediately knew the words to it. A young boy who loved classical music died with his violin on his chest. The recipient of his heart developed a love for classical music. A lesbian who was fond of burgers received the heart of a man-crazy vegetarian lady. The recipient then developed an aversion to meat and married a man shortly after that.

This constitutes more evidence of our holographic nature and that mind is both extraneous to and perfuses the body just like it does a flock of birds and ant colony. (Internet search Dr. Cowan cosmic heart.)

The idea that mind is imbued within and at the same time extraneous to our material reality has been intuitively concluded as far back as the Greek philosophers and before. Words that describe this include animism, panpsychism, enminded, and idealism. Quantum physics buttresses this by revealing that matter at its most fundamental level appears to dissolve into something akin to a timeless mind. Moreover, the design in nature infers inherent mind as do all paranormal, and preternatural phenomena.

Mind is not dependent on matter, but rather matter depends upon a preexistent and timeless mind. That means our physicality would have a pre-body history. That also means we would have a post-body future.

43
DEATH IS A RETURN

We instinctually fear death because survival is programmed into us. It's also feared because some religions have attached the horror of eternal hell to it.

Death is not an unsolved mystery. Nor does life beyond death have anything to do with belief and faith.

Although not absolute proof in itself, the idea of immortality is predominant in virtually every culture and has been as far back in time as records were made. However, although people may say they believe in life beyond death, most can't do so with intellectual pride or confidence. That's because physical existence is all about beginnings and ends, not eternity. That's the way we're used to thinking

As the following proofs of immortality are surveyed, keep in mind that truth doesn't depend upon the veracity of any one assertion examined separately but on the vast improbability of many reasonable assertions from a variety of fields agreeing on the same falsehood.

Intimations of Immortality

1. Origins

Materialism and evolution violate a host of natural laws and are, therefore, false. Rather than a spontaneous mindless mix of mud, we are proven to be the product of intelligent thought. That thought preexisted our creation, and, like all thoughts, does not disappear upon the disassembly of the physical manifestation (the body) of that thought.

2. E=Mc²

Einstein's famous equation shows that the matter of the body is actually nonmaterial. Rearranging the equation with simple algebra, we get Matter=E/c2. Neither energy nor the speed of light is material, they can just temporarily convert to matter.

3. The First Law of Thermodynamics

This law states that energy can neither be created nor destroyed. Since we are comprised of energy, this law, like E=Mc2 implies timelessness and is consistent with human immortality.

4. Timeless Mind Underlies Reality

Way down under our material atomic bodies is a quantum reality that is best likened to mind and thought.

Einstein wrote in his book, *The World As I See It*, that the universe "reveals an intelligence of such superiority that, compared with it, all the systematic thinking and acting of human beings is an utterly insignificant reflection."

Since mind does not have any of the physical constraints of the material world and is timeless, we, being mind, are also timeless.

5. Near-Death Experiences (NDE)

From 5-15% of those resuscitated from clinical death report vivid experiences in a nonphysical realm. Although this is commonly referred to as an NDE, it is better termed an after-death experience in that there is no heartbeat, breathing, reflexes, or brain electrical activity. Many are not only dead but under anesthesia at the same time.

There are NDE accounts recorded throughout history. Such events and others mentioned in this list, are the likely reasons cultures around the globe have such strong beliefs in an afterlife, spirits, and reincarnation.

In modern times, thousands of cases have been scientifically studied. For example, a prospective clinical study in the Lancet medical journal (12-15-2001), reported that 62 out of 344 patients who were revived after being clinically dead from cardiac arrest, had a conscious out of body experience. Most of these, adults and children, described core events of enhanced consciousness, going through a tunnel and into light, life review, telepathic ability, meeting dead friends and family, a sense that it is more real than physical life, a sense of all-embracing love and acceptance, and feeling like they had returned to their true home.

People blind since birth reported seeing themselves lying in state and described things they have never seen.

Follow up study of survivors over many years revealed transformations, including loss of fear of death, increased intuitive senses, rapid healing of injuries, and being more empathetic and less ego-centered. In other reports, children increased IQ scores dramatically after an NDE.

No physical causes such as anoxia, drugs, prior beliefs, resuscitation efforts, or release of endorphins explain the experiences or the transformations.

Naysayers, of course, abound. To see some of their arguments and NDE rebuttals, internet search Dr. Jeffry Long [radiation oncologist], or Dr. Pim van Lommel [cardiologist].)

Some materialists may accede to evidence that consciousness can occur in NDEs, but have faith that science will one day explain how material brains that are dead by all clinical measures can be conscious. But science is not faith, it is observation, testability, and repeatability, none of which skeptics can provide to prove that dead brains are conscious. Although it can't be proven that science will not one day discover such a thing, neither can it be proven that one day science will not discover that cows can jump over the moon. It is logically impossible to disprove a negative.

Moreover, *reduction ad absurdum*, if materialists are correct in their faith that dead brains are conscious, it would be inhumane and murderous to bury or cremate dead people!

6. Out of Body Experiences (OBE)

Some people can enter a trance-like state and then travel with a non-material body into other dimensions. Blind people with no light perception can accurately describe what they see in both the physical and nonphysical worlds during an OBE. One person described a five-digit number on a piece of paper that could only have been seen if she were floating in an out of body state. In a random survey, 339 out of 420 people claimed to have had an OBE. After a heart attack, 26 of 32 patients reported an OBE and gave accurate descriptions of events in the hospital which occurred while they were unconscious.

Of all societies studied, 437 of them (89%) have some tradition of OBEs. Skulls of children have been found with trepanned holes; a practice used to attempt to facilitate OBEs, astral sorties, and mediumship. Aldous Huxley, Goethe, D. H. Lawrence, Strindberg, and Jack London all reported OBE experiences.

OBE abilities can be learned, and there are many teachers and opportunities.

LSD (lysergic acid diethylamide), ayahuasca and other DMT (dimethyl tryptamine) and monoamine oxidase inhibitor (MAOI) carriers, ketamine, mescaline, THC cannabinoids, ibogaine, and other synthetic and natural compounds can induce OBEs. People use drugs for OBEs because it is easier (but not safer) than training the mind to leave the body on its own.

7. Reincarnation and Pre-Birth Memories

Reincarnation was integral to Egyptian culture thousands of years BC. Greek philosophers debated it, it is a tenet of Jewish Kabbalism and was a doctrine of early Christianity until purged by pagan Roman demigods and their clergy. Today, millions of people around the world subscribe to the belief.

Granted, popularity and religious dogma do not constitute proofs. However, ideas that reach as far back as history can be explored, and that persist through millennia certainly can intimate an underlying truth.

But we no longer need to rely on evidence that can be easily dismissed. Reincarnation has now been the subject of serious modern scientific research. The results, although seemingly fantastic, are compelling.

For example, Dr. Ian Stevenson held an endowed professorship at the University of Virginia. (Dr. Jim Tucker has continued his work at the same University). He traveled the world for almost 40 years investigating more than two thousand cases of children who recall previous lives. (That number has increased to over 2,500 with the continuing work of Dr. Tucker.) His voluminous and scholarly scientific works with photographs and documentation give firsthand accounts of children who, from the time they are first able to speak, beg to be taken "home," pine for parents, husbands, and mistresses in a prior life, and know details of another life there is no way for them to have learned in their present life. Some children, once they learn to speak, even describe thoughts of the mother during gestation and memory as far back as conception.

For example, at two, little Daniel said he was a 25-year-old mechanic who died in a car crash. He named the mechanic's hometown and the driver of the car. When the family of the mechanic heard of the little boy's claims, they visited him unannounced. The little boy instantly recognized them and named his "past life" sister.

From the time she was a toddler, Suzy doted on an elderly man she claimed was her husband in a previous life. The man, his wife, and family, could not deny the private details Suzy mysteriously knew about him.

When Preeti began to speak, she begged to be taken to her "real" family. She named her previous mother and father and the distant town where they lived. When she was taken to the home, Preeti immediately named her previous brothers and sisters.

A little suburban Virginia boy insisted he owned a farm in a previous life. He described the farm, cows, and shed. Once, while out driving in the car with his family, he cried out that his farm was just around the bend. When they got there every detail of the farm was just as he had described.

Christian, at the age of two, became obsessed with baseball, insisting on wearing baseball uniforms and sleeping with baseballs. He then told his mom he was Lou Gehrig before becoming her baby. Go to cathy-byrd.com/coast-to-coast to listen to this compelling story.

The internet is replete with documented cases of rein-carnation.

8. Past Life Regression

Hypnotists and psychiatrists help subjects regress to past lives and be cured of emotional problems not alleviated by any other means. Some people suffer sup-pressed carry-over memories of traumas and relationships from previous lives. Healing often results once these events are recalled. Scars and birthmarks have also been ex-plained by such things as gunshots and knife wounds in past lives.

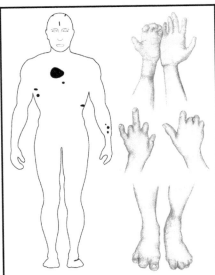

Past Life Defects – The marks on the body and the hand and foot defects shown here are documented as traceable to past life injuries according to the work of professor Ian Stevenson.

© Wysong   Figure 256

PAST LIFE REGRESSION AND HEALINGS

This is a partial list of professionals on a website (induced-adc.com) that use communication with deceased loved ones as a means of healing grief (see Resource Section for others):

Katelyn Daniels, LCPC
Schaumburg, IL 847-490-1295 | katelyndaniels@aol.com

Cynthia Davidson-Reid, M.S., LMSW
New York, NY 212-580-1523 | cdrcoach@rcn.com

Donald Dufford, Ph.D.
San Jose, CA 408-559-9088 | Soquel, CA 831-479-1960 | dondufford@aol.com

Martha Escamilla R Bogota
Colombia | www.traumatreatments.com

Marina Ferrier, Ph.D.,LCPC, MFT
Sandpoint, ID 208-265-2271 | marinaferrier@aol.com

Deborah M. Fish, M.Sc.
Ottawa, Ontario, Canada 819 776-5119 | www.deborahfish.com

Eileen Freedland, MSW, LMSW
Bloomfield Hills, MI 248-647-0050 | efreedland@earthlink.net

Juliane Grodhues,Dipl-Psych.
Saarbruecken, Germany 0049-6805-913368 | jgrodhues@t-online.de

Mo Therese Hannah, Ph.D.
Latham (near Albany) NY 518-210-2487 | mhanah413@aol.com

Jenny Streit Horn, M.S., LPC, NCC
Denton, TX 940-382-6141 | jshorn@websentia.us

Esther Klein, LCSW
Safety Harbor (near Tampa), FL 727-726-5049 | eljklein@gmail.com

Lisa Lane, M.A., LPC
Dallas, TX 214-351-5851 or 214-808-4670 | lilane7@earthlink.net

Dave MacDonald, M.S.W., L.C.S.W.
Atlanta, Georgia & Asheville, NC 404-524-5005 | macaffinc@mindspring.com

Elaine Maher, LCSW
Honolulu, HI 808-551-2251 | emm4602@aol.com

David Mannelli, Psy.D.
Milwaukee, WI 262-542-3255 (x126) | dfmannelli@msn.com

Graham Maxey, M. Div., M.A., LPC
Arlington, TX 817-939-0800 | zephat@swbell.net

Cathy L. Parker, MSW, LCSW
Chattanooga, TN 423-899-0024, Ext 32 | clp1988@charter.net

Kathy Parker, Ph.D.
Roselle, IL 773-259-4239 | kparkerpsy@aol.com

Greg Rimoldi, MSW, LCSW
Gurnee, IL 847-356-5564 | upstreamtravler@sbcglobal.net

Thomas E. Taylor, M.Div., MSW, BCETS
North Bellmore, NY 516-351-1012 | nb650c@aol.com

Carl Totton, Psy.D.
North Hollywood, CA 818-760-4219 | drcarlat@yahoo.com

Gregg Unterberger, M.Ed., LPC
Austin, TX 512-451-9527 | gregmerlyn@aol.com

Laura Winds, MA, LMFT
Bellingham, WA 360-647-1003 | lawinds@nas.com

Pati Zimmerman, MSW, Ph.D.
Clackamas, OR (near Portland) 503-657-7207 | pazimmerman@comcast.net

Figure 257

9. Xenoglossy

Some people, including children, have an inexplicable accent, speak foreign languages and even ancient tongues no longer spoken anywhere in the world. They explain that it's the language and culture from when they lived in another place, in another life, in another body. (Search xenoglossy on Youtube; also <u>reincarnationexperiment.org</u>)

10. Ghosts

Countless people have witnessed apparitions of humans. Sense-presence is a phenomenon whereby a recently passed person is seen, heard, or sensed by another. About 50% of people have experienced this. At Gettysburg, there are ghost tours where numerous sightings have occurred, and voices of the dead have been recorded.

Akiane – born in 1994, began drawing at 4, painting at 6, and teaching herself and learning mostly from her own keen observation and study. An internationally recognized 11-year-old prodigy, she is considered the only known child binary genius in both realist painting and poetry. Selected as 1 of 20 most accomplished visual artists in the world, Akiane speaks four languages: Lithuanian, Russian, English and Sign Language. At age 7 she began writing poetry and aphorisms. Her poems often arrive fully conceived. Her favorite size canvases are 48 x 60 inches. They are reproduced in lots of 500 numbered reproductions and sold for more than $2000 each. She rises at 5 a.m., five to six days a week to get ready to paint in the studio and write; she works for about three hours a day. She often works over a hundred hours on a painting, producing 8 to 10 paintings a year. She has "start-to-finish" demonstration videos of her paintings which prove they are of her hand. Her biggest wish: "that everyone would love God and one another." <u>artakiane.com</u> (For another example of unexplained early artistic talent see <u>kieronwilliamson.com</u>)

Figure 258

© Marla Olmstead

Marla Olmstead – This young lady began painting before her second birthday. The New York Times featured her first major exhibition. Marla's work has been shown on The Today Show, CBS Sunday Morning, 60 Minutes II, The London Observer, BBC World News, Art and Antiques and Time Magazine. Her original and Limited Editions have been acquired by collectors internationally and are valued at up to $25,000 each. Over 200 buyers are lined up from around the world to purchase her stunning works. Using fingers, brush, spatula and even a ketchup bottle, Marla creates vibrant and expressive canvases as large as five feet high. Critics say she rivals the styles of Jackson Pollock and Wassily Kandinsky. It is unknown for a child artist to begin with abstract art. Even Picasso at a young age attempted realism with stick figures and the like first. To view her works in color, go to marlaolmstead.com. To read the debate about whether her work is or is not genius, just plug in "Marla Olmstead Child Prodigy" in the search bar. It would seem that the debate would be easily solved by any child or adult creating an abstract piece and trying to get $25,000 for it.

Figure 259

© Stephen Wiltshire

Stephen Wiltshire – was mute until the age of nine and autistic. Nevertheless he has drawn the whole of central London after a helicopter trip above it. He has also drawn Tokyo on a 10-meter long canvas within seven days following a short helicopter ride over the city. Since then he has drawn Rome, Hong Kong, Frankfurt, Madrid, Dubai, Jerusalem and London (above) on giant canvasses. When Wiltshire took the helicopter ride over Rome, he drew the exact number of columns in the Colosseum.

Figure 260

11. Unexplained Abilities

Henry Ford said, "I believe that we . . . will come back again . . . and we can utilize the experience we collect in one life in the next. Genius is the fruit of long experience in many lives. Some are older souls than others, and so they know more." Children are thus born with extraordinary skills, such as in math, music, art, memory, and language, present in a past life.

12. Family Dissimilarities

Remarkable differences exist among family members. Although genetically of the same mold, siblings have disparate and distinct personalities and life objectives. Regression to previous lives explains present life individuality. Who we are is not just nature and nurture; it's past as well.

13. We Don't Change

If you introspect, the inner you is the same no matter how far back you remember. Your mind, knowledge, and experience grow, the physical body matures, ages, and returns to dust. But, regardless, your essence, the otherworldly nonmaterial you remains the same.

14. Dream Realities

A lucid dream is a dream during which the dreamer is aware that they are dreaming and may have some control over the dream characters, narrative, and environment. In those special dreams, as well as in ordinary ones all of us have, an alternate reality can be as real as physical life. We experience a material world, living creatures, communication, feelings, and senses—even some extraordinary abilities like flying (my favorite). If, in a dream, while the body is "dead" in sleep, a nonmaterial reality can exist in which you are a part, why couldn't consciousness survive similarly after the body dies? We are, as Prospero remarked, "such stuff as dreams are made of."

15. After Death Communication

In after death communication (ADC), the dead reveal details that prove they are who they claim to be. For example, a psychic medium speaks to a dead child and the child tells the medium about a toy hidden in a special place. The parents check and find the toy exactly where described. Thousands of other remarkable examples abound in the literature. Television programs featuring psychics also provide remarkable evidence.

NOTABLES AND EVIDENCE TESTIFYING TO LIFE AFTER DEATH
(In no particular order and by no means a complete listing.)

- Buddha
- Confucius
- Laotse
- Patinas
- Jesus
- Krishna
- Hermes
- Zoroaster
- Ancient culture art such as Stonehenge's after-death tunnel carved on walls
- Out-of-body journeys by twelfth-century Persian Sufis
- Head hunters who believe the soul is in the head so they shrink it and sew the eyes and mouth closed so the slain enemy will not meet them in the next life
- Aborigine dreamtime planers
- Zuni Indians who spend 50% of their wake time in religious ceremony related to after-death life
- Abraham Lincoln
- General Patten
- Charles Dickens

- Henry Ford
- Walt Whitman
- Thomas Edison
- Pierre and Marie Currie
- Edgar Mitchell
- Margaret Mead
- Johannes Kepler
- Isaac Newton
- Kekule
- Descartes
- Tungas Shamans in Siberia
- Malagasy of Madagascar
- Tibetan Buddhists
- World's shamanic traditions
- Hindus
- Japanese Ainu
- Alaskan Tlingit Indians
- Ojibwa, Hopi, Pawnee, Omaha Ogalala Sioux and Algonquin Indians
- Australian Aranda aborigines
- Siberian Gilyak

- Incas
- Zulus
- Nigerian Igbo
- Judaic Kabbalistic traditions
- Dogon spiritualists of the Sudan
- Greek philosophers: Anazimenes, Pythagoras, Heraclitus, Empedocles, Aristotle and Plato
- Ancient Gnostics such as Philo, Judaeus and Maimonides
- Egyptian prophet Hermes
- Trismegistus
- Eighth century Tibetan Book of the Dead
- 2500 year old Egyptian Book of the Dead
- Medieval literature replete with accounts of spiritual excursions out of the body
- Hindu Avatamsaka Sutra
- Fa-Tsang and the Hua-yen school of Buddha
- Leibniz, a seventh century German mathematician

Truth Persists – Ideas that are widely held throughout history should be paid attention to. Truth has a way of hanging around.

© Wysong

Figure 261

In near-death experiences (NDE), out of body experiences (OBE) and after death communication (ADC) via mediums and psychics, the dead describe that they are alive and fully conscious in another dimension. Induction into a state where ADCs can take place reportedly can occur in 98% of those who try. Consider just one of the many websites that offer lessons in this area: induced-adc.com. Allan L. Botkin, Psy.D. says there, "We can very rapidly, reliably, and easily induce an IADC® (induced after death communication) in nearly all people interested in having the experience."

Many after death communications are accurate as to historical detail. People who died in the early 1700s described three-pronged forks, those who died later in the century described four prongs. Clothing, footwear, and foods described were also consistent with the time. These are only a few examples. A study of past-life accounts yields countless others. (Yes there are charlatans in this field as in all others. They do not invalidate those who actually do communicate with the dead.)

Regardless of age, location, time or belief system, virtually all who say they have communicated with the dead describe common features about dying and life thereafter.

Medium communication with the discarnate has been, and is, the subject of rigorous scientific study. Research conducted at <u>windbridge. org</u> has been published in a journal subject to rigorous peer review. One study by Julie Beischel, Ph.D., proves, through quintuple blinded studies and careful statistical methodology (P = .001 [less than .05 is significant]), that mediums can communicate with the dead. This work, worthy of a Nobel Prize, is essentially ignored by mainstream scientific and medical materialists. Her study, in itself, should remove any remaining nails in the coffins people think they are destined for.

Such revelations are nothing new. For example, Wallace (1823-1913), the co-founder of evolution with Darwin, came to an unlikely and astounding conclusion. After personal experiments and examining reports from other scientists that the universe is populated with a hierarchy of nonmaterial spirit beings, he remarked:

"All my preconceptions, all my knowledge, all my belief in the supremacy of science and of natural law were against the possibility of such phenomena. And even when one by one, the facts were forced upon me without possibility of escape from them, still, as Sir David Brewster declared after being at first astonished by the phenomena he saw with Mr. Home, 'spirit was the last thing I could give in to' . . . for twenty-five years I had been an utter skeptic as to the existence of any preter-human or super-human intelligences, and that I never for a moment contemplated the possibility that the marvels related by spiritualists could be literally true. If I have now changed my opinion it is simply by the force of evidence. It is from no dread of annihilation that I have gone into this subject; it is from no inordinate longing for eternal existence that I have come to believe in facts . . ."

The Swedish "Leonardo da Vinci" of his era, Swedenborg (born 1688), developed out of body travel skills. Although tainted by Biblical presuppositions, he filled twenty volumes with the results of these travels.

16. Logic

The inner us—the moral, questioning, creative, volitional part—fits best with the idea that we are nonmaterial creatures who occupy biological bodies in order to develop the ethical character that comes with choice. This particularly rings true in the later years in life when the ethical Indiscretions of youth settle in to haunt conscience and cause painful regret.

It makes more sense that a lifetime's worth of learning from trying to obey conscience—an inherent drive implanted within—is retained rather than to have it all vanish at the moment of death.

Figure 262

If you send your television to the junkyard and it is smashed to smithereens, the broadcast transmissions it used to receive do not cease to exist. Similarly, our conscious essence, a nonmaterial waveform/energy/consciousness, would not cease to exist just because the brain/body tuner was junked—died.

DEATH IS NOTHING AT ALL

I have only slipped away into the next room
I am I and you are you
Whatever we were to each other
That we are still
Call me by my old familiar name
Speak to me in the easy way you always used
Put no difference into your tone
Wear no forced air of solemnity or sorrow
Laugh as we always laughed
At the little jokes we always enjoyed together
Play, smile, think of me, pray for me
Let my name be ever the household word that it always was
Let it be spoken without effort
Without the ghost of a shadow in it

Life means all that it ever meant
It is the same as it ever was
There is absolute unbroken continuity
What is death but a negligible accident?
Why should I be out of mind
Because I am out of sight?
I am waiting for you for an interval
Somewhere very near
Just around the corner
All is well.
Nothing is past; nothing is lost
One brief moment and all will be as it was before
How we shall laugh at the trouble of parting when we meet again!

© 1847-1918 Canon Henry Scott-Holland, Canon of St Paul's Cathedral

Figure 263

It would seem that if previous lives are to learn from, then we should be able to recall them. However, we may have had many, even hundreds of such lives. Carrying those memories would make this life impossible. We could be terrified by some memories, regretful of our missteps, or heartsick missing those we have loved.

The important memories, the ones that can forge us into better people, may not be vividly in mind but are embedded within conscience to help guide our lives.

The foregoing points to one inevitable conclusion: Death is a change rather than an end; a comma, not a period in our life's story. We are not material beings suffering from spiritual illusions, but rather spirit beings suffering from a material illusion. The wisdom of this eulogy is apparent: "Birth til death, we travel between the eternities."

GONE FROM MY SIGHT

I am standing upon the seashore.
A ship, at my side,

spreads her white sails to the
moving breeze and starts

for the blue ocean.
She is an object of beauty and strength.

I stand and watch her until,
at length, she hangs like a speck

of white cloud just where the sea and sky come
to mingle with each other.

~

Then, someone at my side says,
"There, she is gone."

~

Gone where?

Gone from my sight. That is all. She is just as
large in mast, hull and spar as she was when she
left my side.

And, she is just as able to bear her load of
living freight to her destined port.

~

Her diminished size is in me – not in her.

~

And, just at the moment when someone says,
"There, she is gone,"

there are other eyes watching her coming, and
other voices

ready to take up the glad shout,
"Here she comes!"

And that is dying...

© Henry Van Dyke   Figure 279

44
LIFE AFTER DEATH

Facts, logic, and science demand a whole new way of looking at who we are, why we are here, and where we are going.

A Logical Sequence

- The physical world and our bodies are not really solid matter all the way down.

- The "nothingness" of which reality is composed is best explained as being occupied by conscious intelligence.

- In the domain of consciousness (mind/thought), time is not linear, both past and future can be accessed.

- Atoms and evolution do not explain the origin of consciousness, free will, or life.

- The intricacies of the universe and life cry out creation by an extraordinary intelligence, a Creator not properly defined by human-made religions and holy books.

- Our conscious essence is like thought and not reducible to nor explained by the temporal body and brain.

- This implies that we must have preexisted Earth-life and will survive its end.

- In turn, it can be inferred, and it's supported by empirical and experiential evidence, that there is life beyond this physical world that would not be restricted by the limitations of physicality.

- That would mean that we can shed the constraints of this physical world.

- These understandings would explain paranormal phenomena such as out of body experiences, near-death experiences, after-death communications, clairvoyance, telepathy and the whole bag of weird things that fly in the face of the confinements of materialism.

Death is Birth in Reverse

Most people assume that the only way to know about life beyond the grave would be to guess or to listen to those who claim to have a hotline to God. On the contrary, there is a wealth of direct testimony and evidence that gives glimpses of life beyond. Also, we can apply reason, sound scientific principles, and can even weigh direct personal experience. If you can develop paranormal abilities, you might even be able to visit the real life behind the scenes of this physical one and see for yourself. If not, then you should give consideration (critically, of course) to the testimony and evidence from those who claim to have done so.

Put out of mind cultural and religious preconceptions about what death is and what it is like afterward. Don't think in terms of phantasmagoric streets of gold, fire and pitchforks, white beards, wings, and halos. We will settle down to the more matter of fact, mundane, but nonetheless fantastic ideas that emerge from a sober look at the actual evidence.

After Death Anatomy

Dr. Robert Crookall, in a series of meticulous books, examined countless cases of OBEs, NDEs, and psychic communications with those who have died. He found remarkable consistency, regardless of the culture, in accounts of the death process and the transition to a nonmaterial, telepathic, clairvoyant realm.

Crookall's research describes death being as natural as conception, gestation, and birth. His subjects report that at death our true nature is revealed. The nonphysical anatomy is composed of "spirit," "soul," and "vehicle of vitality." During physical life, they are bound together within the Earthly body and are attached to it through a "silver cord."

This cord is sometimes visible to those present at the bed of those dying. Even skeptical doctors have reported seeing this silver cord phenomenon. The discarnate body is apart from the physical one but attached to it by this cord. When people experience OBE or NDE events, and for a time after true mortal death, the cord remains attached, permitting a dual consciousness. The cord is said to be a lifeline connection between the nonmaterial body and the material one.

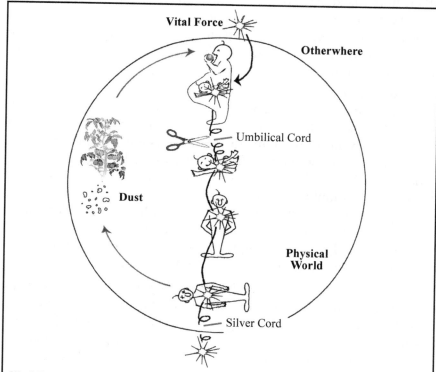

Vital Force - The spark of life, otherwise known as the vital force, lies outside of our physical world and is the source of life. As the child is tied to the mother by the umbilical cord, a person is tied to the vital force by a silver cord. Transition to the physical world requires severing of the umbilical cord, transition to the nonphysical world requires severing of the silver cord. Some people with a 'loose' silver cord are able to enter the nonphysical world and then return to the physical (OBE, NDE, psychics...).

© Wysong

Figure 264

Each type of death—untimely death, natural death in sleep, death by explosion, death after a lingering illness, etc.—creates a different death experience that Crookall has carefully cataloged in a scientific and clinical style.

In sudden unexpected death, the person may find themselves doing what they were doing before they died (driving the car, running across a battlefield . . .) and be wondering why nobody sees them or can hear them talk. A death while sleeping may result in a sense of vivid dreaming. A protracted and exhausting illness may result in a limbo of restful recuperation.

By the time one finishes examining Crookall's works or the many others in this field, it's extremely difficult to view death as mere physical termination, or any mystical experience at all. He and other researchers present a compelling body of evidence demonstrating that when the stopper of Earth-life is pulled, only the material part drains away, not the "vapor" of our essence.

At death, we remain attached to the body by the silver cord while at the same time having a sense of separateness (like a baby in the womb). The dead are said to be able to see their physical body and even observe and hear the events surrounding their death in a hospital room, at home, or the scene of a car accident. When we depart the body, the silver cord remains attached, and there is a clear sense of duality (like a baby after delivery with the umbilical cord still attached). After the silver cord breaks, the corporeal ballast is shed, and we realize we have a life independent and free from the body. In the nonphysical realm we do, however, need nurturing to readjust to the nonphysical realm, just like infants need the care of parents to adjust to their after-womb environment.

Moving on into "adult" life in the nonphysical world has a lot to do with how amenable we are to accept what is happening. If we are fixated in this life with some religious expectation, or in denial of the possibility of life after death because of materialistic indoctrination, the transition can be difficult and slow, appropriately likened to a stubborn and protracted breach birth.

Death is a birth into a form that can be reincarnated. That's no less believable than physical birth on the heels of conception and gestation all of which are miraculous events. Voltaire said, "It is no more surprising to be born twice than once."

Ralph Waldo Emerson wrote, "The soul is an emanation of Divinity . . . a ray of light from the source of light. It comes from without into the human body, as into a temporary abode, and then it goes out of it anew; it wanders in ethereal regions and it returns to visit the Earth where it passes into another body . . . for the soul is immortal."

The After-Death World

The following eclectic description of the after-death world is gathered from the numerous resources listed in the Resource section at the end of this book. When you learn the credentials of the authors and researchers, experience their humility, openness, and lack of agenda, and consider that you are getting the same story from people spread over thousands of years, and from every imaginable culture and circumstance (children, aborigine, farmer, noble, pauper, scientist, doctor), there is every reason to pay attention.

The following is a brief synopsis of the testimony gathered from after death communications and out-of-body and near-death experiences. Variations of the death experience occur and are modeled to individual needs to make the transition as easy and wonderful as possible.

- At death, people feel more alive than ever and have no sense of having died at all. Looking back at the body, it appears as only a fleeting garment of Earth-life.

- The dead say the easiest thing in life is death. Death should not be equated with the pain that often precedes it. There is no pain at the time of death, even with hanging and burning. This is explained by the subconscious leaving because it is aware of what is about to happen to the body.

- Right after physical death, there is a traveling through tunnel experience after which people are met by beings of "light," and sometimes a particular one who knows them deeply. The feeling is one of coming home. Friends are everywhere.

- There is a wondrous sense of peace, comfort, warmth, well-being, and embracing love.

- In the period in between Earth lives in the non-physical realm we are met by friends, relatives, and guides who help us transition and understand the meaning of Earth experiences. Love pervades and there is no punishment or judgment other than what we impose on ourselves for having failed Earth objectives.

- Other beings ("guides") emanate only love and patience. The feeling of acceptance is said to be like being hugged by a mother or father who loves you regardless.

- The nonphysical world has exquisite beauty, perfect temperature, intense light and color, overwhelming smells, and enthralling sounds. It makes Earth seem dull and shadow-like by comparison.

317

Earth becomes the dream, spirit-life the true reality. Things don't create sound, they are sound; things don't emit an odor, they are fragrance; things don't reflect light, they are light. The beauty and sense of reality in the other plane is far beyond anything we experience on Earth. A soldier reports "the most exquisite scenery imaginable. One minute I was blasting away, and then I was in the most beautiful peaceful garden."

- At death, there is a greatly expanded sense of consciousness and a feeling of being part of infinite intelligence and creative power.

- There is a sense of freedom from weight; the real you has been extracted. One seven-year-old boy who died reported back to a medium that death "was like walking into your mind." Things are enormously interesting, delightful, boundless, free, light, and infinite. There are immortal sensibilities, space means nothing, time stands still, but access to any part of it requires mere thought.

- The dead instantly possess special powers such as telepathy, instantaneous travel, and foreknowledge. All they need to do is think a person or place, and there they are.

- Intuitive and imaginative capabilities are fantastically enhanced, intellectual skills unimportant.

- Reality in the nonphysical world is thought forms, just as it is in this, only we are not seduced, blinded, and entranced by the material. Unencumbered by the constraints of the physical world, mind is everything. If you think about food, it will be a part of your life. If you don't, it will disappear. Choose to pick a fight and thought-form wounds will result from the battle. There are golfer's realms as well as those for dancers, runners, hikers, basketball players, and every imaginable religious one, including those for the most piously and smugly assured. If you think about sex, it will be a part of your life. If you don't, it won't. ("Sex" reportedly takes on many different forms, physical-type intercourse being only one of them, and reportedly the least enjoyable of the options.) People are in complete control of their destiny and only move from one experience or plane to another if and when they desire. Moving "up" from only playing golf every day is a choice that comes from within.

- Health returns to its most perfectly youthful state: "My frame seemed to have been remade with some highly malleable rubber that was a huge improvement over (material) bones and joints . . .

I could bend over backward in a perfect 'n' shape . . . I tried bouncing on my feet, a foot, then two foot, then three. All quite effortless . . . How could the Earth (there are said to be perfect duplicates of Earth in this reality) be so like a trampoline? No, it's my new rubbery feet!"

- Creativity is an integral part of our nature. In the non-physical realm, it is at an especially high pitch. One person described practicing creating miniature solar systems. The beauty of the universe and our ability in the physical plane to explore and appreciate it to the degree we do is said to be a testimony to our participation in its creation..

- Everyone experiences a life review in which all of life's experiences are brought to memory. "Judgment" turns out to be an intimate and complete personal exploration (nothing remains hidden) of choices made in Earth-life along with their impact on others, complete with experiencing the pain or joy one has caused. The pangs of conscience we feel in Earth-life are said to be amplified excruciatingly during the life review. The dead see themselves totally uncloaked, naked; their inner motives are fully exposed. No excuses or surprises. Each person turns out to be their own most severe judge. Conscience is revealed as the touchstone for living that we sense it is while on Earth.

- The dead love where they are. If it is an untimely near-death experience, they are reluctant to return to the body. They only return because counselors remind them that their objective on Earth was not completed. But the choice is theirs. We control our destiny and are never victims.

- The transition after death is easy if the mind is open, difficult, and confusing otherwise. There are various levels of existence after death, and they match—to begin at least—the death expectation of the person so as to make the transition as easy and comfortable as possible. Those expecting to see Jesus, Mohammed, Buddha, or saints, may do so. (The variety of religious figures to match a person's expectation is another proof that religions do not reflect reality.) Those expecting a paradise will find that. Those in disbelief that death can be anything other than oblivion will flounder in a state of believing they are only dreaming. Some who cannot give up the idea of Earth-life or refuse to admit their new dimensional state, wander the Earth interfering either mischievously or maliciously with the unsuspecting (as ghosts, spooks, possessions, and so on).

- Ascent to higher levels of learning, growth, and experience, or to the decision to try another material sojourn on Earth or elsewhere, comes after counseling with guides and personal reflection. But people are in control of their destinies, and there is an eternity of patience.

319

- The same personality and characteristics that differentiated people from others while on Earth are retained. The inner us does not ever change other than (hopefully) becoming better—meaning closer to what we all sense we should be if we listen to conscience.

- Those still on Earth draw the dead to them by their thoughts or by mourning. Those on the other side keenly feel the grieving of those on Earth. One passed individual talked about the empathetic pain he felt for a person on Earth grieving: "being able to feel the raw edge of her wound as if it were my own" This pull is a distraction to those passed, since life beyond is filled with interesting activity. Besides, they know those on Earth will be with them momentarily. Earth-life is seen as but a tiny blip in the eternity of existence, so time is not relevant to them as it is for those on Earth.

- The reason those who have passed do not usually communicate with those on Earth is that they are in a different dimension at a different "vibration." Spirit life is extremely fast and complicated due to its telepathic nature. On the other hand, Earth-life is extremely slowed, permitting us to experience slowed, time-sensitive physical reality. The earthly physical body acts as a governor, permitting us more measured contemplation and experience.

- As smart as we may think we are with our physical brains, we are in no way capable of comprehending and sorting out the volume of data present in a dimension where there is the fluidity of infinite interconnectedness. The sharply focused morsel of reality presented by our senses on Earth, with beginnings and ends, causes and effects, does not compare to the infinite dynamics of the nonphysical world. All mediums express the speed difficulty between those in the spirit world and Earth world. Material humans cannot speed up enough, and the spirits have trouble slowing down. If you observe a medium in action, this difficulty in tempo between the two worlds is often obvious. Also, the dead do not speak to mediums in sentences, but rather with impressions that the medium often struggles to interpret and relate in sentence form.

- To the dead, life on Earth is like a few minutes and almost inconsequential. They feel no need to communicate with us on Earth since we will be with them in the blink of an eye, their time. The job in Earth-life is to engage its reality and live well, not be preoccupied with life beyond. Although those in the after-death reality may occasionally intercede in human affairs, the task at hand for humans in physical Earth-life is to reach within and conquer the tests before them, not be supplicants to those beyond to solve problems.

• The choice to come to Earth is ours. We also choose our parents. We merge with the developing fetus. In the early stages in the womb, we make to and fro visits. There is work to be done in joining with the growing child. A child's inabilities and awkwardness may, in part, reflect the difficulty in melding spirit with physical.

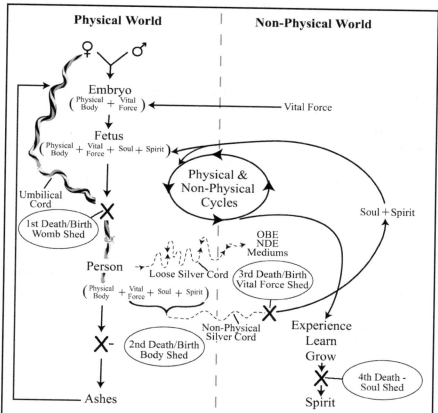

Physical, Non-Physical Births and Deaths – A schematic of births and deaths (X) in the physical and non-physical worlds. In the physical world the physical body recycles at death. The body turns to dust which nourishes the food to build a new body. In the nonphysical world, vital force-spirit-soul are said to recycle. The processes of death (note there are four possible) and birth (four possible), are not supernatural events but natural processes. There is even a spiritual equivalent to the umbilical cord, called the silver cord. The cycling is said to occur endlessly for the purpose of experience and learning to grow the inner self.

© Wysong

Figure 265

- Visits to Earth in human form are for the express purpose of utilizing slowed experience on Earth to implant moral lessons needed to advance to another higher plane of being in the spirit world. A physical body and brain permit us the opportunity for discovery and error and with that the pleasure of success and the pain of failure. Such experience can more effectively forge character. This helps explain why people tend not to learn by being told, but only through personal experience.

- The purpose of life on Earth is to develop morally and learn. Multiple existences facilitate this process. A whole life, or series of lives, may be necessary to get through a person's thick skull (being) that one must be honest to oneself before they can be honest to others, or that theft, conceit, violence, and selfishness are counterproductive to inner development. Earth-life is like a forging furnace. People come, go through the fire and get hammered a bit, take a cooling-off break in the non-Earth plane, come back, get hammered some more—until they have learned all that is possible by Earth experience or decide to learn by some other means.

- Learning in the spirit realm continues endlessly and is aided by libraries, movies, sage teachers, mentors, and boundless friends and helpmates. Some do all their learning in the non-physical dimension and never come to Earth or go to other physical worlds. However, that choice is said to result in slower and more difficult growth. Similarly, we can talk to our children until we're blue in the face about safe driving, but nobody ever fully understands until they experience the pain of an accident or lose a loved one in a crash. It is an unusual person who can learn without experience. That is the value of a difficult and trying Earth-life.

- The lessons we set out for ourselves before coming to Earth are guided by the conflicts of conscience we feel.

- All levels of beings come to Earth. Some are of exceptional character, others are best described as evil. The terrible things that occur here and the interactions with which we are faced on Earth permit opportunities to exert our moral character. If all were peaches and cream, nothing would be learned. Regardless of how bad life is, it will be but a blink of the eye in retrospect against a backdrop of infinite existence. Nevertheless, Earth-life is tough; it requires significant courage to come here, and no little recuperation after.

- Other worlds and dimensions could be chosen aside from Earth. The reports are that we can even be entirely different creatures. Some worlds are paradisiacal, some very difficult (like Earth), others are aqueous and in others we can be airborne. Some of our weird dreams, reportedly, give us glimpses of these other lives and environments.

- In deep sleep, we may be visiting the nonmaterial realm for rejuvenation. But awareness is blocked when we awaken so that realm does not interfere with experiencing this one as a reality.

- Relationships in the spirit realm are totally open and honest. There are no secrets or pretenses. Hypocrisy does not exist. We are fully exposed to ourselves and to others for who we are.

- There are no enemies. Love, understanding, and patience pervade. After death, people instantly access friends, relatives, and others who are at a similar level of development and interest. There are countless other beings in the non-physical realm. They are all at different stages of development and in the appropriate developmental spheres. Those at very high levels do not return to physical life. Those at very low levels suffer from the hell they create for themselves. Hades (hell) or whatever one may call a less than ideal place, is not torture, but a condition of limbo for those resistant to development or confused about the transition from physical life. But help and love are always there for the asking.

- People tend to associate with the same group and recycle to Earth into different roles in association with them. These pre-Earth relationships are said to be the reason we gravitate to the people we do on Earth. A mother may end up as the child of her husband. A murder victim may be the father of a murderer. A rich person may return as a servant in the home of a former beggar.

- Soul mates may be just that—intimately close people in the other plane who recognize one another almost instantly on Earth and are powerfully attracted.

- Of the thousands of people who have been studied and claim to have had other Earth lives, almost all recall mundane and boring lives as peasants, laborers, farmers, and primitive food gatherers. Very few recall life as an aristocrat or being famous. This defeats the argument that such recollections are fantasies. If you are going to make up a previous life, why not say you were Napoleon or Aristotle?

- All the Big Questions are more fully answered once we leave Earth's confining dimensions. We will comprehend timelessness, infinity, and ultimate causes more fully.

- The ethical pull and the desire for truth we feel while on Earth are reflections of our greater purpose of being. We have been created as companions. As good companions we must have free will to either join (love) or separate from (hate) our neighbors and Creator. Relentlessly pursuing truth shows our respect for and desire to join with the ultimate truth, our very source. In this regard, it is interesting that the Egyptians pictured an accounting at death in the form of a scale. On one side of the scale was truth represented by a feather. On the other side was one's heart. If they balanced, life in the afterworld was good. If truth was not properly pursued, there was a penalty to be paid. Surrender to the pure mind of truth, a formless, genderless "angelic" state of pure love and contentedness, is the ultimate goal. This process, for as long as it takes, is what our existence is all about.

Death is a part of life, not its end or some abstract religious experience requiring faith. Contemplating a continuing life on the other side of death—where loved ones reside, learning is endless, challenge and creativity are everywhere, love is boundless, pretense does not exist, and energy and growth is unlimited—is undoubtedly a wonderful prospect. But our enthusiasm for it should be in proportion to the evidence on its behalf and the degree to which we open-mindedly pursue it as if thinking matters.

45
WHY THERE IS SUFFERING

Other than the record and irrationality of man-made religions which are thought to be a reflection of the creator, perhaps the greatest impediment to recognizing that an intelligence is responsible for our reality, is suffering. The argument is that if there is an intelligence with unlimited capabilities, it would have compassion and prevent catastrophes and suffering.

Such thinking emerges from anthropomorphizing the Creator, attributing human qualities to it. Also, blaming others, in this case the Creator, is always too convenient for us humans. Let's think it through.

Suffering in Nature

First, consider the reality of our Earthly circumstance. We are part of a gigantic interconnected natural machine. To enjoy Earth's benefits, we must assume our role in that machine. We are not an extrinsic toy infected with evil and punished by a sadistic god hungry for worship.

Natural disasters are just the necessary workings of the nature machine obeying nature's laws. Yes, we can suffer if we get in the way. But Earth has to do its thing. Nature is a creature doing what it must, no more fair or cruel than cat or man killing plants and animals for food to survive. Nature is a dynamic of rock, water, air, magma, mud, fire, ice, and myriad other physical elements and forces that result in atmospheric, hydrological, and geological change.

If this and the resultant cataclysms did not happen to relieve tensions, pressures would build that could make the whole planet barren of life. For example, without plate tectonics, volcanoes, and earthquakes, the contour of Earth's surface would be level, resulting in the entire planet covered with water almost two miles deep.

So, it is one thing to wish nature would behave differently. It's quite another to define what that would be without creating consequences direr than what we do face.

Moreover, all disasters bring benefits. Floods fertilize the land, ice ages carve out lakes and make soil, volcanoes create land and seed the Earth with minerals, and forest fires create the opportunity for new growth. If the Creator interfered with these events, events that may even take billions of lives (human and other), natural law would need to be set aside. But that can't be done without disrupting everything else since everything is connected. Such cheating is also not the nature of a true and just Creator. A rigged system with constant miraculous interventions would be unpredictable and unreliable. Natural law, upon which we depend for everything, would be meaningless.

Nature is not in our debt for the mere act of living. So, it's inappropriate to claim victimization if we don't use good sense and take care not to live on a fault line or at the foot of a volcano. If we don't and suffer from lava flowing into our bedroom or the whole house sinking into a fissure, the Creator is not the culpable party.

The biological world can also seem cruel. Each second, billions of creatures suffer and die. Predation, parasitism, competition, pathogenesis, and food harvesting (killing) pervade. It's not a matter of good, evil, divine obliviousness, or vengeance. It's the necessary functioning of the interconnected creature called life. It must behave as it does for the whole to survive. If the whole didn't survive, neither could we.

Nature is no crueler in its acts than we are when we inadvertently squash insects underfoot or shred the life out of lettuce when we chew a salad. Life just is; it must function and obey natural law. Lions kill zebras, humans kill food animals, and plants can kill insects and even us.

In fact, killing and death are necessary. Without death, life is not possible. Try as we might, it's not possible to work out feasible details of how a world without death could exist. If we were able to prevent all death, the world would soon be buried miles deep with starving, suffocating, and suffering creatures.

Our Own Worst Enemy

Much of life's travail is not about forces of nature over which we have no control. Rather, it's about bearing the consequences of our own beliefs and acts. We (individually and as a collective) clamor for freedom to believe and do what we choose. But that freedom also means we own the consequences for what we choose to believe and do. Unfounded belief and faith, greed, laziness, impatience, shortsightedness, reliance on others, and ego all block the flow of truth and impact behavior. With that comes a deserved nest of woes such as war, terrorism, Crusades, Inquisitions, communism, Nazism, and so on.

Modern medicine is falsely based upon the invented creeds of materialism and evolution. This results in the pretense and hubris of knowledge that is simply not there. With impunity, bodies are manipulated with drugs and other interventions as if they were mere machines and profit centers. The result is that modern medicine is the number one killer and maimer. Self-serving and ignorant humans do this, and willingly uninformed humans submit to it. Blame does not lie with the Creator.

© Wysong   Figure 267

We foul our air, water, land, and food. We cover our skin with toxic clothes, hide from the sun (avoiding its critical health benefits), wear shoes not permitting skin-to-Earth contact (avoiding the health benefits of electrons flowing up through the feet), and flood our world with toxins, artificial light, electromagnetism, and other pollutants. The result is rampant cancer, heart disease, obesity, diabetes, Alzheimer's, and other chronic degenerative and deadly conditions. Blame does not lie with the Creator.

Sow with ignorance, reap with tears.

A host of crippling and cruel genetic conditions occur in religions that insist on inbreeding because their man-made god tells them they are more special than the rest of us. The Bible and Qur'an

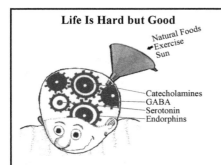 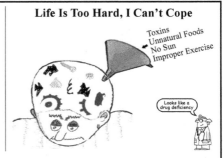

Life Is Hard but Good

Natural Foods
Exercise
Sun

Catecholamines
GABA
Serotonin
Endorphins

Life Is Too Hard, I Can't Cope

Toxins
Unnatural Foods
No Sun
Improper Exercise

Looks like a drug deficiency

Attitude Toward Life – has a lot to do with how we eat, sunlight, exercise and the like. Correct living causes the release of feel-good, positive-attitude chemicals in the brain. Too many people ignore their duty to their own bodies and the health of their brains, then wonder why they can't seem to cope with life and exacerbate the problem further with drugs.

© Wysong — Figure 269

say that pain and suffering are the results of Adam and Eve eating forbidden fruit in the Garden of Eden. We supposedly inherited this moral infraction from them, and the only way out of misery is through Jesus or Mohammed religions. But submission to such religions has caused incalculable human misery and death through the ages. Blame does not lie with the Creator.

Moreover, nothing is learned from the religious practice of playing the victim, supplicating, begging, importuning, and blaming the Creator. Nor is it befitting a dignified Creator of the universe to need such "worship," or to respond to pleadings from those who will not take responsibility for themselves. Praying is fine but people need to keep their brains alert and hands and feet moving.

The evolution/materialist mindset that we are mere animals unleashes the selfish, egoistic, might-makes-right, and reproductive animal forces rising from the hindbrain. Theft, violence, domination, sexual conquest, undeserved gain, and other selfish

This is the last one... maybe we should let it be - our kids will need something to kill.

Big Game Conservation – Present environmental problems are a result of living today is if tomorrow didn't matter.

© Wysong — Figure 268

328

desires undiminished by free will and conscience—which are denied by evolutionists and materialists or ignored by those who believe they do have them— result in terrible wars, crime, and suffering.

Figure 270

Such misery is not the result of a malevolent or dispassionate god. It's our choice to ignore facts, reason, and conscience. If we marry ourselves to insidious beliefs and faiths, justice doesn't demand that we are saved from ourselves.

Suffering Creates Opportunity

If everything was always hunky-dory and blissful, or someone always intervened to save us from acting out base or irrational thoughts and from any resulting pain, failure, or disappointment, we would learn little. We need challenges and discomfort, not just euphoria. If sticking our hand in a bonfire didn't hurt, we'd have a lot of people minus hands. Pain is, perhaps, life's greatest teacher.

Being tested, tasting failure, tragedy, pain, joy, conflicts of conscience, frustration, guilt, compassion, injustice, cruelty, missed shots at the buzzer, and all of the other contents in life's mixed bag create the opportunity for learning and growing. Most of us, upon reflection, must admit we have grown in some way from even the most terrible of experiences.

Even the best of lives can experience tragedy and pain. A heartless murder, an accident, premature death, and other unfortunate calamities over which we have no control can bring pain and suffering to us or others. But they also create an opportunity for empathy, compassion, love, and gaining perspective on life's true values.

The world is only ruthless and cruel if we don't intervene. If we do, the world can become quite wonderful. An abused child creates an opportunity for others to step in and show love. A famine permits others to be kind and share their food. Paraplegia can create the circumstances for a person to learn skills they would have otherwise never known, and an opportunity for caregivers to learn the joy of compassion and selflessness. Out of misery can come happiness, out of ugliness, beauty, and out of unspeakable cruelty, love. It's up to us.

This reminds me of a wonderful feral mother cat that befriended my family. We would feed her and give her some pats, but she was soon off into the woods doing her wild thing. We lost track of her for a time and feared that she had been killed or captured by a pound. But then one day she returned with a youngster, the proud accomplishment of her absence. On one occasion I walked out the back door to be faced with wild kingdom. She had caught a mouse and brought it to her kitten. The mouse was unharmed and almost as big as the kitten. The kitten had it at bay but was getting bitten. Which one was prey was hard to discern. The mother just reclined quietly nearby, nonchalantly, occasionally glancing over at her youngster. The kitten was learning valuable and painful lessons, lessons that could never be learned by just watching the mom, and eating pre-killed harmless meals. Since the kitten's survival would one day depend upon such lessons, the mother's actions showed true love, not apathy and cruelty.

The Choice Was and Is Ours

The battle between conscience and hind-brain animal instincts is in large part the challenge we choose for Earth life. It's a war between the ethics within and the biological forces of the creature we chose to inhabit. The degree to which we learn to master the evil that can rise from within and take responsibility for our acts determines to a large extent the quality of our lives and the fulfillment of our purpose here.

A Creator constantly removing all risk would make free will and learning pointless. Also, think of the dullness of a world where, regardless of the choices made, everything happened in a predictably safe and beneficial way.

As immortal beings, we plan our Earth-life, including its pain and suffering. We also can change that plan while on Earth. Suicide, for instance, would be a dramatic example of a person's choice to abort their Earth effort due to the extreme difficulty that was chosen.

Such free will is the necessary ingredient for moral development. A person may decide that the best way to learn compassion is to come to Earth and experience abuse in some way. Another person may want to be more selfless, so they choose to be miserably poor. Yet another may want to understand generosity better, so they are born into a starving family. A person desiring to know the emptiness of wealth may live a life burdened by riches. In some cases, people choose a relatively easy Earth life as a rejuvenator after a previously very difficult or traumatic life. W.C. Fields, the boozing comedian, said that when he comes back, he'll live over a saloon.

Since we choose our Earth-life and its challenges with eyes wide open, we have nobody to blame but ourselves for whatever circumstances befall us. The fact that we are free to make our own decisions to come here, live a life we plan, and carry the responsibility and consequences for that life is the epitome of justice. It is the way of the perfectly just Creator, not evidence of cruelty and indifference.

Moreover, since everyone is at a different stage of moral development, and everyone has a different script for learning by experience, and free will is always at play, Earth will always be a mix of good and bad. We know that before entering the bargain.

Choosing to come to Earth to experience pain may—with a narrowed materialistic and human view—seem ridiculous. But if the goal is to become a better person and pain is the only way we think we can achieve that, it's not ridiculous at all. Moreover, as immortal beings, this sojourn on Earth in the perspective of infinity is but a blink.

We freely and wisely choose that blink for the eternity of benefit we think it can bring.

46
WHAT THE CREATOR IS
AND IS NOT

There is a natural yearning to know our Source. We'd like to understand why we were created, of course, but there is also awe and thankfulness. After all, we didn't make ourselves or the world that makes life possible.

We might think a sit-down conversation with the Creator would be great. But that's naïve and pretentious. An infinite Creator responsible for the incomprehensible physical and nonphysical reality, can't be humanized. Attempts to do so are what created thousands of conflicting religions plaguing humans from our beginnings.

Besides, if we could do it, and the Creator multiplied itself so each of us could have a duplicate as a pal, we would be irrevocably distracted from Earth life and its purpose. Curiosity, challenges, learning, conscience, career, and personal relationships would all be sated by simply talking to the ultimate guru who knows all, including the future. With such access, we would likely retire into a monastic life perfectly content with the ultimate friend and mentor.

Tao Te Ching tried to capture the conundrum of trying to know our indefinable source: "The Tao that can be spoken is not the eternal Tao. The name that can be named is not the eternal name."

Nevertheless, people looking for a buddy Creator turn to religions that claim to be its representative. Then, knowing becomes synonymous with duty, fear, holy book study, prayer, and obedience to religious dos and don'ts with hell and heaven consequences.

Religions conjure names for the Creator, like Elohim, Allah, Atman, Brahma, Buddha, Christ, Yahweh, Jehovah, Jesus, Ein Sof, Eshwara, God, Krishna, OM, Shakti, Shiva, Tao, Vishu, Raan . . . and hundreds of others. A name has the effect of reducing the Creator to something we can be familiar with, like a fellow human. Holy books are then created with recordings of conversations with the named anthropomorphized creator telling us what it thinks, how it feels, and rules it demands be followed.

Nobody Has Seen God

© Wysong   Figure 159

Such attempts at the impossible, for so many good-hearted seekers, consume them with worship rituals, institutions, exegesis, hermeneutics, rules, clergy, proselytizing, and all the associated religious rigmarole rather than the personal responsibility of pursuing truth and reaching within to conscience.

What can be surmised about the Creator is deduced from the creation itself and its laws. Reality is the reflection of the Creator. Unlike religions pretending to be that reflection, the Creator (reality) is intelligent, true, reliable, and just. Moreover, since everything is one, we are connected to and part of the source, and more so to the extent we merge with the truth and justice of reality.

Agnosticism and atheism take root due to materialistic and evolutionary indoctrination. The inability to materialistically perceive or analyze the Creator is taken as proof of its nonexistence. It also follows that if matter explains our origin, we are nothing more than biological robots in a meaningless universe.

Atheists and agnostics think they have put the final nail in the Creator's coffin by seeing through religious nonsense. They, rightly so, cannot swallow the idea of a personage who writes books copying pagan mythologies, demands belief in irrationality, and justifies horrific acts that should shock the conscience of any reflective person.

Then, wedded to materialism and evolution and thinking religion is the only way to think about the Creator, agnostics and atheists declare that the Creator does not exist, or that they cannot know.

Looking for God in Matter

© Wysong   Figure 181

This forces them into untenable positions. The atheistic claim that they know that the Creator does not exist is logically false. To know such a thing would require looking in every nook and cranny in the universe from the beginning of time up to now. Until that has been done, no declaration of nonexistence is valid. A belief and faith in atheism can be claimed, but that's it.

For agnostics, "I don't know" is their first cause. We must agree that "I don't know" is the correct position to take for the Creator's essence, motives, power, and eternal nature. But "I don't know" is an intellectually dishonest position concerning the existence of a Creator. It denies the staggering functional complexity and roiling mystery of our world which is totally inexplicable other than by invoking intelligence. That, can clearly be known.

If we found a shoe on Mars but no obvious source, we would still conclude it was made by intelligence even if we didn't know the nature of that intelligence or its origin. Every star in the universe, atom on Earth, and every creature is a shoe that demands intelligent causation, even if we can't know the nature of that intelligence or its origin.

OA thinking person comes to understand that religions do not have dominion over knowledge. On the other hand, the heady progress in material sciences and industries has led to the conclusion that all answers to all questions lie in scientific discovery. The doctrines of materialism, abiogenesis, and evolution constitute a new religion. Instead of a mythical human-created god in the sky, humans have, in essence, become their own god.

Keep in mind that humans, no matter their technological prowess, only can discover what is already here. We are responsible for no natural laws, no energy, no matter. We simply discover and tinker with what has been given to us.

"And so, I have proven that the chicken not only came before the egg, but before the universe as well.."

© Wysong

Figure 282

The underlying doctrines of the new religion all fail. For example, no life can arise from lifeless matter. That denies the doctrine of abiogenesis. No cell can transform over time into the panoply of life forms on Earth. That denies the doctrine of evolution. Matter at its smallest, as quantum physics proves, disappears into a nothingness best characterized as mind, not tinier matter. Thus the doctrine of materialism is denied.

These doctrines can be believed, but without solving the thorny problem of proof, such belief is mere faith.

When the materialistic, abiogenetic, and evolutionary legs are cut out from under agnostics and atheists, and human-made religions are not pushed in their face as the only alternative, truth can be revealed.

Removing the clutter of unproven beliefs and faiths is the necessary thinking reset. Then hubris must be replaced by perspective as in the following.

The point is that finite beings constricted by physical dimensions and brains cannot know the infinite. Our physical reality is like an island in an endless inconceivable sea. We must be content in knowing the existence of things we cannot fathom, such as infinity, oneness, timelessness, spiritual existence, immortality, and a Creator without beginning or end and limitless capabilities.

335

SMALLEST TO BIGGEST IN KNOWN UNIVERSE

Perspective – Consumed by our day-to-day lives, and with scientists and religionists giving us the impression they have things all figured out, it's easy to inflate human importance. The scope of known physical reality begins to put things into perspective. On the universe and multiverse scale, the Earth is so diminutive that it is invisible. We are less than that. Yet it all, what we know and that beyond our comprehension, had a creative cause. We can learn about that Creator from the creation itself, but anthropomorphizing the Creator, or denying it, is the ultimate hubris.

Infinitely Small

Invisible, seen with mathematics and logic
- Space-time fabric: Quantum foam (1.6 x 10^{-35} m) atop one-dimensional quantum strings, smaller would defy laws of physics
- Planck particle: smallest particle (1.5 x 10^{-34} m)
- Elementary particles, responsible for mass, electromagnetism, gravity, radioactive decay, e.g., electron neutrino (1×10^{-24} m)
- Smallest quark (5.8 x 10^{-22} m)
- Lowest gamma ray wavelength from photon light particle (1×10^{-19} m)
- Electron (1×10^{-18} m)
- Higgs Boson—responsible for mass (8×10^{-18} m)
- Protons & Neutrons (8.4×10^{-16} m)
- Largest nucleus— Oganesson Element 118 (1.7×10^{-14} m)

Visible with transmission electron microscope
- Largest atom Caesium (596 pm); Human body contains one octillion atoms (10^{27})

Visible with light microscope
- DNA (1.5 nm)—20 billion pairs/genome
- Bacteriophage (200 nm)
- Virus (440 nm)
- Bacteria E. coli (2 μm); Human body has 100 trillion bacteria.
- Mitochondria (3 μm)
- Nucleus (8 μm)
- Skin cell (20 μm); Human body has 40 trillion cells.
- Visible to naked eye
- Smallest particle visible to the human eye (50 μm)
- Human hair, about the size of an 8 point period (100 μm)
- Human Ovum (130 μm)
- Sand grain (200 μm)
- Mite (400 μm)
- Head of a pin (1.5 mm)—holds a human if all atomic spaces collapsed
- flea (2 mm)
- Penny (1.9 cm)
- Blue whale— largest animal (98 ft. long, 173 tons)
- Hyperion Sequoia tree—tallest of 3 trillion trees on Earth (381 ft.)

continued on next page

Figure 274

continued from previous page

- Moon (3,474 km diameter)
- Earth (12,742 km)—can hold 50 moons
- Sun (1.39 million km)—can hold a million Earths
- VY-Canis Majoris star (1.98 billion km)—It would take a thousand years for a plane traveling a thousand mph to circumnavigate it.
- UY scuti star (2.4 billion km)—can hold a billion Suns; too faint to see
- Solar system (10 billion km diameter)—equals four UY scutis side-by-side

Things measured in light years
- Nebula—NGC 262 is over 2.6 million light years across and contains over 50 billion solar masses worth of hydrogen. clouds and stardust
- Light could travel around Earth 7 times/sec.
- Nearest star, Proxima Centauri— 4.22 light-years from Earth.
- Farthest star we can see with our naked eye is V762 Cas in Cassiopeia—16,308 light-years away.
- Andromeda Galaxy is the most distant object seen with the naked eyes—2,000,000 light-years away
- Milky Way—100 bilion stars; 100,000 light-years across
- Galaxies—two trillion in observable universe
- Largest galaxy IC1101—5.8 million light-years across, with 100 trillion stars
- Galaxy clusters—may look like one star—Laniakea supercluster of 100K galaxies is 550 million light-years across
- Supercluster complex—10 billion light-years across (10 million superclusters in universe)
- Universe, Cosmic web of clusters—93 billion light-years across
- Multiverse—countless parallel universes comprising everything that exists: the entirety of space, time, matter, energy, the physical laws and the constants that describe them.

Our puniness – Arrow points to an invisible small point representing Earth and humans on the scale of the Universe.

Infinitely Big

Definitions:

- $10^{-1} = 1/10$; $10^{-2} = 1/100$, etc.
- $10^1 = 10$; $10^2 = 100$, etc.
- m = meter (= 3.28 ft.)
- cm = hundredth of a meter (10^{-2} m)
- mm = thousandth of a meter (10^{-3} m)
- μm (micron) = millionth of a meter (10^{-6}m)
- nm = billionth of a meter (10^{-9} m)
- pm = trillionth of a meter (10^{-12} m)
- Speed of light = 186,000 miles per second
- Earth circumference = 24,901 mi

Figure 274

Trying to understand the first cause without a beginning is frustrating because of an endless regression of the first cause needing a cause which needs a cause, which needs a cause . . . Such cause-effect reasoning that this physical reality demands, prevents the comprehension of the infinite.

Infinity is a perfect way to understand our limitations. We can't comprehend it, yet we know it exists. Neither can we really know gravity, atoms, space, or anything else at its fundamental level or how it came into existence. Knowing they exist or using them to make trinkets is not true knowing.

So, everyone knows things that they can't fully comprehend. We can also know, but not comprehend, that there is an intelligent Source responsible for creating natural laws, the Universe, infinity, and us. That does not close our minds with a belief, it opens them to exploring truth to the degree our physical limits permit. By openly exploring truth, we get a glimpse of the Creator since truth and Creator are the same.

47
THINKING'S DESTINATION

Our thinking journey has led to the obvious answers to the Big Questions:

Where did we come from? An intelligence far exceeding ours is our source. That's clear because no human understands or can create even the simplest of living creatures. We don't see them spontaneously emerging from lifeless matter nor do they increasingly transform into functionally complex organisms.

Where are we going? Given that matter does not have free will or consciousness, as we have, we must be other than matter and thus not mortal. If we examine the hundreds of studies confirming, or we have a near death experience, out of body experience, are able to communicate with those who have passed, are regressed into past lives, have paranormal experiences, or consider the direct testimony of those who have had such experiences, our nonmaterial nature and immortality become confirmed.

Why are we here? Since we were created by intelligent will, that act must have a purpose. If we look inward, that purpose speaks to us from our conscience. It says to be honest with ourselves, self-reliant, do good things, treat others as we would have them treat us, and seek and follow truth. We may ignore that voice, but it is always within, nagging, directing, and penalizing with guilt and shame for disobedience.

Once we solve the question of our origin and true nature--we are immortal created beings--the question of why we exist remains.

That answer, in its fullest, would require peering into the incomprehensible mind of the Creator. Since that isn't possible, we are left with what we do have, our own minds.

If we look inward, our purpose speaks to us from our conscience. It says to be honest with ourselves, self-reliant, do good things, treat others as we would have them treat us, and seek and follow truth. That purpose can be obscured by ego, self-interest, pleasures, travails, fear, and the necessities of day-to-day material life. We may ignore our inner voice, but it's always there, nagging, directing, and penalizing with guilt and shame for disobedience.

The best word for our purpose is love. When we love things, we want to care for and be connected to them. The need for the connection of love is why so much of life is spent trying to be accepted, respected, and recognized. We don't want to be alone and apart. It neither feels good nor is it healthy. Isolate infant humans, chimps, or elephants, and they will languish into death. Hold them close, and they thrive.

Love creates the terrible pain of loss. That implies that our earthly, temporal existence of beginnings and ends, where time causes separations, is unnatural and counter to our essence. The dread and ache of loss also tell us that we belong elsewhere where there is no loss.

That's the nature of the real world, our home before and after physical Earth life. Because time is irrelevant there, things neither end nor disappear. It's the place where there is never separation or loss, and love, our ultimate purpose, can flourish.

Feel free to contact me with your thoughts or questions.

drwysong@asifthinkingmatters.com

$1 MILLION REWARD

Evolution, materialism, atheism, and religion are widely held beliefs. They are better-termed faiths since nobody can prove the underlying premises (foundations) upon which they depend. Ponder the following premises and see if you can prove any of them. You'll find it to be impossible. The greatest minds, the most erudite scholars, philosophers, and scientists are by your side in abject failure.

Proving even one of these would qualify for a million-dollar Nobel Prize. But no takers in spite of countless attempts since the prize began in 1895.

On the other hand, as this book demonstrates, there is clear proof, not faith, of creative intelligence, a reality that extends beyond the material, and human consciousness that survives bodily death. They are the truths deserving of Nobel prizes.

Essential Premises for Evolution, Materialism, and Atheism

1. Matter and energy account for all aspects of our reality and experiences.

2. Matter, energy, and scientific laws can come to be from nothing.

3. Functional Information and complexity on the scale found in even the simplest living organism can arise spontaneously absent intelligence.

4. Every minute aspect of every living creature arose spontaneously through known, incremental, atomic, and molecular steps, each increment being more beneficial to survival than its predecessor.

5. Over time, all populations become more functionally complex, rather than degrading in form and function.

6. Free will and self-awareness can be traced to the properties of atoms or molecules.

7. All the thoughts humans experience are initiated by the brain, and a specific neuronal and biochemical mechanism and structure can explain the origin and makeup of each thought.

8. There is something within the scope of scientific facts that would preclude paranormal and preternatural abilities and events.

9. All psychic abilities can be duplicated by mere guessing.

10. Human consciousness and self-awareness cease at death.

Essential Premises for Religion

1. A particular book is the literal word of the Creator of the universe and can be understood by everyone the same.

2. The Bible can be traced to its original manuscripts.

3. A human has the logical and ethical right to attribute a human-created book to the Creator of the universe.

4. There is a book containing information that cannot be attributed to human authors and human capabilities.

5. There is a book that claims to be authored by the Creator of the universe and is logical, consistent with itself and known facts, just, and ethical.

6. Ethics and actions beneficial to life, society, and the world cannot come from individuals using only reason and conscience.

7. Humanmade religions have a history demonstrating they have not impeded human enlightenment nor caused suffering and death.

8. People following the lessons and commands of the Bible would not kill unbelievers, stone disobedient children, and all the other horrendous acts outlined in chapter 28.

9. Jesus—claimed to be the same as and/or one with the Bible god—can't be held responsible for all the horrendous, unjust, and unethical acts and commands of the god of the Old Testament.

10. Faith, as opposed to reason guided by evidence, is the best path to truth and the best means for guiding humanity to health and happiness.

RESOURCES

The following informal listings provide links, key names, titles, and words that can be Internet searched for more specific information. Active links can be found at: asifthinkingmatters.com/resources.

1. Rules for Finding Truth

Bauer, Henry, Scientific Literacy and the Myth of the Scientific Method; Science Is Not What You Think, How It Has Changed, Why We Can't Trust It, How It Can Be Fixed; Dogmatism in Science and Medicine, How Dominant Theories Monopolize Research and Stifle the Search for Truth.

Broad, William, Betrayers of the Truth, Fraud and Deceit in the Halls of Science.

Clifford, W., The Ethics of Belief and Other Essays. Amherst, Prometheus Books, 1999.

Nietzsche, Friedrich, On Truth and Lie in an Extra-Moral Sense. New York, Viking Penguin Inc, 1976.

Popular Mechanics. Debunking the 9/11 Myths, A Special Report. 29 Apr 2008. popularmechanics.com/technology/military_law/1227842.html.

2. Truth Is Real and Accessible

Broughton, R., Parapsychology, The Controversial Science. London, Random Century, 1992.

Harris, S., The End of Faith, Religion, Terror, and the Future of Reason. New York, W. W. Norton and Company, Inc, 2004.

Kuhn, T. S., The Structure of Scientific Revolutions. 2nd ed. Chicago, Chicago University Press, 1970.

Nagel, T., The Last Word. Oxford, Oxford University Press, 1997.

Wysong, R. L., Living Life as if Thinking Matters; Lipid Nutrition, Understanding Fats and Oils in Health and Disease; The Truth About Pet foods. asifthinkingmatters.com.

4. The Laws of Thermodynamics

Eddington, A., The Nature of the Physical World. New York, Macmillan, 1930.

Wysong, R. L., The Creation-Evolution Controversy. Midland, Inquiry Press, 1976.

5. The Law of Information

Digital information and its growth. tobb.org.tr/BilgiHizmetleri/Documents/Raporlar/Expanding_Digital_Universe_IDC_WhitePaper_022507.pdf.

DNA information storage capacity. nature.com/news/how-dna-could-store-all-the-world-s-data-1.20496#storage.

6. The Law of Impossibility

Dawkins, R., The God Delusion. New York, Houghton Mifflin Company, 2006.
Wysong, R. L., The Creation-Evolution Controversy. Midland, Inquiry Press, 1976.

7. The Law of Biogenesis

Pinto-Correia, Clara. The Ovary of Eve, Egg and Sperm and Preformation. Chicago, University of Chicago Press, 1997.

8. The Laws of Chemistry

Anfinsen, C. B., et al., Experimental and theoretical aspects of protein folding. Advances in Protein Chemistry, 29 (1975), 205-300.
Baker, D., A surprising simplicity to protein folding. Nature, 405 (2000), 39-42.
Creighton, T. E., Experimental studies of protein folding and unfolding. Progress in Biophysics and Molecular Biology, 33 (1978), 231-97.
Karplus, M., The Levinthal paradox yesterday and today. Folding and Design, 2 (1995), 569-76.
Levinthal, C., Are there pathways for protein folding? Estrait du Journal de Chimie Physique, 65 (1968), 44.
Pellagrino, C., Ghosts of Vesuvius. New York, HarperCollins Publishers, 2004.
Shapiro, R., Life's humble beginnings. Science and Technology News, Jul/Aug 2006.
Wysong, R. L., Lipid Nutrition, Understanding Fats and Oils in Health and Disease; The Cholesterol Myth, Believe It to Your Peril. asifthinkingmatters.com.
Zhou, Y., et al., Interpreting the folding kinetics of helical proteins. Nature, 401 (1999), 400-3.

9. The Law of Time

Age of The Earth
Cook, M. A., Prehistory and Earth Models. London, Max Parrish, 1966.
Wysong, R. L., The Creation-Evolution Controversy. Midland, Inquiry Press, 1976.
Time and Change
Arrhenius, G., Evidence for life on Earth before 3800 million years ago. Nature, 384,55, 1996.
Crick, F., Life Itself, Its Origin and Nature. New York, Simon & Schuster, 1981.
Harold, F., The Way of the Cell, Molecules, Organisms and the Order of Life. Oxford, Oxford University Press, 2001.
Milton, R., Shattering the Myths of Darwinism. Rochester, Park Street Press, 1997.
Morowitz, H., Energy Flow in Biology. New York, Academic Press, 1968.
Nahle, Nasif, Conference "Abiogenesis." Addressed to scientists and students of the biological sciences faculty, U. A. N. L.; San Nicolas de los Garza, N. L., Mexico. 5 Oct 2004.
Pellegrino, C., Ghosts of Vesuvius. New York, HarperCollins Publishers, 2004.
Sagan, C., Life. Encyclopedia Britannica, 22,964-981.
Schidlowski, M., A 3800-Million Year Isotopic Record of Life from Carbon in Sedimentary Rocks. Nature, 333,313,318, 1988.
Taylor, G. R., The Great Evolution Mystery. London, Secker and Warburg, 1983.
Wysong, R. L., The Creation-Evolution Controversy. Midland, Inquiry Press, 1976.

10. Fossil Problems

Cremo, M. A., Human Devolution. Los Angeles, Bhaktivedanta Book Publishing Inc., 2003.
Darquea, J., Cabrera. The Message of the Engraved Stones of Ica. labyrinthina.com.
Dawkins, R., The God Delusion. New York, Houghton Mifflin Company, 2006.
McGuinness. T., mysteryspheres.com.
Tuttle, R., The Pattern of Little Feet. American Journal of Physical Anthropology, 78 (1989), 316.
Tuttle, R., The Pitted Patter of Laetoli Feet. Natural History, (1990), 60-65.
Watson. L., The Water People. Science Digest, 90 (1982), 44.
West, J., Serpent in the Sky. New York, Harper and Row, 1979.
Wysong, R. L., The Creation-Evolution Controversy. Midland, Inquiry Press, 1976.

11. Have Humans Evolved

Albo, Frank, Alternative history. frankalbo.com.
Alternate Earth and Human History
Ancient Stone Circle Energy Technology
michaeltellinger.com.

Numerous photographs of skeletons and artifacts. pinterest.com/pin/71142869085869584.
Quayle, Stephen, stevequayle.com.
Schoch, Robert, robertschoch.com.
Townsend, Mitchell, Pictographic stones.
Von Daniken, Erich, daniken.com.
Willis, Jim, ancient-origins.net/opinion-author-profiles/jim-willis-008080.

Architecture
Bullard, J., Waiting for Agnes, Inspired by the True Story of Coral Castle. Kearney, Morris Publishing, 2004.
Cotterell, M., The Lost Tomb of Viracocha, Unlocking the Secrets of the Peruvian Pyramids. Rochester, Bear & Company, 2003.
Hamilton, R., The Mystery of the Serpent Mound, In Search of the Alphabet of the Gods. Berkeley, Frog, Ltd, 2001.
Weidner, J., et al., The Mysteries of the Great Cross of Hendaye. Rochester, Destiny Books, 2003.

Giants
ancient-origins.net/unexplained-phenomena/top-ten-giant-discoveries-north-america-005196.
hiddenincatours.com/strange-alien-hand-found-coast-peru.

Megaliths
beforeus.com.
Evidence of Machining. youtu.be/HrBs5Jcq0Pk.
hiddenincatours.com.
lamarzulli.ne t.
mcremo.com.

Skulls
ancient-origins.net/ancient-places-americas-opinion-guest-authors/elongated-human-skulls-peru-possible-evidence-lost.
humansarefree.com/2014/01/the-ancient-elongated-skulls-are-not.html.

12. Are We Selected Mutants?

Denver, D. R., et al., High direct estimate of the mutation rate in the mitochondrial genome of Caenorhabditis elegans. Science, 289 (2000), 2342-4.
Milton, R., Shattering the Myths of Darwinism. Rochester, Park Street Press, 1992.

13. Favorite Evolutionist Proofs

Atheists of Silicon Valley. godlessgeeks.com.
Braden, G., The God Code, The Secret of Our Past, the Promise of Our Future. Carlsbad, Hay House, Inc, 2004.
Callahan, K. L., Our Origin & Destiny, An Evolutionary Perspective on the New Millennium. Virginia Beach, A. R. E. Press, 1996.
Collins, F., The Language of God, A Scientist Presents Evidence for Belief. New York, Simon & Schuster, 2007.
Cremo, M. A., Human Devolution, A Vedic Alternative to Darwin's Theory. Badger, Torchlight Publishing, 2003.
Cremo, M. A., The Hidden History of the Human Race. Los Angeles, Bhaktivedanta Book Publishing, 1999.
Dawkins, R., et al., Climbing Mount Improbable. New York, W. W. Norton & Company, Inc, 1996.
Dayhoff, MD, Atlas of protein sequence and structure. National Biomedical Research Foundation, Silver Spring, Maryland, Vol. 5, Matrix 1, D-8, 1972.
De Beer, G., Homology, An Unsolved Problem. London, Oxford University Press, 1971.
Denton, M., Evolution, A Theory in Crisis. London, Burnett Books, 1985.
Duke University Medical Center Common Parasite Overturns Traditional Beliefs About the Evolution and Role of Hemoglobin. ScienceDaily. 5 Jun 2008. sciencedaily.com/releases/1999/10/991005071327.htm.
Ferguson, A., Biochemical Systematics and Evolution. Glasgow, Blackie, 1980.
Fujiyama, A., et al., Construction and analysis of a human-chimpanzee comparative clone map. Science, 295 (2002), 131-134.
Glynn, P., God the Evidence. Roseville, Random House, Inc, 1999.
Godfrey, L., Scientists Confront Creationism. New York, W. W. Norton & Co, 1983.
Grant, B., Seafloor to Bench Top. The Scientist, 01 Oct 2007.

Harrub, B., Ph.D. The Truth About Human Origins, An Investigation of the Creation/Evolution Controversy as it Relates to the Origin of Mankind. Montgomery, Apologetics Press, 2003.

Jackson, D., et al., Sponge Paleogenomics Reveals an Ancient Role for Carbonic Anhydrase in Skeletogenesis. Science, 316 (2007),1893-4.

Kuska, B., Should scientists scrap the notion of junk DNA? Journal of National Cancer Institute, 90 (1998), 1032-3.

Mayr, E., Population, Species and Evolution. Cambridge, Harvard University Press, 1970.

Miller, K. R., Finding Darwin's God, A Scientist's Search for Common Ground Between God and Evolution. New York, HarperCollins Publishers, 2007.

Milton, R., Shattering the Myths of Darwinism. Rochester, Park Street Press, 1992.

Pellegrino, C., Ghosts of Vesuvius. New York, Harper Perennial, 2004.

Roux, K. H., et al., Structural analysis of the nurse shark (new) antigen receptor (NAR), Molecular convergence of NAR and unusual mammalian immunoglobulins. Proceedings of the National Academy of Science USA, 95 (1998), 11804-11809.

Schwartz, M., et al., Paternal inheritance of mitochondrial DNA. New England Journal of Medicine, 347 (2002), 576-580.

Spetner, L., Not by Chance! – Shattering the Modern Theory of Evolution. Brooklyn, The Judaica Press, Inc, 1998.

Weidersheim, E., The Structure of Man. London, Macmillan, 1895.

Wysong, R. L., The Cholesterol Myth-Believe it to Your Peril. 31 Jul 2008. asifthinkingmatters.com.

Wysong, R. L., The Creation Evolution Controversy. Midland, Inquiry Press, 1976.

14. Why Evolution Is Believed

Hundreds of scientists skeptical of evolution, dissentfromdarwin.org.

Belief in Materialism

Davies, P., et al., The Matter Myth. London, Viking, 1991.

Horgan, J., The End of Science, Facing the Limits of Knowledge in the Twilight of the Scientific Age. London, Little, Brown and Co, 1996.

Kant, I., Critique of Pure Reason. London, J. M. Dent, 1969.

Bullying Is Not Science

International Society for Complexity, Information, and Design. 13 Jun 2008. iscid.org.

Evolution's Legacy

Berlinski, D., Darwinism versus Intelligent Design. Commentary, Mar 2003.

Davies, P., Superforce, The Search for a Grand Unified Theory of Nature. New York, Simon & Schuster, 1984.

Davies, P., The Cosmic Blueprint. Philadelphia, Templeton Foundation Press, 2004.

Denton, M., Evolution, A Theory in Crisis. London, Burnett Books, 1985.

Denton, M., Nature's Destiny. New York, Simon & Schuster, 1998.

Fuller, Buckminster, Only Integrity Is Going to Count. Audio CD. Critical Path Publishing, 2004.

Harrub, B., et al., The Truth About Human Origins. Montgomery, Apologetics Press, 2003.

Hoyle, F., The Intelligent Universe. New York, Holt, Rinehart, and Winston, 1984.

Lewis, C. S., Miracles. New York, The Macmillan Co, 1947.

Lipson, H. J., and F. R. S., A Physicist Looks at Evolution. Physics Bulletin, 31 (1980). 138.

Pearce, J., The Biology of Transcendence. Rochester, Park Street Press, 2002.

Wysong, R. L., The Creation-Evolution Controversy. Midland, Inquiry Press, 1976.

Science Critique

Bruner, J. S., et al., Journal of Personality, 18 (1949), 206-23.

Conway, A. V., The research game, A view from the field. Complementary Medical Research, 3 (1988), 29-36.

Dembski, W. A., Intelligent Design, The Bridge Between Science and Theology. Downers Grove, InterVarsity Press, 1999.

Dembski, W. A., The Design Revolution, Answering the Toughest Questions About Intelligent Design. Downers Grove, InterVarsity Press, 2004.

Festinger, L., A Theory of Cognitive Dissonance. Palo Alto, Stanford University Press, 1962.

Horrobin, D., In Praise of Non-experts. New Scientist, 24 (1982), 842-4.

Kuhn, T. S., The Structure of Scientific Revolutions. 2ed. Chicago, Chicago University Press, 1970.

Medawar, P., The Limits of Science. New York, Oxford University Press, 1985.

Milton, R., Alternative Science, Challenging the Myths of the Scientific Establishment. Rochester, Inner Traditions, 1996.

Science Fraud
Broad, W., et al., Betrayers of the Truth, Fraud and Deceit in Science. Oxford, Oxford University Press, 1985.
Hansel, C. E., M. ESP and Parapsychology, A Critical Re-evaluation. Buffalo, Prometheus, 1980.
Melton, J. G., et al., Skeptics and the New Age. New Age Encyclopedia. Detroit, Gail Research, 1990.
Science Is Not Ideology
Dawkins, R., The God Delusion. New York, Houghton Mifflin Company, 2006.
Dembski, W., The Design Revolution. Dovers Grove, InterVarsity Press, 2004.
Harris, S., Letter to a Christian Nation. New York, Knopf, 2006.
Why Evolution is Believed
Dawkins, R., The God Delusion. New York, Houghton Mifflin Company, 2006.
Lewontin, R., Billions and Billions of Demons. The New York Review, 9 Jan 1997.
Penrose, R., The Emperor's New Mind. New York, Oxford University Press, 1989.
Why Not Believed
Broad, W., et al., Betrayers of the Truth, Fraud and Deceit in Science. Oxford, Oxford University Press, 1985.
Carroll, R. T., The Skeptic's Dictionary, A Collection of Strange Beliefs, Amusing Deceptions, and Dangerous Delusions. New York, John Wiley & Sons, 2003.
Ehrman, B., Misquoting Jesus, The Story Behind Who Changed the Bible and Why. New York, HarperOne, 2007.
Evans, C., Cults of Unreason. London, George G. Harrap, 1973.
Flynn, D. J., Intellectual Morons, How Ideology Makes Smart People Fall for Stupid Ideas. New York, Crown Forum, 2004.
Hall, R., Pathological Science. Physics Today, Oct 1989, 36-48.
Haught, J., 2000 Years of Disbelief, Famous People with the Courage to Doubt. Amherst, Prometheus Books, 1996.
Kurtz, P., Committee to scientifically investigate claims of the paranormal and other phenomena. The Humanist, May/Jun 1976, 28.
Lafleur, L. J., Cranks and Scientists. Scientific Monthly, Nov 1951, 284-90. Randi, J. The Magic of Uri Geller. Ballantine, New York, 1975.
Reuchlin, A., The True Authorship of the New Testament, Bellevue, Abelard Reuchlin Foundation, 1979.
Sabbagh, K., A Rum Affair, A True Story of Botanical Fraud. London, Allen Lane, 1999.
Sheldrake, R., Could Experimenter Effects Occur in the Physical and Biological Sciences? Skeptical Inquirer, May/Jun 1998c, 57-58.
Sheldrake, R., Experimenter Effects in Scientific Research, How Widely Are They Neglected? Journal of Scientific Exploration, 12 1998b, 73-78.
Shermer, M., Why People Believe Weird Things, Pseudoscience, Superstitions, and Other Confusions of Our Time. New York, W. H. Freeman & Co, 1997.
Sturrock, P., Brave New Heresies. New Scientist, 24/31(1988), 49-51.
Taylor, J., Science and the Supernatural. London, Temple Smith, 1980.
The Theosophical Society in America – Encouraging the study of religion, philosophy and science so that we may better understand ourselves and our relationships within this multidimensional universe. The Society stands for complete freedom of individual search and belief.
Wynn, C. M., et al., Quantum Leaps in the Wrong Direction. Washington D. C., Joseph Henry Press, 2001.
Why Origins Matters
McCutcheon, M., The Compass in Your Nose and Other Astonishing Facts About Humans. Los Angeles, Jeremy P. Tarcher, Inc, 1989.

16. Design

Consciousness in Universe
Graneau, P., Is dead matter aware of its environment? Frontier Perspectives, 7, Fall/ Winter 1998.
Jahn, R. G., et al., Margins of Reality, The Role of Consciousness in the Physical World. Orlando, Harcourt, Brace, Jovanovich, 1987.
Pearce, J., From Magical Child to Magical Teen. Rochester, Inner Traditions, 2003.
Pearce, J., The Biology of Transcendence, A Blueprint of the Human Spirit. Rochester, Park Street Press, 2002.
Ring, K., The Omega Project, Near-Death Experiences, UFO Encounters, and Mind at Large. New York, William Morrow, 1992.
Swartz, E. R., et al., The Living Energy Universe, A Fundamental Discovery that Transforms Science & Medicine. Charlottesville, Hampton Roads Publishing Company, Inc, 1999.

Design
Ciardi, J., The Collected Poems of John Ciardi. Fayetteville, The University of Arkansas Press, 1997.
Dawkins, R., The God Delusion. New York, Houghton Mifflin Company, 2006.
Harris, S., Letter to a Christian Nation. New York, Knopf, 2006.
Russell, B., Why I Am Not a Christian. New York, Simon & Schuster, 1965.
Ress, M. J., Just Six Numbers, The Deep Forces That Shape the Universe. New York, Basic Books, 2000.
Intelligence
Gawrylewski, A., The bytes behind biology. The Scientist, Aug 2007.

17. Biological Machines
APOPO. Ratting out tuberculosis. Science, 303 (2004), 166.
Behe, M., Darwin's Black Box. New York, Simon & Schuster, 2006.
Boxma, B., et al., An aerobic mitochondrion that produces hydrogen. Nature, 434 (2005), 74-9.
Church, J., et al., Another sniffer dog for the clinic? Lancet, 358 (2001), 930.
Dawkins, R., The God Delusion. New York, Houghton Mifflin Company, 2006.
Pembroke, W., Sniffer dogs in the melanoma clinic? Lancet, 1 (1989), 734.
Pincock, S., Cockroaches, nature's petri dish. The Scientist, 20 (2006), 17-8.

18. Nuts, Bolts, Gears, and Rotors Prove Intelligent Design
van de Kamp T., et al., A biological screw in a beetle's leg. Science. Jul, 2011.
Berg, H. C., The rotary motor of bacterial flagella. Annual Review of Biochemistry., 72 (2003), 19-24.

19. Humans Defy Evolution
Looking Within
BBC News. Man Breaks pi Memory Record. 11 Jun 2008. news.bbc.co.uk/1/hi/world/asia-pacific/4644103.stm.
Dawkins, R., The Blind Watchmaker. London, Longmans, 1986.
Flatow, I., Rainbows, Curve Balls. New York, Harper & Row, 1988.
Linker et al., The Kaleidoscopic Brain. The Scientist, 11-17, 41.
McCutcheon, M., The Compass in Your Nose and Other Astonishing Facts About Humans. Los Angeles, Jeremy P. Tarcher, Inc, 1989.
Pearce, J., The Biology of Transcendence. Rochester, Park Street Press, 2002.
Penrose, R., The Emperor's New Mind. New York, Oxford University Press, 1989.
Talbot, M., Beyond the Quantum. New York, Bantam Books, 1988.
Treffert, D., Extraordinary People, Understanding Savant Syndrome. New York, Authors Guild, 2006.
Von Ward, P., Gods, Genes, and Consciousness. Charlottesville, Hampton Roads, 2004.
Megaliths
Newman, Hugh, megalithomania.co.uk/hughnewman.html.

20. The Anthropic Universe
Lemley, B., Guth's Grand Guess. Discover, 23 (2002), 32-39.
Hawking, S., A Brief History of Time. New York, Bantam Books, 1988.
Penrose, R., The Emperor's New Mind. New York, Oxford University Press, 1989.

23. How Religion Begins and Develops
History
Bargeman, L., The Egyptian Origin of Christianity. Bloomington, 1st Books Publishing, 2002.
Henry, W., Cloak of the Illuminati. Kempton, Adventures Unlimited, 2003.
Johnson, P., A History of Christianity. Harmondsworth, Penguin Books, 1980.
Madaule, J., The Albigensian Crusade. New York, Fordham University Press, 1967.
Pagels, E., The Gnostic Gospels. New York, Vintage Books, 1981.
Rudolph, K., Gnosis. San Francisco, Harper & Row, 1983.
Runciman, S., The Medieval Manichee. Cambridge, Cambridge University Press, 1955.
Sunderland, J., The Origin and Character of the Bible. Boston, The Beacon Press, 1947.
Tyson, D., The Power of the Word, The Secret Code of Creation. St. Paul, Llewellyn Publications, 2004.
Modern belief in geocentrism, theprinciplemovie.com.
Institutions and Rules
York, B., Moyers proves that the left can be blinded by zeal. The Hill. 18 Jun 2008. thehill.com.

Religion as Materialism
Hardy, K. R., Social Origins of American Scientists and Scholars. Science, (1974).
Russell, B., An Outline of Philosophy. New York, The New American Library, 1960.
The Origins and Stages of Religion
Gawrylewski, A., Ph.D.s and Parishioners. The Scientist, 1 (2007), 22.
Lewis, C. S., Miracles. New York, The Macmillan Co, 1947.
White, A., The Warfare of Science with Theology. New York, Appleton, 1996.

24. Religions Cross Pollinate
ancientfacts.net/5-holy-books-predate-bible/?view=all.
George, G. M., James' Stolen Legacy, The Egyptian Origins of Western Philosophy.
Hebrew earliest writings. livescience.com/8008-bible-possibly-written-centuries-earlier-text-suggests.html.
Jackson, John, Christianity Before Christ, and Pagan Origins of the Christ Myth.
Judaism, Pagan Origins. youtube.com/watch?v=ZECezMYug8c.
Religions Predating the Bible. oldest.org/religion/religious-texts.
Holy Book History
Johnson, P., A History of Christianity. Harmondsworth, Penguin Books, 1980.
Pagels, E., The Gnostic Gospels. New York, Vintage Books, 1989.
Sunderland, J., The Origin and Character of the Bible. Boston, The Beacon Press, 1947.
Religious History. truthbeknown.com.

25. Gods Writing Books
Dawkins, R., The God Delusion. New York, Houghton Mifflin Company, 2006.
Graves, Kersey, The World's Sixteen Crucified Saviors (Christianity Before Christ).
Higgins, Godfrey, (1772–1833), Anacalypsis.
New-Life.net. 18 Jun 2008. new-life.net/talmud.htm.
Reuchlin, A., The True Authorship of the New Testament. Kent, The Abelard Reuchlin Foundation, 1986.
Jesus as a warrior king living in the 60s. edfu-books.uk

26. Questionable Foundations of Christianity
Acharya, S., The Christ Conspiracy, The Greatest Story Ever Sold.
Acharya, S./Murdock, D.M., freethoughtnation.com.
Atwill, Joseph, Caesar's Messiah.
Carotta, Francesco, Jesus Was Caesar, On the Julian Origin of Christianity.
Carrier, Richard, On the Historicity of Jesus, Why We Might Have Reason for Doubt.
Dyer, Jay, Christian apologist refuting those who doubt the Bible and Jesus' existence, jaysanalysis.com/category/apologetics.
Ellerbe, Helen, The Dark Side of Christian History.
Fitzgerald, David, Nailed: Ten Christian Myths That Show Jesus Never Existed at All.
Freke, Timothy, The Jesus Mysteries, Was the "Original Jesus" a Pagan God?
Humphreys, Kenneth, Jesus Never Existed, An Introduction to the Ultimate Heresy.
Jabbar, Malik H., The Astrological Foundation of The Christ Myth, Book One.
Murdock, Dorothy, Scholarly examination of the history of pagan and Christian religions and their parallels. truthbeknown.com.
Piso, Roman, Piso Christ, A Book of the New Classical Scholarship.
Reuchlin, Abelard, The true authorship of the New Testament.
Robinson, D. C., Caesar's Messiah - Why the Church MUST Answer, A Discourse/Reflection on Joseph Atwill's Caesar's.
Valliant, James, Creating Christ, How Roman Emperors Invented Christianity.
Wikipedia. Christ Myth Theory, an exhaustive and documented discussion of pros and cons, proponents and critics. wikipedia.org/wiki/Christ_myth_theory.
Williams, Walter, The Historical Origin of Christianity.

27. How to Measure Holy Books
Ehrman, Bart, Jesus Interrupted, Revealing the Hidden Contradictions.

29. Religion Unleashed
ALOR. 18 Jun 2008. alor.org.
Bergman, J., 18 Jun 2008. premier1.net/~raines/mental.html.

Chapman, M., Social and Biological Aspects of Ethnicity. Oxford, Oxford University Press, 1993.

Goodman, R. M., Genetic Disorders Among Jewish People. Baltimore, The John Hopkins University Press, 1979.

Nuenke, M., Reproductive perspectives, A review of some recent books on the ethics of manipulating human genes. The Mankind Quarterly. 61 (2001).

Potter, R., A social psychological study of fundamentalist Christianity. England, Sussex University, Ph.D., dissertation, 1985.

Prophecy: See Clairvoyance/Premonition under chapter 35 resources.

Sack, U., Case studies of voluntary defectors from intensive religious groups. University of California, Ph.D. dissertation, 1985.

Salzman, D., A study of isolation and immunization of individuals from the larger society in which they live. Chicago, University of Chicago, Masters thesis, 1951.

Shachtman, T., Medical Sleuth. Smithsonian, Feb 2006.

Tiffany, J., The Khazars, Non-Semitic Jews. The Barnes Review, Jul 1997, 9-12.

30. Ends of the World

Colavito, M., The Heresy of Oedipus and the Mind-Mind Split. New York, Edwin Mellen Press, 1995.

Doland, P., Another Case Not Made, A Critique of Lee Strobel's 'The Case for a Creator' (2005). 23 Jun 2008. infidels.org/library/modern/paul_doland/creator.html.

Festinger, Leon, et al., When Prophecy Fails, a study of cognitive dissonance in those who believe in Prophecy.

Pearce, J., The Biology of Transcendence. Rochester, Park Street Press, 2002.

Pellegrino, C., Ghosts of Vesuvius. New York, HarperCollins Publishers, 2004.

Rapture Ready. raptureready.com.

Religious Tolerance. religioustolerance.org.

Prophecy not unique: See Clairvoyance/Premonition under chapter 35 resources.

31. Defending Holy Books

Agards Bible Timeline. 18 Jun 2008. agards-bible-timeline.com.

Bageant, J., What the Left Behind Series Really Means. News Intelligence Analysis. 13 Dec 2005.

Halsell, G., Prophecy and Politics. Village Voice, 18 May 2004.

32. Faith

Dawkins, R., The God Delusion. New York, Houghton Mifflin Company, 2006.

Ehrman, B. D., Lost Christianities, The Battles for Scripture and the Faiths We Never Knew. New York, Oxford University Press, 2003.

Ehrman, B., Lost Christianities. New York, Oxford University Press, 2003.

Flemings, H., A Philosophical Scientific and Theological Defense for the Notion that a God Exists. Lanham, University Press of America, 2003.

Harris, S., The End of Faith, Religion, Terror, and the Future of Reason. New York, W. W. Norton and Company, Inc, 2004.

Harris, S., The End of Faith, Religion, Terror, and the Future of Reason. New York, W. W. Norton and Company, Inc, 2004.

Harris, S., The End of Faith. New York, W. W. Norton & Company, Inc, 2004.

Leidloff, J., The Continuum Concept. Reading, Addison Wesley Press, 1977.

Osman, A., Jesus in the House of the Pharaohs, The Essene Revelations on the Historical Jesus. Rochester, Bear & Company, 1992.

Pearce, J., The Biology of Transcendence. Rochester, Park Street Press, 2002.

Pearce, J., The Death of Religion and the Rebirth of Spirit, A Return to the Intelligence of the Heart. Rochester, Park Street Press, 2007.

Schadewald, R. J., The Flat-Earth Bible. Reprinted from The Bulletin of the Tychonian Society, 44 (1987).

Schneider, R. J., Does the Bible teach a spherical earth? Berea college, ASA3 org; from PSCF 53 (Sep 2001), 159-169.

Spencer, R., The Politically Incorrect Guide to Islam (and the Crusades). Washington, D. C., Regnery Publishing, Inc, 2005.

Teeple, H., How Did Christianity Really Begin? Evanston, Religion and Ethics Institute, 1992.

Vining, M., Jesus the Wicked Priest, How Christianity Was Born of An Essene Schism. Rochester, Bear & Company, 2008.

Wolff, R., Original Wisdom. Rochester, Inner Traditions, 2001.

Wysong, R. L., Living Life As If Thinking Matters. Midland, Inquiry Press, 2008.

33. The Source of Goodness
Fuller, Buckminster, Only Integrity Is Going to Count. Audio CD. Critical Path Publishing, 2004.

34. Matter is an Illusion
Holism and Holographic Universe
Bohm, D., Unfolding Meaning. London, Ark Paperbacks, 1987.
Bohm, D., Wholeness and the Implicate Order. New York, Routledge Classics, 1980.
Bohm, N., et al., On the intuitive understanding of nonlocality as implied by quantum theory. Foundation of Physics, 5 (1975), 93-109.
Lanza, R. A., New Theory of the Universe. The American Scholar, Mar 2007.
Lewels, J., Over the rainbow, Quantum physics discovers the holographic universe. MUFON Symposium Proceedings, Jul 1995, 119-134.
Lewis, C. S., Miracles, A Preliminary Study. New York, The Macmillan Company, 1947.
Science and Technology Facility Council. The Large Hadron Collider. 31 Jan 2008. lhc.ac.uk.
Talbot, M., Beyond the Quantum. New York, Bantam Books, 1988.
Talbot, M., Synchronicity and the Holographic Universe. Thinking Allowed Productions, 1992.
Talbot, M., The Holographic Universe. New York, HarperCollins Publishers, 1991.
Parallel Universes
Wolf, F. A., Parallel Universe, The Search for Other Worlds. New York, Simon and Schuster, 1988.
Quantum Physics
Capra, F., The Tao of Physics, An Exploration of the Parallels Between Modern Physics and Eastern Mysticism. Boston, Shambhala, 2000.
Davies, P., et al., The Matter Myth. London, Viking, 1991.
Eddington, Sir Arthur, Defense of Mysticism. In Ken Wilber, Quantum Questions, Mystical Writings of the World's Greatest Physicists. Boston, Shambhala, 1984.
Ganz, J., Scientists bring light to full stop, hold it, then send it on its way. New York Times, 18 Jan, 2001, A21.
Hawking, S., A Brief History of Time. New York, Bantam Books, 1988.
Huyghe, P., Antimatter. Omni. Oct 1994, 101.
Itano, W., et al., Quantum Zeno Effect. Physical Review A, 41 (1990), 2295-2300.
Laszlo, E., Science and the Akashic Field, An Integral Theory of Everything. Rochester, Inner Traditions, 2004.
LeShan, L., The Medium, the Mystic, and the Physicist. New York, The Viking Press, 1966.
Masgrau, et al., Biochemical Quantum Tunneling. Science, 312 (2006), 155.
Nosh, J. M., Unfinished symphony. Time, 31 Dec 1999, 86.
Penrose, R., The Emperor's New Mind, Concerning Computers, Minds and the Laws of Physics. New York, Oxford University Press, 1989.
Rees, M., Just Six Numbers, The Deep Forces That Shape the Universe. New York, Basic Books, 2000.
Roberts, J., The "Unknown" Reality - Volume One. San Rafael, Amber-Allen Publishing, 1977.
Roberts, J., The "Unknown" Reality - Volume Two. San Rafael, Amber-Allen Publishing, 1979.

35. Weird Things Disprove Materialism
Bem, Dr. Daryl, news.cornell.edu/stories/2010/12/study-looks-brains-ability-see-future, skeptiko.com/daryl-bem-responds-to-parapsychology-debunkers, Feeling the Future: A Meta-analysis of 90 Experiments on the Anomalous Anticipation of Random Future Events. [Under Editorial Review] Feeling the Future: Experimental evidence for anomalous retroactive influences on cognition and affect. Journal of Personality and Social Psychology, 100, 407-425. Must psychologists change the way they analyze their data? A response to Wagenmakers, Wetzels, Borsboom, & van der Maas (2011). Response to Alcock's "Back from the Future: Comments on Bem."
CIA use of remote viewing: bibliotecapleyades.net/vision_remota/esp_visionremota_6.htm.
Dossey, Larry, MD (books): The Science of Premonitions, One Mind: How Our Individual Mind Is Part of a Greater Consciousness and Why It Matters (Explains why premonition and other seemingly extraordinary abilities are actually ordinary in the underlying reality.)
Kuhn, T. S., The Structure of Scientific Revolutions. 2ed., Chicago, Chicago University Press, 1970.
Universe is timeless, permitting access both ways, platonia.com/barbour_emergence_of_time.pdf, popsci.com/science/article/2012-09/book-excerpt-there-no-such-thing-time, discovermagazine.com/2007/jun/in-no-time.
Wysong, R. L., Controlled Clinical Studies. Wysong e-Health Letter, November 1987.

Dowsing
raymongrace.us, learndowsing.com.
Lottery Dowsing. mariawheatley.com, bluesunenergetics.net, myhusbandhasadd.com.
ESP
Hart, H., ESP Projection, Spontaneous Cases and the Experimental Method. Journal of the American Society for Psychical Research, 48 (1954), 121-146.
Puthoff, H., et al., Information Transmission Under Condition of Sensory Shielding, SRI Report, 1974.
Radin, Dean, Ph.D., Entangled Minds, Extrasensory Experiences in a Quantum Reality.
Reed, Henry, henryreed.com.
Swann, I., Everybody's Guide to Natural ESP. Los Angeles, Jeremy P. Tarcher, 1991.
Targ, Russel, watkinsmagazine.com/the-reality-of-esp-a-physicists-proof-of-psychic-abilities.
Vassey, Z., Method for Measuring the Probability of I Bit Extrasensory Information Transfer Between Living Organisms. Journal of Parapsychology, 42 (1978), 158-160.

36. Even Weirder Things

Hernandez, Rey, Consciousness, UFOs, etc. consciousnessandcontact.org.
Mahabal, Vernon, Hand analysis is by far the most scientific and dependable system of self-awareness. palmistryinstitute.com.
Mitchell, Edgar, Dr., Consciousness, UFOs, etc. consciousnessandcontact.org.
Morse, Melvin, MD, Remote viewing. melvinmorsemd.com.
Mossbridge, Julia, The Science of Precognition. thepremonitioncode.com.
Neimology, knowthename.com.
Precognition/clairvoyance, appliedprecog.com.
Utts, Jessica, Professor, Scientific proof of remote viewing and psychic phenomena. ics.uci.edu/~jutts.
Aliens/UFOs/Abductions
Anka, Darryl, Channels entity known as Bashar. bashar.org.
Bachmann, Steve, Bigfoot and E.T.'s. bizarrebigfoot.blogspot.com.
Dropa, A Race of Dwarf-Like Extraterrestrials. Wikipedia, wikipedia.org/wiki/Dropa.
Haley, L., Unlocking Alien Closets, Abductions, Mind Control, and Spirituality. Murfreesboro, Greenleaf Publications, 2003.
Hart, W., The Genesis Race, Our Extraterrestrial DNA and the True Origins of the Species. Rochester, Bear & Company, 2003.
Hopkins, B., et al., Sight Unseen, Science, UFO Invisibility and Transgenic Beings. New York, Atria Books, 2003.
Hopkins, Bud, How to Report a UFO Experience, intrudersfoundation.org.
Kitei, L. D., The Phoenix Lights. Charlottesville, Hampton Roads Publishing Company, Inc, 2004.
Kloetzke, Chase, UFO Investigation. chasekloetzke.com.
Larkins, L., Calling on Extraterrestrials, 11 Steps to Inviting Your Own UFO Encounters. Charlottesville, Hampton Roads Publishing Company, Inc, 2003.
Larkins, L., Listening to Extraterrestrials, Telepathic Coaching by Enlightened Beings. Charlottesville, Hampton Roads Publishing Company, Inc, 2004.
Larkins, L., Talking to Extraterrestrials, Communicating with Enlightened Beings. Charlottesville, Hampton Roads Publishing Company, Inc, 2002.
Leir, R. K., The Aliens and the Scalpel, Scientific Proof of Extraterrestrial Implants in Humans. Columbus, Granite Publishing, 1998.
Lewels, J., The God Hypothesis, Extraterrestrial Life and its Implications for Science and Religion. Mill Spring, Wild Flower Press, 1997.
Mack, J. E., Abduction, Human Encounters with Aliens. New York, Charles Scribner's Sons, 1994.
Mack, J. E., Passport to the Cosmos, Human Transformation and Alien Encounters. New York, Random House, Inc, 1999.
Sanderson, I., Uninvited Visitors, A Biologist Looks at UFOs. New York, Cowles Educational Corp, 1967.
Von Ward, P., Gods, Genes, and Consciousness. Charlottesville, Hampton Roads Publishing Company, Inc, 2004.
Wallace, S., From the Motherland to the Mothership. Dallas, Crystal City Publications, 2001.
Alternate Realities
Alexander, John, johnbalexander.com.
Steinfeld, Alan, newrealities.com.

Apparitions
Bartulica, N., Medjugorje, Are the Seers Telling the Truth? Chicago, Croatian Franciscan Press, 1991.
Groeschel, B., A Still, Small Voice. Ignatius Press, 1993.
Hill, E., Mysticism. Garden City, Doubleday, 1990.
Maindron, G., The Apparitions of Our Lady at Kibeho. Marian Spring Centre, 1996.
Smith, Jody, The Image of Guadalupe, Myth or Miracle? Garden City, Doubleday & Company, 1983.
Sullivan, R., The Miracle Detective, An Investigation of Holy Visions. New York, Atlantic Monthly Press, 2004.
Woodward, K., Making Saints, How the Catholic Church Determines Who Becomes a Saint, Who Doesn't, and Why. New York, Simon & Schuster, 1990.
Zimdars-Swartz, S., Encountering Mary. New Jersey, Princeton University Press, 1991.
Astrology
Fisher, W., et al., Some Laboratories Studies of Fluctuating Phenomena, International Journal of Biometeorology, 12 (1968), 15-19.
Gauquelin, M., The Cosmic Clocks. London, Peter Owen, 1969.
Grasse, R., Signs of the Times. Charlottesville, Hampton Road Publishing Company, Inc, 2002.
Oshop, Renay, Scientific study of astrology.
Athletics
Garfield, C., Peak Performance, Mental Training Techniques of the World's Greatest Athletes. New York, Warner Books, 1984.
Gauquelin, M., The Cosmic Clocks. Chicago, Henry Regenery Company, 1967.
Global Consciousness Project. noosphere.princeton.edu.
Gurney, E. F., et al., Phantasms of the Living. London, Kegan Paul, Trench, Trubner, 1886.
Auras
Hunt, V., Infinite Mind, Science of the Human Vibrations of Consciousness. Malibu, Malibu Publishing Co, 1996.
Belief in Paranormal
Gallu, G. H., et al., Belief in Paranormal Among American Adults. Skeptical Inquirer, 15 (1991), 137-146.
Cell Memory
Schwartz, Gary, Cell memory in transplants.
Child Prodigy
Carroll, L., et al., The Indigo Children, The New Kids Have Arrived. Carlsbad, Hay House, 1999.
Montgomery, R., Strangers Among Us. New York, Coward, McCann, Geoghegan, 1979.
Randles, J., Star Children, The True Story of Alien Offspring Among Us. New York, Sterling Publishing Co, 1995.
Clairvoyance/Precognition/ Premonition/Presentiment/Prophecy
Barker, J. C., Premonitions of the Aberfan Disaster. Journal of the Society for Psychical Research, 55 (1967), 189-237.
Behe, G., Titanic, Psychic Forewarnings of a Tragedy. Wellingborough, Patrick Stephens, 1988.
Bem, Dr. Daryl, news.cornell.edu/stories/2010/12/study-looks-brains-ability-see-future; skeptiko.com/daryl-bem-responds-to-parapsychology-debunkers.
Boundary Institute. Premonitions of 9/11. 1 Feb 2008. boundaryinstitute.org/premon911.htm.
Brennan, J. H., Time Travel. St. Paul, Llewellyn Worldwide, 2003.
Cayce, Edgar, edgarcayce.org/the-readings/ancient-mysteries/seven-prophecies-that-came-true.
Cox, W. E., Precognition, An Analysis, II. Journal of the American Society for Psychical Research, 50 (1956), 99-109.
discovermagazine.com/2007/jun/in-no-time.
Dossey, Larry, The Science of Premonitions.
Dunne, B. J., et al., Precognitive Remote Perception. Princeton Engineering Anomalies Research Laboratory (Report), Aug 1983.
Feeling the Future, A Meta-analysis of 90 Experiments on the Anomalous Anticipation of Random Future Events. [Under Editorial Review]. dbem.org/FF Meta-analysis 6.2.pdf; Experimental evidence for anomalous retroactive influences on cognition and affect. Journal of Personality and Social Psychology, 100, 407-425. dbem.org/FeelingFuture.pdf.
hogueProphecy.com.
Honorton, C., et al., Future-telling, A meta-analysis of forced-choice precognition experiments. Journal of Parapsychology, 53 (1989), 281-209.
Mossbridge, Julie, The Premonition Code, The Science of Precognition. noetic.org.

Must psychologists change the way they analyze their data? A response to Wagenmakers, Wetzels, Borsboom, & van der Maas (2011). dbem.org/ResponsetoWagenmakers.pdf.

One Mind, How Our Individual Mind Is Part of a Greater Consciousness and Why It Matters (Explains why premonition and other seemingly extraordinary abilities are actually ordinary in the underlying reality.)

Paquette, Andy, Dreamer, 20 years of psychic dreams and how they changed my life. popsci.com/science/article/2012-09/book-excerpt-there-no-such-thing-time.

Response to Alcock's "Back from the Future, Comments on Bem." dbem.org/ResponsetoAlcock.pdf.

Rosenblatt, Marty, Physicist, appliedprecog.com.

Saltmarsh, H., The Future and Beyond, Paranormal Foreknowledge and Evidence of Personal Survival from Cross Correspondences. Charlottesville, Hampton Roads, 2003.

Schmeidler, G., An Experiment in Precognitive Clairvoyance, Part I, The Main Results and Part 2, The Reliability of The Scores. Journal of Parapsychology, 28 (1964), 1-27.

Snow, C. B., Mass Dreams of the Future. Sedona, Deep Forest Press, 1989.

Stratton, J. A., Electromagnetic Theory. New York, McGraw-Hill, 1941.

Townshend, C. H., Indisputable clairvoyance of M. Adolphe Didier. The Zoist, XI, Apr 1853, 75-78.

Townshend, C. H., Recent Clairvoyance of Alexis Didier. The Zoist, IX, Jan 1852, 402-411.

Universe is timeless, permitting access both ways. platonia.com/barbour_emergence_of_time.pdf.

Crop Circles

Gazecki, William, imdb.com/title/tt0331225; cropcirclesthemovie.com/ufos.html.

Diagnosis

Chen, M., et al., Non-Invasive Detection of Hypoglycaemia Using A Novel, Fully Biocompatible and Patient Friendly Alarm System. British Medical Journal, 321 (2000), 1565-66.

Evil Eye

Dundes, A., The Evil Eye, A Casebook. Madison, University of Wisconsin Press, 1992.

Elsworthy, F., The Evil Eye. London, Murray, 1895.

Group Intention (group willing events)

Alexander, John, Alternate realities. johnbalexander.com.

Taggart, Lynn, lynnemctaggart.com.

Healing

Astin, J., et al., The Efficacy of Distant Healing, A Systematic Review of Randomized Trials. Annals of Internal Medicine, 132, (2000), 903-910.

Bengston, William, Ph.D., Healing by touch. bengstonresearch.com.

Benor, D. J., Spiritual Healing, Scientific Validation of a Healing Revolution. Southfield, Vision Publications, 2001.

Benor, D., Survey of Spiritual Healing Research. Complementary Medical Research, 4 (1990), 9-33.

Bodine, E., Hands That Heal. Novato, New World Library, 2004.

Born, J., et al., Timing the End of Nocturnal Sleep. Nature, 397 (1999), 29-30.

Braud, W., Distant Mental Influence. Charlottesville, Hampton Roads, 2003.

Braud, W., et al., Consciousness Interactions with Remote Biological Systems, Anomalous Intentionality Effects. Subtle Energies, 2 (1993), 1-47.

Braud, W., On the Use of Living Target Systems in Distant Mental Influence Research. Psi Research Methodology, A Re-examination. (L. Coly, ed.) New York, Parapsychology Foundation, 1991.

Braud, W., Wellness Implications of Retroactive Intentional Influence, Exploring an Outrageous Hypothesis. Alternative Therapies in Health and Medicine, 6 (2000), 37-48.

Buxton, S., The Shamanic Way of the Bee, Ancient Wisdom and Healing Practices of the Bee Masters. Rochester, Destiny Books, 2004.

Dean, D., Plethysmograph Recordings as ESP Responses. International Journal of Europsychiatry, 2 (1996), 439-446.

Dossey, L., Healing Beyond the Body. Boston, Shambhala, 2001.

Dossey, L., Healing Words, The Power of Prayer and the Practice of Medicine. New York, Harper Collins, 1993.

Dossey, L., Prayer is Good Medicine. New York, Harper Collins, 1996.

Orloff, J., Intuitive Healing. New York, Three Rivers Press, 2000.

Pearl, E., The Reconnection, Heal Others, Heal Yourself. Carlsbad. Hay House, Inc, 2001. drericpearl.com.

Prayer. applesforhealth.com/prayerhelps1.html.

Schlitz, M., et al., Distant Intentionality and Healing, Assessing the Evidence. Alternative Therapies in Health and Medicine, 3 (1997).

Stelter, A., PSI-Healing. New York, Bantam Books, 1976

Targ, E., Evaluating Distant Healing, A Research Review. Alternative Therapies in Health and Medicine, 3 (1977).

Tiller, W. A., Subtle Energies in Energy Medicine. Frontier Perspectives, 4 (1995).

Wesselman, H., et al., Spirit Medicine, Healing in the Sacred Realms. Carlsbad, Hay House, Inc, 2004.

Homeopathy

Malerba, Larry, Homeopathy. spiritsciencehealing.com.

Melton, J. G., et al., Skeptics and the New Age, in New Age Encyclopedia. Detroit, Gail Research, 1990.

Hypnosis

Temple, R., Open to Suggestion, The Uses and Abuses of Hypnosis. London, Aquarian Press, 1989.

Watson, L., Supernature. London, Hodder & Stoughton, 1973.

Levitation

Grosso, Michael, The Man Who Could Fly, St. Joseph of Copertino and the Mystery of Levitation.

Lucid Dreaming (dreaming while wide awake)

Brown, David Jay, mavericksofthemind.com.

Magnet Sensitive

Reichenbach, K., Researches on Magnetism, Electricity, Etc. London, Taylor, Walton & Maberly, 1850.

Meditations

Dyer, W. W., Getting in the Gap, Making Conscious Contact with God Through Meditation. Carlsbad, Hay House, Inc, 2003.

Miracles

Kreiser, B. R., Miracles, Convulsion, and Ecclesiastical Politics in Early Eighteenth-Century Paris. Princeton, Princeton University Press, 1978.

Montgeron, L. B. Carre de, (1737). La Verite des Miracles. Vol. 1, 380, Paris, as quoted in Blavatsky, H. P., Isis Unveiled, 1, (374). New York, J. W. Bouton, 1987.

Morphic Resonance

Sheldrake, R., A New Science of Life, The Hypothesis of Morphic Resonance. Rochester, Park Street Press, 1981.

Phantom Limbs

Bromage, P. R., et al., Phantom Limbs and The Body Schema. Canadian Anaesthetists' Society Journal, 21 (1974), 267-74.

Feldman, S., Phantom Limbs. American Journal of Psychology, 53 (1940), 590-92.

Melzack, R., et al., Experimental Phantom Limbs. Experimental Neurology, 39 (1973), 261-69.

Psychic Detectives

Baldwin, Dan, The Psychic Detective Guide Book.

Baldwin, D., Find Me, How Psychic Detectives from Around the World Have Banded Together to Find Missing People. Woonsocket, New River Press, 2007.

Proffitt, Elaina, devawhispers.com.

Thomas, Robbie, robbiethomas.net.

Ryan, Marisa, marisaryan.com.

Psychic Spies

McMoneagle, Joe, U. S. Army Remote Viewer explains how his near-death experience led to being selected for the government's psychic spy program. monroeinstitute.org/node/1321.

Puthoff, H. E., CIA-Initiated Remote Viewing Program at Stanford Research Institute. Journal of Scientific Exploration, 10 (1996), 63-76.

Schnabel, J., Remote Viewers, The Secret History of America's Psychic Spies. New York, Dell, 1997.

Smith, P. S., Reading the Enemy's Mind. Manhattan, Tom Dougherty Books, 2005.

Psychical Research

Honorton, C., et al., PSI Communication in The Ganzfeld. Experiments with an Automated Testing System and a Comparison with a Meta-Analysis of Earlier Studies. Journal of Parapsychology, 54 (1990), 99-139.

Wallace, A. R., Harmony of Spiritualism and Science. Light, 5 (1885b), 352.

Psychokinesis/Metal Bending

Brain Waves Move Computer Cursors. New York Times, 1995.

Christensen, K. R., Philosophy and Choice. New York, McGraw Hill, 2002.

Eysenck, J., et al., Explaining the Unexplained. London, Weidenfeld & Nicolson, 1982.

Gallenberger, Joseph, synccreation.com.

Hasted, J., The Metal Benders. London, Routledge & Kegan Paul, 1981.

Jahn, R. T., et al., Margins of Reality, The Role of Consciousness in the Physical World. Orlando, Harcourt, Brace, Jovanovich, 1987.

McCreery, C., Science, Philosophy and ESP. London, Faber & Faber, 1967.

Nash, C. B., Psychokinetic Control of Bacterial Growth. Journal of the American Society for Psychical Research, 51 (1982), 217-21.

Puthoff, H., et al., Information Transmission Under Condition of Sensory Shielding. Nature, 252 (1974), 602-607.

Radin, D., et al., Consciousness-Related Effects in Random Physical Systems. Foundations of Physics, 19 (1989), 1499-1514.

Radin, D., The Conscious Universe, The Scientific Truth of Psychic Phenomena. New York, Harper Collins, 1997.

Schmidt, H., Observation of a Psychokinetic Effect Under Highly Controlled Conditions. Journal of Parapsychology, 57 (1993), 351-372.

Schmidt, H., Observation of A Psychokinetic Effect Under Highly Controlled Conditions. Journal of Parapsychology, 57 (1993), 351-372.

Schmidt, H., PK Effect on Pre-Recorded Targets. Journal of the American Society for Psychical Research, 70 (1976), 267-291.

Schmidt, H., Random Generators and Living Systems as Targets in Retro-PK Experiments. Journal of the American Society for Psychical Research, 91 (1976), 1-14.

Stenger, V. J., Physics and Psychics, The Search for a World Beyond the Senses. Buffalo, Prometheus Books, 1990.

Targ, R., et al., Mind-Reach, Scientists Look at Psychic Abilities. Charlottesville, Hampton Road Publishing, Inc, 1977.

Taylor, J., Superminds. London, Pan, 1976.

Varvoglis, M., Goal-Directed-and Observer-Dependent PK, An Evaluation of the Conformance-Behavior Model and the Observation Theories. The Journal of the American Society for Psychical Research, 80 (1986).

Remote Viewing

Bem, D., et al., Does PSI Exist? Replicable Evidence for an Anomalous Process of Information Transfer. Psychological Bulletin, (1994).

Brown, C., Cosmic Voyage. New York, Dutton Books, 1996.

CIA use of remote viewing. bibliotecapleyades.net/vision_remota/esp_visionremota_6.htm.

Cottrell, Douglas, Clairvoyance, telepathy, intuitive healing, remote viewing, prophecy. conspiracy-unlimited. blubrry.net/tag/douglas-james-cottrell.

Dames, Edward, Major, U. S. Army (ret.), LearnRV.com.

Dunne, B., et al., Information and Uncertainty in Remote Perception Research. Journal of Scientific Exploration, 17 (2003), 207-242.

Learn to remote view. learnrv.com.

McMoneagle, J., Remote Viewing Secrets. Charlottesville, Hampton Roads Publishing Company, Inc, 2000.

McMoneagle, J., The Stargate Chronicles, Memoirs of a Psychic Spy. Charlottesville, Hampton Roads Publishing Company, Inc, 2002.

Puthoff, H., et al., A Perceptual Channel for Information Transfer Over Kilometer Distances, Historical Perspective and Recent Research. Proc. IEEE, 64 (1976).

Radin, D., The Conscious Universe, The Scientific Truth of Psychic Phenomena. New York, HarperCollins, 1997.

Schlitz, M., et al., Ganzfeld Psi Performance Within an Artistically Gifted Population. Journal ASPR, 86 (1992), 83-98.

Schlitz, M., et al., Transcontinental Remote Viewing. Journal of Parapsychology, 44 (1980), 305-15.

Smith, Paul, Instructional Courses on Remote Viewing. rviewer.com.

Targ, R., et al., Information Transfer Under Conditions of Sensory Shielding. Nature, 252 (1974), 602-607.

Targ, R., et al., Mind-reach, Scientists Look at Psychic Abilities. Charlottesville, Hampton Road Publishing Company, Inc, 1977.

Targ, R., Limitless Mind, A Guide to Remote Viewing and Transformation of Consciousness. Novato, New World Library, 2004.

Targ, R., Remote Viewing at Stanford Research Institute in the 1970s, A Memoir. Journal of Scientific Exploration, 10 (1996), 77-88.

Targ, Russell, Books and Workshops on Remote Viewing, PSI / Psychic Science, Spiritual Healing. espresearch.com.

Reverse Speech
Oates, David, reversespeech.com.
Sense of Being Stared At
Baker, R., Can We Tell When Someone Is Staring at Us from Behind? Skeptical Inquirer, (2000), 34-40.
Braud, W., et al., Reactions to An Unseen Gaze (Remote Attention), A Review, With New Data on Autonomic Staring Detection. Journal of Parapsychology, 57 (1993a), 373-90.
Colwell, J. S., et al., The Ability to Detect Unseen Staring, A Literature Review and Empirical Tests. British Journal of Psychology, 91 (2000), 71-85.
Coover, J. E., The Feeling of Being Stared At – Experimental. American Journal of Psychology, 24 (1913), 570-5.
Cottrell, J. E., et al., Beliefs of Children and Adults About Feeling Stares of Unseen Others. Developmental Psychology, 32 (1996), 50-61.
Sheldrake, R., Dogs That Know When Their Owners Are Coming Home, and Other Unexplained Powers of Animals. New York, Three Rivers Press, 1999.
Sheldrake, R., The Sense of Being Stared At. New York, Crown Publishers, 2003.
Senses
Cytowic, R. E., The Man Who Tasted Shapes, a Bizarre Medical Mystery Offers Revolutionary Insights into Emotions, Reasoning, and Consciousness. New York, Tarcher/Putnam, 1993.
Staring
Drummond, P., et al., Staring at One Side of The Face Increases Blood Flow on That Side of The Face. Psychophysiology, 41 (2004), 281.
FindMe2. 31 Jan 2008. findme2.com.
Synchronicity
Krige, E. J., Girls' Puberty Songs and Their Relation to Fertility, Health, Morality and Religion Among the Zulus. Africa, 38 (1968), 173-198.
Peat, D., Synchronicity, The Bridge Between Matter and Mind. New York, Bantam Books, 1987.
Strogatz, S., Sync, The Emerging Science of Spontaneous Order. New York, Theia Books, 2003.
Swanson, C., The Synchronized Universe, New Science of the Paranormal. Poseidia Press, 2003.
Telepathy
Boone, J. A., The Language of Silence. New York, Harper & Row, 1970.
Gallup, G. H., et al., Belief in Paranormal Phenomena Among American Adults. Skeptical Inquirer, 15 (1991), 137-46.
Kogan, I. M., Information Theory Analysis of Telepathic Communication Experiments. Radio Engineering, 23 (1968), 122.
Kogan, I. M., Is Telepathy Possible? Radio Engineering, 21 (1966), 75.
Kogan, I. M., Telepathy, Hypotheses and Observations. Radio Engineering, 22 (1967), 141.
Persinger, Michael, Proof of telepathy. skeptiko.com/michael-persinger-discovers-telepathic-link/.
Playfair, G. L., Twin Telepathy, The Psychic Connection. London, Vega, 2003.
Targ, R., et al., Information Transfer Under Conditions of Sensory Shielding. Nature, 251 (1974), 602-607.
Ullman, M., et al., Dream Studies and Telepathy, An Experimental Approach. New York, Parapsychology Foundation, 1970.
Telephone Call Anticipation
Brown, D., et al., The Anticipation of Telephone Calls, A Survey in California. Journal of Parapsychology, 65 (2001), 145-56.
Time Travel
Basiago, Andrew, JD, projectpegasus.net.
Bolduc, H., Journeys Within, A True Story of Time Travel, Past Life Regression, and Channeling. Independence, Adventures into Time Publishers, 1988.
Brennan, J. H., Time Travel, A Guide for Beginners. St. Paul, Llewellyn Publications, 2003.
Grace, Sanja, sonjagrace.com.
Quit, Jason, thecrystalsun.com.
Randles, J., Breaking the Time Barrier. New York, Paraview Pocket Books, 205.
Seifer, M., Transcending the Speed of Light, Consciousness, Quantum Physics, and the Fifth Dimension. Rochester, Inner Traditions, 2008.
Wolf, F. A., The Yoga of Time Travel, How the Mind Can Defeat Time. Adyar, Theosophical Publishing House, 2004.
Zukav, G., The Dancing Wu Li Masters. London, Fontana Books, 1982.

Twins
Playfair, G. L., Telepathy and Identical Twins. Journal of the Society for Psychical Research, 63 (1999), 86-98.
Yawns
Joly-Mascheroni, R. M., et al., Dogs catch human yawns. Biology Letters, 4 (2008), 446-448.

37. Creature Testimony
Baker, R., The Mystery of Migration. London, McDonald, 1980.
Bekoff, M., Minding Animals, Awareness, Emotions, and Heart. New York, Oxford University Press, Inc, 2002.
Buxton, S., The Shamanic Way of the Bee, Ancient Wisdom and Healing Practices of the Bee Masters. Rochester, Destiny Books, 2004.
Downer, J., Supernatural, The Unseen Powers of Animals. London, BBC, 1999.
Droscher, V. B., The Magic of The Senses, New Discoveries in Animal Perception. London, Panther, 2003.
Edney, A. T. B., Dogs and Human Epilepsy. Veterinary Record, 132 (1993), 337-38.
Farmer, S. D., Power Animals, How to Connect with Your Animal Spirit Guide. Carlsbad, Hay House, 2004.
Fort, Charles, (1874-1932), famous chronicler of paranormal events, coined as Fortean phenomena.
Grant, B., Do Chimps Have Culture? The Scientist, Aug 2007, 29-35.
Hampshire, M., Pets That Saved Our Lives. Daily Mail, 30 Mar 1999, 40-42.
Harman, W., et al., Testing the Morphogenic Field Hypothesis. iShift (Institute of Noetic Sciences), 1983.
Harpignies, J., Visionary Plant Consciousness, The Shamanic Searchings of the Plant World. Rochester, Park Street Press, 2007.
Hopkin, K., How Bacteria Talk. The Scientist, 1 (2006), 61.
Marais, E., The Soul of the White Ant. Harmondsworth, Penguin Books, 1973.
McDougall, W., An Experiment for the Testing of the Hypothesis of Lamarck. British Journal of Psychology, 17 (1927), 267-304.
McDougall, W., Fourth Report on a Lamarckian Experiment. British Journal of Psychology, 28 (1938), 321-345.
McDougall, W., Second Report on a Lamarckian Experiment. British Journal of Psychology, 20 (1930), 201-218.
McFarland, D., The Oxford Companion to Animal Behavior. Oxford, Oxford University Press, 1981.
Mitchell, Dr. Edgar, Cofounder of Foundation for Research into Extraterrestrial and Extraordinary Encounters (FREE); Worldwide academic study of thousands of ET encounters.
Mosa, D., A Day in the Life of Oscar the Cat. New England Journal of Medicine, 357 (2007), 328-329.
Myers, A., Communicating with Animals. Chicago, Contemporary Books, 1997.
Parrot Intelligence, Griffin and Einstein.
Peoc'h, R., Telepathy Experiments Between Rabbits. Foundation Odier de Psycho-Physique Bulletin, 3 (1997), 25-28.
Psychic Dogs. youtube.com/watch?v=SvOzdqnTE2I.
Rodwell, Mary, The New Human, Awakening to Our Cosmic Heritage.
Rubik, B., Volitional Effects of Healers on a Bacterial System. In Rubic, B. Life at the Edge of Science. Philadelphia, Institute for Frontier Science, 1996.
Sheldrake, R. and Morgana, A., Testing a Language-Using Parrot for Telepathy. Journal of Scientific Exploration, 17 (2003).
Sheldrake, R., A New Science of Life, The Hypothesis of Morphic Resonance. Rochester, Park Street Press, 1981.
Sheldrake, R., Dogs That Know When Their Owners Are Coming Home. New York, Three Rivers Press, 1999.
Sheldrake, R., New Science of Life, The Hypothesis of Formative Causation. 2ed. Los Angeles, J. P. Tarcher, 1985.
Sheldrake, R., The Sense of Being Stared At. New York, Crown Publishers, 2003.
Smith, P., Animal Talk. Tulsa, Council Oak Books, 2004.
Smith, P., Animals in Spirit. Hillsboro, Beyond Word Publishing, 2008.
Species Link. The Journal of Interspecies Telepathic Communication. animaltalk.net.
Summers, P., Talking with the Animals. Charlottesville, Hampton Roads Publishing, 1998. sheldrake. org/papers/Animals/parrot_abs.html.
Watson, L., Lifetide. New York, Bantam, 1980.
Whiten, A., et al., Culture in Chimpanzees. Nature, 399 (1999), 682-5.

Flocks, etc. Movement
Huth, A., et al., The Simulation of the Movement of Fish Schools. Journal of Theoretical Biology, 156 (1992), 365-85.
Niwa, H., Self-Organizing Dynamic Model of Fish Schooling. Journal of Theoretical Biology, 171 (1994), 123-26.
Nonlocal Biocommunication
Aspect, Dalibard Roger, Experimental Test of Bell's Inequalities Using Time-Varying Analyzers. Phys. Rev. Lett., 25, 1982, p. 1804.
Backster & White, Biocommunications Capability, Human Donors and In Vitro Leukocytes. Int. J. of Biosoc. Res., Vol. 7(2), p. 132-46, 1985.
Backster, Cleve, Biocommunication and the Oneness of All Life. Intercontinental Metaphysical Conference, 1990 (Videotape from HPC, Ltd., 409 Marquette Drive, Louisville, KY 40222).
Backster, Cleve, Evidence for a Primary Perception at the Cellular Level in Plants and Animals. AAAS Annual Meeting, NYC, Jan. 26-31, 1975.
Backster, Cleve, Evidence of a Primary Perception in Plant Life. Int. J of Parapsych., Vol. X, No. 4, 1968, p. 329 (See also The Secret Life of Plants, by Bird & Tompkins, which documents Backster's lie detector style of work with plants extensively.).
d'Espagnat, Bernard, The Quantum Theory and Reality. Scientific American, Nov. 1979, p. 158.
Klinkhamer, James, Explanatory Guide to the Spectrophotometric Determination of the Orogranutocytic Migratory Rate for Dental Students and Dental Hygienists. Unpublished (available from the Backster Res. Foundation, 861 Sixth Ave., San Diego, CA 92101).
Morowitz, Harold, Do Bacteria Think? Psychology Today, Feb., 1981, p. 10.
O'Leary, Brian, Exploring Inner and Outer Space. North Atlantic Books, Berkeley, CA, 1989.
Valone, Dr. Thomas, A physicist, electrical engineer, retired college teacher and a licensed professional engineer. He presently is the President of Integrity Research Institute and a board member of USPA. iri@erols.com.
Parrots
Berger, J., The Parrot Who Owns Me. New York, Villard Books, 2001.
Plant Sentience
Backster, Cleve, Primary Perception.
Bose, Jagadis, Plant Response and Plant Autographs and Their Revelations.
Dixon and Fitch, Personality of Plants.
Geddis, Patrick, The Life and Work of Jagadis C. Bose.
Kranich, Ernst, Planetary Influences Upon Plants.
Plants have childhood memories. New Scientist, 13 Jan 1983.
Staddon, H., Man, Moon, and Plant.
Tompkins and Bird, The Secret Life of Plants
Telepathy, Animal
Blake, H. N., Talking with Horses, a Study of Communication Between Man and Horse. London, Souvenir Press, 1975.

38. Personal Weirdness

Capra, F., The Tao of Physics, An Exploration of the Parallels Between Modern Physics and Eastern Mysticism. Boston, Shamghala, 2000.
Huxley, Aldous, The Perennial Philosophy. New York, Harper and Brothers, 1945.
LeShan, L., The Medium, the Mystic and the Physicist. New York, The Viking Press, 1966.
Penrose, R., The Emperor's New Mind. New York, Oxford University Press, 1989.
Schmicker, Michael, Best Evidence, An Investigative Reporter's Three-Year Quest to Uncover the Best Scientific Evidence for ESP, Psychokinesis, Mental Healing, Ghosts and Poltergeists, Dowsing, Mediums, Near Death Experiences, Reincarnation, and Other Impossible Phenomena That Refuse to Disappear.
Siegel, B., 365 Prescriptions for the Soul, Daily Messages of Inspiration, Hope and Love. Novato, New World Library, 2004.
Stenger, V., Physics and Psychics, The Search for a World Beyond the Senses. New York, Prometheus Books, 1990.

39. Proving Weird Things

Broad, W. and Wade, N., Betrayers of The Truth, Fraud and Deceit in Science. Oxford, Oxford University Press, 1985.
Eysenck, H. J., and C. Sargent, Explaining the Unexplained. London, Weidenfeld & Nicolson, 1982.
Radi, D. I., and Nelson, R. D., Consciousness-Related Effects in Random Physical Systems. Foundations of Physics, 19 (1989), 1499-1514.

Sabbagh, K., A Rum Affair, A True Story of Botanical Fraud. London, Allen Lane, 1999.
Sheldrake, R., Could Experimenter Effects Occur in The Physical and Biological Sciences? Skeptical Inquirer, May/June (1998), 57-58.
Sheldrake, R., Experimenter Effects in Scientific Research, How Widely Are They Neglected? Journal of Scientific Exploration, 12 (1998), 73-78.
Targ. R., Remote Viewing and Spiritual Healing. 15 Feb 2008. espresearch.com.
Wysong, R. L., Living Life As If Thinking Matters. Midland, Inquiry Press, 2008.

40. Skeptics and Debunkers

CSICOP. Committee for Skeptical Inquiry, a materialistic approach to scientific inquiry, education, and the use of reason. csicop.org.
Dunning, Brian, Debunking and Critical Analysis of Pop Phenomena from a materialistic and conventional thought perspective. skeptoid.com.
Harrison, Guy, Books on reason and critical thinking. guypharrison.com.
Milton, R., Alternative Science. Rochester, Park Street Press, 1994.
Mars and athletes. erenow.net/common/astrology-for-dummies/20.php
Plait, Phil, Ph.D., Debunking and skepticism of astronomy ideas that conflict with conventional and materialistic thought. badastronomy.org.
Randi, James, JREf, James Randi Educational Foundation, debunking and skepticism of ideas that conflict with conventional and materialistic thought, web.randi.org.
Shermer, M., Why People Believe Weird Things. New York, Henry Holt and Company, 2002.
Skepticality. Debunking and skepticism of ideas that conflict with conventional and materialistic thought. skepticality.com.
Skeptics' guide to the universe, debunking and skepticism of ideas that conflict with conventional and materialistic thought. theskepticsguide.org.
Tsikaris, Alex, Critical analysis of materialistic debunkers and skeptics, consciousness research, religion critiques. skeptiko.com.
The Grip of Materialism
Harrub, B., and Thompson, Bert, The Truth About Human Origins. Montgomery, Apologetics Press, 2003.
Milton, R., Alternative Science. Rochester, Park Street Press, 1994.

41. Free Will Proves We Are Other

Hawking, S., A Brief History of Time. New York, Bantam Books, 1988.
Penrose, R., The Emperor's New Mind. New York, Oxford University Press, 1989.

42. Mind Outside Matter
Artificial Intelligence/Computers
Penrose, R., Shadows of the Mind, A Search for the Missing Science of Consciousness.
Radin, D., The Conscious Universe, The Scientific Truth of Psychic Phenomena. New York, Harper Collins, 1997.
Reichenbach, K. V., Researches on Magnetism, Electricity, Heat, Light, Crystallization, & Chemical Attraction, Etc. London, Taylor, Walton and Maberly, 1850.
Talbot, M., Mysticism and the New Physics. New York, Penguin Books, 1981.
Walker, E. H., The Physics of Consciousness, The Quantum Mind and the Meaning of Life. Cambridge, Perseus Books, 2000.
Consciousness Not Brain or Body
Pearce, J., The Crack in the Cosmic Egg. Rochester, Park Street Press, 2002.
Penrose, R., The Emperor's New Mind. New York, Oxford University Press, 1989.
Pribram, K., Languages of the Brain. Monterrey, Wadsworth Publishing, 1977.
Dual Nature
1st Books. 25 Jun 2008. 1stbooks.com.
Armour, J. A., Neurocardiology. Lakewood, Acropolis Books, 1997.
Crick, F., The Astonishing Hypothesis. New York, Touchstone, 1994.
Feuillet, F., Brain of a White-Collar Worker. Lancet, 21 (2007), 262.
Harrub, B., and Bert Thonpson. The Truth About Human Origins. Montgomery, Apologetics Press, 2003.
Mishlove, J., Thinking Allowed, Conversations on the Leading Edge of Knowledge. Tulsa, Council Oak Books, 1992.
Pearce, J., The Biology of Transcendence. Rochester, Park Street Press, 2002.

Penrose, R., The Emperor's New Mind. New York, Oxford University Press, 1989.
Roach, M., Spook. New York, W. W. Norton & Company Inc, 2005.
Sheldrake, R., The Sense of Being Stared At. New York, Crown Publishers, 2003.
Talbot, M., Beyond the Quantum. New York, Bantam Books, 1988.
Talbot, M., The Holographic Universe. New York, HarperCollins Publishers, 1991.
Schwartz, James, meetmattfraser.com.

Maternal Mind Influences Child
Hammond, W. A., On the Influence of the Maternal Mind Over the Offspring During Pregnancy and Lactation. Quarterly Journal of Psychological Medicine and Medical Jurisprudence, (1868), 1-28.
Stevenson, I., A New Look at Maternal Impressions, An Analysis of 50 Published Cases and Reports of Two Recent Examples. Journal of Scientific Exploration, 6 (1992), 353-373.

Mind Control of Body
Bartrop, R. W., et al., Depressed Lymphocyte Function. Lancet, 16 Apr 1977, 834-6.
Church, Dawson, mindtomatter.club.
Delgado, M. R., Physical Control of the Mind, Toward a Psychocivilized Society. New York, Harper & Row, 1969.
Eysenck, H. J., Personality, Stress and Cancer, Prediction and Prophylaxis. British Journal of Medical Psychology, 61 (1988), 57-75.

Out-of-Body Experience (OBE)
Astral Projection, wikipedia.org/wiki/Astral_projection.
Banks, Leslie, Retired Police Lieutenant, Psychic Medium, thereceptivityproject.com.
Blackmore, S., Beyond the Body, An Investigation of Out-of-Body Experiences. Chicago, Academy Chicago Publishers, 1982.
Buhlman, W., Adventures Beyond the Body, How to Experience Out-of-Body Travel. New York, HarperCollins Publishers, 1996.
Crookall, R., The Study and Practice of Astral Projection. Hackensack, Wehman Brothers, 1960.
Dening, M., et al., Astral Projection, The Out-of-Body Experience. St. Paul, Llewellyn Publications, 2001.
Leland, K., Otherwhere, A Field Guide to Nonphysical Reality for the Out-of-Body Traveler. Charlottesville, Hampton Roads, 2001.
McCoy, E., Astral Projection for Beginners. Saint Paul, Llewellyn Publications, 1999.
Monroe, R., Journeys out of the Body. New York, Broadway Books, 1973.
Moss, R., Dreamways of the Iroquois, Honoring the Secret Wishes of the Soul. Rochester, Destiny Books, 2004.
Tart, Charles, Psychologist, near-death.com/experiences/out-of-body/charles-tart.html.
Taylor, Albert, Astral Projection, scribd.com/doc/56644685/Taylor-Soul-Traveler-1998.
Wesselman, H., The Journey to the Sacred Garden, A Guide to Traveling in the Spiritual Realms. Carlsbad, Hay House, Inc, 2003.

Panpsychism
Koch, Christof, Consciousness, Confessions of a Romantic Reductionist. MIT Press, 2012.
Koch, Christof, Is Consciousness Universal? Scientific American, Jan 1, 2014.
Skrbina, David, Panpsychism in the West. MIT Press, 2005.
Tononi, Giulio, Integrated Information Theory of Consciousness, An Updated Account. In Archives Italiennes de Biologie, Vol. 150, No. 4, pages 293–329; December 2012.

Parapsychology
McClenon, James, jamesmcclenon.com.

Psychoactive Drugs
Grof, S., Beyond the Brain, Birth, Death and Transcendence in Psychotherapy. Albany, State University Press of New York, 1985.
Grof, S., The Adventure of Self-Discovery. Albany, State University of New York Press, 1988.
Harpignies, J. P., Visionary Plant Consciousness, The Shamanic Teachings of the Plant World. Rochester, Inner Traditions Bear & Company, 2007.
Heaven, R., Plant Spirit Shamanism, Traditional Techniques for Healing the Soul. Rochester, Inner Traditions Bear & Company, 2006.
Holland, J., Ecstasy, The Complete Guide, A Comprehensive Look at the Risks and Benefits of MDMA. Rochester, Inner Traditions Bear & Company, 2001.
Metzner, R., Sacred Mushroom of Visions, Teonanacatl, A Sourcebook on the Psilocybin Mushroom. Rochester, Inner Traditions Bear & Company, 2005.
Metzner, R., Sacred Vine of Spirits, Ayahuasca. Rochester, Inner Traditions Bear & Company, 2005.
Ratsch, C., The Encyclopedia of Psychoactive Plants, Ethnopharmacology and Its Applications.

Rochester, Inner Traditions Bear & Company, 2005.
Ravalec, V., et al., Iboga, The Visionary Root of African Shamanism. Rochester, Park Street Press, 2004.
Schultes, R., et al., Plants of the Gods, Their Sacred, Healing, and Hallucinogenic Powers. Rochester, Inner Traditions Bear & Company, 2001.
Strassman, R., DMT, The Spirit Molecule, A Doctor's Revolutionary Research into the Biology of Near-Death and Mystical Experiences. Rochester, Inner Traditions Bear & Company, 2001.
Toro, G., et al., Drugs of the Dreaming. Rochester, Park Street Press, 2007.
Backman, Dr. Linda, Past Life Therapy, dannionandkathrynbrinkley.com.
Masino, Susan, Children's memories of past lives.
Newton, M., Journey of Souls, Case Studies of Life Between Lives. St. Paul, Llewellyn Publications, 2001.
The I Is Elsewhere
Talbot, M., The Holographic Universe. New York, HarperCollins Publishers, 1991.
Sheldrake, R., The Sense of Being Stared At. New York, Crown Publishers, 2003.
Piaget, J., The Children's Conception of the World. London, Granada, 1973.

43. Death is a Return
Hoag, Craig, Your Eternal Self. afterlifeinstitute.org.
Myers, F. W. H., Human Personality and its Survival of Bodily Death. New York, Longmans, Green and Co, 1903.
Newton, Michael, past life regression therapy and near-death experiences. youtube.com/watch?v=Vk5bSG78pbQ.
Varghese, Rog, There Is Life After Death, Compelling Reports from Those Who Have Glimpsed the Afterlife.
Medium/Psychics - After Death Communication
Allen, M., The Survival Files, The Most Convincing Evidence Yet Compiled for the Survival of Your Soul. Momentpoint Media, 2007.
Anderson, G., Lessons from the Light, Extraordinary Messages of Comfort and Hope from the Other Side. New York, Berkeley, 2000.
Dalzell, G. E., Messages, Evidence for Life After Death. Charlottesville, Hampton Roads Publishing Company, Inc, 2002.
Edward, J., One Last Time, A Psychic Medium Speaks to Those We Have Loved and Lost. New York, Berkley, 2002.
Gauld, A., Mediumship and Survival, A Century of Investigations. Chicago, Academy, 1984.
Guggenheim, B., & Guggenheim, J., Hello from Heaven, A New Field of Research Confirms That Life and Love Are Eternal. New York, Bantam Books, 1996.
Martin, J., et al., Love Beyond Life, The Healing Power of After-Death Communications. New York, Bantam Books, 1988.
Northrop, S., et al., Séance, Healing Messages from Beyond. New York, Dell Books, 1996.
Radin, D., The Conscious Universe, The Scientific Truth of Psychic Phenomena. New York, HarperCollins, 1997.
Raudive, Konstantin, Breakthrough, An Amazing Experiment in Electronic Experimentation with the Dead. Scotland, Electronic Voice Phenomena Research Association, 1971.
Rothschild, J., Signals, An Inspiring Story of Life After Life. Novato, New World Library, 2001.
Schwartz, G. E., The Afterlife Experiments, Breakthrough Scientific Evidence of Life After Death. New York, Pocket Books, 2002.
Smith, S., The Afterlife Codes, Searching for Evidence of the Survival of the Soul. Charlottesville, Hampton Roads Publishing Co., Inc, 2000.
Stromberg, Hanie, freewebs.com/haniastromberg.
Bardos
Findlay, A., Looking Back. London, Psychic Press, 1955.
Findlay, A., The Psychic Stream. London, Psychic Press, 1939.
Newton, M., Journey of Souls, Case Studies of Life Between Lives. St. Paul, Llewellyn Publications, 2001.
Bible Support
BL.uk. A site that explores sacred texts and offers pro and con arguments. Also provides interesting videos and podcasts on how scribes prepared manuscripts. bl.uk/sacred.
Flemings, H., A Philosophical Scientific and Theological Defense for the Notion That a God Exists. Lanham, University Press of America, Inc, 2003.
Rothschild, J., Signals, An Inspiring Story of Life After Life. Novato, New World Library, 2001.
Birthmarks and Wounds

Stevenson, I., Birthmarks and Birth Defects Corresponding to Wounds on Deceased Persons. Journal of Scientific Exploration, 7 (1993), 403-416.

Stevenson, I., Reincarnation and Biology, A Contribution to the Etiology of Birthmarks and Birth Defects. 2 Vols. Westport, Praeger Publishers, 1997.

Phinn, G., Eternal Life and How to Enjoy It. Charlottesville, Hampton Roads Publishing House, 2004.

Ward, S., Matthew, Tell Me About Heaven. Philadelphia, Xlibris Corporation, 2000.

Dead Animal Communication

Anderson, Karen, Animal psychic, animalcommunicating.com.

Cuthbertson, Nikki, nikkicuthbertson.com/animal-communication.

Kinkade, Amerial, Animal communicator, ameliakinkade.com.

Reed, Crystal, Hope, crystalhopereed.com.

Seidelmann, Sarah, MD, followyourfeelgood.com.

Death Is Not the End

Chopra, D., The Book of Secrets, Unlocking the Hidden Dimensions of Your Life. New York, Harmony Books, 2004.

Ho, M. W., The Entangled Universe. Yes! A Journal of Positive Futures, Spring 2000.

James, W., William James and the Denial of Death. (Cited in M. Ferrari.) Journal of Consciousness Studies, 2002.

Laszlo, E., Science and the Akashic Field. Rochester, Inner Traditions, 2004.

Martin, J., et al., We Don't Die, Conversations with the Other Side. New York, The Berkley Publishing Group, 1988.

Morse, D., Searching for Eternity, A Scientist's Spiritual Journey to Overcome Death Anxiety. Memphis, Eagle Wing Books, Inc, 2000.

Roach, M., Spook. New York, W. W. Norton & Company Inc, 2005.

Wambach, H., Reliving Past Lives. New York, Harper & Row, 1978.

Death Process

Cox, R., Creating the Soul Body. Rochester, Inner Traditions, 2008.

Crookall, R., Intimations of Immortality. Cambridge, James Clarke & Co. Ltd, 1965.

Crookall, R., The Supreme Adventure, Analyses of Psychic Communications. Cambridge, James Clarke & Co. Ltd, 1961.

Future Life Incarnation

Goldberg, B., Time Travelers from Our Future, A Fifth Dimension Odyssey. Sun Lakes, Book World, Inc, 1999.

Guides and Angels

Chamberlain, D. B., Babies That Remember Birth, and Other Extraordinary Scientific Discoveries About the Mind and Personality of Your Newborn. Los Angeles, Tarcher, 1988.

Chamberlain, D. B., The Expanding Boundaries of Memory. Pre- and Peri- Natal Psychology Journal, 4 (1990), 171-189.

Graf, S., Realms of the Human Unconscious. New York, E. P. Dutton, 1976.

Nesbitt, M., Ghosts of Gettysburg, Spirits, Apparitions, and Haunted Places of the Battlefield. Volumes 1-6. Gettysburg, Thomas Publications, 1991-2004.

Virtue, D., Messages from Your Angels. Carlsbad, Hay House, 2002.

Near Death Awareness

Callahan, M., et al., Final Gifts, Understanding the Special Awareness, Needs, and Communication of the Dying. New York, Simon & Schuster, 1992.

Tart, Charles, Psychologist. near-death.com/experiences/out-of-body/charles-tart.html.

Taylor, Albert, Aeronautical Engineer. scribd.com/doc/56644685/Taylor-Soul-Traveler-1998.

Passages

Levinson, D. J., The Seasons of a Man's Life. New York, Ballantine Books, 1978.

Hypnotherapy, Past Life Experience Therapy

Botkin, A., et al., Induced After Death Communication, A New Therapy for Healing Grief and Trauma. Charlottesville, Hampton Roads Publishing Company, Inc, 2005.

Botkin, A., et al., Reconnections, The Induction of Afterdeath Communication in Clinical Practice. Charlottesville, Hampton Roads, 2004.

Goldberg, B., Quantum Physics and its Application to Past Life Regression and Future Life Progression Hypnotherapy. Journal of Regression Therapy, 7, (1993), 89-93.

Goldberg, B., Regression and Progression in Past Life Therapy. National Guild of Hypnotists Newsletter, 1, Jan/Feb 1994.

Goldberg, B., The Clinical Use of Hypnotic Regression and Progression in Hypnotherapy. Psychology – A Journal of Human Behaviour, 27, (1990), 43-48.

induced-adc.com.

Newton, M., Life Between Lives, Hypnotherapy for Spiritual Regression. St. Paul, Llewellyn Publications, 2004.

Weiss, B., Many Lives, Many Masters. New York, Simon & Schuster, 1988.

Weiss, B., Meditation, Achieving Inner Peace and Tranquility in Your Life. Carlsbad, Hay House, 2002.

Weiss, B., Mirrors of Time. Carlsbad, Hay House, 2002. iarrt.org, pastlife@empirenet.com.

Schwartz, James, meetmattfraser.com.

Prebirth Life

Carman, E. M., et al., Cosmic Cradle, Souls Waiting in the Wings for Birth. Fairfield, Sunstar Publishing Ltd., 1999.

Chamberlain, D. B., Babies Remember Birth, and Other Extraordinary Scientific Discoveries About the Mind and Personality of your Newborn. Los Angeles, Tarcher, 1988.

Chamberlain, D. B., The Expanding Boundaries of Memory. Pre- and Peri-Natal Psychology Journal, 4, (1990), 171-189.

Hallett, E., Soul Trek, Meeting Our Children on the Way to Birth. Hamilton, Light Hearts Publishing, 1995.

Hinze, S., Coming from the Light, Spiritual Accounts of Life Before Birth. New York, Pocket Books, 1994.

Lundahl, C., et al., The Eternal Journey, How Near-Death Experiences Illuminate Our Earthly Lives. New York, Warner Books, 1997.

Prebirth Memory

Chamberlain, D. B., Babies Remember Birth, and Other Extraordinary Scientific Discoveries About the Mind and Personality of your Newborn. Los Angeles, Tarcher, 1988.

Cheek, D. B., Are Telepathy, Clairvoyance and "Hearing" Possible in Utero? Suggestive Evidence as Revealed During Hypnotic Age-Regression. Journal of Pre- & Peri-Natal Psychology, 7 (1992), 125-137.

Verny, T., et al., The Secret Life of the Unborn Child. New York, Dell, 1981.

Psychic

Psychic medium directory. Over 700 psychics vetted and screen by a private investigator, bestpsychicdirectory.com.

Anka, Darryl, ET Psychic Communicator. Channels entity known as Bashar, bashar.org.

Banks, Leslie, Retired Police Lieutenant, thereceptivityproject.com.

Bella, Sloan, Psychic Medium, sloanbella.com.

Bodine, Michael, Psychic and Ghostbuster, michaelbodine.com.

Caputo, Theresa, TV "Long Island Medium," Psychic Medium, theresacaputo.com.

Coasttocoastam.com. Search psychic medium on the site for numerous interviews. coasttocoastam.com.

Diamond, Debra, PhD., Psychic Medium. debradiamondpsychic.com

Fraser, Matt, Psychic Medium, Television and Personal Medium Contact With the Dead, meetmattfraser.com.

Hamilton-Parker, Craig, psychics.co.uk.

Holland, John, johnholland.com.

Robinett, Kristy, kristyrobinett.com.

Russo, Kim, Psychic Medium, kimthehappymedium.com.

Ryan, Marisa, marisaryan.com.

Salvin, Linda, Psychic and NDE, lindasalvin.com.

Tart, Charles, paradigm-sys.com.

Wilson, Susanne, Psychic Medium, carefreemedium.com.

Reincarnation/Regression

Barker, E., Letters from the Light, An Afterlife Journal. Hillsboro, Beyond Worlds Pub., Inc, 1995.

Bolduc, H., Journeys Within, A True Story of Time Travel, Past Life Regression, and Channeling. Independence, Adventures into Time Publishers, 1988.

Bolduc, H., Life Patterns, Soul Lessons and Forgiveness. Independence, Journeys into Time, Inc, 1994.

Bowman, C., Children's Past Lives, How Past Life Memories Affect Your Child. New York, Bantam Books, 1998.

Bruce, R., et al., Mastering Astral Projection, 90-Day Guide to Out-of-Body Experience. St. Paul, Llewellyn Publications, 2004.

Cerminara, G., Many Mansions. New York, Sloane, 1970.

Children's Past Lives. childpastlives.org.

Church, W. H., Edgar Cayce's Story of the Soul, Trace the Fascinating Footsteps of Your Evolving Soul from Its Origins to Its Destination. Virginia Beach, A. R. E. Press, 1989.

Cunningham, J., A Tribe Returned. Crest Park, Deep Forest Press, 1994.

Drewes, A., Parapsychological Research with Children. Blue Ridge Summit, The Scarecrow Press, Inc, 1991.

Gershom, Y., Beyond the Ashes, Cases of Reincarnation from the Holocaust. Virginia Beach, A. R. E. Press, 1992.

Gershom, Y., From Ashes to Healing, Mystical Encounters with the Holocaust. Virginia Beach, A. R. E. Press, 1996.

Goldberg, B., Past Lives – Future Lives, Accounts of Regressions and Progressions Through Hypnosis. New York, Ballantine Books, 1982.

Gregory, T., The Meaning of Life, Spiritual Insights and Practical Advice on the Big Questions We All Ask. Walnut Creek, Living Spirit Press, 2000.

Hodson, G., Reincarnation, Fact or Fallacy? Wheaton, The Theosophical Publishing House, 1967.

Lane, B., 16 Clues to Your Past Lives! Virginia Beach, A. R. E. Press, 1999.

Lane, B., Echoes from Medieval Halls, Past-Life Memories from the Middle Ages. Virginia Beach, A. R. E. Press, 1997.

Lane, B., Echoes from the Battlefield, First-Person Accounts of Civil War Past Lives. Virginia Beach, A. R. E. Press., 1996.

Langley, N., Edgar Cayce on Reincarnation. London, Howard Baker, 1969.

Linn, D., Past Lives, Present Dreams. New York, Ballantine Books, 1997.

Lucas, S., Past Life Dreamwork, Healing the Soul Through Understanding Karmic Patterns. Rochester, Bear & Company, 2008.

Lucas, W., Regression Therapy, A Handbook for Professionals, I & II. Crest Park, Deep Forest Press, 1993.

Moody, R., et al., Reunions, Visionary Encounters with Departed Loved Ones. New York, Ivy Books, 1993.

Moss, P., Encounters with Past, How Man Can Experience and Relive History. Garden City, Doubleday & Company, Inc, 1980.

Mossbridge, J., Unfolding, The Perpetual Science of Your Soul's Work. Novato, New World Library, 2002.

Netherton, M., et al., Past Lives Therapy. New York, William Morrow, Inc, 1978.

Novak, P., The Lost Secret of Death. Charlottesville, Hampton Roads Publishing.

Rieder, M., Mission to Millboro. Nevada City, Blue Dolphin Publishing, Inc, 1993.

Rogo, D. S., The Search for Yesterday, A Critical Examination of the Evidence of Reincarnation. Englewood Cliffs, Prentice Hall, 1985.

Schwartz, Gary. E., Ph.D., The Afterlife Experiments, Breakthrough Scientific Evidence of Life After Death. New York, Pocket Books, 2002.

Sherman, H., The Dead Are Alive, They Can and Do Communicate with You! New York, Ballantine Books, 1981.

Shroder, T., Old Souls, The Scientific Evidence for Past Lives. New York, Simon & Schuster, 1999.

Smith, S., The Afterlife Codes, Searching for Evidence of the Survival of the Soul. Charlottesville, Hampton Roads Publishing Co., Inc, 2000.

Snow, R. L., Looking for Carroll Beckwith, The True Story of a Detective's Search for His Past Life. Emmaus, Daybreak Books, 1999.

Stevenson, I., Reincarnation, Field Studies and Theoretical Issues – Handbook of Parapsychology. New York, Reinhold Co, 1977.

Stevenson, I., Twenty Cases Suggestive of Reincarnation. 2nd Edition. Charlottesville, University Press of Virginia, 1974.

Stevenson, I., Where Reincarnation and Biology Intersect. Glenview, Praeger, 1997.

Wambach, H., Reliving Past Lives, The Evidence Under Hypnosis. New York, Harper & Row, 1978.

White, S., The Unobstructed Universe. New York, E. P. Dutton & Co. Inc, 1941.

Woolger, R., Other Lives, Other Selves, A Jungian Psychotherapist Discovers Past Lives. New York, Bantam, 1988.

Religions/Mystics

Pearce, J., The Biology of Transcendence, A Blueprint of the Human Spirit. Rochester, Park Street Press, 2002.

Price-Williams, D., et al., Shamanism and Altered States of Consciousness. Anthropology of Consciousness, 5 (1994), 1-15.

Sitchen, Z., Genesis Revisited, Is Modern Science Catching Up with Ancient Knowledge? Santa Fe, Bear & Co, 1990.

Scientific Research Proving Mind Beyond Matter

Institute of Noetic Sciences (IONS). Research into universal interconnectedness not bounded by space and time. noetic.org.

Radin, Dean, Ph.D., Real Magic, Ancient Wisdom, Modern Science, and a Guide to the Secret Power of the Universe; Entangled Minds, Extrasensory Experiences in a Quantum Reality; Supernormal, Science, Yoga, and the Evidence for Extraordinary Psychic Abilities. deanradin.com.

Schwartz, Gary, Ph.D., The Afterlife Experiments, Breakthrough Scientific Evidence of Life after Death. opensciences.org/gary-schwartz.

Tart, Charles, Ph.D., Archives of Scientists' Transcendent Experiences; The Secret Science of the Soul; The End of Materialism. paradigm-sys.com.

Soul Research

ianlawton.com.

Spiritual

Seidelmann, Sarah, MD, Spiritual coach, followyourfeelgood.com.

Wagner, Rick, myhauntedreality.com.

Spiritual Believers

badastronomy.com.

Milton, R., Alternative Science, Challenging the Myths of the Scientific Establishment. Rochester, Inner Traditions, 1996.

Wilber, K., A Brief History of Everything. Boston, Shambhala Publications, Inc, 1996.

Time Travel

Basiago, Andrew, Attorney, projectpegasus.net.

Grace, Sonja, sonjagrace.com.

Quit, Jason, thecrystalsun.com.

Xenoglossy

Stevenson, I., Unlearned Language, New Studies in Xenoglossy. Charlottesville, University Press of Virginia, 1984.

44. Life After Death

Elsen, Pieter, Ph.D., past life regression to find the true purpose in life. elsenhypnotherapy.com.

Fraser, Matt, Psychic Medium, Television and Personal Medium Contact with the Dead, meetmattfraser.com.

Ghosts

Bodine, Michael, Psychic and Ghostbuster, michaelbodine.com.

Gauld, A., et al., Poltergeists. London, Routledge & Kegan Paul, 1979.

International Ghost Hunters Society. ghostweb.com

Nesbitt, M., Ghosts of Gettysburg, Spirits, Apparitions, and Haunted Places of the Battlefield. Volumes 1-6. Gettysburg, Thomas Publications, 1991-2004.

Nicola, J. J., Diabolical Possession and Exorcism. Rockford, Tan Books and Publishers, Inc, 1974.

Pearson, Patricia, Sense presence; Opening Heaven's Doors.

Playfair, Guy, Parapsychology investigator of poltergeists, after-death communication and the telepathy of twins. skeptiko.com/139-are-ghosts-real-guy-lyon-playfair/.

Mediums

Banks, Leslie, Retired Police Lieutenant, thereceptivityproject.com.

Beischel, Julie, Ph.D., Controlled Experimental Scientific Proof That Mediums Communicate with Dead People windbridge.org.

Bella. Sloan, sloanbella.com.

Caputo, Theresa, TV "Long Island Medium", theresacaputo.com.

Frees, Marla, marlafrees.com.

Hamilton-Parker, Craig, psychics.co.uk.

Holland, John, johnholland.com.

Noe, Karen, karennoe.com.

Robinett, Kristy, kristyrobinett.com.

Rubenstein, Ian, Consulting Spirit, A Doctor's experience with practical mediumship. drianrubensteinmd.com.

Russo, Kim, kimthehappymedium.com.

Wilson, Susanne, carefreemedium.com.

Near Death Experiences (NDE)

Afterlife Knowledge. afterlife-knowledge.com.

Alexander, Eben, ebenalexander.com/about/my-experience-in-coma, ndestories.org/dr-eben-alexander.

American Society for Psychical Research. ASPR is the oldest psychical research organization in the United States and has supported the scientific investigation of extraordinary or yet unexplained phenomena that have been called psychic or paranormal. aspr.com.

Anava, Alon, ndestories.org/alon-anava.
Atwater, PMH, Many Books on NDE and Afterlife Studies. ndestories.org/pmh-atwater.
Aware Study. nourfoundation.com/events/Beyond-the-Mind-Body-Problem/The-Human-Consciousness-Project/the-AWARE-study.html.
Benedict, Mellen-Thomas, ndestories.org/mellen-thomas-benedict.
Bennett, David, ndestories.org/david-bennett.
beyondtheveil.net.
Blackmore, S. J., Dying to Live, Near-Death Experiences. Buffalo, Prometheus Books, 1993.
Brinkley, Dannion, dannionandkathrynbrinkley.com, ndestories.org/dannion-brinkley.
Brodsky, Beverly, ndestories.org/beverly-brodsky.
Call, Amy, ndestories.org/amy-call.
Clark, G., The Man Who Tapped the Secrets of the Universe. Waynesboro, University of Science and Philosophy, 1996.
CoasttoCoastam.com. Search NDE on the site for numerous interviews. coasttocoastam.com.
Colton, Burpo, ndestories.org/colton-burpo.
Danison, Nanci, ndestories.org/nanci-danison.
Eadie, Betty, ndestories.org/betty-j-eadie.
Fenwick, Peter, Neuropsychologist, Neurophysiologist, Near Death Experience Research.
Galland. Leo, Experiences After Death of Son, drgalland.com.
Greyson, Bruce, Handbook of NDE, Over 100 Peer Reviewed References.
Haynes, Jessica, ndestories.org/jessica-haynes.
Holden, Jan, Thirty Years of NDE Research.
Horn, Anne, ndestories.org/anne-horn.
Howard, Storm, ndestories.org/howard-storm.
Ian, McCormack, ndestories.org/ian-mccormack.
International Association for Near-Death Studies, Inc. iands.org.
Introductory Bibliography of Near-Death Experiences. iands.org/oldbib.html.
Journal of Near-Death Studies. iands.org/pubs/jnds.
Kagan, Jeremy, ndestories.org/jeremy-kagan.
Kinman, Raymond, ndestories.org/raymond-kinman.
Koch, Dr. Christof, President and Chief Scientific Officer of the Allen Institute for Brain Science, christofkoch.com/who-am-i.
Kopecky, Robert, Three NDEs, robertkopecky.com.
Krippner, Stanley, stanleykrippner.weebly.com.
Leland, K., The Unanswered Question, Death, Near-Death, and the Afterlife. Charlottesville, Hampton Roads, 2002.
Long, Dr. Jeffry, Radiation Oncologist, nderf.org.
Long, Jeffrey, Largest Database of NDE, NDE research, nderf.org.
McKenzie, Erica, ndestories.org/erica-mckenzie.
Milarch, David, ndestories.org/david-milarch.
Moody, Raymond.
Moorjani, Anita, ndestories.org/anita-moorjani.
NDE podcast (NDE Research Foundation)- hundreds of interviews with experiencers. neardeathexperiencepodcast.org.
Neal, Mary, Explores Her Own NDE and Provides a Website Gateway to the NDE Experiences of Many Others. ndestories.org/dr-mary-neal.
Noratuk, Vicki, ndestories.org/vicki-noratuk.
Olsen, Jeff, ndestories.org/jeff-c-olsen.
Osis, Karlis, aspr.com/osis.html.
Parnia, Sam, World's Largest Near-Death Experiences Study Page. southampton.ac.uk/news/2014/10/07, neardeathexperience.us.
Parti, Dr. Rajiv, ndestories.org/dr-rajiv-parti.
Pasarow, Reinee, ndestories.org/reinee-pasarow.
Petro, Andy, ndestories.org/andy-petro.
Piper, Don, ndestories.org/don-piper.
Rapini, Jo Mary, ndestories.org/mary-jo-rapini.
Renfrow, Cami, ndestories.org/cami-renfrow.
Ring, Kenneth, kenring.org.
Ritchie, Dr. George, ndestories.org/george-ritchie.

Rob, Wood, ndestories.org/rob-wood.
Robinson, Mickey, ndestories.org/mickey-robinson.
Rodonaia, George, ndestories.org/dr-george-rodonaia.
Ross, Elisabeth Kubler, ekrfoundation.org.
S., Duane, ndestories.org/duane-s.
Salvin, Linda, lindasalvin.com.
Sartori, Dr. Penny, Intensive Care NDE Experiences. drpennysartori.com.
Sneeden, Yvonne, ndestories.org/yvonne-sneeden.
Sudman, Natalie, ndestories.org/natalie-sudman.
Swanson, Claude, physicist, Scientific proof of life after death, synchronizeduniverse.com.
Tanous, Alex, alextanous.org.
Tart, Dr. Charles, near-death.com/experiences/out-of-body/charles-tart.html.
Van Lommel, Pim, Peer-Reviewed Research Proving NDE. pimvanlommel.nl/en.
Whitfield, Harris Barbara, ndestories.org/barbara_harris_whitfield.

Past Life Regression

Gabriel, Linda, hypnotherapist for life between lives (LBL) and past lives. lindagabriel.com.
Haraldsson, Erlendur, past life regression, The Departed Among the Living, An Investigative Study of Afterlife Encounters.
Tucker, Jim, Life Before Life, A Scientific Investigation of Children's Memories of Previous Lives. jimbtucker.com.

The Real Life

Crookall, R., Intimations of Immortality; The Supreme Adventure. Greenwood, The Attic Press, Inc, 1961.
Phinn, G., Eternal Life and How to Enjoy It. Charlottesville, Hampton Roads Publishing Company, Inc, 2004.
Roach, M., Spook. New York, W. W. Norton & Company Inc, 2005.
Walker, E., The Physics of Consciousness, The Quantum Mind and the Meaning of Life. New York, Perseus Books Group, 2000.

WYSONG

INDEX

GRAPHIC INDEX

Index

BY THE SAME AUTHOR

Living Life As If Thinking Matters
Why dissent is crucial to health, happiness, hope, and a better world.

Living life better and solving its dilemmas requires putting thinking ahead of popular beliefs.

We are all born on the starting line of life with blank mental slates. Then each of us has our mind filled in by parents, schools, peers, and experts. The result is a society stuffed with given beliefs, none of which we own, and—as you will learn in this book—most of which are wrong.

Although important questions are often debated, there seems to be no satisfying solutions. Instead, shortsighted agendas prevail, money dictates decisions, and ethics seems a thing of the past. We all sense this misdirection and can feel helpless as the world spirals out of control.

Since ultimately everything in life happens because of the way we think, solutions depend upon thinking too. That does not mean playing the victim and relying on others, but reaching within to see the sense, goodness, and direction that lie there.

Dr. Wysong helps readers tap into their unlimited resources and take control. All of life's important topics are discussed in this encyclopedic, wise, and helpful book, including: how to achieve optimal health, think correctly about politics, family, love, sex, the environment, economics, government, and social issues, and how to self-improve and cultivate conscience.

If you would like to understand life better, be healthier, happier, have meaning, contribute to a better world, and avoid some bumps and bruises along the way, this is your guidebook.

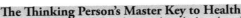

The Thinking Person's Master Key to Health
An entertaining and thought-provoking look at how human and pet health should be approached.

This one-hour CD encapsulates over 30 years of Dr. Wysong's thought and research on health, medicine, and prevention.

Few people realize that the modern paradigm of health care is dangerously flawed. The solution is not cheaper drugs, lower medical insurance rates, or free universal health care. More of the same is not the solution.

As Dr. Wysong proves, using the medical profession's own scientific literature, modern health care is the number one killer in modern society. That's because doctors are not taught about what creates health, but are rather immersed in a technology that focuses on naming diseases and treating symptoms. Medical intervention flouts the body's own healing mechanisms and introduces disruptions in the form of surgery and allopathic drugs that often do more harm than good.

Dr. Wysong explains that the key to health is to understand our genetic roots in prehistory and respect them. By (figuratively) returning to the wild we tune to our proper place in the natural order of things and permit our minds and bodies to reverse disease and achieve the true health we were designed for.

This is not yet another formula of dos, don'ts, and rigid arbitrary rules. Rather, Dr. Wysong employs the highest ideal of teaching: helping those who want to learn reach within to understand and obey what they already intuitively know.

In this thought provoking discourse you will learn how to make day-to-day choices so you, your family, and pets can achieve optimal health.

The Cholesterol Myth – Believe it to Your Peril

A revealing and concise critique of the prevailing belief that fat and cholesterol cause cardiovascular disease.

In 1923 President Harding died of a heart attack. The disease was so uncommon that doctors had difficulty with the diagnosis. How could this be? People up to that time were eating fat, eggs, lard, butter, and other high cholesterol foods with gusto.

Today, atherosclerotic heart disease is the number one killer. This is in spite of every attempt to vilify cholesterol as the culprit. People by the millions now attempt to rid the diet of fat and cholesterol, have their blood cholesterol regularly checked, monitor ratios of HDL and LDL, and make cholesterol lowering medications number one sellers. Obliviously, heart disease continues its epidemic march.

Clearly, something does not add up. In this eye-opening book, Dr. Wysong sets aside the politically correct view of cholesterol as villain and brings to bear common sense and an array of scientific and medical facts.

Here you will learn that not only is cholesterol not your enemy and not the cause of heart disease, but rather it is a vital component of healthy metabolism. Every second of every day the body is busily synthesizing this essential component of health and life. Ignoring this fact and instead focusing on cholesterol as the enemy can mean disease and death, not life and health.

Once the cholesterol myth is set aside and the facts examined, the true cause of heart disease becomes clear. The reversal and prevention of heart disease is as simple as coming to understand and respecting the body's natural processes and supporting them with simple lifestyle and nutritional changes.

This book can save your life.

Lipid Nutrition

Understanding fats and oils in health and disease.

Fats in foods and fat on the body have become national obsessions. Increasing research is now showing complex and far-reaching relationships between lipid (fat and oil) consumption and a wide range of health concerns. With each new discovery there is controversy between belief, disbelief, and overbelief.

To the public or average professional, the rapid influx of information related to health and nutrition may seem impossible to sort through. This is to be expected since even the most informed of researchers cannot keep adequately abreast. Herein lies the value in Dr. Wysong's book. He has done the homework for us. Lipid Nutrition skillfully assembles detailed information from the most current research, combines this with simple reasonings and wisdom to give answers and guidance of excellent practicality.

Lipid Nutrition is more than a book which teaches current understandings of the role of fats and oils in health and disease. It is also more than just another diet book with new claims about another nutrient that is either the fountain of youth or an insidious poison lurking in our food supply. It is more a book of reasoning and common sense.

This book will also help the reader appreciate the relationship between nutrition and environmental concerns. Our food is part of the environment upon which we depend, as much as the air, water, land, sun and biota. Pollute our larger environment, and the Earth is in jeopardy; pollute or otherwise vitiate our food and our bodies are in jeopardy. Dr. Wysong helps us to see that everything is intertwined and that respect for natural balances is critical.

Read carefully. Lipid Nutrition can be one of those rare books which replaces the reading of dozens of others.

The Synorgon Diet
How to achieve healthy weight in a world of excess.

Once in a while there is a book that obsoletes all its contemporaries and predecessors. Dr. Wysong's Synorgon Diet is such a book. It provides the philosophic filter through which all other diet plans will be understood and judged.

The Synorgon Diet is the definitive answer for achieving and maintaining healthy weight. If you think the present epidemic of obesity is a result of eating too much, little exercise, lack of self-discipline or that people are simply victims of metabolic disorders, you are partly right but mostly wrong. These things are symptoms of the problem, but not the cause.

Understanding is the key to any solution. Obesity is no exception. Yet modern diet approaches not only do not create understanding, an essential element in any behavioral modification, but actually compound the problem by perpetuating myths and half truths, and promising quick and easy cures.

Much like the correct combination can open the vault door to a trove of riches, the synorgon understanding opens the door to healthy weight and a new life of vitality riches.

You'll learn:

- How to lose weight without dieting
- That the cause of diet lose-regain cycles is not you. but a fundamental flaw in almost all diet programs
- Secrets of prehistory that are essential for healthy weight today
- Why excess weight is not a private matter
- The real dangers in modern processed foods which are being kept secret
- Fats and oils in the diet that are essential to your diet success
- A kind of exercise that is essential
- A one-day diet plan that guarantees success
- Why your understanding of such things as pollution, recycling, and deforestation is required
- Natural foods that can rai e your metabolic rate so you burn more calories while at rest
- How to turn off a powerful but little known physiological obesity switch
- Why obesity is nonexistent in wild human and animal populations
- Hundreds of foods you can eat all you want of and not become obese
- . . . and much more to empower you with control over your own weight and health destiny.

The Creation-Evolution Controversy
A daring adventure between two emotionally charged spheres of thought.

Who has not wondered about the origin of the universe and life? And, for certain, this is a question that should be taken with the utmost seriousness and sense of duty. After all, how can we know why we are here or what we should be doing if we do not know where we came from?

Although religions have their belief (creation), and materialists have their belief (evolution), beliefs are not what truth is about. This is a book of daring adventure between these two emotionally charged belief systems. Rather than advocate, Dr. Wysong pits one belief against the other using the only weapons that should be used if truth is the objective: reason and evidence.

Dr. Wysong's rational, philosophic, and scientific probings make this book a reservoir of thoughtful and factual information that will not draw dust on your bookshelf.

Now in its twelfth printing, this 1975 book has been read worldwide, is widely cited on the web, and continues to be used in schools. It has helped lay the groundwork for a rational dialogue between religion and science and remains current to this day because of its even handed treatment of the subject and because reason should never fall out of fashion.

All who profess a love of knowledge, thirst for answers about our origins, seek scientific and logical clarity, and can come to this subject with a truly open mind will find The Creation-Evolution Controversy refreshing, illuminating, and worthy of more than the usual attention.

"The man is going against the stream. But he seems to be big enough to do it and he appears to have done his homework. In these times of shaking institutions and falling idols, maybe this is a book whose time has come . . .a mountain of a job." – M. Cole, author

"*A work well documented and presented in the spirit of the search for truth which has been one of man's noblest pursuits down through the ages.*" – E. Uhlan, Exposition Press

"*The book contains some very carefully documented and closely reasoned arguments and reaches some genuinely intriguing conclusions.*" – N. Waxman, Harper and Row

"*A performance of unusual merit and scope.*" – R. Morse, Philosophical Library

"*We are fascinated by the very thorough and meticulous job.*" – W. Cannon, Thomas Nelson, Inc.

"*The work is a highly informative and well supported examination of all the aspects . . . The writing style is interesting, relaxed, and in spite of the subject matter, fairly free from heavy technical terminology and without pedanticism.*" – D. Warmouth, editor

Creation by a supernatural being, which is considered mythology in scientific circles, and evolution, which is considered blasphemy in many religious circles, have never been compared in this way before. And never has a method for resolving the issue in a rational manner been so clearly outlined.

Dr. Wysong's probings into disciplines from chemistry to philosophy to geology, and the fascinating array of 138 illustrations, make this book a reservoir of information that will not draw dust on your bookshelf.

Rationale for Animal Nutrition
An interview with Dr. R.L. Wysong.

Rationale for Animal Nutrition is the seminal book that started the natural pet food movement.

Most controversial topics in animal nutrition and health have not been adequately examined. Rationale for Animal Nutrition addresses these critical issues by capturing the fascinating views and experience of Dr. Wysong.

Although nutrition is thought to be a completed science, it is not, neither in theory nor practice. Rationale for Animal Nutrition addresses the incorrect ideas and unsettled issues, and goes far beyond the standard, protein-builds-muscle and vitamin-A-is-good-for-the-eyes, nutritional pabulum.

Dr. Wysong's experience in veterinary surgery and medicine, nutritional and food science research, and building and running food manufacturing facilities gives him the 'in the trenches' insight to take issue with a wide variety of common nutritional givens. These are some of the myths he challenges:

- Processed packaged pet foods are "100% complete and balanced"
- Synthetic nutrients are the same as natural
- Better digestibility equals better food
- Supplementing commercial pet foods is dangerous
- NRC requirements are well founded in fact
- A food's merit can be determined by its list of ingredients or analyses
- Foods in paper bags can have a six month or greater shelf-life
- Modern nutrition is better than that of our ancestors
- More technology and more medicine will mean less disease
- Science knows what nutrients we require

Dr. Wysong gives readers fundamental, philosophic understandings of their place—and that of their companion animals—in the natural order of things. This empowers people with the insight needed to make independent, healthful decisions when confronting the confusing and dangerous commercial marketplace.

The Truth About Pet Foods

A groundbreaking book exposing the dangerous myths of today's pet food industry.

For more than fifty years people have been filling their pets' bowls with processed foods. This is done with full confidence that manufacturers have things all figured out. After all, the label says, "100% complete and balanced."

It would seem that the case is closed on pet nutrition. But this exposé, by a veterinary surgeon, clinician, teacher, researcher, and food scientist, tells another story. Pets exclusively fed processed foods are in jeopardy. Untold thousands of animals have suffered disease and death at the hands of this modern feeding practice. Neither nutritionists tweaking percentages, so-called "natural" foods, or eliminating boogeyman ingredients have solved the disaster.

Such disease—cancer, arthritis, obesity, dental degeneration, and so on—is not always immediate, but rather insidious and progressive. So the cause—singularly fed processed food—is not identified as the culprit it is. The tragedy is that modern degenerative diseases are not only largely preventable, but in many cases reversible by simple dietary and life-style changes.

In an easily read format, Dr. Wysong explains what's wrong and what to do to take control of pet health. Along the way, readers will learn how to better care for their own and their family's health as well.

This is a provocative, no-holds-barred look at one of the world's largest food industries and its regulatory sanctions. But it is fair, documented, logical, thought provoking and definitely eye opening.

The solution to the epidemic of degenerative health problems facing pets is knowledge. This important book brings that critical knowledge by unveiling to the reader what they already intuitively know but have not yet discovered . . . the truth about pet food.

The Wysong e-Health Letter Bound Volumes

Each book contains a year of Dr. Wysong's Health Letters covering health and socially important topics. Complete with scientific references.

As If Thinking Matters Newsletter

asifthinkingmatters.com/newsletter

Examining the fundamental problems of human existence — The Origin of Life, Ethics, Health, Governance — and the rational means for their solution. Without an understanding of where we came from, we cannot know where we are going. Without ethics, there is no hope for peace and security. Without health, a full life is not possible. Without liberty, human potential is but a wish.

Dr. Wysong's Podcast
asifthinkingmatters.com/podcast

Dr. Wysong's YouTube Channel
youtube.com/AsIfThinkingMatters

Dr. Wysong's Posts on Quora
quora.com/profile/Randy-Wysong

Dr. Wysong's Posts on Parler
parler.com/profile/thinkingmatters

Websites
asifthinkingmatters.com
wysonginstitute.org
inquirypress.com

ABOUT THE AUTHOR

Dr. Wysong (BS, DVM) is author of thirteen books, numerous scientific articles, and newsletters on the origin of life, philosophy, logic, self-improvement, fitness, nutrition, prevention, alternative holistic health, embryology, and surgical techniques. (Much of this work is catalogued at asifthinkingmatters.com.) He has practiced veterinary surgery and medicine, taught college courses in human anatomy, physiology, and the origin of life, directed research in health education and product development, guides the philanthropic non-profit Wysong Institute, and is an iconoclastic free thinker, natural health and fitness advocate, athletic competitor, and do-it-yourselfer. Contact is at: drwysong@asifthinkingmatters.com.

Science/ Religion/ Metaphysics

Solving the age-old dilemmas by putting thinking ahead of belief

Nothing could be more fundamental than the questions of: Where did we come from? Why are we here? Where are we going? Nothing could be more true than the fact that virtually no one has answers they can rationally defend with evidence and consistency with natural laws. If we do not know our origin or destiny, then we cannot know how to properly live. The world's precarious state, and the prevailing sense of futility and meaninglessness are symptoms of either having no answers, or having the wrong ones. Experts have reached no consensus in spite of thousands of years of trying. So the average person either latches onto some convenient and attractive belief propped up with desire, hope, and faith, or gives up and ignores the topics altogether. This book offers the promise of turning that all around. It is the only book that sets aside evolutionary and religious bias to reveal the truth manifest by reason, evidence, and experience. If read openly and honestly, what you hold in your hands has the potential to totally revolutionize the scientific, philosophic, and religious worlds. When we approach the big questions as if thinking matters, we are led to exactly where the world needs to go, a place of honesty, truth, confidence, solutions, and love. Dr. Wysong masterfully teaches us how to reach within, use our own minds, consider the evidence honestly, and remain open-minded. The result is beautiful in its simplicity and wonderful in the hope, meaning, and purpose it brings.

Reader Comments

"Mind opening, life altering. My world was turned upside down, but I found out it was not right side up after all."

"This was hard to read at times. But as I continued I began to realize that my bristling was simply because of my passion for beliefs that I had never really examined. He helped me see that the only thing I had to fear was the fear of losing beliefs I had no business owning in the first place."

"Each of us stubbornly holds to ideas implanted in our brains by society. We seem to fear truly thinking for ourselves... I even felt tears well up as I discovered the promise that existed in my own mind—and for the world."

"The first book of its kind that does not end up trying to shackle the reader to some presupposed given truth. A true open-thinking journey; a real inspiration."

"Eloquent—hopeful and moving, too. A tone builds through the book that leaves one anticipating real insight and real answers. It's thrilling that the difficult steps through science and reason culminate in the heart."

"A daring tonic teaching fundamental truths. A masterful journey through science and logic."

"I felt chills and the hair rising on the back of my neck. Not because of fear but because of the rush created by enlightenment and the possibility for answers to questions that I had long ago shelved as unanswerable."

"This is a good book; it is surprisingly reasonable given the 'weirdness' of some of the content. It successfully causes the reader to reevaluate the old givens."

"Iconoclastic and intellectually honest."

"...virtually soaked with illuminating ideas and fascinating information."

ISBN 978-0-918112-30-9
51495

9 780918 112309